T&T CLARK HANDBOOK OF THOMAS F. TORRANCE

T&T CLARK HANDBOOK OF THOMAS F. TORRANCE

Edited by
Paul D. Molnar and Myk Habets

t&tclark
LONDON • NEW YORK • OXFORD • NEW DELHI • SYDNEY

T&T CLARK
Bloomsbury Publishing Plc
50 Bedford Square, London, WC1B 3DP, UK
1385 Broadway, New York, NY 10018, USA
29 Earlsfort Terrace, Dublin 2, Ireland

BLOOMSBURY, T&T CLARK and the T&T Clark logo are trademarks
of Bloomsbury Publishing Plc

First published in Great Britain 2020
This paperback edition published in 2022

Copyright © Paul D. Molnar, Myk Habets and contributors, 2020

Paul D. Molnar and Myk Habets have asserted their right under the Copyright,
Designs and Patents Act, 1988, to be identified as Editors of this work.

For legal purposes the Acknowledgments on p. xvii constitute an
extension of this copyright page.

Cover design: Terry Woodley
Cover image © zentilia / iStock

All rights reserved. No part of this publication may be reproduced or transmitted in
any form or by any means, electronic or mechanical, including photocopying,
recording, or any information storage or retrieval system, without prior
permission in writing from the publishers.

Bloomsbury Publishing Plc does not have any control over, or responsibility for,
any third-party websites referred to or in this book. All internet addresses given
in this book were correct at the time of going to press. The author and publisher
regret any inconvenience caused if addresses have changed or sites have ceased
to exist, but can accept no responsibility for any such changes.

A catalogue record for this book is available from the British Library.

Library of Congress Cataloging-in-Publication Data

Names: Molnar, Paul D., 1946– editor. | Habets, Myk, editor.
Title: T&T Clark handbook of Thomas F. Torrance / edited by Paul D. Molnar and Myk Habets.
Description: New York: T&T Clark, 2020. |
Includes bibliographical references and index.
Identifiers: LCCN 2019039600 (print) | LCCN 2019039601 (ebook) |
ISBN 9780567670519 (hardback) | ISBN 9780567670526 (pdf) |
ISBN 9780567670533 (epub)
Subjects: LCSH: Torrance, Thomas F. (Thomas Forsyth), 1913–2007
Classification: LCC BX4827.T67 .T28 2020 (print) |
LCC BX4827.T67 (ebook) | DDC 230/.044092–dc23
LC record available at https://lccn.loc.gov/2019039600
LC ebook record available at https://lccn.loc.gov/2019039601

ISBN: HB: 978-0-5676-7051-9
PB: 978-1-3503-2038-3
ePDF: 978-0-5676-7052-6
ePUB: 978-0-5676-7053-3

Typeset by Integra Software Services Pvt. Ltd.

To find out more about our authors and books visit www.bloomsbury.com
and sign up for our newsletters.

*Dedicated to The Very Reverend Professor Thomas F. Torrance (1913–2007):
preeminent scholar, churchman, ecumenist, pastor, and advocate of
"scientific theology."* In Memoriam.

CONTENTS

Notes on Contributors ... ix

Foreword
   George Hunsinger ... xiii

Acknowledgments ... xvii

1 Introduction ... 1
   Paul D. Molnar

Part One Contexts

2 Why Read Torrance Today? ... 11
   Ivor J. Davidson

3 Thomas F. Torrance as a Scottish Theologian ... 37
   David Fergusson

4 Thomas F. Torrance and Ecumenism ... 51
   Joel Scandrett

5 Thomas F. Torrance and Karl Barth: Similarities and Differences ... 67
   Paul D. Molnar

6 Thomas F. Torrance's Influence upon Ray Anderson's Paradigm
   of a Practical Theology of Ministry ... 85
   Todd Speidell

7 Thomas F. Torrance: Historian of Dogma ... 101
   Jason R. Radcliff

8 Theological Science Then and Now ... 111
   Travis Stevick

Part Two Dogmatics

9 Thomas F. Torrance on the Doctrine of Revelation ... 127
   John C. McDowell

10 The Importance of the Personal in the Onto-relational Theology
    of Thomas F. Torrance ... 143
    Gary W. Deddo

11 Thomas F. Torrance and the Trinity *Christopher R. J. Holmes*	161
12 Incarnation and Atonement *Thomas A. Noble*	173
13 The Innovative Fruitfulness of *an/en-hypostasis* in Thomas F. Torrance *Robert T. Walker*	189
14 "Jesus Christ Is Our Human Response to God": Divine and Human Agency in the Theology of Thomas F. Torrance *Christian D. Kettler*	207
15 Thomas F. Torrance and Ecclesiology *Kate Tyler*	223
16 "Not I, but Christ": Thomas F. Torrance on the Christian Life *E. Jerome Van Kuiken*	243
17 *Theologia* Is *Eusebia*: Thomas F. Torrance's Church Homiletics *Myk Habets*	259
18 The End of Ministry: Thomas F. Torrance and Eschatology *Andrew Purves*	277
NAME INDEX	291
SUBJECT INDEX	294

CONTRIBUTORS

Ivor J. Davidson is Honorary Professor of Theology, University of Aberdeen. Ivor held Personal Chairs in Systematic and Historical Theology at the University of Otago and the University of St Andrews, where he was also previously Dean of the Faculty and Head of the School of Divinity and Principal of St Mary's College. He has taught and supervised extensively in Christian doctrine and in Patristic theology and history. His publications include the definitive critical edition of the first "systematic" treatise on Christian ethics, the *De Officiis* of Ambrose of Milan (2002), and two widely used volumes on early church history. And he is contracted to produce a volume on eschatology for Zondervan Academic's *New Studies in Dogmatics* (2020).

Gary W. Deddo is President and Professor of Theology, Grace Communion Seminary, Grace Communion International, Charlotte, NC. Gary is Founding President of the Thomas F. Torrance Theological Fellowship. His publications include *Karl Barth's Theology of Relations: Trinitarian, Christological, and Human. Towards an Ethic of the Family* (1999/2015).

David Fergusson is Professor of Divinity at New College, University of Edinburgh. He has delivered the Bampton Lectures in Oxford (2001), the Gifford Lectures in Glasgow (2008), the Warfield Lectures in Princeton (2009), the Birks Lectures in Montreal (2013) and has lectured in the United States, Europe, Hong Kong, Japan, Korea, Taiwan, South Africa, and Australia. His publications include *The Providence of God* (2018), and he is the coeditor of *The History of Scottish Theology*, 3 vols. (forthcoming).

Myk Habets is Head of School of Theology and Senior Lecturer in Systematic Theology, Laidlaw College, Auckland, New Zealand and Senior Research Fellow, Australian College of Theology. His research covers the theology of Thomas F. Torrance, doctrines of *theosis*, Third Article Theology, Evangelical Calvinism, C. S. Lewis, and Baptist theology. Myk is past Co-Vice President of the Thomas F. Torrance Theological Fellowship and is coeditor of the *Journal of Theological Interpretation*. His publications include *Theosis in the Theology of Thomas Torrance* (2009), *Theology in Transposition: A Constructive Appraisal of T. F. Torrance* (2013), and *The Progressive Mystery: Tracing the Elusive Spirit in Scripture and Tradition* (2019). He has edited over fifteen volumes including *Third Article Theology: A Pneumatological Dogmatics* (2016).

Christopher R. J. Holmes is Head of the Theology Programme, School of Arts, University of Otago, Dunedin, New Zealand. Christopher is Associate Professor of Systematic Theology and an Anglican Priest. He is the author of four books and many journal articles and book chapters on various Christian doctrines. His latest book is *The Lord Is Good: Seeking the God of the Psalter* (2018).

Christian D. Kettler is Professor of Theology and Religion, Friends University, Wichita, Kansas, USA. Chris is past President of the Thomas F. Torrance Theological Fellowship and was awarded the St. John of Damascus Award for cultural renewal by the Eighth Day Institute in 2018. His publications include *Reading Ray S. Anderson: Theology as Ministry, Ministry as Theology* (2015) and *The Breadth and Depth of the Atonement: The Vicarious Humanity of Christ in the Church, the World, and the Self* (2017).

John C. McDowell is Director of Research and Professor in Theology, Philosophy, and Ethics, University of Divinity. His published writings cover twentieth-century German theology, in particular the work of Karl Barth, theological ethics, the philosophical theology of Donald MacKinnon, theology and the tragic, neoliberalism and higher education, and hope and violence in popular culture. His publications include *Hope in Barth's Eschatology: Interrogations and Transformations beyond Tragedy* (2000), *Theology and the Globalized Present: Feasting in the Presence of God* (2019), with Scott Kirkland, *Eschatology: Christian Hope*, Guides to Theology (2018), *The Gospel According to Star Wars: Faith, Hope and the Force*, 2nd edition (2017; 1st edition, 2007), *The Ideology of Identity Politics in George Lucas* (2016), and *The Politics of Big Fantasy: Studies in Cultural Suspicion* (2014).

Paul D. Molnar is Professor of Systematic Theology, Department of Theology and Religious Studies, St. John's University, Queens, New York. He has published six books, including *Thomas F. Torrance: Theologian of the Trinity* (2009; reissued 2016), *Faith, Freedom and the Spirit: The Economic Trinity in Barth, Torrance and Contemporary Theology* (2015), and *Divine Freedom and the Doctrine of the Immanent Trinity: In Dialogue with Karl Barth and Contemporary Theology*, 2nd edition (T&T Clark, 2017); he has also published many articles including "The importance of the doctrine of justification in the theology of Thomas F. Torrance and of Karl Barth," *Scottish Journal of Theology* 70 (2): 198–226 (2017), "Thomas F. Torrance and the problem of universalism," *Scottish Journal of Theology* 68 (2): 164–86 (2015), and "The obedience of the Son in the theology of Karl Barth and of Thomas F. Torrance," *Scottish Journal of Theology* 67 (1): 50–69 (2014). He is a past president of the Thomas F. Torrance Theological Fellowship, Editor of the *Karl Barth Society of North America Newsletter*, Consulting Editor with the *Scottish Journal of Theology*, Contributing Editor with *Cultural Encounters*, and Consulting Editor with *Participatio*: The Journal of the Thomas F. Torrance Theological Fellowship.

Thomas A. Noble is Research Professor of Theology at Nazarene Theological Seminary in Kansas City, where he has taught for twenty years. He was previously Dean at Nazarene Theological College, Manchester, where he is now Senior Research Fellow supervising PhD research for Manchester University. His publications include a history of Tyndale House, the biblical research library in Cambridge (2006), and *Holy Trinity, Holy People* (2013). He has edited several volumes, was President of the Wesleyan Theological Society (2009–10), and President of the T. F. Torrance Theological Fellowship (2016–19).

Andrew Purves is Jean and Nancy Davis Professor Emeritus of Historical Theology, Pittsburgh Theological Seminary. His most recent book is *Christology and Atonement: Theological Engagements with John McLeod Campbell, Hugh Ross Mackintosh, and*

Thomas Forsyth Torrance (2015). Other books include *The Search for Compassion: Spirituality and Ministry*, *Union in Christ* (with Mark Achtemeier), *A Passion for the Gospel* (with Achtemeier), *Encountering God: Christian Faith in Turbulent Times* (with Charles Partee), *Pastoral Theology in the Classical Tradition*, *Reconstructing Pastoral Theology: A Christological Foundation*, *The Crucifixion of Ministry*, and *The Resurrection of Ministry*.

Jason R. Radcliff teaches at The Stony Brook School, a college-preparatory boarding school in New York. He is also on the faculty of The George Mercer, Jr. Memorial School of Theology, and serves as Assistant Editor of *Participatio: The Journal of the Thomas F. Torrance Theological Fellowship*. His publications include *Thomas F. Torrance and the Church Fathers* (2014) and *Thomas F. Torrance and the Orthodox-Reformed Theological Dialogue* (2018).

Joel Scandrett is Assistant Professor of Historical Theology and Director of the Robert E. Webber Center at Trinity School for Ministry, Ambridge, Pennsylvania. Joel is former Co-Vice President of the Thomas F. Torrance Theological Fellowship and former Associate Academic Editor for IVP Academic. His editorial projects include the *Dictionary of Major Biblical Interpreters* and the *Reformation Commentary on Scripture*. His own publications include *Salvation Means Creation Healed* (with Howard A. Snyder, 2011) and *Mapping Atonement* (with William Witt, forthcoming).

Todd Speidell is Editor, *Participatio: The Journal of the Thomas F. Torrance Theological Fellowship,* General Editor, The Ray S. Anderson Collection. His publications include *Fully Human in Christ: The Incarnation as the End of Ethics* (2016), coeditor, *T. F. Torrance and Eastern Orthodoxy: Theology in Reconciliation* (2015), editor, *Trinity and Transformation: J.B. Torrance's Vision of Worship, Mission, and Society* (2016), editor, *On Being Christian ... and Human* (2002), and coeditor, *Incarnational Ministry: The Presence of Christ in Church, Society, and Family* (2009).

Travis Stevick is Independent scholar and Elder in the Iowa Annual Conference of the United Methodist Church. Travis is Assistant Editor and Technology Director of *Participatio: The Journal of the Thomas F. Torrance Theological Fellowship*. His publications include *Encountering Reality: T. F. Torrance on Truth and Human Understanding* (2015).

Kate Tyler is College Director, Bishopdale College, Nelson, New Zealand. Her publications include *The Ecclesiology of Thomas F. Torrance: Koinonia and the Church* (2019). Other publications include articles in *Missiology, Participatio,* and *Stimulus*.

E. Jerome Van Kuiken is Dean of School of Ministry and Christian Thought, Oklahoma Wesleyan University, Bartlesville, USA. Jerome is Executive Committee member of the Thomas F. Torrance Theological Fellowship. His publications include *Christ's Humanity in Current and Ancient Controversy: Fallen or Not?* (T&T Clark, 2017) and chapters in *Reconsidering Arminius* (2014), *Leadership the Wesleyan Way* (2016), and *Methodist Christology* (2020).

Robert T. Walker is Honorary Fellow in Systematic Theology at New College, School of Divinity, University of Edinburgh. Robert is retired Instructor in Outdoor Sports (water sports, skiing, hillwalking, mountain biking), Edinburgh University (1984–2014) and Lecturer in Christian Theology, Edinburgh University Office of Life-long Learning (1984–2009). His publications include the edited works of T.F. Torrance: *Incarnation* (2008) and *Atonement* (2009), and articles in *Participatio*.

FOREWORD

GEORGE HUNSINGER

Thomas Forsyth Torrance (1913–2007) was arguably the greatest Reformed theologian since Karl Barth, with whom he studied, and an eminent twentieth-century ecumenist. Having served for twenty-seven years as Professor of Christian Dogmatics at New College, he was elected Moderator of the General Assembly of the Church of Scotland in 1976; and in 1978, he was awarded the Templeton Prize for Progress in Religion for his contributions to the emerging field of theology and science.

In theology, he generally placed himself somewhere between Calvin and Barth, though also moving well beyond them. An accomplished patristics scholar, he devoted himself to Eastern Orthodox-Reformed dialogue, being highly esteemed among the Orthodox for his ecumenical spirit and his grasp of primary sources in the original languages. He was even consecrated a Protopresbyter in the Patriarchate of Alexandria by the Archbishop of Axum in 1973. He once surprised me by saying that his favorite theologian was Athanasius, whom he placed in illuminating relationship with Karl Barth. An icon of the great Alexandrian appears as the frontispiece to his *The Trinitarian Faith* (1988), an exposition of the Nicene Creed, which remains perhaps the most accessible of his numerous learned works.

Besides the theologian, the ecumenist, and the church leader, there were at least three other Torrances: the translator, the interdisciplinary theologian, and the historian of doctrine. English-speaking theology stands greatly in his debt for his monumental efforts in editing and translating not only Calvin's New Testament commentaries but also Barth's voluminous dogmatics. His interest in Einstein and modern physics from the standpoint of Nicene Christianity has yet to be adequately assessed.[1] Least well known, perhaps, is his work as an intellectual historian. Scattered throughout many journals (some of them obscure) is a series of essays on virtually every major figure in the history of doctrine.[2] Alongside Athanasius he had a special fondness for Gregory Nazianzen, Cyril of Alexandria, and Hilary of Poitiers. In breadth of learning, depth of scholarship, quality of output, ecumenical conviction, and devotion to the Nicene faith, theology and church will not soon see another like him.

No theologian in recent times has made a clearer connection than Torrance between the Incarnation and the Cross, and between Christ's bodily Resurrection and his Ascension. Torrance states repeatedly that the Incarnation is the precondition of the Atonement as fulfilled in the Cross, and that the Cross is the inner completion of the Incarnation.

---

[1] However, the stellar work by Stevick goes far to rectify earlier, less than satisfactory treatments of Torrance on theology and science. See Travis M. Stevick, *Encountering Reality: T. F. Torrance on Truth and Human Understanding* (Minneapolis, MN: Fortress, 2016).

[2] It would be useful if they could be collected into a single volume.

Neither can be had without the other. Moreover, the Cross of Christ, for Torrance, as grounded in the Incarnation, necessarily carries intercessory and vicarious significance for the world's salvation. Finally, Christ's Resurrection serves uniquely not only to reveal him as the Incarnate Son, but also to elevate him into eternal life, where he intercedes perpetually for the church and the world until the end of all things.

No Reformed theologian since John Owen has had a firmer grasp than Torrance of Christ's priestly mediation. His contributions here, which I believe surpass Barth, are of inestimable significance. Barth is arguably less solid than Torrance about how to grant proper centrality to the New Testament's cultic metaphors—blood, sacrifice, access, intercession, vicarious representation, expiation, etc.—in a way that rightly displaces the forensic metaphors dominant in the West, while still affirming and preserving them. Torrance's grasp of the eucharist is therefore of greater ecumenical promise than anything to be found in Barth.

In this regard, it is worth noting that Torrance manages to hold together three great themes that are often split off from one another in contemporary theological discussion: substitution, participation, and exchange. When substitution is divorced from participation, it can seem as if substitution is merely a transaction that takes place over our heads—as if substitution had to come first and participation entered in only later. When participation is divorced from substitution, on the other hand, the result can effectively be sanctification without justification (or more subtly the absorption of justification into sanctification), which is arguably what happens in much modern liberal theology as well as in much high sacramental ecclesiology. By contrast, Torrance argues not only that "objective justification" precedes "subjective justification," but also that both are already participatory in themselves—by grace alone—before they are actualized subjectively through faith (Eph 2:8-9). For Torrance, therefore, Christ's humanity is not only vicarious but also all-inclusive at the same time.[3] He is "the man for others" in a unique sense, not just an ethical sense. For us and our salvation, he is the one true substitutionary and all-inclusive human being.

In his concept of the "faithfulness of Christ" (*pistis Christou*)[4]—a much disputed term in contemporary biblical scholarship—Torrance combines not only elements of "substitution" and "participation" (with both objective and corporate aspects) but also the indispensable "pattern of exchange."

> This reconciliation took place through a "wondrous exchange" ... in which Christ took our place, that we might have his place. ... The Son of God substituted himself in our place, ... taking all our shame and curse upon himself, ... that he might stand in humanity's place and work out in himself humanity's reconciliation.
>
> In that he thus took our place of sin and shame and death, he freely gives us his place of holiness and glory and life, that we through his poverty might become rich, that we through his being made sin and a curse for us, might be reconciled to God clothed

---

[3] Thomas F. Torrance, "Justification: Its Radical Nature and Place in Reformed Doctrine and Life," in *Theology in Reconstruction* (Grand Rapids, MI: Eerdmans, 1965), 150–68, esp. 153–60.

[4] I would say that the severe critique of Torrance by James Barr regarding the phrase *pistis Christou* may be regarded as philologically correct but theologically irrelevant. Torrance's judgments rest on a wider base than his mistaken philology. Like Barth, but unlike many New Testament scholars today, Torrance interprets the contested phrase vicariously, not merely in terms of participation without substitution. See Barr, *Semantics of Biblical Language* (London: Oxford University Press, 1961), 161–205.

with his righteousness and stand before God in his person. He came in our name, that we in his name might have access to the presence of the Father and be restored to him as his children.[5]

Like Barth, Torrance stresses that there is no system (no "ontology") by which such affirmations can be explained. They are either understood out of themselves or not at all.

Torrance's idea about "ontological healing" is an attempt to re-think the doctrine of sanctification. He attempts to place it within the frame of Christ's incarnational mediation, in which, to use Barth's words, our Lord "took this conflict into his own being" and "took part in it from both sides,"[6] including therefore from the human side.[7] Like Barth, only more so, Torrance explains both our justification and our sanctification by means of Christ's obedient humanity. For sanctification, this means that regeneration takes place in Christ before it takes place in us. For Torrance, there is one sanctification common to Christ and the church, and it is ours only by virtue of our participation in him (*unio mystica*).

As far as I can see, however, Torrance would have done better to describe the regeneration of fallen humanity in Christ by adopting Calvin's terms of "mortification" and "vivification." Instead he resorted to the metaphor of "ontological healing," apparently inspired by Nazianzen's famous saying that "the unassumed is the unhealed." Torrance's proposal was arguably better than the metaphor he used to advance it. His grasp of sanctification's objective pole as anchored in the Incarnation is largely an elaboration of (not a contradiction to) objective sanctification as developed by Barth. Admittedly, the actualistic motif is sharper in Barth than in Torrance, but it is by no means absent from the Scottish theologian. What Torrance arguably lacks, however, is a more robust "apocalyptic" sense of the drastic and inconceivable transition in Christ (and in baptism) from death to new life with God, a transition that the term "healing" does not quite grasp.

I believe that the future of Torrance studies will need to sort out some of his central ideas by elevating them to a higher level of analytical clarity. The problem lies not only with his less-than-crisp writing style. (It can often seem that he never met a relative clause he didn't like. He once confided to me, "My younger brother James writes better than I do." The elder brother might have profited from a good editor.) Beyond the numbing syntax, however, Torrance sometimes seems to operate at a highly intuitive level that can veer off into sheer cloudy vagueness. A prime example, it seems to me, can be found in his incessant polemic against something called "dualism." Kye Won Lee has usefully gathered a number of the instances into one place. He writes:

> For Torrance, the term "dualism" is generally applied to bipolarity distinctions such as the spiritual/physical (material), the spiritual (the non-given)/the sensuous (the given), the eternal/temporal (mutable), the intelligible/sensible, *noumena* (unknowable)/*phenomena* (knowable), the supernatural/natural, the other-/this-worldly, the inward (invisible)/outward (visible), the religious/moral, meaning/reality, interpretation (meaning)/fact (occurrences), the conceptual/non-conceptual, explanation/understanding, subject/object, sign/reality, the mythological/scientific, form/matter (being), structure/substance, the formal/ontological, the determinate/indeterminate, the theoretical/empirical,

---

[5] Torrance, *Atonement*, 128–9 (slightly modified; italics added).
[6] Barth, *Church Dogmatics* II/1, 397.
[7] See also Torrance, *The Mediation of Christ* (Colorado Springs: Helmers & Howard, 1992), 39–41, 67–9, 112–14.

theology/experience, theology/natural science, *Geschichte/Historie*, faith/sight, Gospel/law, the doctrine of the One God/Triune God, God/the world, God the Father/*Logos, anabatic/katabatic* Christology, the Person/work of Christ, redemption/creation, Giver/Gift, Offerer/Offering, water-/spirit-baptism, space and time as a three-dimensional/one-dimensional continuum, etc.[8]

Lee sums up: "Torrance describes dualism more extensively as atomistic, analytic, static, external, causal, determinate, closed, mystical, mythological, anthropocentric, moral, existential, subjective, and so on. Whatever is modified with these adjectives, therefore, is constantly rejected by his theology."[9] It seems fair to conclude that Torrance's sweeping rejections of "dualism" lack the necessary clarity because they are overly broad. There may be some good ideas in there struggling to get out, but all-purpose dismissals of "dualism" will in the future need to be more carefully unpacked.[10]

In conclusion, like his distinguished contemporaries Hans W. Frei and Eberhard Jüngel, Torrance thought with Barth and through Barth, while also going beyond him and against him. Barth himself had more than one occasion to remark: "*Ich bin kein Barthianer!*" Torrance shows himself to be a true "Barthian," because Barth would have it no other way. The contributors to this fine Handbook will do much to stimulate the careful and critical attention to Torrance that his achievement so richly deserves.

---

[8]Kye Won Lee, *Living in Union with Christ: The Practical Theology of Thomas F. Torrance* (New York: Peter Lang, 2003), 14n.15.
[9]Ibid., 14.
[10]When I wrote my study of Torrance on the sacraments, I felt compelled to filter out all the blooming, buzzing confusion about "dualism," because I felt it was detracting from the ecumenical reception of his ground-breaking work. See my "The Dimension of Depth: Thomas F. Torrance on the Sacraments of Baptism and the Lord's Supper," in Hunsinger, *Conversational Theology* (London/New York: T&T Clark, 2015), 21–43.

ACKNOWLEDGMENTS

The editors would like to thank the contributors to this important volume on a theologian we all greatly admire. Thanks are due for their expertise, time, and wisdom. The editors would also like to thank the entire team at Bloomsbury T&T Clark for their ongoing support of quality academic publications, with special thanks to our editor, Anna Turton, for her personal support and encouragement of our respective scholarship. The Thomas F. Torrance Theological Fellowship continues to be a vehicle for scholarly exchange and collegial fellowship, and we are deeply grateful for its ongoing work and for its support of this project. I (Myk) acknowledge as ever the support of my wonderful wife, Odele, and my two children, Sydney and Liam, and thank them for cheering me on from the sidelines. I would also like to thank Paul Molnar for his friendship over many years and for what I have learnt and continue to learn from him and his work. I (Paul) would like to thank Thomas F. Torrance himself not only for his friendship and support over many years but for his assistance in helping me to learn what it really means to think from a center in God. I would also like to thank Iain R. Torrance for his consistent friendship, support, and encouragement, especially as that relates to my work on his father's remarkable theology. Finally, I would like to thank Myk Habets not only for his contributions to this project but for his friendship and collegial collaboration over many years.

CHAPTER ONE

Introduction

PAUL D. MOLNAR

In his comprehensive biography of Scottish theologian Thomas Forsyth Torrance (August 30, 1913–December 2, 2007), who was an ordained minister in the Church of Scotland, Alister McGrath noted that Torrance was "one of the most productive, creative and important theologians of the twentieth century"[1] and "the most significant British academic theologian of the twentieth century."[2] While he is perhaps best known for his pioneering work in the study of science and Christian theology, it is clear that Torrance was equally respected both as a dogmatic or academic theologian and as a minister of the Gospel. He once stated: "I am primarily interested in the Gospel; and preaching. I am a missionary. And all my thinking is missionary and evangelistic. My theology is evangelistic and missionary. I am concerned in that kind of way with the Gospel."[3] Additionally, it has been said that Torrance's understanding of the sacraments offers a new synthesis of Calvin and Barth and improves on them such that his is "the most creative Reformed breakthrough on the sacraments since Calvin."[4]

TORRANCE AND BARTH

Torrance is also well known as a student of Karl Barth whom he described as "by far the greatest theologian of the modern era," and of whom he further stated that "it may well be that Barth's ultimate influence upon the whole Church will be comparable with that of Athanasius the Great."[5] Indeed, Torrance maintained that Barth "was unquestionably the greatest theologian that has appeared for several hundred years" noting that "Pope Paul [Pope Paul VI] used to say that he was the greatest theologian since Thomas Aquinas."[6] That of course did not mean that he was uncritical of Barth, as he himself raised questions to Barth's later view of the sacraments; to some of his explication of

---

[1] Alister E. McGrath, *Thomas F. Torrance: An Intellectual Biography* (Edinburgh: T&T Clark, 1999), 107.

[2] Ibid., xi. Recently, Torrance has been appropriately referred to as "arguably the greatest twentieth-century dogmatic theologian in the English-speaking world," in *Karl Barth, the Jews, and Judaism*, ed. George Hunsinger (Grand Rapids, MI: Eerdmans, 2018), 178.

[3] Cited in Myk Habets, *Theology in Transposition: A Constructive Appraisal of T. F. Torrance* (Minneapolis, MN: Fortress Press, 2013), 86–7.

[4] George Hunsinger, "The Dimension of Depth: Thomas F. Torrance on the Sacraments of Baptism and the Lord's Supper," *Scottish Journal of Theology* 54, no. 2 (2001): 160.

[5] Thomas F. Torrance, *Karl Barth, Biblical and Evangelical Theologian* (Edinburgh: T&T Clark, 1990), xi.

[6] Ibid., 1.

trinitarian doctrine, especially what he saw as the element of subordinationism within his position;[7] and to his more general reference to the "humanity of God" rather than a more specific focus on the humanity of the risen, ascended, and advent Lord.[8] He was never thrilled with Barth's choice to speak of the persons of the Trinity as modes of being and also moved beyond Barth in his own understanding of the *Filioque*.[9] Moreover, he thought that Barth's critique of Calvin's view of election did not do "full justice" to Calvin's own Christocentric emphases.[10] The positive eschatological point that Torrance wanted to stress with Calvin was that Christ came to save and not condemn humanity. Thus, there was no "twofold will of God for salvation and reprobation" but only God's gracious will to save us. This is what will be disclosed at the *parousia*.[11] Finally, according to McGrath, Torrance thought Barth's most serious weakness was his "failure to engage with the natural sciences,"[12] and this led Torrance to construct his own "new natural theology" in spite of Barth's thoroughgoing rejection of natural theology.[13]

TORRANCE THE PROFESSOR AND ECUMENIST

For twenty-seven years Torrance was professor of Christian Dogmatics at New College in the University of Edinburgh. He authored, edited, or translated a massive amount of material—more than 360 pieces before his retirement in 1979 and over 250 more after that; this included most famously his editing the English translation of the thirteen-volume *Church Dogmatics* written by Karl Barth, as well as John Calvin's New Testament *Commentaries*. He read the Church Fathers in their original Greek and often

---

[7]See Paul D. Molnar, "The importance of the doctrine of justification in the theology of Thomas F. Torrance and of Karl Barth," *Scottish Journal of Theology* 70, no. 2 (2017): 198–226, and "The obedience of the Son in the Theology of Karl Barth and of Thomas F. Torrance," *Scottish Journal of Theology* 67, no. 1 (2014): 50–69.

[8]See Torrance, *Karl Barth*, 134. See also Paul D. Molnar, Introduction to the Cornerstones edition of Thomas F. Torrance's *Space, Time and Resurrection* (London: T&T Clark, 2018), xxxv–xxxvi.

[9]George Hunsinger, *Evangelical, Catholic and Reformed* (Grand Rapids, MI: Eerdmans, 2015), 27–8. For a discussion of Barth and Torrance on the *Filioque*, see Paul D. Molnar "Theological Issues Involved in the *Filioque*," in *Ecumenical Perspectives on the Filioque for the 21st Century*, ed. Myk Habets (London: Bloomsbury T&T Clark, 2014), 24–34.

[10]See Thomas F. Torrance, *The School of Faith: The Catechisms of the Reformed Church*, trans. and ed. with an Introduction by Thomas F. Torrance (Eugene, OR: Wipf & Stock, 1996), lxxvii. Nonetheless, it is worth noting that Torrance was also critical of Calvin's view of predestination since he conceived the kingdom of God "too generally in terms of an overarching sovereignty of God" so that "Calvin's doctrine of election is conceived in terms of an act of predestination which is pushed back to some still point before and behind time, rather than as the living action of the eternal in time," Thomas F. Torrance, *Incarnation: The Person and Life of Christ*, ed. Robert T. Walker (Downers Grove, IL: IVP Academic/Milton Keynes: Paternoster, 2008), 302. Indeed, he also mentioned that in the end there was a problem in Calvin's polemical writings "in defence of predestination, for there is a tendency in them toward abstracting the work of God in election from the work of Christ," *The School of Faith*, lxxviii.

[11]Torrance, *The School of Faith*, lxxviii. That is why election and reprobation could not be held in any kind of equilibrium and conceptualized logically or systematically. To do so would obviate the fact that election is God's active love of humanity in time and space such that salvation refers to the salvation of humanity and of history and time and election therefore must not be allowed to undermine eschatology with a deterministic and static view tied to some "pre-temporal eternity" which would then undermine the importance of the "advent Christ," *Incarnation*, 302.

[12]McGrath, *Intellectual Biography*, 197.

[13]For a discussion of Torrance's "new natural theology," see Chapter 5.

provided his own translation of such important figures as Athanasius to advance his own understanding of essential doctrines. In 1978 he received the Templeton Foundation Prize for Progress in Religion. Torrance served as Moderator of the General Assembly of the Church of Scotland from 1976 to 1977. He worked determinedly toward visible and not just spiritual ecumenical unity with Anglicans, Lutherans, Eastern Orthodox, and Roman Catholics throughout his career; was consecrated a Protopresbyter in the Patriarchate of Alexandria in 1973 in recognition of his work with the Eastern Orthodox Church; became personal friends with the Roman Catholic cardinal and renowned ecumenist, Yves Congar; was founding editor of the *Scottish Journal of Theology* in 1948; led a colloquy discussing Karl Rahner's theology of the Trinity in 1975;[14] worked toward improved relations between Christians and Jews; and contributed to discussions with Roman Catholics and Reformed theologians regarding the doctrine of justification by faith and by grace. Torrance was instrumental in the development of the historic agreement between the Reformed and Eastern Orthodox Churches on the doctrine of the Trinity, which resulted in a joint statement of agreement on that doctrine issued between the World Alliance of Reformed Churches and the Orthodox Church on March 13, 1991.[15] He represented the Church of Scotland in dialogues with the Church of England from 1949 to 1951, was Convener of the Church of Scotland Commission on Baptism from 1954 to 1962, and was present at the World Council of Churches meeting in Evanston, Illinois, in 1954. From 1955 to 1959 he worked to publish five interim reports, and the final report on Baptism in 1960.[16] Torrance also served on the Reformed-Roman Catholic Study Commission on the Eucharist in Woudschoten, Holland, in 1974.

EARLY YEARS

Torrance was born of missionary parents in Chengdu, West China, where he attended a school established by Canadian missionaries from 1920 to 1927.[17] He later studied classics, philosophy, and the philosophy of science at the University of Edinburgh and began the formal study of theology in New College in 1934. Having read Schleiermacher's theology and appreciated its beauty, Torrance nonetheless believed Schleiermacher's fundamental presuppositions were not in harmony with the Christian Gospel and that "the propositional structure he imposed upon the Christian consciousness lacked any realist scientific objectivity."[18]

---

[14]See Thomas F. Torrance, *Trinitarian Perspectives* (Edinburgh: T&T Clark, 1994), 77–102.

[15]See Jason Radcliff, "T. F. Torrance and Reformed-Orthodox Dialogue," in *T. F. Torrance and Eastern Orthodoxy: Theology in Reconciliation*, ed. Matthew Baker and Todd Speidell (Eugene, OR: Wipf & Stock, 2015), 32–53 and *Thomas F. Torrance and the Orthodox-Reformed Theological Dialogue* (Eugene, OR: Wipf & Stock, 2018).

[16]McGrath, *Intellectual Biography*, 99–100.

[17]Ibid., 13.

[18]Torrance, *Karl Barth*, 121. Torrance forcefully argued that "the Ebionite-adoptionist theory of Christology is the only possible account of Christ's person, when the start is made from the naturalistic-historical point of view, which has so characterised modern theology since F.D.E. Schleiermacher," *The Doctrine of Jesus Christ* (Eugene, OR: Wipf & Stock, 2002), 65.

SCIENTIFIC THEOLOGY

Against this perspective, Torrance intended to pursue what he called a "scientific theology," that is, a theology whose propositions were determined by the unique nature of the object of reflection "and not according to arbitrary convention."[19] Hence, "In all scientific knowledge, including theology above all, man is unconditionally bound to his object, for to be bound and determined by what is objective is the core of rationality."[20] Because that object of reflection is God in his self-revelation as he meets us in his Word and Spirit one simply could not engage in scientific theology if theology is understood merely as a discussion of one's God-consciousness or one's religious experiences. What Torrance wanted to avoid at all costs was a theology that dissolved into a form of anthropology "in which meaning is expressed in the symbolic or mythological objectification of inward experience."[21] What he wanted to affirm as a scientific theologian was that the subject matter of theology must be controlled by the reality of God who reveals himself in Christ and through his Holy Spirit; theology is thus "controlled ... by reference to the ontological structures of realities being investigated."[22] That applies not only to revelation but to the eternal Trinity such that a proper understanding of the Trinity, which for Torrance was the ground and grammar of theology, must finally be governed by the internal relations within God himself as known in and from the economic Trinity.[23] Torrance famously opposed every form of dualistic thinking, both ancient and modern, since such thinking tended to separate God from the world in deistic fashion and made a proper understanding of God's interactions with us in history impossible by failing to take seriously the incarnation as the point of contact for God's actual relations with us in space and time (history) as the "medium of his self-revelation and self-communication to mankind." Taking the incarnation seriously meant simultaneously opposing both dualism and monism (pantheism). For Torrance, "Everything would go wrong if the creaturely reality of this world were confused with or mistaken for the reality of God, or if the contingent rationality of this world were denied its reality and overwhelmed by the transcendent rationality of God."[24] That is one reason why Torrance followed Athanasius and held that "we do not know God in disjunction from his relation to the

---

[19] Thomas F. Torrance, *The Trinitarian Faith: The Evangelical Theology of the Ancient Catholic Church* (Edinburgh: T&T Clark, 1988), 51.

[20] Thomas F. Torrance, *Theological Science* (Oxford: Oxford University Press, 1978), 303. Torrance persistently, powerfully, and quite properly opposed confusing the Holy Spirit with the human spirit as did "a great deal of modern Protestant theology" when theologians equated the Holy Spirit with "subjective awareness of God or religious self-understanding," Thomas F. Torrance, *Theology in Reconstruction* (London: SCM Press, 1965), 231. Torrance even noted that this confusion "means that modern religious man is afflicted with a deep-seated mental disease" since "failure to distinguish between objective realities and subjective conditions, or a confusion between them, is the primary mark of irrational behavior or mental disorder," ibid.

[21] Thomas F. Torrance, *Reality and Evangelical Theology* (Philadelphia, PA: Westminster Press, 1982), 29.

[22] Ibid.

[23] See, for example, Paul D. Molnar, *Thomas F. Torrance: Theologian of the Trinity* (Farnham: Ashgate, 2009), 44, 55–7. Torrance held that the doctrine of the Trinity was "the nerve and centre" of "all the other doctrines," Thomas F. Torrance, *The Christian Doctrine of God, One Being Three Persons* (London: Bloomsbury T&T Clark, 2016), 31, and that the epistemological function of the incarnation was to enable knowledge of the immanent Trinity, Thomas F. Torrance, *Theology in Reconciliation: Essays towards Evangelical and Catholic Unity in East and West* (London: Geoffrey Chapman, 1975), 222. That is why he also insisted that the Nicene *homoousion* was "the epistemological linchpin" of theology, *Christian Doctrine of God*, 95.

[24] Torrance, *Theology in Reconciliation*, 222.

world, as if this world were not his creation or the sphere of his activity towards us" while firmly rejecting the idea that we could know God "by way of logical inference from the world."[25]

TORRANCE, BARTH, AND HIS CHRISTOCENTRIC THEOLOGY

In 1936 Torrance was awarded the Blackie Fellowship to study in the Middle East. After returning to Scotland he graduated *summa cum laude* with his Bachelor of Divinity from the University of Edinburgh, having specialized in systematic theology.[26] With an Aitken Fellowship, he was able to study with Karl Barth in Basel, taking his seminar during the academic year 1937–38. He planned to continue studying with Barth, but he was needed to teach at Auburn Theological Seminary in upstate New York where he presented his important lectures in Christology, which were finally published in 2002.[27] These lectures are as relevant today as they were eighty years ago. Torrance explains why he thought "much modern theology" seemed "only to advance to the belief in the deity of Christ after much reflection, and then states it in such a guarded way and couched in such hesitating words that it appears evident that they have not really seen the Lord of Glory."[28] What he argued against was the idea that one could understand Jesus properly from a neutral or purely historical perspective without acknowledging his uniqueness as the incarnate Word who, as the living Lord who died on the cross and rose from the dead, was the only one who could actively disclose himself through his Holy Spirit by enabling people to believe in him as the Lord and Savior of the world. Hence, in his Edinburgh lectures in Christology he insisted:

> We cannot earn knowledge of Christ, we cannot achieve it, or build up to it ... In the very act of our knowing Christ he is the master, we are the mastered. He manifests himself and gives himself to us by his own power and agency, by his Holy Spirit, and in the very act of knowing him we ascribe all the possibility of our knowing him to Christ alone, and none of it to ourselves.[29]

Thus, to know Christ in his uniqueness "is the act of Christ himself, the miracle of his Holy Spirit" while relying on "our own experience and thought all we can arrive at here is the realisation that here is a fact beyond our natural powers to grasp."[30]

---

[25]Ibid.

[26]McGrath, *Intellectual Biography*, 42.

[27]See Torrance, *The Doctrine of Jesus Christ*.

[28]Ibid., 22.

[29]Torrance, *Incarnation*, 2. In his act of grace in giving himself to us "he remains not only our Lord but the Lord of our knowing of him, who certainly gives himself as the object of our knowledge yet in such a way that the gift is a continuous self-giving in which the gift and the Giver are identical, and therefore in such a way that he *retains his objectivity*, so that he may be known only in and through constant communion with him and ever fresh appropriation of his self-revelation," Thomas F. Torrance, *Space, Time and Resurrection* (London: T&T Clark, 2019), 173–4. This is not only how Jesus revealed himself to his contemporaries but how the risen and ascended Lord reveals himself here and now. It is precisely the historical Jesus with whom we are in communion through faith who is God's self-revelation such that it is "the historical reality of Jesus resurrected in his human integrity in such a way that the risen Lord remains in indissoluble unity and continuity with the incarnation in space and time, the same yesterday, today and for ever," ibid., 174.

[30]Torrance, *The Doctrine of Jesus Christ*, 22.

DISTINGUISHING FAITH FROM ITS OBJECT

With his scientific approach to theology, Torrance consistently and rigorously insisted that it was the object of faith and not faith itself that was the basis of truth in Christology, the doctrine of God and in understanding revelation in its identity with Christ the revealer. With Barth, he insisted that Jesus was not the revealer in his humanity as such, but that the revealing power was the power of the Word and the action of the Spirit. Hence, he wrote, "The Manhood of Jesus as such is not divine, nor the revelation of God. The human Jesus is never as such the 'locale' of revelation in the New Testament."[31] He maintained that the "modern" approach to Jesus was "entirely naturalistic" and for that reason simply conveyed "an idea" because it approached Jesus "in the spirit of an undertaker!"[32] Against this approach he insisted that the disciples were not "swept off their feet by the friendship and impact or spell of the man Jesus" but "encountered in him the power of God's Spirit, and it was this that enabled them to call him 'the Christ', 'the Son of the Living God.'"[33] Consequently, they were not simply people who valued Jesus because of his influence upon them, since their coming to believe in him was a "sheer miracle" through the Holy Spirit.[34]

TRINITARIAN THEOLOGY

In connection with contemporary discussions about trinitarian doctrine, some of which deny the possibility of knowing the immanent Trinity or overtly collapse the immanent into the economic Trinity, thus undermining the very possibility of a scientific theology, Torrance's own thinking was clear and firmly grounded in a proper understanding of the doctrine of the Trinity and Christology. He argued:

> We do not say that God is Father, Son, and Holy Spirit because he becomes Father, Son and Holy Spirit to us, but while we only know him because he becomes so to us,

---

[31] Ibid., 10.

[32] Ibid.

[33] Ibid. Torrance insists that the revelation of God in Christ "is a matter for the Spirit ... of Christ" and that "revelation came fully at Pentecost, but there were anticipations of it such as we find in Peter's confession: 'Thou are the Christ, the Son of the living God,'" ibid., 35. For Torrance, "The manifestation of the Son of God was an act of the Spirit to faith," thus Jesus's human teaching and historical activity are the "media through which the Holy Spirit supervenes in witness to Christ and thus to reveal to us the Father," ibid., 36. Nonetheless, there is no Nestorian separation of Jesus's humanity and divinity in Torrance's thinking. Thus, Jesus's entire teaching "is saturated with the consciousness of his Sonship and it all directs attention towards his own Person as the Son," ibid., 37, and Jesus "obtruded his own Person always into the field of his teaching, and all was calculated to concentrate attention on himself. In him was to be found the data of Christianity," ibid., 38. This, because he was not just a messenger of the truth but that he himself *is* the truth (Jn. 14:6) (ibid., 39). Faith, which acknowledges Christ's unique Person and actions, is "*Christ's own action*, his encounter with us, he who has come to save us ... It is thus through the action of Christ himself that we know him" (18). Indeed, for Torrance "the doctrine of the Holy Spirit has not a special content of its own; its content is the Person of Christ, Christ clothed with his own Truth," ibid., 49.

[34] Ibid. Torrance avoided any sort of Monophysitism or Nestorianism (which would espouse an adoptionist view of Jesus by disregarding the fact that he *is* the Word of God, God himself), ibid., 68–70, arguing that "revelation could not be made in such a way that the humanity as such and in itself was given out as or taken to be divine," ibid., 34; he wrote: "It was not the flesh and blood that revealed Christ and the true significance of his Person, not even the flesh and blood of Christ himself. What constitutes the revelation is ... the Divine within Christ—*God in Christ*," ibid., 35.

he only becomes Father, Son and Holy Spirit to us precisely because he *is* first and eternally Father, Son and Holy Spirit in himself alone. The doctrine of the Trinity which involves the very root and ground of Christian truth all in itself is the guard of truth here. If there is no such dogma as the Pre-existence of Christ, there can be no Trinity: and the central basis of Christianity would then be cut out. The Trinity and Pre-existence of Christ are tenets of faith that stand and fall together.[35]

Instead of holding the misguided view that history somehow constitutes Jesus's eternal Sonship,[36] Torrance quite properly held that while there is no God behind the back of Jesus Christ,[37] and while we cannot know the eternal Trinity except through him, all of God's actions for us are grounded in who God is eternally in himself as Father, Son, and Holy Spirit.[38] In other words Torrance opposed any idea of a dependent deity as undermining God's free grace. As he indicated in his doctoral thesis written under Karl Barth and completed *magna cum laude* in 1946, Torrance held that "grace is in fact identical with Jesus Christ in person and word and deed ... neither the action nor the gift is separable from the person of the giver."[39] After his service in the Second World War providing pastoral and practical support to Scottish soldiers in North Africa and Italy, Torrance eventually became minister at Beechgrove Church in Aberdeen and married Margaret Edith Spear on October 2, 1946.

TORRANCE'S FAMILY

The family eventually included Thomas Spear Torrance (born in 1947) who became an economist and philosopher of science at Heriot-Watt University in Edinburgh and is now retired; Iain Richard Torrance (born in 1949) who is a Church of Scotland minister, theologian and academic, pro-chancellor of the University of Aberdeen, dean of the Chapel Royal in Scotland including chaplain-in-ordinary to Her Majesty Queen Elizabeth II in Scotland, and honorary professor of Early Christian Doctrine and Ethics at the University of Edinburgh. Like his father, Iain was also Moderator of the General Assembly of the Church of Scotland (2003–04), former president and professor of Patristics Emeritus at Princeton Theological Seminary, Professor Emeritus, Aberdeen University, and was co-editor of the *Scottish Journal of Theology* from 1982 to 2015; Alison Meta Elizabeth Torrance (born in 1951) who is a medical doctor in general practice in Edinburgh.

---

[35] Ibid., 107.

[36] Torrance firmly asserted: "The idea held by Origen that God's relation to the created universe is necessary to his own Being was comprehensively destroyed by Athanasius," *Christian Doctrine of God*, 4. Thus, "we cannot think of the ontological Trinity as if it were constituted by or dependent on the economic Trinity," ibid., 108–9. George Hunsinger captures Torrance's thinking here perfectly: "Although Torrance agrees that God is involved in history, he holds that this is so only contingently, in other words not by ontological necessity, but strictly by free grace alone. In no sense did God need the world (or the cross of Christ) to constitute himself as the Trinity," *Evangelical, Catholic and Reformed*, 28.

[37] Torrance, *The Doctrine of Jesus Christ*, 15. See also *Christian Doctrine of God*, 5, 17, 24, 108, 177.

[38] Thus, "in the Gospel God does not just *appear* to us to be Father, Son and Holy Spirit, for he really *is* Father, Son and Holy Spirit in himself, and reveals himself as such," *Christian Doctrine of God*, 7. This thinking is in harmony with Barth's important assertion that "we cannot say anything higher or better of the 'inwardness of God' than that God is Father, Son and Holy Spirit," Karl Barth *Church Dogmatics*, I/2, 377.

[39] Thomas F. Torrance, *The Doctrine of Grace in the Apostolic Fathers* (Eugene, OR: Wipf & Stock, 1996), 33.

SUMMARY

This volume covers the wide range of Torrance's extensive work both in dogmatic theology and in connection with theology and science. Among the topics treated are his theological relationship with his mentor, Karl Barth; his continued pastoral activity preaching the Gospel; his emphasis upon practical ministry which greatly influenced his student, Ray Anderson; his specific contributions to the Orthodox–Reformed dialogue on the Trinity; his relational theological ontology; his understanding of divine and human agency along with his understanding of the incarnation (including Christ's vicarious humanity), his trinitarian theology, and his specific theology of revelation, atonement, and justification. Included is a discussion of specific Christological emphases such as his innovative use of the Patristic concepts of *enhypostasis* and *anhypostasis* and his specific hermeneutics. There is also an important discussion of Torrance's eschatology with special emphasis on how his understanding of the ascension shapes and should shape Christian theology. Finally, his ecumenism, ecclesiology along with his focus on the Christian life, and his relation to Scottish theology are discussed.

Overall, readers will find that this wide-ranging volume will provide a thorough and engaging overview of the theology of Thomas F. Torrance that will only entice more and more serious students of theology to engage his thought with a view toward the future of dogmatic theology and the relationship between theology and science. Torrance's theology is profoundly Christological and trinitarian and offers a thoroughly compelling and sensible explanation of the Christian faith that is certainly becoming appreciated by a growing number of doctoral students as well as by members of the Thomas F. Torrance Theological Fellowship, which was formed in 2004 and continues to thrive well into the first quarter of the twenty-first century.

PART ONE

Contexts

CHAPTER TWO

Why Read Torrance Today?

IVOR J. DAVIDSON

There is little reason to fear that Thomas F. Torrance will stop being read. His place among the most significant English-speaking theologians of the second half of the twentieth century is scarcely in doubt. A commanding presence in Scottish Divinity for thirty years and more, the exceptional energy of his scholarly and churchly activities generated a substantial literary output, which extended well beyond his formal retirement from academic life: a good many of his best-known books were produced over the two decades thereafter. His contributions to the study of theology's relations with the natural sciences were groundbreaking well before that; those ventures were also extended in maturity, establishing an unavoidable reference-point for reflection upon the terms on which theology and other kinds of human enquiry might seek to converse. Leading mediator of Barth to the English-speaking world, sponsor of enduring instruments of theological scholarship, pioneer of a particular rendition of Patristic and Reformed catholicity, passionate communicator, architect of ecumenism, advocate of an integrated account of nature, rationality, and knowledge in light of divine transcendence, Torrance's stature in the landscape of modern theological endeavor can hardly be missed.

Torrance's thought has engaged the attention of leading figures in academic theology, and his influence has been widely diffused. Individual themes in his work have given rise to a steady stream of doctoral projects, monographs, and journal literature; his major and lesser-known texts continue to be reissued, translated, and appreciated around the world. A scholarly society is devoted to the study of his theology; his archive and library bequest in Princeton are of attraction to researchers; conferences and study-groups discuss his work; lectureships and awards commemorate his name. His ideas continue to stimulate in theology and science, dogmatics, practical theology, hermeneutics, culture, and aesthetics.

In the present volume, a bare protreptic to Torrance's writings is hardly required. Yet for all the study of particular topics in his thought, critical panorama on his work remains fairly inchoate. A number of guides seek to show us his core convictions and rightly emphasize their interconnection;[1] an intellectual biography charts his career;[2] major

---

[1] Elmer M. Colyer, *How to Read T.F. Torrance: Understanding His Trinitarian and Scientific Theology* (Downers Grove, IL: InterVarsity Press, 2001); *The Nature of Doctrine in T. F. Torrance's Theology* (Eugene, OR: Wipf & Stock, 2001); Paul D. Molnar, *Thomas F. Torrance: Theologian of the Trinity* (Farnham and Burlington, VT: Ashgate, 2009); Myk Habets, *Theology in Transposition: A Constructive Appraisal of T. F. Torrance* (Minneapolis, MN: Fortress Press, 2013); see also Elmer M. Colyer, ed., *The Promise of Trinitarian Theology: Theologians in Dialogue with T. F. Torrance* (Lanham, MD: Rowman and Littlefield, 2001). Stephen D. Morrison, *T. F. Torrance in Plain English* (Columbus, OH: Beloved Publishing, 2017), offers a recent basic treatment.

[2] Alister E. McGrath, *Thomas F. Torrance: An Intellectual Biography* (Edinburgh: T&T Clark, 1999).

aspects of his thought are treated in an expanding literature and explored further in this *Handbook*. But granted the acknowledged relationships between many of these themes, and the extensive scope of Torrance's efforts to demonstrate that method, content, and form in theology go together, it is important to consider what it is about his approach to theology at large that remains worth reading and what it might mean to begin to read him well.

The challenges to measured appraisal are substantial: the sheer size of the *oeuvre*, and its erudition, which ranges in freedom across extensive tracts of biblical, historical, and dogmatic theology, philosophy, and science; the magisterial manner, inclined to large-scale analytical categorization, a frank and schematic construal of rights and wrongs in Christian tradition and the history of ideas; the density of style, fast-moving, repetitive, at times impatient of the reader's likely wants or tolerance of the jargon; the tight integration of convictions, which can make it seem as if the account of truth and error must stand or fall as a single package, incapable of assimilation in any alternative version or selection of its parts. The genres vary; the topic of the moment is ever vital and far-reaching in its entailments: apprehension in the proposed terms is generally emblematic of holistic discernment. The idiom reflects the personality: pastoral, generous, eager to initiate; also combative, blunt, uncompromising. Renewal of the church's teaching, preaching, and practice is ever the candid aim—that, and (or as) mission to the world. The tasks are serious. For various reasons, a final doctrinal synthesis is never produced, but the aspiration to articulate a comprehensive approach, and to ward off corrosion of its essentials, is never a matter of doubt. The ventures across conventional boundaries, and the pervasive insistence on the proper way to travel, pose issues for specialists in several fields. Categorical depictions involve compression on the one hand, huge claims on the other. The Torrancian can be torrential; structural complexity is unavoidable; the vision is never small.

Reception history attests the demands. The task of rendering fair account of all that Torrance's audiences have taken from him or had to say in response to his work would make for a large study in itself, but at a superficial level the choices have often appeared stark, not least because the central tenets are so tightly woven.

Both in his day and since, his work has held considerable persuasive power, commanding strong allegiance as expression of a Christian theology that is intellectually serious, spiritually rich, and practically engaged. Its influence has been disseminated internationally by former students and colleagues from diverse traditions. A number of its recurring themes, or ones related to them, have of course also been spread through the work of the wider Torrance family. It is unclear that his theology ought in fact to be treated as but the most elaborate or seminal expression of a genus, less clear still that its principles deserve to be associated with more distant sorts of dynastic influence; T. F. Torrance and his work belong in a class of their own and require to be considered on their own terms. Still, in as much as there may be said to be such a thing as "Torrance theology" or a "Torrance tradition,"[3] and other members of the family or those close to them have occupied positions within academy and church, the impact of his thought has been variously extended. Plenty of readers have come to Torrance's writings for themselves and discovered in them great appeal; his ideas have also afforded inspiration to theologians whose backgrounds have been quite different or whose career paths have barely or never

---

[3] Gerrit Scott Dawson, ed., *An Introduction to Torrance Theology* (London and New York: T&T Clark, 2007).

crossed with his. In all this, though, a fair proportion of the scholarship has been produced by those who have found his vision compelling and are understandably keen to advertise its strengths. Among enthusiasts, the sharper edges of critical questions have tended to be handled in fairly defensive terms, as failure to appreciate the depth of his wisdom or subtlety of its nuances; warm exposition has remained a dominant register.

For Torrance's critics, by contrast, the whole package looks a lot more problematic. Torrance's approach, for all its investments in texts and history, mishandles Scripture's language and literary forms, collapses the complexity of theology's temporal stories, projects a great tradition that never was half so simple—or a quarter so innocent of the dynamics of power. It also underestimates the realities of our present location, on modernity's steeper slopes. At its most ambitious—in engagement with philosophy, science, or the history of ideas—it seems perilously akin to an attempt to trump intellectual differences with dogma or co-opt other discourses as ill-fitting instruments for the public elaboration of private fiduciary claims. In the malformation of strategy, Barth—as Torrance understood him, at any rate—plays a prominent part, supported by other unlikely prophets of liberation for our times. To Torrance, Calvin—seldom a hero of progressive Scotland—was a giant; Athanasius the greatest "modern" theologian. Old concepts generate obvious reductions and no less obvious tensions. Torrance was, admittedly, no uncritical reader of Barth; but even where he seeks to go beyond (his) Barth in pursuit of other possibilities, the results are dubious: the quest for a "scientific theology" both ancient and modern yields only a philosophically unsatisfying account of God, nature, and knowledge—variously diagnosable as foundationalist or exclusive; a trivialization at any rate of the diverse methods and aims of the contemporary natural sciences, perhaps even of classical theology itself. On these kinds of judgments, Torrance's work emerges, in all its learning, as exercise in conservative hubris or at any rate wishful thinking. The idiom of its pleas for reform remains austere. Academic scourge of a more liberal faith, the program underestimates the challenges posed by serious biblical and historical work, conjures up an epistemology far too neat, fails to reckon with legitimate diversity in the church or the messy realities of a late modern world. In so far as it appears resistant to selective reconstruction, the enterprise can only be viewed from afar; an approach less definite or all-encompassing makes for a gentler life.

To be carried along in a mightily powerful flow or radically to dissent? The contrasts need hardly be quite that simplistic. Still, as Torrance's immediate students and colleagues found, reactions have tended to the polar; "preaching for a verdict"[4] generates results. Torrance could enthrall, and he could overwhelm. His didactic style eschewed pretensions to academic detachment, the supposedly neutral survey of a range of possibilities; open advocacy lay at its heart, polemical analysis a part of it, irony nowhere in sight. The writing is of a piece: it can be accessible; it can also be pretty hard work. Faced with intellectual energy and personal conviction of such an order, sifting the contents of the whole, celebrating and assimilating the strengths while legitimately probing the weaker points, has never been all that easy. The range and complexity of the material, and the forcefulness of its expression, are reflected in the diversity of responses to its general weight; the issues may also be affected by judgments as to the ways in which the ideas have assumed shape in ecclesiastical and academic life.

---

[4] Principle of his cherished teacher, H. R. Mackintosh.

Even where Torrance's passion for classical doctrine has been warmly endorsed, his criticisms of Calvinist scholasticism and its perceived legacies have invited rejoinder as construal of a Reformed faith. On this tack, Torrance's hostility to venerable themes of seventeenth-century confession typifies the prejudices of Barthian "neo-orthodoxy," a pernicious modern force whose repudiation or quirky reconstruction of historic Reformed investments evinces a fair measure of confusion in general. In Torrance's case, the deficiencies are evident in expositions of the knowledge of God which take pots at certain versions of objectivist biblicism; they are found in larger letters in readings of doctrinal history, not least its Scottish chapters, which willfully espouse positions on incarnation, atonement, and evangel that knew, in proximate versions, no shortage of controversy in days gone by. On his part, it remains a matter of firm profession that *his* accounts of the themes, not those of Westminster and its champions, are consistently evangelical: faithful to Scripture and creed, true to Calvin at his trinitarian and participatory best, in line with Scottish instincts in their richest authentic forms. The Greek Fathers opened up vistas that federalism and legalism, afflicted by recurring ailments of the Latin West, failed to behold; the wiser among the Reformed managed to get the panorama. To those unpersuaded of the history, or yet uneasy with the name of Barth or his alleged effects, the realities are more stark: noble the ambitions, brilliant the achievements—Torrance's theology remains, alas, a mixture of the congenial and the dodgy.

As the debates illustrate, Torrance can be read along many tracks: as dogmatician; as historical theologian; as exegete of Scripture; as reader of Barth; as interpreter of Reformed traditions; as exponent of a reconstructed natural theology; as epistemological realist and advocate of "scientific" method; as ecumenist; as theologian of church, ministry, and proclamation. What we make of his work along any of these paths will of course depend in part on what we bring to the task and on our willingness to call into question our own assumptions about the ways, means, and ends of theological activity: about the nature of Scripture's authority, the place of creeds and confessions, the weight of history and tradition, the identity of the church, the roles of experience, reason, and culture, the do's and don'ts of responsible handling of texts and ideas.

Sensitively engaged, Torrance's thought, for all its associative features, need hardly stand or fall as a whole: it has, inevitably, genuine strengths and genuine weaknesses; whatever the demands, substantive assessment entails appreciation and critique. But the sorts of appeal or difficulty we perceive in the details involves determinations about what might be of core significance in theological work; and it is here that Torrance's approach at large may be said to press for our attention. Everything does not quite—after all—rely on everything else in his thinking; certain procedural things, however, matter a very great deal—and to their importance we do well to pay heed. Some of the principles have perhaps started to be appropriated a little better today than when he first advanced them; others, arguably, have not, or at any rate their counsel is ever pertinent. To give Torrance's fundamental approach the consideration it deserves, and to do so whatever that may mean for our own habits, is to move beyond mere rehearsal of his obvious thematic moves: it is to begin to consider what his method in theology may have to offer to constructive work today.

The musings that follow are entirely subjective and very basic. The simplicity will not surprise; if the impressions find an echo or so in the judgments of others, that would, I guess, be reassuring.

I

First, what exactly is it we encounter if we begin to read him?

A huge amount, written over a long life. Students often ask where to start. Interests and aptitudes vary, as do supervisory prejudices. In terms of general access, a case might be made for the Christology–soteriology–pneumatology, then the trinitarian studies, then the theology and science, in all its incremental spread; a selection of the (arguably more dated) historical exercises and work on Barth perhaps last of all. But that of course risks leaving out a very great deal on church, ministry, sacraments, and ecumenism; on biblical interpretation, creation, theological anthropology, eschatology; on the Christian life, preaching, physical science, knowledge, ethics, law, education, and more. All this too has much to say to those prepared to give it their energy. The ongoing collection and reissuing of out-of-print and lesser-known material is an important enterprise, as is the distribution of his work in electronic form.[5]

To follow any purely thematic approach is to ignore chronology: texts and ideas float free of their original locations. Self-evidently, Torrance's theology changed a great deal less than some. Synthesis, a quest to identify a unitary structure in faithful confession of the gospel, was an early impulse; bold opinions were ventured from the first. Looking back, he considered a good many of his philosophical and theological principles already formed in student years: a deep investment in the reality of divine revelation, in biblical exegesis, and in the power of theology to converse with all things else on its own terms rather than as exercise in vague theistic correlation; an abiding antipathy to the perceived

---

[5] One idiosyncratic, distinctly non-chronological, sequence for selected reading, as a bare minimum: Thomas F. Torrance, *The Mediation of Christ* (Exeter: Paternoster, 1983); *Incarnation: The Person and Life of Christ*, ed. Robert T. Walker (Downers Grove, IL: IVP Academic/Milton Keynes: Paternoster, 2008); *Atonement: The Person and Work of Christ*, ed. Robert T. Walker (Downers Grove, IL: IVP Academic/Milton Keynes: Paternoster, 2009); select chapters in *Theology in Reconciliation: Essays towards Evangelical and Catholic Unity in East and West* (London: Geoffrey Chapman, 1975) [above all: "The Mind of Christ in Worship"], *Theology in Reconstruction* (London: SCM, 1965); *Gospel, Church, and Ministry*, ed. Jock Stein (Eugene, OR: Pickwick, 2012); *Trinitarian Perspectives: Toward Doctrinal Agreement* (Edinburgh: T&T Clark, 1994); *The Trinitarian Faith: The Evangelical Theology of the Ancient Catholic Church* (Edinburgh: T&T Clark, 1988); *The Christian Doctrine of God, One Being Three Persons* (Edinburgh: T&T Clark, 1996); *Theological Science* (London: Oxford University Press, 1969; 2nd edition, Edinburgh: T&T Clark, 1996); *God and Rationality* (London: Oxford University Press, 1971); *Christian Theology and Scientific Culture* (Belfast: Christian Journals/New York: Oxford University Press, 1980); *The Ground and Grammar of Theology: Consonance between Theology and Science* (Charlottesville: University Press of Virginia/Belfast: Christian Journals, 1980); *Reality and Evangelical Theology* (Philadelphia, PA: Westminster Press, 1982); *Divine and Contingent Order* (Oxford and New York: Oxford University Press, 1981); *Transformation and Convergence in the Frame of Knowledge: Explorations in the Interrelations of Scientific and Theological Enterprise* (Belfast: Christian Journals/Grand Rapids, MI: Eerdmans, 1984); *The Christian Frame of Mind* (Edinburgh: Handsel Press, 1985); *Reality and Scientific Theology* (Edinburgh: Scottish Academic Press, 1985); *Scottish Theology: From John Knox to John McLeod Campbell* (Edinburgh: T&T Clark, 1996); *Divine Interpretation: Studies in Medieval and Modern Hermeneutics*, ed. Adam Nigh and Todd Speidell (Eugene, OR: Pickwick, 2017); *Divine Meaning: Studies in Greek Patristic Hermeneutics* (Edinburgh: T&T Clark, 1992); *The Hermeneutics of John Calvin* (Edinburgh: Scottish Academic Press, 1988); *Karl Barth, Biblical and Evangelical Theologian* (Edinburgh: T&T Clark, 1990). The mature dogmatics are best sampled in *The Trinitarian Faith* (the book Torrance considered his best) and *The Christian Doctrine of God*. These two books may well, along with *Theological Science*, remain his most enduring. Some of us are unlikely to stop sending our students to *Space, Time and Incarnation* (London: Oxford University Press, 1969) and *Space, Time and Resurrection* (Edinburgh: Handsel Press, 1976), brief as these studies are; *Royal Priesthood*, Scottish Journal of Theology Occasional Papers, no. 3 (Edinburgh: Oliver & Boyd, 1955; 2nd edition, London and New York: T&T Clark, 1993), deservedly remains a short classic as an ecumenical endeavor to derive a high doctrine of the church's ministry and sacraments from the priestly work of Christ.

legacies of Augustine, Schleiermacher, and Ritschl. As his academic teaching and writing took form, his depictions of the Christian past featured recurring sets of heroes and villains; in the former case, the collective imprint of Athanasius, Cyril of Alexandria, Calvin, and Barth is unmistakable.

It can seem as if all the really formative determinations came early: parental example—deeply devotional, evangelistic, interconfessional; the influence of particular teachers—H. R. Mackintosh above all; Daniel Lamont also; the pull of Barth in the 1930s and a sense of the alternatives in Scotland; disappointment with the moderatism of his distinguished professor and future colleague John Baillie. A year under Barth in Basel was worth several elsewhere; the United States, Oxford, small-town parish ministry, war service, and Aberdeen added much in intellectual as well as practical terms, not least confirmation that serious study could be prosecuted amid a life of intense activity. The scholarly ventures were under way well before appointment to New College: the founding of the Scottish Church Theology Society; the launching of the *Scottish Journal of Theology*; publishing, including the early issue of his doctoral work on grace in the apostolic fathers[6] and the completion of a monograph on Calvin's anthropology (part of its context the enduring burdens of the Barth–Brunner debate).[7] Missionary zeal was strong; the vocation to a teaching ministry was no preference for academy over church, only the integral fulfilment of a calling to evangelize and renew. In pursuit of the goal, the professional moves would be few: extensive travels and lecturing aside, beyond a short spell at Auburn Seminary Torrance elected to remain in Scotland (on its eastern side at that) throughout his career.

Nevertheless, Torrance's work unfolded across several decades of substantial evolution in society, church, and academy; it was inevitably affected by the circumstances in which he operated, and went on learning, over that extended period. One of the tasks which remains to be taken more seriously than it has is the contextualization of his thought in the particular influences, challenges, and concerns of a working life that stretched well into his later years. Periodization of the relationships between his own research or interactions and his written work is hardly clear-cut. His papers, diaries, interviews, and autobiographical reflections offer important reference-points; a tiny part of his reading year by year can also be glimpsed in his extensive work as reviewer, commentator, translator, and editor. But he could himself be prone to overstate continuities; a fuller picture of his intellectual development still waits to be built up from contextual analysis of his writings text by text and from the cultural histories of the overlapping worlds in which he worked.

The major themes of his scholarship and teaching from the early 1950s to the late 1970s—grace, anthropology, ecclesiology, ministry, sacraments, eschatology, incarnation, atonement, resurrection and ascension, pneumatology, space and time, epistemology, theological science, creation, natural theology, and hermeneutics—are situated in multiple contexts: the promotion of Barth and Barth studies, often in the face of misunderstandings; efforts to move beyond Barth as well as with him, not just in navigating controversy over natural theology but also on human agency in response to grace; wide-ranging participation in ecumenism and the opportunities it afforded for deepening research in Patristics; the effects of postwar "biblical theology," invested afresh (controversially) in canon, linguistic revelation, and alternatives to historical skepticism;

---

[6]Thomas F. Torrance, *The Doctrine of Grace in the Apostolic Fathers* (Edinburgh: Oliver and Boyd, 1948).
[7]Thomas F. Torrance, *Calvin's Doctrine of Man* (London: Lutterworth Press, 1949).

endeavors for renewal in sacramentalism and liturgy; the politics of the Church of Scotland and Torrance's several roles as (sometimes frustrated) reformer among the Reformed; the expansion of religious studies as an academic discipline; relationships with colleagues in Edinburgh and elsewhere; wide-ranging engagements in philosophy and the sciences.

Genres differed: for many years, essays, journal articles, and shorter studies were the primary instrument. The groundbreaking *Theological Science* appeared in 1969; most of the larger books came later. Preaching was an enduring passion, in lecture-room as well as church; Torrance's convictions on what it meant to proclaim Christ, and some of the sermons which enacted them, deserve study in their own right. The obligations of teaching, speaking, or church committee work were often initial impetus for scholarly explorations. Quite a number of published texts would evolve from lecture-series, their final form affected by some of the interactions to which those occasions gave rise. Responses to inept or lazy questions could be devastating; Torrance could also be a listener and a generous encourager of the keen. The pastoral dimensions to the theological instruction were never too far away. Early counsel for students on what it meant to proceed well—rather than badly—could be found in the lengthy introduction to his book of Reformed catechisms.[8]

In all of it, influences and targets varied; the wider theological landscape also evolved. Torrance's views of Calvin, and certainly his readings of Barth, ought not to be assumed to be static, far less ever somehow uncritical. His doctoral project aside, the Fathers feature surprisingly little in some of his earlier writing: even Athanasius, his favorite theologian, though the subject of major essays from the mid-1970s, is quoted a lot less in the 1960s and 1970s as a whole than we might expect; much more substantial work in Greek Patristics came later. A history of theology in his homeland—or an expanded set of soundings on prominent characters of the Kirk from the sixteenth to the nineteenth centuries—was written up last of all, after years of amassing "old Scottish books";[9] only in later life was there opportunity to explore the territory in something of the depth earlier desired.

A large part of Torrance's dogmatic oeuvre was wrought in his maturity, over the 1980s and early 1990s. The investments, particularly in trinitarian theology, were of long standing, the methods hardly new,[10] but the arguments were the work of one who had thought about the issues over many years and gone on reading a great deal. He had variously heard or dismissed objections to his convictions and observed alternatives in practice. He had engaged closely with the Orthodox world over a lengthy period; his ways of construing Reformed history, and his efforts to shape his own church, had also known diverse effects. His study of the Fathers had significantly expanded. Broader disciplinary changes had begun to occur: theology had come to evince far more interest in trinitarianism, and in doctrine generally, than it had in the 1960s or 1970s; biblical scholarship was no longer at risk of general domination by narrowly textual and historical studies, unrelated or hostile to constructive theological conclusions; preoccupations with

---

[8] Thomas F. Torrance, *The School of Faith: The Catechisms of the Reformed Church* (London: James Clarke/New York: Harper & Row, 1959). Torrance's regular lecturing style in Edinburgh can be sampled in *Incarnation* (2008) and *Atonement* (2009); a sample of his lectures at Auburn were issued as Thomas F. Torrance, *The Doctrine of Jesus Christ* (Eugene, OR: Wipf & Stock, 2002).

[9] Torrance, *Scottish Theology*, ix.

[10] Division of labor (only) between chairs in New College meant he had been unable to lecture on the doctrine as fully as he might have wished during the 1960s and 1970s.

(so-called) prolegomena—theology's "problems"; faith and history; the place of reason; religious language—had begun to recede somewhat, at least in their mid-century versions; social, political, and moral questions loomed larger, as did the relationship between Christian confession and other religious faiths in increasingly complex societies.

Torrance's interests in these developments were differential: some of the changes in attitudes to doctrine and Scripture were to him welcome indeed, other cultural concentrations much less so. His ambitious arguments on the relation between theology and the natural sciences staked their own claims in a world conscious of intellectual advance, urging theologians in particular to catch up. What it meant to be a missionary to a scientific culture had certainly expanded. He did not produce any of his work in a vacuum; treatments which move casually between texts and situations may fail to reckon with important dimensions of its shape.

Along any path in his thought, what is on offer is an expressly positive theology, but also, at every stage, a counterproposal to other ways of proceeding. To some of his colleagues, especially in the 1960s and 1970s, the counsel could seem pretty old-fashioned, its prescriptions out of step with "modern thinking." To him, assumptions about what was culturally conservative and what was not remained moot. Throughout his career, he showed interest in interrogating contemporary conventions, plotting their genealogies, and venturing assessment of their fruits. The labors are constructive—never in any open-ended imaginative sense but as expansive testimony to truth that sets free. At the same time, the summons to heed the Word involves warnings against ways of thinking and acting that might compromise its liberating clarity or lose sight of the wonder of which it speaks. "Cutting through confusion" is, one way or another, a familiar refrain. A certain stance *contra mundum* continued to be necessary.

Torrance was never merely a commentator on religious trends: current fashions were to be treated with caution, viewed in light of longer history; current problems the more so. His energies are regularly devoted to tackling underlying causes as much as symptoms of present pathologies: that way, the assumption goes, disease is thrown off best. Political situations or the ideologies which underpinned them elicited firm diagnoses and proposals on various fronts, but it would be quite incorrect to imagine that concerns with the contemporary dominate everything. No small part of Torrance's reasoning is a steady case that good theological work avoids obsession with immediate cultural circumstance, in so far as it has other, more potent investments: in the capacities of divine purpose and agency, which lie far beyond identifiable restrictions on the creaturely side. Still, a measure of critical work was ingredient in attesting the splendor of God's desire to be known by creatures and his self-movement to make that happen; theology's attention to the miracle of grace involved its deliverance from modes of operating which variously engendered self-importance or despair.

If Torrance was ever the evangelist, he was evangelist not least to a discipline which evinced recurring tendencies to get things wrong. As he saw it, liberal Protestantism of the nineteenth and early twentieth centuries, its roots in older problems, had signally failed to recognize that God is God in his own right and on his own terms; that it is on the basis of God's free and gracious action within temporal history that creatures are given to know him as he really is. The domestications of idealism and subjectivism—brilliantly diagnosed by Barth—had not remotely disappeared; they rumbled on in diverse successor forms. A large proportion of contemporary theological writing remained severely inhibited by biblical and doctrinal criticism, essentially anxious about the church's confession, unclear about what it was possible for theology to say under the philosophical conditions of modernity. In Torrance's judgment, the discipline's most significant challenges lay not so much in pressures from without as disarray within: in theologians' loss of confidence in the self-authenticating glory of their subject and in the riches of its proper resources.

The authority of Scripture, tradition, and the church's witness might slide away for various reasons; one way or another, a basic question prevailed: Was God to be sought where he might be found, or was he not? Where the actuality of divine revelation was matter for doubt as much as faith, projects of correlation naturally prevailed. In some of these might appear, on the surface, pleasant and worthy aspirations; underneath lay a deadly anthropocentrism and in real terms intellectual bondage rather freedom. In practice, the valorized bore more than passing resemblance to the conventional; where revisionist theology's content was not merely negative, a denial of what could be espoused by the respectable, it emerged as all-too-generic moralizing—personal or civic virtue baptized, doctrine as cipher for endeavor, the pursuit of aspirations whose formulae had been established on other grounds. Sometimes, too, as history showed, the face of theology's cultural alignments was far worse: associations with ideals that evinced no virtue whatsoever, only the worst forms of political wickedness as quasi-religious scheme. In real terms, all projections of human devising, whatever their form, were exercises in idolatry; bad news indeed for those without prospect whatever of clawing their own way to the divine.

The gospel declared something far more radical when it spoke of the presence of the living God in Jesus Christ. The uniquely liberating power of that reality demanded bold proclamation. It could not be domesticated as some dangerously amorphous appeal to personal experience or to the values of a broken world. The church, and not least its theologians, was summoned to heed the call, for that world's sake.

II

What might it mean, though, to read him *today*?

We do not pick up any of Torrance's work in the situations in which he produced it; the cultural circumstances in which Christian theology is undertaken both locally and globally have changed quite significantly since then. The demography is different: obvious structural decline and increasing marginality in traditional heartlands; rapid expansion elsewhere, not least in parts of the world where prospects seemed quite otherwise not so long ago. New patterns in mission and theological education have emerged in turn. A number of the big themes of Torrance's era in British theology—the legacies of Bultmannian demythologizing; the existential or symbolic approaches of Paul Tillich or John Robinson; the death-of-God theologies of the 1960s; the revisionist accounts of Christian doctrine which hit the headlines in the 1970s; the relationship between Christianity and Marxism—are not the kinds of reference-points they were; the expressions of the underlying issues have at any rate moved on.

It is no longer the case that *wissenschaftlich* approaches seem destined to possess unchallenged prestige in biblical scholarship, or that serious reading of early Christian texts has to occur chiefly as study of late antiquity, or that the Reformers must be heroes only to sectarians, or that the arguments of medieval intellects are necessarily left to those with little else to consider. Even the theology of Scotland has begun to receive fresh attention. Science has continued to develop very rapidly and in some of the ways Torrance himself anticipated; the vestiges of an Enlightenment project such as he felt reason to critique them in the 1960s and 1970s have at the same time continued to crumble fast.

Compared with some of its expressions at Torrance's mid-career, systematic theology has, amid the cultural upheavals, experienced a measure of invigoration. The societal and institutional environments may be very different; at least some aspects of theology's work are also undertaken in a greater degree of intellectual articulacy, in more ecumenical styles, and with wider sorts of engagement, than might have been anticipated—in Britain in particular—a generation or two ago. Profound challenges persist: cultural relativism, indifference, and hostility are as real as ever they have been; the instincts, demands, and cynicism of consumerist societies are ever present; patterns of recruitment to theological study and teaching are far less ecclesial; curricular structures have shifted, adding useful things in some areas, removing plenty in others, not least on the particularity of theology's methods. There is no shortage of faddishness on display; regular preoccupations may be the demonstration of respectability or survival of audit. Yet biblical work in theologically constructive modes shows at least some signs of flourishing; philosophical theology of positive rather than reductive sorts has found renewed energy; endeavors in theology's significance for the arts, sciences, politics, economics, and other fields may be more ambitious than they were. A number of the doctrinal themes which Torrance started to unpack in his major essays and commended at length in his dogmatic texts of the 1980s and 1990s have been championed by others; the fruits have been evident in patterns of graduate study and the subsequent teaching styles of its beneficiaries. It is no longer necessarily a sign of atavistic behavior to pursue research in trinitarianism, incarnation, atonement, or pneumatology, or to study Barth, or to suppose that doctrinal work might indeed bear crucial yields in ecumenism, worship, ethics, or mission.

Some of this might be said to make Torrance's legacy more rather than less appealing; several of the positive changes have discernible debts to his influences. Hardly all of what is fashionable is, however, great; the contemporary practices of theology go on evincing plenty of interests and attitudes that might be deemed ill-conceived, a misappropriation of history or ignorance of its pedagogy. Nor is it hard to see why some of the grander activities of contemporary theologians might matter a great deal less to the life of the churches, never mind the world in general, than self-important academics are inclined to suppose. Torrance for his part liked to say he was not really an academic at all and pressed his students not to approach theological thinking as any sort of detached exercise. But what might commitment mean, and what are its criteria?

If theology in Torrance's time was heavily affected by questions of context and experience, the perceived challenges or opportunities of a modern world, the presence of such questions today is greater still. Issues of race, culture, gender, poverty, and ecology, of religious and philosophical pluralism, of militant atheism, of globalization and empire, of geopolitics, ideology, and terrorism, have come to loom far larger in theological consciousness; so too have diverse expressions of postmodern irony. The relationship between theologies substantially driven by questions of personal situation or local identity, and a catholic confession which transcends expressivism or political constraint and can indeed be shared with the whole world, is a question of some importance. Profound changes to the map of Christianity in global terms make the matter all the more significant. How are theologians today to identify and express what really matters, and how should their work proceed if they are to speak aright of God and all things else in relation to God?

If Torrance's theology is to be understood at all in the settings in which we may find ourselves, one of its fundamental convictions—learned in particular from Barth—requires to be seized. In Torrance's logic, the church at large—the sphere in which theologians ought to see their primary vocation—must take its broader cultural environment seriously, but not with the wrong kinds of seriousness. As far as Christian theology is concerned, whatever else is going on, there is the evangel of God, its authority, content, and ends his. The church's intellectual and social context is real indeed and must be treated as such; it is not, however, a fate, nor do its putative opportunities or imperatives establish the possibilities of faith's confession. What the evangel announces is, for faith, interpretative of all things and comprehensively redemptive. Confession never floats free of its cultural forms; but these forms are, for faith, responsible in so far as they are—humbly, gladly—transparent to the reality declared in divine action. Wherever we may be, the primary determinants of theology's substance and of its tasks must themselves be theological; its essential resources and critical norms remain those of gospel and church. Here are the criteria for faith's commitment today, as ever.

Torrance delighted in the vitality of Christian confession in a changing world; well into his old age he went to great lengths to promote it internationally. But, as the testimony of the faithful in Chengdu and Wenchuan in the mid-1990s showed, the conditions for the church's flourishing do not lie in human hands, nor can their fulfilment be reduced to a story of human inventiveness. If theology is to view its vocation correctly, it must recall that its work is at every point located within the divine economy, and subject to its sovereign authority, wondrous and untamable all at once. In any situation, Torrance insists, theology is obligated to pursue its business in certain kinds of ways, in as much as these are essential corollaries of the gospel's realism. Where theologians lose sight of them, as they persist in doing, they need to be redirected.

Whatever our world looks like as compared with Torrance's, his work continues to press at least four things upon us as crucial. In a thorough exposition, each of these themes would need to be traced out properly in his writings over time, its development plotted in detail according to context. All can however be said to be widely characteristic of his overall approach and basic to its message. We note them in barest outline only.

1. The Essential Nature of Theological Reasoning

Dogmatic theology, as Torrance discerns it, is the church's endeavor to give faithful conceptual account of God's self-communicative presence. Only God reveals God; in free and merciful divine movement toward us, creatures are granted creaturely taste of God's perfect knowledge of himself. If revelation occurs as reconciliation, theology is a positive and joyful science, set free from the perils of experientialism or merely aspirational endeavors to approach divinity. Theology is not condemned to seek God under its own steam or by its own imaginative energies; nor is it obliged to confine itself to apophatic silence or negativity in the face of inscrutable mystery. Relativism of all kinds is to be repudiated. Thinking "from a center in God" rather than a center in the human mind means taking the purposes, means, and ends of divine self-presence in the particularity of its occurrence with seriousness and with delight.

As Torrance sees it, it is not possible to speak rightly of the nature of Scripture or faith or reason or experience, or of the church's responsibilities in worship, ministry, fellowship, or proclamation, without speaking immediately of the determinate purposes and action of the God who wills to be known. Theology's authority, its resources, contexts, aims, and ends can only be identified in light of the history of God's creating, reconciling, and perfecting ways. Doctrinal theology seeks to pick out the details of that history in specific terms, under the instruction of God's Word. The connections between its themes are indeed significant in as much as these themes together necessarily refer beyond themselves to their divine Subject. The task of doctrinal exposition is no exercise in abstraction; it is a wondering attempt to give orderly confession of God's self-disclosure, without which we can properly say nothing. The quest is not for a system as such, normed by some overarching set of principles (the reality of God can never be so reduced); it is for faithful and clear attestation of what is and is not presented in the reality of divine self-giving.

All of the really big moves in Torrance's mature dogmatics are intended to set forth the coherence and proportions of that matter. The Nicene *homoousion* is "ontological and epistemological linch-pin" of the revolution wrought in human knowledge by the presence of God's true being in the personal act that is his enfleshed Word, Jesus Christ, among us, made known in the Spirit's power. The Holy Spirit is crucial to our personal apprehension of the knowledge of God in Christ, the essential agent of our access in faith to God as he really is, our great divine deliverer from the hopelessness of reliance on ourselves. The Trinity is "ground and grammar" of Christian theology from first to last.

For Torrance, the careful articulation of all this has unavoidably sharp edges. God makes himself known in time as he really is, his inner being corresponding to his external acts—but his inner being is not collapsed into temporal history. The immanent Trinity, the being of the God who is "onto-relationally" Three-in-One, is eternally complete and realized in itself; there is trinitarian order in God's action toward creation, but the action is also God's free and gracious movement toward us: it neither constitutes nor jeopardizes his being. What God is toward us he is eternally in himself, but it is not possible to read back into his immanent being any ontological subordination of the Son or the Spirit to the Father. The Father is first in the order of divine persons, but not the cause or source of deity.[11] In Torrance's theology of creation, the creator–creature relation is strictly secondary to the essential relations of God as he is in himself, the one who creates in accordance with the good pleasure of his eternally boundless plenitude; once more, the fellowship of God's triune life awaits no external relation in order to be complete. At the same time, contingent creation also possesses a freedom, integrity, and intelligibility that derive from its divine origin and purpose as declared in Jesus Christ.

Again: theology must be insistent on the "double relation" of the enfleshed Son: eternal and ontological co-equal with God the Father; one also—as movement of free grace—with us in our humanity. The twofold reality of the mediator is essential to his reconciling significance; his work is vitally integrated with his person. Theology must render ontological—not "mythological"—account of the incarnation, pointing up its vital connection to a constitutive—not merely exemplary—atonement for sins. It must say that the humanity of the enfleshed Word is not external or instrumental to his saving action but essential to it. It must speak of the bodily resurrection of Jesus as utterly unique and miraculous act of God, its objectivity self-validating and beyond demonstration in any terms other than its own; of his bodily ascension and continuing high priestly ministry in heaven; of the new creation as eschatological completion of the one *parousia* initiated in his first advent in flesh. It must articulate a doctrine of justification that underscores the gracious, unconditional, and all-sufficient nature of God's love for sinners, which has made complete provision for them in the singular action of Christ.

---

[11]Torrance held that his views in this territory were closer to those of Gregory of Nazianzus than Basil; he believed Barth remained Basilian.

Governed by revelation, Torrance's approach to doctrine prizes faithful performance rather than composition as the theologian's vocation; commentary and synthesis hold firm rein over any temptation to personal creativity. A number of themes in Torrance's reasoning nevertheless yield, by any standards, significant constructive accounts. His efforts to give a tightly integrated treatment of revelation, justification, and the work of the Spirit in the knowledge of God; his construal of the vicarious humanity of Christ and its implications for human response to God in the gospel; his understanding of the sacraments of baptism and the Lord's Supper as participation in the mystery of Christ, and specifically in the reality of his obedience and worship—all these continue to merit close attention. The theme of union with Christ, an emphasis absorbed deeply from his teacher H. R. Mackintosh in particular, is immensely significant to his ways of connecting incarnation, soteriology, ecclesiology, and sacramental theology; the importance of union with Christ as ascended High Priest is also fundamental to his understandings of prayer, of Christian ministry and ordination. The evolving renditions of these emphases over time continue to make for rich study.

Important also is Torrance's proposed solution to the impasse of the *Filioque* as a (professedly Athanasian and Epiphanian) case that it is from the being rather than the person of the Father that the Son is generated and the Spirit proceeds, hence Son and Spirit proceed inseparably in as much as the Spirit is from the Father in the Son, the unity of the Three grounded in their coinherent relational being rather than in the person of the Father as principle of the Godhead.[12] So too is his endeavor to present a (heavily qualified) Reformed account of *theosis* as participation through the Spirit in the incarnate Son's communion with the Father, and as such a genuine fellowship with God's triune life which perfects rather than dissolves human integrity. So too is his concern to focus discussion of human personhood in Christology rather than in a commendation of social trinitarianism as some might see it; Patristic theology could indeed richly fund a contemporary theological anthropology, but not in the ways that crasser invocations of divine plurality proposed.

The *kind* of trinitarian and Christological dogmatics Torrance commends is quite different from expressions of systematic theology which affect to use doctrinal categories to underwrite approaches to contemporary questions or to determine doctrine's substantive content in light of such concerns. His pervasive insistence on "objectivity" is impossible to miss; whatever else he takes that theme to involve, a vital aspect of its force is that theology must not be reduced to a cipher for human ideas. Torrance's theology certainly entails practical consequences, but it remains a world away from the reduction of the doctrine of God to a sociopolitical program, or the governance of incarnational or soteriological teaching by themes such as suffering, hospitality, violence, or egalitarianism. Its modes of study are also well removed from approaches to theology which focus primarily on the philosophical dissection of doctrinal themes, with little interest in their scriptural foundations; conceptual precision and coherence are of high importance, but analytical treatment as he sees it pursues transparency to revelation as encountered in and through a text.

Dogmatic theology may be in somewhat better heart today than it was, but contemporary theology continues to face versions of a number of the impulses against which Torrance

---

[12]Torrance was of course instrumental in the formulation of the agreed statement of the World Alliance of Reformed Churches and the Orthodox Church in March 1991. See now Jason Robert Radcliff, *Thomas F. Torrance and the Orthodox-Reformed Theological Dialogue* (Eugene, OR: Wipf & Stock, 2018).

protests: pressures to seek its resources, methods, and objectives somewhere outside of the reality enacted in the majesty of divine self-movement toward us in all its momentous effect. Theological speech and its functions continue to be tackled in terms that are taken to be subject to, rather than normative of, the assumptions and interests with which theological enquiry is to be approached. The types of principled relativism which Torrance deplores have proliferated rather than declined, the assumed cogency of the cause in both intellectual and political terms a cultural given. Torrance's work stands as a powerful statement of why such forces remain objectionable for Christian theology, and of why theological exposition ordered by the specificity of God's self-disclosure is indispensably necessary, not only for theology's material content but also for its form, and for the representation of what its practices must in any situation involve.

2. The Significance of the Church's History of Confession

If Torrance's approach to theology attests anything, it is a conviction that the history of the church's confession is a gift, not burden. Torrance began his academic career in a chair of ecclesiastical history; though he soon transferred to dogmatics his teaching remained pervasively shaped by his ways of reading historical theology. Torrance is never interested in reading doctrinal history as an historian *simpliciter*, but as a dogmatician, and it is this which leads him to seek resources in Christian tradition. Divine instruction is to be found supremely in Scripture; it is to be found also in the wisdom of the vast company who have sought to listen to the Word before us, and whose language and modes of argument at their best model fidelity to revelation. Through such testimonies God continues to instruct us today.

Torrance is nourished by the past, not embarrassed by it. He sees historical theology as freeing modern theological work from some of the inhibitions by which it is too often bound. A *consensus patrum* in particular, for Torrance the classical confession of an undivided church, is a rich inheritance indeed, within which lie immense conceptual resources for present challenges.[13] Catechesis, immersion in the vast spiritual and intellectual assets of the church's theological history, is a fundamental blessing. However out of step with late modern instincts the approach may be, an essentially commentarial style of theology remains appropriate. Torrance's work as a whole is saturated with primary references as compared with secondary literature.

The principles were present in Orthodoxy and in *ressourcement* theologies; they were, for Torrance, all too rare in modern Protestant (or more fashionable Roman Catholic) divinity, which remained heavily preoccupied with the present and with personal experience. Torrance saw clear problems in the shifting expressivism of symbolic or moralistic religion, taken up with immediacy and its perceived possibilities. He saw dangers also in much more sophisticated accounts of transcendental experience, such as those of Joseph Maréchal or Karl Rahner, or the fluid experientialism that lurked in Edward Schillebeeckx's depictions of redemptive encounter with divinity. Those approaches may not have been guilty of the present-centered inanities of some contextual theologies, yet in their attempts to generalize or existentialize immediate human experience they ventured construals of divine being and action that appeared substantially removed from the church's classical claims regarding the radical nature of God's self-disclosure in temporality. Perspectives of that sort not

---

[13]See further Jason Robert Radcliff, *Thomas F. Torrance and the Church Fathers: A Reformed, Evangelical, and Ecumenical Reconstruction of the Patristic Tradition* (Eugene, OR: Pickwick Publications, 2014).

only risked the projection of present human intuitions or agendas as divine; they appeared to forget that where we happen to be is only a phase within a much more dramatically decisive history: that of God's ways with his creatures. For Torrance as for Barth, the gospel as heard by the church before us delivers from such restrictions and from the dangerous subjectivities to which they drive us. Our practices of confession, like those of our forebears, occur in the presence of the God who is and acts; his authority, agency, and purposes enclose all that they and we together can ever be about.

As Torrance's accounts of tradition and the deposit of faith make clear, and as his negative readings of aspects of classical Augustinian and Reformed theology illustrate, he does not idealize the past or treat its legacy uncritically; nor (contrary to caricature) does he invoke a romanticized lineage in the interests of a narrow present inhabitation. He traces strong Patristic archetypes for Reformed and evangelical convictions, but as his labors in the 1950s had already proposed, attention to the church's historic doctrine is for him vital to the overcoming of differences between traditions, and in turn to the transcendence of parochial contextualizing, whether in old settings or in new. The study of the church's teaching does not promote ecclesial hyperinflation: it warns us precisely against the arrogation of truth as sectional property, the confusion of contingent parts of the tradition with the one true gospel, or of all-too-fallible local ministries with the effectual purposes that are God's alone. One of the crucial dimensions of a large-scale approach to historical theology as Torrance commends it is its capacity to call into question particular elements of one's own inheritance; that is certainly a feature of his views of Scottish Calvinism. Torrance's version of his own Reformed faith is the confession of an active interpreter, concerned to reflect upon as well as within his tradition, to theologize out of it and about it at once. His Reformed investments are, as we have noted, quite different from others: intensely critical of the legacies of Dort and Westminster, strongly enthusiastic about an alternative trajectory on the articulation of election, atonement, and divine forgiveness.

Whether he is right in all of this and whether his arguments are careful enough to avoid raising unnecessary specters in the minds of some of his Reformed interlocutors are questions that deserve to be discussed. A good deal of what he has to say owes much less to Barth's influences as such than some have assumed; its relationship to outlying witnesses in the Scottish tradition may also be more complicated than meets the eye. What is not in doubt is his desire to remind the Reformed as much as anyone else that their arguments must look back to older resources if they are to avoid isolation from core contentions of a classical faith. Torrance's understanding of these contentions as elaborated in Greek Patristic reasoning is itself open to appraisal, but early Christian theology is intended as instrument of a critical as well as a principled self-identification (and in turn as an expression of authentic Reformed instincts rather than any abandonment of the heritage). His ecumenism, and his eschewal of culturally narrow or nationalist attitudes in ecclesiology, typifies the principle: retrieval involves recognition of the proportions of God's church in history and of the extent to which faithful confession means participation in a genuinely catholic testimony to the glory of the God made known in Jesus Christ.

Theology today may show signs of having begun to take some of these points seriously: lazy present-centeredness is assuredly ever with us, but at other levels there are some encouraging evidences of a closer intersection of systematic and historical work, of much deeper respect for the Fathers, medievals, and early-modern thinkers, and of the relevance of the churchly interpretation of Scripture for contemporary biblical studies. Greek Patristic resources are a good deal more prized than they were in many places a generation or so ago; there is increasing recognition that Protestants, Catholics, even evangelicals, have much to gain from recovering their riches; Orthodoxy has found new attention and appeal in Western contexts. The ecumenical potential which Torrance saw in such study is indeed vast, and his practical exemplification of its capacities remains impressive.

Still, as ongoing debates suggest, renewal of interest in the texts or concepts of former ages does not mean that the readings are always reliable or that present theological agendas are necessarily faithful to the logic of those they invoke. Theology continues to be afflicted by temptations to deploy the arguments of history in dubious contemporary terms, or to ignore the exegetical as well as didactic or polemical work that may have produced them, or to treat casually their connections to a rhetoric of doxological contemplation. If it is to avoid some of the mistakes, patient and contextually sensitive reading is indispensable, as is candor about the complexities of interpretative traditions and the sediments they bestow. Torrance's own construals, like others, remain open to questions; what matters is his reminder that we think and speak on a field in which God has ever been communicative and do our work surrounded by a great cloud of witnesses. Torrance urges us to engage that testimony expectantly, heirs of its instruction; obsession with ourselves in detachment from the faith of the faithful is an exercise in folly.

3. Theology as Participatory

Torrance's accounts of the knowledge of God, of the nature of salvation, of Christology, pneumatology, church, and Christian life are intensely participatory. True knowledge of God is essentially bound up with the theology of justification and with the revelatory and perfecting work of the Holy Spirit; union with Christ, living by virtue of the faith of Christ and by his vicarious humanity, means irreducibly personal relationship with the risen and ascended Savior through the Spirit and being led by him to his Father.

Doctrinal work is for Torrance intellectually all-absorbing, but it is not a scholarly game; if revelation and reconciliation are of a piece, theology's fundamental setting is fellowship with the triune God. Dogmatics is not a bulwark against the possibility that we could ever be wrong; it is the confession impelled when revelation breaks into our minds and makes us repent. Heresy and mythology, by contrast, are grounded in impiety, the proud and ungodly detachment of thought and speech about God from the specific modes of God's self-disclosure. Where divine self-movement is essentially involved, there can for theology be no dispassionate intellectual stance where we summon ideas before us in order to appraise them coolly then proceed on our way. There is the pathos, and the joy, of participation in the regeneration wrought for otherwise broken and estranged humanity by the mediator. The version of theology Torrance commends is an unavoidably engaged, praying, worshipping activity, governed by disciplines of repentance, gratitude, and obedience, not as human works in completion of divine conditions but as trusting acknowledgment of the decisive conversion of humanity that has occurred in Jesus Christ. Faith means glad confession; it means recognition also of the limitations of our creaturely position *coram Deo*, beneficiaries in Christ of a privilege that is ever greater than we can conceive, and entirely beyond our domestication. A certain kind of apophatic reserve[14] in wondering acknowledgment of mystery that remains transcendent of our capacities is necessary. The triune God of glory gives himself truly, personally, wonderfully but does not—*qua* God—give himself away.

---

[14] For Torrance, Athanasian as distinct from pseudo-Dionysian.

The doxological confession of all this is, however, for Torrance, a matter of *rational* worship as commended by apostolic counsel (Rom. 12:1). To think out of a center in God rather than a center in ourselves is assuredly to do serious mental work; it is also to have our minds renewed in accordance with truth, a process that involves radical *metanoia* and conformity to the mind of Christ. Intellectual and spiritual asceticism is ingredient in that process: an essential submission to divine authority. At the heart of such submission is listening: above all, a continuing hearing of the Word of God as spoken in Holy Scripture. To read Scripture faithfully is to engage its "depth dimension" as instrument of divine speech in human language commandeered as embassy of God's eloquence. The *scopus* of the Bible is Christ; the end of exegesis is communion. The virtues formed here cannot be secured by human effort: they are the Spirit's work. But reason may indeed pray for and expect divine illumination.

Academic prestige aplenty came Torrance's way, and the flourishing of universities mattered to him, but he saw his scholarly activities as enactment of ministerial vocation. His concerns to remind the church to take theological study seriously, and to offer the academy in turn a picture of unapologetic commitment, may in various respects be yet more challenging today; they are surely none the less vital. His approach continues to press upon theologians that there must be no either/or to intellectual work and spiritual discipline; that theology which, either as a matter of (perverse) principle or by default, cuts itself off from the only culture in which it can properly flourish is guaranteed to wither. If theology is to serve both church and academy well, it is obligated to pursue its tasks on its own terms. If theology does not recognize that it is a participatory matter at its core, if its academic study does not in practice value prayer, worship, and disciplined attentiveness to the Word, and if it does not bear fruit in Spirit-generated transformation of character and practical witness, urgent questions deserve to be asked. If theology does not really think that its work goes on—anywhere, anytime—in the presence of the living God, whose livingness makes all the difference in the world to its activities, something has gone badly awry. The discipline's greatest need in human terms, Torrance reminds us, is the enactment of the sanctification of its practitioners. For that, its unavoidable recourse remains prayer.

4. The Contours of Theology's Engagement with Other Discourses

Torrance's missionary energy is an unmistakable element in his work. There is no bracketing of *didache* from *kerygma*; the endeavors to evangelize academic culture are of a piece with the vision. His quest for a scientific theology is insistent that a theology of classical particularity, strongly committed to an epistemology of revelation, has nothing whatever to do with intellectual or cultural insularity. To see Torrance's refusals of correlation as in any way retreatist, or the pursuit of intellectual security courtesy of a naïve pietism, is entirely mistaken. His work contrasts sharply with other ways of engaging, but it does so precisely because it refuses their terms. Torrance proceeds in no fear of the possibility that philosophy or science might sink theology's claims, but in confidence in the untamable power of the truth concerning God and creatures, and in the boundless capacity of that truth to seize the mind.

Torrance's bold elaboration of a unified method may not be to everyone's taste, but the desire to identify such a thing clearly animated him from a very early stage. His landmark study *Theological Science* remains a remarkably accomplished text, which deserves still to be pondered yet more widely. The multiple expansions of the case for a scientific theology over the two decades thereafter are, in their concern to explore first principles of enquiry and to set out the "frame of mind" which applies to the intellectual activities of genuine scientists in any field, a vast articulation of the point that theology has no reason whatever to cut itself off. Leaving behind the false cultural "split" between theology and other kinds of science is vital, and there is all the more basis to do this in the world of contemporary scientific discoveries. For Torrance, Albert Einstein and James Clerk Maxwell help to remind theologians that a number of their paranoias about the world of nature, or the possibilities of divine action within spatiotemporal order, or the processes by which human minds apprehend and communicate, may in fact trade upon seriously outdated physics. In turn, theologians may, with a little philosophical help perhaps from Michael Polanyi and John Macmurray, press upon scientists a long-standing Christian case (John Philoponos one of its heroes) concerning contingency: that Aristotelian or deistic assumptions about the natural world and what it means to study its layers of phenomena may well be gratuitous.

The reasoning is for Torrance entirely bound up with the ontological and epistemological significance of the triune God's self-disclosure; in so far as theology is directed by that reality, it is properly scientific, taking its shape—"*kata physin*"—from its object. Torrance's ways of expressing the relationship of theology to other sciences are nothing like "evidentialist" apologetics, an endeavor to erect a public discourse upon supposed points of contact or pre-understandings that might be common to human minds with or without faith. Torrance expressly cautions theology against the wrong kinds of dialogue, in which the discipline pursues some vague common language in surrender of its particularity, or collapses its subject matter within the boundaries imposed by research in other fields. It is by articulating, not suppressing, the logic of Christian doctrinal claims that theology will rightly fulfil its calling.

On this reckoning, the terms upon which theologians and other scientists might converse require to be identified in more candid fashion. If there is a quarrel here with modernity, it is with the false polarities into which it has often driven us and with the elision of differences that these in turn prescribe. If there is indeed a real world outside of the human mind, and if that world is discerned rather than constructed by critical reason, the kind of unified method that matters might be said to be simply an agreement that enquiry must proceed in accordance with that after which it reaches. Such *is* "science." If that can be recognized, and if it is indeed the case that knowledge attained is in crucial ways inseparable from the ways in which knowledge is pursued, then theology and other disciplines have much indeed to talk about in their differing engagements with reality.

Whatever is to be said about the many steps in Torrance's reasoning—and the work evolves in range and clarity over time—the sheer scale of his labors in theology as science merits ongoing close study as a hugely ramified set of accounts of how it might at least be possible—if not essential—for a theology of revelation to pursue critical engagement with other intellectual fields by dint of its own realist assumptions about God and the world. Whatever the particular strengths and weaknesses of his efforts to articulate a "new" natural theology, the enterprise at no point overtakes the basic investments in a trinitarian account of creation; it is noteworthy that reference to natural theology as such scarcely features in his mature work on the Trinity. In the end, for Torrance, the elaboration of a natural theology is not necessarily to be thought of as a bid for autonomy, as Barth feared; carefully expressed, it might, after all, coexist with a strong commitment to positive[15]

---

[15]Never general; Torrance expressly shuns reduction of the relationship of science and theology to a dialogue of "science and religion" at large.

religion. Whatever the ultimate pros and cons of his endeavors to reconstruct an account of God and nature after Barth, Torrance's exposition of the possible relationship between theology and the scientific investigation of nature offers an enduringly weighty manifesto; here are some at least of the essential terms upon which theology might seek to interact with other discourses of exploration in a fast-moving intellectual world.

III

To take these four burdens of Torrance's theology seriously is, we have suggested, to recognize that their expression within the body of his work as a whole naturally evinces both high points and weaknesses. For Torrance himself, some of the critical interactions with his arguments were worthy of appreciation; quite a few were not. Too often the objections seemed to him pretty inept: a failure to grasp "depth structures," an imposition of "logico-causal" reasoning, a reflection of the vestigial effects of "dualist" or "instrumentalist" assumptions. The precise nature of his claims about divine revelation and its entailments for an account of human apprehension of reality was regularly misunderstood. While he remained distinctly hostile to the wrong kinds of appeal to "mystery," he emphasized also that the actuality of divinely afforded knowledge is necessarily determinative of what can be said concerning the empirical or theoretical structure of that knowledge. Second-order conceptualization of theological truths must itself be undertaken in expressly theological terms, as must exposition of the associations of these concepts one with another. Not everyone got the point.

Like all of us, Torrance evinced more tacit assumptions than he knew; his tendencies to append generic labels to arguably disparate phenomena (versions of "dualism" in particular), or to plot lengthy trajectories of dispositions that might be said to be variously represented in philosophy, cosmology, and theology, doubtless reflect his own desires for organization and analysis of complex intellectual histories. A pervasive binary of divine versus human starting-points, compelling as it can sound, may pose issues as a grid through which to approach so much. The preference for primary sources is laudable but may involve a certain neglect of other ways of interpreting them. Critical questions deserve to be pursued.

It is entirely legitimate for contemporary readers to consider whether Torrance's emphasis on vicarious grace makes sufficiently careful distinctions between Christ's human action and ours or whether there are possible difficulties in his ways of expounding the evangelistic, sacramental, and moral implications of the incarnate Son's faith. It is appropriate to go on asking whether the scriptural reading which undergirds Torrance's accounts of the mediator's achievement is well founded. His theology bears upon scholarly debates about *pistis Christou*, which have expanded substantially over the past twenty-five years, and upon assessments of the relationship between "apocalyptic" construals of participation and classical Lutheran or Reformed ways of parsing Paul's accounts of justification by faith. Torrancian interpretations have been variously implicated in the arguments of biblical scholars regarding narratival participation in Christ as Paul envisions it. It is right for students to be invited to consider what the exegetical and historical strengths and weaknesses of Torrance's soteriology might entail for other expositions of a sharp contrast between a Pauline vision of mediation and putative reckonings of the benefits of Christ in extrinsic or quasi-conditional terms, and to ask whether the issues may have been qualified by continuing discussions in biblical and historical work since Torrance's time.

It is reasonable to probe the details of Torrance's ways of understanding the connection between incarnation and atonement: to consider what it might and might not mean to say that the Word assumes fallen flesh yet lives a sinless human existence; or to depict the incarnation as dynamic atoning event; or to talk of vicarious repentance; or to do theological justice to the Savior's human history and its background in Israel's story; or to subordinate forensic categories to ontological ones; or to affirm that not only all humanity but all creation is redeemed, resurrected, and consecrated in the mediator's personal action. It is valid to explore also whether Torrance's ways of expressing resistance to subordination and causality within the Godhead and his articulations of perichoretic relations sometimes risk at least a measure of compromise to the particularity of trinitarian persons, or whether his accounts do enough to avoid a subtle sort of modalism,[16] or whether (even) he always articulates a consistent sort of distinction between essence and economy. It is reasonable to ask if the attempts to develop a new natural theology do ultimately sit—*malgré tout*—in at least a degree of tension with the centrality of the incarnation as celebrated elsewhere. How well Torrance reads Scripture in particular ought to be crucial in all of these questions; for all his emphasis on the accommodation of the divine Word to human form and the deployment of that form as instrument of God's economic presence, the substantive exegesis in some (though not all) of his work does remain quite compressed. His dogmatics deserve such careful assessment precisely out of respect for their depth and for the integrity with which they are pursued.

The accounts of the development of doctrine, learned as they are, remain heavily dominated by their author's perceptions of the outcomes or nodal points of historical processes; they certainly tend to be arranged schematically in light of his perduring convictions. Thus presented, theology's history seems to emerge as a history of correct and incorrect apprehensions of truth, its saints and heretics abstracted somewhat from the worldly factors which in providence affected them. As has often been observed, there is a certain "timeless" quality to the narrative. The engagements with Patristic, medieval, and Reformation theologies tend to focus on conceptual themes more than on the scriptural exegesis which frequently played a major role in shaping the arguments.

The approach is heuristically potent; it is also reductive. Torrance's studies of the history of biblical interpretation, incomplete as they remain, continue to make for fascinating reading but clearly evince his recurring ways of classifying wisdom versus folly. In general: Torrance fashions effective conversations between voices from an array of premodern and modern contexts, but proposes interests or assumptions they may or may not have demonstrably shared, and arguably neglects other significant features of their formation. Intellectual as distinct from sociopolitical or cultural factors are undoubtedly dominant (the characterization of Barth in particular offers a fairly clear example; there are many much older cases). It is quite in order to ask whether Torrance's dogmatic arguments are necessarily reliant on his ways of reading all of the history or whether the *grandes lignes* of his theology may yet stand in more chastened terms.

Scholarship in his own time could already pose challenges to some of his historical judgments and the conceptual stories which they fund, a number of the objections

---

[16]According to that criticism, Torrance's reading of the Cappadocians (or enthusiasm for Gregory of Nazianzus rather than Basil of Caesarea or Gregory of Nyssa) remains curiously Augustinian in the end, preoccupied still with an undivided *monarchia* at the expense (it is said) of the particularity of divine persons, not least on account of his strong emphasis on the *homoousion*. Whether almost any of the terms of such a critique are right is an open question.

might be all the stronger today. Whether the reading of Augustine's "inherent dualism" (or indeed various other alleged features of his thought) is remotely right; or whether there ever was in fact a "Latin heresy"; or whether the deployment of *anhypostasis* and *enhypostasis* involves somewhat generous expansion of late-Patristic categories; or whether the putative differences between Calvin's theology and the assumptions of Reformed Orthodoxy is even faintly correct—all these are valid matters for discussion.

Torrance's account of a Patristic *consensus* is very much his own, heavily inclined toward Greek as distinct from Latin authorities and much inflected by his own interests. Sharp polarities of Greek and Latin ways of doing trinitarian theology are widely repudiated in scholarly work these days, and rightly so; some of Torrance's ways of characterizing the virtues of his favored approach versus its deviants may well look all the more problematic now in evidential terms. The issues can be multiplied. Torrance's Calvin, never mind his "Calvinism," certainly continues to invite critical appraisal. The idea that the sixteenth century saw recovery of a Patristic soteriology of grace from the ruins of late-medieval Augustinianism, only for the achievement to be effectively a matter of dark contest in Reformed theology ever after, may be, after all, somewhat overwrought.

Some may yet be inclined to think the theologies of the seventeenth century in particular scarcely half so bleak, their methods and legacies not necessarily as here presented. The relational glory of the triune God may not always have been quite so heavily displaced by didactic exposition of the metaphysics of the One God; an alleged contractual occlusion of covenantal logic—beguiling though that interpretative narrative has proved—is hardly the only way to read the evidence; the watchdogs of a crippling legalism, and their brave escapees, might at least sometimes be viewed in other terms, the conceptual achievements in each instance appraised in more balanced terms.

In the modern story, Barth is chief hero; there, too, however, the construal of Barth's development now looks distinctly dated, and the readings of Barth's theology (which are admittedly far more nuanced than some of Torrance's critics have appreciated) include reckonings of their subject's strengths and weaknesses, and of his place in the history of Reformed theology (including his relationship to Schleiermacher), which are clearly not beyond contest. The magisterial treatment of theology as scientific activity might also perhaps be said to press Barth's highly energized celebrations of positive revelation (whether as early theology of crisis or in the terms of his later actualism) into a somewhat clinical register.

One corollary of Torrance's ways of framing human participation in Christ might be that he struggles to do justice to the strength and range of Barth's concerns for moral theology; it is certainly possible to argue that his criticisms of Barth's mature doctrine of baptism as dualistic reflect a degree of misreading which has something to do with that challenge. At the least, Torrance appears to wrestle a good deal with themes which run deep in the *Church Dogmatics*. In the end, it can seem as if, for all his desire to emphasize the participatory dimensions of the theology of the gospel, Torrance has *relatively* little to say about the gospel's fundamentally moral fabric: he writes widely on ethical themes, most certainly, but in comparison with Barth's renditions of covenantal correspondence at any rate the dogmatics that assert the main moves remain—perhaps—a little one-sided. The significance of the humanity of the Savior appears at times to threaten to absorb ours rather a lot.

Like Barth, Torrance is ever wary of Pelagian self-inflation, or of churchly identity or ministerial activities as putative completion of rather than participation in the crucified, risen and ascended Lord's effectiveness in the Spirit's power. Creatures assuredly do not fashion themselves; it is in the union of God and humanity in Christ that proper relation to our creator is actualized. There can be no substitution of the uniquely constitutive being and act of Christ by the movements of human agents. The church is the visible presence of the exalted Christ in temporal history; its reality is at no point reliant on its institutional structures. The trinitarian and Christological investments which underwrite Torrance's ecclesiology and sacramental theology are spelt out with great power. It is worth asking, however, if at least some of Torrance's ways of expounding vicarious humanity do risk a dissolution of creaturely response in incarnational grace, or if the depictions of the church's worship and ministry in present, human, bodily forms are at the last as textured as they might be. Their relationship to classical Reformed arguments certainly deserves to go on being explored, as does their relative strength compared with Barth's deep insistence that election and reconciliation involve appointment to and establishment in ways of authentically human being and doing.

To read Torrance today is to read him in light of a great deal of other work in theological ethics, not least in and after Barth's huge exposition of God-centered humanism; there are conceivably ways of talking about human agency, church, ministry, and sacraments there which honor aspects of Scripture's testimony in yet richer terms or which could usefully be brought into dialogue with Torrance's writing. Not all attempts to articulate creaturely response as constituted by divine action need compromise the unsubstitutable perfection of Christ's achievement; not all accounts of the church's ontology and its visible expression need descend into dangerous talk of human efforts or an inflated discourse of general participation in God as counterweight to alleged extrinsicism; not all depictions of the duties of holiness in fellowship with the living Lord need—of course—be commendations of introspection or perilous exercises in technocracy of the self (the disciplines of Torrance's own faith knew it well).

There are ways of speaking of the relationship of divine and human agency, of ecclesial being and becoming, of sacramental fellowship and of human worship and witness which may not require quite the polarities of objectivity and subjectivity which Torrance's reasoning regularly sets up. Still stronger accentuation of Scriptural emphasis on union with Christ in covenantal terms in particular might well secure a great deal. And yet: the spiritual impact of Torrance's exposition of the mind of Christ in worship, and of the ministry of the ascended Christ as divine–human advocate with the Father, remains profound indeed, as does his concern to commend scriptural interpretation as spiritual task. The emphases on participatory prayer and doxology, the obligations to contemplate, to study, and to obey are clear. The church's life below on the (entire) basis of its life above is indeed real and so is its summons to serve. It is hardly the case that Torrance ever leaves the believer wondering how to proceed.

Torrance's formulations of a natural theology and his presentation of theology as science take him by any measure well beyond Barth. Torrance knew far more about natural science, its philosophy and practices, than most modern theologians who have seen fit to write on the matter, and the key moves in his arguments are often considerably more careful than some of their hastier critics have supposed. It remains true nevertheless that he engaged much more with the physical sciences than the biological or social ones; he also ventured relatively little into the social processes in which scientific investigation takes place. In these areas, his work can today seem somewhat inchoate. Its ultimate dream remains impressive indeed—a massive new synthesis in which false cultural differences between the sciences, theology, and the humanities would be overcome. Among other things, the realization awaits, even at a theoretical level, much fuller consideration of the complex ways in which different kinds of human enquiry might be said to function within the natural sciences themselves, never mind elsewhere, and of their potentially differential investments in a correspondence between knowledge and "reality."

Whether Torrance's strong insistence on the factuality of knowing is sufficient to encompass all of these, or whether it risks sliding into a version of occasionalism in which some are granted deep knowledge while others are not, remain valid matters for debate. So too does the relationship of his thought in this area also to the real or perceived legacies of Barth's actualism. How such questions are tackled may bear directly upon the success or otherwise of his version of a natural theology and of its potential applications in contemporary theological practice. The relationship between, on the one hand, the strongly inclusive and universally constitutive dimensions in his theology, and, on the other, his acknowledgment of fallen humanity's capacity for ignorance and perverse self-exclusion from true knowledge of the creator and sustainer of all things invites continuing scrutiny here as elsewhere. In the end, we are unlikely to make much headway in understanding Torrance's concerns if we miss the force of his case that the apprehension of truth occurs in consequence of God and God's action in the world in any event. Still: whether the vision can say enough about the necessary *differences* of theology from other things in all of the ways that Torrance's central doctrines might be said to require is a matter to go on pondering.

IV

Torrance's theology clearly requires to be read alongside other approaches in its time and since. His methods continue to contrast strongly with symbolic, existential, or experientially reflexive accounts of a modern Christian faith, or with treatments of doctrine in which Scripture's referential authority is set aside in favor of nominalism, or with theological styles in which negativity is sounded as final if not opening note. His rendition of trinitarian dogmatics also contains differences from other versions of modern trinitarian theology which bid similarly to emphasize revealed mystery yet make moves to which he remains firmly resistant. If it can be argued that quite a bit of the later twentieth century's trinitarianism has ventured in directions that are in truth quite at odds with some core assumptions of Patristic and medieval Christian reasoning—on the relation of being and time, on divine simplicity and plurality, on the nature of divine personhood, on the knowability of the divine essence—Torrance's work regularly stands over against a good many of these instincts. His arguments are ultimately far more alert to the precision of Patristic thought, and of what it encouraged theology *not* to say as well.

Torrance's mature work in particular refuses to collapse the doctrine of God's essential perfection into the economy of temporal history or to draw unbroken lines between the knowledge of God and any putative creaturely experience of self-transcendence or relationality. The insistence on the plenitude of God's triune life in himself as essential basis of his free and loving communication of himself to creatures is such that the disclosure specifies but does not exhaust divine ontology. God is known as triune because he makes himself known as such in his particular actions in time and space; these actions do not constitute his triune being, nor does God somehow determine his being as triune for the purposes of his fellowship with creatures. Torrance's depictions of revelation arguably become yet more careful over time, concerned to avoid misrepresentation or false extension of the principle that the immanent and the economic are one. The immanent is not dissolved into the economic, nor is there mutual conditioning of God as well as us in consequence of God's determination to have fellowship with us. Torrance retains notably stronger investments in divine aseity and offers much more careful exposition of what is not happening in the temporal missions of the Word and the Spirit than some have succeeded in doing.

In turn he is able, arguably, to offer better resources for a theology of creaturely experience of God: a matter of wondrous intimacy and God-given assurance, but not a dissolution of difference between God and us, far less any crass identification of God with our intuitions or relations. His ways of construing divine metaphysics and mystery, and of reading the later Barth, stand some way removed from approaches which have been elaborated since his time. If he is to be assessed as a theologian after Barth, his expositions of Trinity, history, and freedom place him much closer to some Barth interpreters than others; he in any case remains committed to the force of classical contentions regarding the fullness of the relations in which God's life essentially subsists.

Comparative study is an important part of considering Torrance's significance. The place of Barth in the entire landscape is unavoidable: much of what Torrance did *not* attempt as well as what he did can only be understood in view of his towering shadow. But other theologies, whether in Barth's wake or propelled by different forces, have also invested deeply in Scripture and historical theology, and in theology's essential tasks of ecclesial service, concerned not to reduce the subject or its works of engagement to the kinds of explanatory and critical modes which have dominated so much mainstream academic activity in modern times. Torrance's stature, distinctiveness, and influences undoubtedly bear comparison with theirs.

Students need to learn how to read Torrance's contributions as compared (often radically) with those of, say, Wolfhart Pannenberg, or Eberhard Jüngel, or Robert Jenson; or to consider his various kinds of links to, influences upon, and differences with figures such as Georges Florovsky, or John Zizioulas, or Donald MacKinnon, or Colin Gunton, or John Webster; or to think about the evidences of his effects upon the work of many other distinguished colleagues, relatives, and former students from different confessional backgrounds. His relationship with Orthodoxy in particular was unique among Protestant theologians in his time, though of course he also had his enduring differences with Orthodox scholars on many issues, venturing his own contributions in the process to a perennial debate about Patristic interpretation; his work continues to make fascinating reading in dialogue with Eastern voices.[17]

His interactions with the theologies of Karl Rahner, Yves Congar, and other Roman Catholic theologians also make for interesting study in assessment of his thinking about justification, church, sacraments, and Trinity, and his ways of framing what is and is not at stake in human experience of God revealed. Torrance could combine warm celebration of the ecumenical potency of the *homoousion* with tough language about impersonal grace, sacerdotalism, and the pernicious effects of scholastic reason—delighting also in passion for the Fathers and for a Christ-centered piety of sacrament as well as Word wherever he found it. Vatican II or no, dualism and phenomenalism and "mechanistic" habits of thought remained a problem, the objectivity of the one enfleshed mediator still not always taken with full seriousness; Edward Schillebeeckx and Hans Küng could illustrate the point. Torrance's contributions to ecumenism invite detailed consideration

---

[17]See further Matthew Baker and Todd Speidell, eds., *T. F. Torrance and Eastern Orthodoxy: Theology in Reconciliation* (Eugene, OR: Wipf & Stock, 2015).

of wide-ranging conversation-partners and assessment of (often in the end politically successful) counterarguments as well as his own proposals.

He very much needs to be appraised, too, as a distinctively Scottish theologian. He merits a place among the greats of his own tradition, its most distinguished twentieth-century exemplar: understanding his significance in that line requires us to delve into its historic riches as well and to consider how his work sits alongside that of his Scottish heroes, his teachers, and his modern interlocutors.

Whatever dialogues are to be posited, Torrance's literary legacy is in the end *sui generis* in modern English-language theology, particularly in a Reformed register. The moves and proportions in his reasoning are surely not always right; some of the judgments can well be contested; the idiom can undoubtedly be demanding. Some parts of the corpus are inevitably much weightier than others; the overlaps can be tiring. He remained deeply suspicious of the "psychologizing" of theology or the implication that theological arguments ought ever to be evaluated on terms other than their ostensive conformity to truth. His work seldom comes across as less than fully assured, but it was his conviction also that theologians are obligated to point away from themselves. On that principle, it is necessary to set all of Torrance's work and our thoughts as we consider it under the judgment of that which it is given to theology to say in light of God's self-exposition in Jesus Christ, made known in the Spirit's power. That is precisely what Torrance's deepest investments urge us to go on doing.

Torrance deserves to be read and read better. In that cause, debates about how to understand all of the details in his arguments or how to set his ideas in relation to others—or indeed how to begin to assess the impacts of his work empirically—important as they may be, ought not to be the endgame. What matters more is attentive engagement with the vision set before us of theology's vocation and of how its commitments ought to be pursued. If aspects of Torrance's oeuvre are dated, overreaching, or problematic, that vision at large is not: it continues to be of very considerable pertinence, encouraging theology on some enduringly vital paths, warning it firmly away from others. Critical assimilation of something of the spirit of his thinking, and of its potential to inform our own constructive work, is the appropriate way to take the message seriously.

If Torrance's writings continue to matter, they do so in so far as they direct our worship, wonder, and works of testimony to the reality of the God who announces himself in the gospel. We begin to read Torrance well when we pay heed to the implications of his insistence that the knowledge of this One is theology's calling, the wondering attestation of his splendor our highest privilege as creatures.

CHAPTER THREE

Thomas F. Torrance as a Scottish Theologian

DAVID FERGUSSON

Thomas F. Torrance was a Scottish theologian by virtue of his formation, context, and intellectual concerns. Among the wider ecumenical and international reception of his work today, this may not be well understood. But it is worth exploring to gain insight into an important dimension of his life and work. Most of Torrance's intellectual formation was in Edinburgh where he graduated in Arts and Divinity. Brief spells of study in Oxford and Basel ensured that other influences were absorbed, but the stamp of Edinburgh teachers, especially H. R. Mackintosh and Daniel Lamont, was enduring. Apart from time spent teaching in North America (1938–39) and as an army chaplain in Europe (1944–45), his ministry and academic work were exercised in his homeland, where he made a significant contribution to the life of the Church of Scotland. In a teaching career that spanned almost thirty years at New College, Torrance and Edinburgh became almost synonymous in the theological world. At times, he may have been tempted to ply his trade elsewhere—in 1961, Oscar Cullmann encouraged him to apply for Barth's chair in Basel—but he chose to remain in Edinburgh, perhaps for family as well as professional reasons. And he did so despite some frustration with elements of life at New College, not least the public attack upon his work by his colleague James Barr in *Semantics of Biblical Language* (1961).[1] Later, in 1996, during a productive retirement, he produced a major study of the history of Scottish theology which revealed his lifelong preoccupation with its key figures and movements.[2]

This chapter will explore several ways in which he can be considered a Scottish theologian—his indebtedness to Mackintosh, his close reading of the history of Scottish theology particularly through the 1950s, his immersion in the life of the Kirk, and the consonance of his own convictions with the more catholic expressions of Scottish Reformed theology. A final section will examine the epistemological realism of his theological science.

---

[1] James Barr, *The Semantics of Biblical Language* (Oxford: Oxford University Press, 1961).
[2] Thomas F. Torrance, *Scottish Theology: From John Knox to John McLeod Campbell* (Edinburgh: T&T Clark, 1996).

TEACHER AT NEW COLLEGE: HUGH ROSS MACKINTOSH (1870–1936)

Like his Marburg teacher, Wilhelm Herrmann, Mackintosh has suffered some neglect through characterization as a transitional figure between nineteenth-century liberalism and the dialectical theology that gripped the Reformed world after the 1920s. Yet he should be considered a distinctive and original figure in his own right. As the leading Scottish theologian of the early twentieth century, Mackintosh exercised a strong influence upon later and better-known figures such as the brothers John and Donald Baillie, as well as Torrance himself. Contemporary theological labels do not serve us well in characterizing Mackintosh's approach. In his own time, he was characterized as a "right wing liberal" and "left wing conservative."[3] A Free Church theologian, he belonged to a denomination that had largely departed from the strictness of its earlier adherence to the Westminster Confession of Faith after the Disruption of 1843.[4] Studying in Freiburg, Halle, and Marburg for successive summers, he acquired a facility in German and remained in close contact with developments on the continent, especially through his teacher and friend Wilhelm Herrmann. His training in Scottish philosophy under Pringle-Pattison together with his theological formation at New College enabled Mackintosh to combine a strong realist epistemology with a commitment to natural theology and biblical criticism. Yet when allied to his own Reformed sympathies, the influence of Herrmann pulled Mackintosh toward a reinvigoration of dogmatic themes in expounding the centrality of the incarnation and the atonement. These were to be integrated at the heart of Christian theology, the one elucidating the other. Much of this revealed a strong pastoral dimension in Mackintosh's work. Having served for some years as minister in Tayport, he regarded his theological work as a form of service to the church. Mackintosh indeed continued to preach regularly and to conduct classes in homiletics for his students. He served as Moderator of the General Assembly in 1934, shortly before his sudden death.

In part, Mackintosh's theology was a corrective project. Liberal approaches to the person of Christ risked minimizing the work of Christ, particularly with respect to his death and resurrection. By contrast, the Reformed orthodox tradition had isolated the penal substitutionary account of Christ's work and limited its application to the elect only. In stressing the need to integrate person and work, Mackintosh sought to steer a course between a narrow conservatism and a reductive liberalism. In some respects, he follows John McLeod Campbell's *The Nature of the Atonement* (1856) which insisted upon interpreting the work of Christ in light of the relations that were established in his incarnate life. While McLeod Campbell had been deposed from the ministry of the Church of Scotland in 1831 for teaching a "universal pardon" of sinners—a view that was judged to be at odds with the Westminster Confession of Faith—Mackintosh was able to work within a later theological and ecclesiastical climate that was more hospitable to such emphases. Readers of Torrance will have little difficulty in recognizing these themes. The incarnational approach to the atonement, the stress on the unconditional and universal scope of God's love in Christ, the criticism of the seventeenth-century Reformed tradition, these all are recurrent emphases in Torrance's own writings. And

---

[3] A. B. Macaulay, "Memoir," in H. R. Mackintosh, *Sermons* (Edinburgh: T&T Clark, 1938), 24.

[4] Mackintosh himself participated in two important church unions—the merger with the United Presbyterian Church in 1900 and then of the resultant United Free Church with the Church of Scotland in 1929. As a result of this process, his career ended as Professor of Systematic Theology within the University of Edinburgh.

students from his second-year dogmatics class will recall that the set essay for the first term was an exploration of the relationship between the incarnation and the atonement.

One of his last pupils, Torrance never tired of extolling Mackintosh and his significance; there is no doubt that he was Torrance's most influential teacher. His papers in the library of Princeton Theological Seminary include a substantial set of notes taken in Mackintosh's classes, alongside a complete set of the typed lecture synopses that Mackintosh made available to his students. With some hyperbole, he wrote, "Here was a theology that matched and promised to deepen that in which I had been brought up by missionary parents. I was far from being disappointed. To study with H. R. Mackintosh was a spiritual and theological benediction, for he was above all a man of God, full of the Holy Spirit and of faith."[5]

It was Mackintosh who first introduced Torrance to Barth and encouraged him to engage his work more fully. This was around the time of the appearance of the first part volume of the *Church Dogmatics*, translated by G. T. Thomson who was later appointed as Mackintosh's successor in Edinburgh. Given Mackintosh's own herculean efforts in translating Ritschl and Schleiermacher, it is unsurprising that Torrance felt himself similarly called to oversee the *Church Dogmatics*, having successfully persuaded Thomas Clark, the Edinburgh publisher, to invest in the project. The influence of Barth on Torrance is elsewhere discussed in this volume, but what may be of interest in this context is Mackintosh's assessment of Barth together with Torrance's later softening of his critique.

An avid reader of German theology, Mackintosh was aware of the work of Barth from an early stage. Though impressed, he was also reserved and on occasion expressed some pointed criticisms. These were summarized in his final work, the posthumously published *Types of Modern Theology* (1937). Barth's significance was noted, together with a recognition that he had important work in front of him. His stress on sin and the atoning work of Christ as disruptive were welcomed, as was his rehabilitation of the language of Christian dogmatics. His break with nineteenth-century liberal theology in some ways resonated with Mackintosh's own development of Herrmannian insights.[6] But in other respects Mackintosh remained faithful to the inheritance of the nineteenth century. In particular, his commitment to natural theology persisted as did his evangelical sense that the gospel needed to address people who were in part already conscious of a troubled relationship with God. Here the doctrine of the *imago Dei* continued to do important apologetic work in his theology. Though rejected by Barth, there remained an account of general revelation in Mackintosh which functioned as a preparation for the gospel or at least provided a setting within which the proclamation of the Christian faith took place. This is most apparent in his claims that the revelation of God is present in nature, history, and conscience.[7] Though Jesus is the supreme and final medium of revelation, he is not the only one.[8] To this extent, Mackintosh may have found himself closer to Brunner, an impression that is confirmed by his unpublished correspondence with Norman Porteous,

---

[5] Thomas F. Torrance, "Hugh Ross Mackintosh: Theologian of the Cross," in H. R. Mackintosh, *The Person of Jesus Christ* (1912, Edinburgh: T&T Clark, 2000), 72.
[6] James W. Leitch, *A Theology of Transition: H. R. Mackintosh as an Approach to Barth* (London: Nisbet, 1952).
[7] H. R. Mackintosh, *The Christian Apprehension of God* (London: SCM, 1929), 69.
[8] Ibid., 78.

who worked with Barth in Münster in the late 1920s.⁹ This anxiety surfaces again in Mackintosh's final work when he charges Barth with an "excessive actualism" in his theology.¹⁰ The same concern transposes into critical remarks about Barth's failure to deal adequately with the continuity and growth in the Christian life through the power of the Spirit.

Although Torrance was himself to reintroduce natural theology within a Barthian paradigm, he tended to view Mackintosh's criticism of Barth as a misunderstanding. The suggestion seems to be that, under the impact of reading Barth, Mackintosh continued to revise his residual liberalism in favor of a more dialectical approach to sin and redemption.¹¹ Yet this reading of Mackintosh may underestimate his points of departure from Barth, particularly on general revelation, the church, and the Christian life. A reconsideration of the standard thesis that Mackintosh is a transitional figure between a discredited liberalism and the richer theology of Barth may now be required.¹² Intriguingly, the later shape of Torrance's theology, while deeply indebted to Barth, also reflected similar points of departure. This is evident, I think, in what follows. Indeed, one might venture the claim that Torrance's theological dispositions were as much shaped by H. R. Mackintosh as by Karl Barth.

UNION WITH CHRIST THROUGH WORD AND SACRAMENT

On close inspection, the affinity between Torrance and his teacher is even more striking. In an early essay, Mackintosh defended the "unio mystica" against the standard charges of liberal Protestantism,¹³ while in his mature work on Christian forgiveness he writes of how "all Christianity comes down to two companion truths—God in Christ for us, and we in Christ for God. It is part of Christian experience at its highest, that what may perhaps be designated an 'organic' connexion is felt to subsist between Christ and His people."¹⁴ While Torrance expounded this idea in closer contact with the theology of the hypostatic union and Chalcedonian Christology—Mackintosh had largely eschewed the metaphysics of two-natures Christology—his theological convictions never strayed far from this dominant theme of union with Christ. Torrance imbibed this from Mackintosh's lectures and writings. Theologies which threatened this central orientation of Christian faith were roundly criticized for dealing in abstractions and logico-deductive terms that prescinded from this central conviction. His relentless criticism of the Westminster Confession of Faith, the subordinate standard of the Scottish Kirk, must be seen in this light.

The stress on union with Christ also generated an intense sense of the real presence in the celebration of the Lord's Supper. Again, there is a crossover from Mackintosh to Torrance. According to the former, it is at the reception of the sacramental elements that

---

⁹I owe this insight to the research of Craig Meek on the Porteous–Mackintosh correspondence, which is held in the Porteous Papers at New College, Edinburgh.

¹⁰H. R. Mackintosh, *Types of Modern Theology* (London: Nisbet, 1937), 314.

¹¹Torrance, "Hugh Ross Mackintosh," 88–93.

¹²John McPake, "H. R. Mackintosh, Thomas F. Torrance and the Reception of the Theology of Karl Barth in Scotland" (Edinburgh: PhD Thesis, University of Edinburgh, 1994).

¹³H. R. Mackintosh, "The *Unio Mystica* as a Theological Concept," *Expositor* 7 (1909): 138–55; and Robert R. Redman Jr., *Reformulating Reformed Theology: Jesus Christ in the Theology of Hugh Ross Mackintosh* (Lanham, MD: University of America Press, 1997), 183–200.

¹⁴H. R. Mackintosh, *The Christian Experience of Forgiveness* (London: Nisbet, 1927), 223–4.

we are most conscious of judgment on sin and God's love for us as we are united with Christ. "It is vain to choose a doctrine of atonement which in the main overlooks the greatest things that come home to us as we take in our hands the bread and wine."[15]

This doctrine of union with Christ is also replayed in Torrance's strong sacramentalism which places him at the Catholic end of the Reformed tradition. Again, we can see this as emerging from a distinctively Scottish context with his commitment to the work of the Scottish Church Society, founded in the late Victorian period by leading figures such as William Milligan, Professor of Divinity and Biblical Criticism in Aberdeen, whose work on the significance of the ascended Christ in worship Torrance frequently commended.[16] The goals of the Scottish Church Society included a more Catholic reading of the Reformed tradition that sought liturgical renewal, frequent celebration of the Lord's Supper, and a Calvinist (as opposed to a Zwinglian) account of sacramental grace and the real presence of Christ in the eucharistic elements. It is this configuration of influences that enabled Torrance to move beyond Karl Barth in some important respects. In particular, his commitment to the ministry of the ascended Christ made present by the Holy Spirit led to a stronger ecclesiology, sacramentalism, and eschatology than we find in Barth. This is apparent in works such as *Royal Priesthood*[17] and also in those friendly criticisms he ventures of Barth. In recalling their last conversation, his words carry echoes of Milligan.

> I then ventured to express my qualms about his account of the ascended Jesus Christ in CD IV/3, in which Christ seemed to be swallowed up in the transcendent Light and Spirit of God, so that the humanity of the risen Jesus appeared to be displaced by what he had called "the humanity of God" in his turning toward us. I had confessed to being astonished not to find at that point in Barth's exposition a careful account of the priestly ministry of the ascended Jesus in accordance with the teaching of the Epistle to the Hebrews about the heavenly intercession of the ascended Christ.[18]

The sermons of Robert Bruce (*c*.1554–1631) were known to Torrance through his family upbringing and then under the tutelage of Mackintosh at New College. Preached in the High Kirk of Edinburgh (St Giles) in 1589, they rank among the finest devotional literature in Scottish theology. In his 1958 volume, Torrance provided a fresh English translation from the original Scots.[19] It is not difficult to understand the appeal of Bruce for Torrance. His exposition of the sacrament is evangelical yet almost mystical. Christ gives himself to us in the sacrament, the whole Christ both flesh and blood. In the conjunction of sign and thing signified, the grace and mercy of God are sealed for us. Bruce writes, "In this union Christ Jesus, who is the thing signified, is as truly delivered to the increase of our spiritual nourishment as the signs are given and delivered to the body for our temporal nourishment."[20] Torrance discerns here an account of the saving and sanctifying union with Christ, an objective and subjective reality—this is the hallmark of

---

[15] Ibid., 197.

[16] William Milligan, *The Ascension and Heavenly Priesthood of Our Lord* (London: Macmillan, 1894).

[17] Thomas F. Torrance, *Royal Priesthood* (Edinburgh: Oliver and Boyd, 1955).

[18] Thomas F. Torrance, "My Interaction with Karl Barth," in *How Karl Barth Changed My Mind*, ed. Donald K. McKim (Grand Rapids, MI: Eerdmans, 1986), 62.

[19] Thomas F. Torrance, "Preface to the First Edition (1958)," in Robert Bruce, *The Mystery of the Lord's Supper: Sermons on the Sacrament Preached in the Kirk of Edinburgh in A.D. 1589*, ed. and trans. Thomas F. Torrance (Ross-shire: Christian Focus Publications, 2005), iv.

[20] Bruce, *The Mystery of the Lord's Supper,* 106.

Calvin and the early Scottish reformers. The focus on the whole Christ, the Word of God incarnate, is a feature of Bruce's preaching. In the context of the Lord's Supper, there is an intensification and deepening of our relationship with Christ. This is the same Christ present in the Word, but there is a sense in which the sacrament enriches a relationship that would otherwise be less intense. This is worth quoting at some length, since it places Bruce (and Torrance) at the higher sacramental end of the Reformed tradition.

> The Sacrament is appointed that we may get a better hold of Christ than we got in the simple Word, that we may possess Christ in our hearts and minds more fully and largely than we did before, by the simple Word. That Christ have more room in which to reside in our narrow hearts than He could have by the hearing of the simple Word, and that we may possess Him more fully, is a better thing. Even though Christ is the same in Himself, yet the better hold you have of Him, the surer you are of His Promise. The Sacraments are appointed that I may have Him more fully in my soul, that I may have the bounds of it enlarged, and that He may make the better residence in me. This no doubt is the reason why these seals are annexed to the evidence of the simple Word.[21]

While the Word of God retains its foundational role, the Christian life is so oriented toward the sacrament of the Lord's Supper that the language of "seal" and "annex" becomes scarcely adequate to its significance. Torrance's success in translating and editing these sermons coincided with several other church-related projects in which he was deeply involved at that time. In surveying these, one gains an appreciation of the extraordinary energy that he brought to his work, coupled with an ability to meet deadlines and targets on several fronts.

As Convener of the Special Commission on Baptism from 1953, Torrance played the lead role in preparing a succession of substantial reports to the General Assembly of the Church of Scotland. These included extensive summaries of the baptismal teaching of Scottish theologians from the late middle ages to the twentieth century. The reports of 1958 and 1959 offered a comprehensive account of the older evangelical Reformed tradition which was placed in opposition to a later declension into forms of hyper-Calvinism and semi-Pelagian moralism. It is easy to discern the authorial presence of Torrance in this material, much of which would reappear in his later study of Scottish theology.[22] Once again, the doctrine of union with Christ is stressed alongside the integration of incarnation and atonement. According to John Knox, the sacraments are signs and seals of our union with Christ. These do not constitute this union, so much as signify what has already been accomplished by Christ's incarnation, his death, and resurrection. The sacraments thus make visible among God's people what has already been established by Jesus Christ. Again, a strong sacramentalism is presented in the exposition of the older Scottish Reformed tradition in Knox, Craig, and Bruce all of whom are valorized by Torrance. The sacraments "bring the immediate presence of God to us." Neither Word nor sacrament should be isolated. "The sacraments without the Word have no soul but the Word needs the sacraments to make our faith sure."[23] How far this is a constructive interpretation of Knox should not detain us here. What is significant

---

[21]Ibid., 64.

[22]Torrance, *Scottish Theology*.

[23]*Reports to the General Assembly of the Church of Scotland* (Edinburgh: General Assembly Publications, 1958/9), 694.

is the extent to which Torrance's theological convictions, both positive and polemical, are presented in this engagement with the Scottish tradition. There is little doubt that such passages represent his own position, including the view that both sacraments should be regarded as "converting ordinances."

Nevertheless, the extent to which the work of the Baptismal Commission actually resolved confusion and uncertainty about the relationship between the once for all baptismal incarnation of Christ and the act of water baptism administered by the church has been debated.[24] Concerns around its "questionable linguistic analysis" and "elusiveness" were apparent[25] with the distinction between *baptisma* and *baptismos* in particular failing to persuade biblical scholars.[26] These difficulties may explain why the General Assembly deflated the proposed deliverance. Instead of accepting the report as "an authoritative interpretation of the Biblical and Reformed doctrine of Baptism" and establishing study days throughout the Presbyteries, the Assembly agreed merely to recognize this as a "valid statement" and commended it for general consideration.[27] Questions around the efficacy and administration of baptism would continue to be raised within the Church of Scotland. Torrance himself would later worry that the subsequent Act of the Assembly, requiring that at least one parent be a communicant member or adherent of the church, had proved too restrictive in relation to the universality of the gospel. His commitment to the practice of infant baptism as a powerful visible display of the grace of God in the incarnate Christ remained unwavering, though his correspondence reveals that he was unable to persuade Karl Barth of this.

Throughout the 1950s Torrance was involved in a series of bilateral and multilateral theological dialogues, many of his own contributions later being gathered into two volumes entitled *Conflict and Agreement in the Church* (1959–60).[28] These reflect his commitment to establishing a rapprochement between the Church of Scotland and the Church of England. His 1955 study *Royal Priesthood* is dedicated "to the Church of England, the church of my mother and my wife, and to the Church of Scotland, the church of my father, in the earnest prayer that they may soon be one."[29] The final chapter offers a defense of the episcopal office from a Reformed perspective. The bishop represents not a separate order of priestly ministry but one in which oversight is exercised at a regional level, so as to signify the unity and continuity of the church. Torrance describes the ways in which a bishop may function as the presiding figure within a presbytery, thus blending elements of Episcopalian and Presbyterian Church government.[30]

In 1957, he was a supporter of the so-called Bishops Report to the General Assembly of the Church of Scotland. Had this been approved it would have introduced bishops into presbyteries, thus preparing the way for the union of the Church of Scotland with the Church of England. Despite the advocacy of Torrance, John Baillie, Archie Craig,

---

[24] John Scott, "Recovering the Meaning of Baptism in Westminster Calvinism in Critical Dialogue with Thomas F. Torrance" (Edinburgh: PhD Thesis, University of Edinburgh, 2015); and Ruth Helen Bell Morrison, "A Study of the Special Commission on Baptism (1953–63) and Developments in Baptismal Doctrine and Practice since 1963" (Glasgow: PhD Thesis, University of Glasgow, 2016).

[25] David Wright, *Infant Baptism in Historical Perspective* (Milton Keynes: Paternoster, 2007), 305.

[26] Barr, *Semantics of Biblical Language,* 140–4.

[27] Wright, *Infant Baptism,* 305.

[28] Thomas F. Torrance, *Conflict and Agreement in the Church*, vol. 1: *Order and Disorder* (London, Lutterworth, 1959), vol. 2: *The Ministry and the Sacraments of the Gospel* (London, Lutterworth, 1960).

[29] Torrance, *Royal Priesthood,* v.

[30] Ibid., 104.

and other leading churchmen of the day, the proposals were eventually defeated after a campaign by the *Scottish Daily Express* championed opposition to episcopacy as vital to Scottish identity. Yet Torrance continued to advocate a catholic reading of the Reformed tradition in his own work.

A further text indicative of his Scottish theological context is the revised version of Wotherspoon and Kirkpatrick's *Manual of Christian Doctrine* which Torrance edited with his ministerial colleague and friend, Ronald Selby Wright. Originally produced in 1920, this volume offered a catholic and ecumenical reading of the Reformed tradition. By 1960, Torrance not only recognized the importance of a new edition of *The Manual of Church Doctrine* but was ready to amend and add new sections to it. Again, there is evidence of an explicit commitment to a strong sacramentalism, not least in his producing a new chapter on the sacraments of the Old Testament—circumcision and Passover—that foreshadow baptism and the Lord's Supper. "The Sacraments result from the fact that Salvation operates by Incarnation; and they import that our relation to Christ is a living relation embracing our whole nature, bodily as well as spiritual."[31] This sacramental theology with its focus on our union with Christ is supported with a range of excerpts from Calvin and other Reformation writers, including Robert Bruce. Torrance stresses the incarnational approach to the atonement adopted in the original text but replaces the rather impersonal and mechanical language of grace by a description of the work of the whole Christ. "Jesus Christ in His grace condescends to give us Himself in a form suitable for us, and so makes Himself accessible to our frailty and weakness. Here He comes to us under the sign and veil of physical objects specially appointed by Him to represent Him and specially sanctified by Him as instruments of His self-communication."[32]

SCOTTISH THEOLOGY: FROM JOHN KNOX TO JOHN MCLEOD CAMPBELL

Written late in his retirement, Torrance's study of the history of Scottish theology is intended as a series of essays on selected thinkers rather than a comprehensive synopsis. Its dominant themes will be familiar to those acquainted with his other writings. Formidable in its knowledge of the highways and byways of the Scottish Reformed tradition, this reads as a work of constructive theology as much as historical exegesis; in doing so, it reveals a good deal about what made Torrance tick as a Scottish theologian. The older Reformed tradition is again championed for its stress on the incarnation, union with Christ, and a more evangelical account of predestination. The gospel is to be offered to all. The whole Christ is to be properly proclaimed. The sacraments are powerful converting ordinances which can generate and intensify our faith by their sensible form of witness to the person and work of Christ. According to Torrance, this original evangelical Calvinism gave way to a lamentable federal systematizing after the Synod of Dort. Its moral and spiritual effects were baleful—though some protested and struck more positive notes, it was not until John McLeod Campbell in the nineteenth century that a significant breakthrough was achieved. This came about by his stressing the centrality of the incarnation for

---

[31] H. J. Wotherspoon and J. M. Kirkpatrick, *A Manual of Church Doctrine according to the Church of Scotland*, revised and enlarged by T. F. Torrance and R. Selby Wright (Oxford: Oxford University Press, 1960), 15.

[32] Ibid., 15, Scott, "Recovering the Meaning of Baptism," 261. John Scott has provided a detailed comparative analysis of the old text with the newer edition amended by Torrance. This reveals substantial adjustments to the original by Torrance. See Scott, "Recovering the Meaning of Baptism," 240–406.

an understanding of God and our humanity. In doing so, Campbell avoided the legal abstractions that beset Reformed orthodoxy in the seventeenth century. Torrance's work continues a Scottish tradition of attaching a very high estimate to *The Nature of the Atonement* (1856).[33] James Denney regarded it as one of only three "really original" books on the subject—the others were by Anselm and Grotius.[34]

The following themes recur throughout Torrance's 1996 study. We will examine each through offering some critical remarks on his reading of Scottish theology.

1. The Incarnational Approach to the Atonement

Torrance writes repeatedly about the whole Christ whose incarnate life, death, and resurrection constitute his atoning work through assuming, healing, and sanctifying our human flesh. This is discerned in several Scottish theologians, including Knox, Leighton, John Forbes of Corse, and McLeod Campbell. The stock criticism of this approach is that it minimizes the apostolic focus on the death of Jesus. Torrance's response, I believe, is not to deny the significance of the crucifixion but to underscore its location within this wider framework; otherwise it becomes distorted through an exclusive and isolated use of forensic categories. The stress on the *totus Christus* is marked in his treatment of Knox on the resurrection and ascension. Noting the sacramental significance of the ascension for his understanding of the Lord's Supper, Torrance is able to describe the sacrament as an event in which we are raised up by the Holy Spirit to union with the ascended Christ. "Ascension introduced the 'distance' between the symbols of bread and wine on earth and the ascended Christ, but nevertheless a 'distance' bridged by the real presence of the risen and ascended Christ through the Spirit."[35] At the same time, our incapacity to imagine the ascended Christ at the right hand of the Father redirects us to the story of Jesus. "There is no way to Jesus, no contact with the risen Lord, but by way of the crucified—no *theologia gloriae*, but first a *theologia crucis* and then on that basis a *sursum corda* following the movement of the ascension."[36]

2. Election in Christ

Torrance contrasts the Scots Confession (1560) with the Westminster Confession (1646), arguing that its setting of election beside Christology achieves a stronger stress on the love of God for all. Here he follows Barth who commended the Scots Confession in this respect in his Aberdeen Gifford Lectures.[37] This again reflects Torrance's relentless insistence that there is no God behind Jesus, no inscrutable divine will that is enacted only in part by the life and death of Christ. One criticism leveled against Torrance is that this represents a revision of the classical Reformed tradition rather than a retrieval of an original conviction that was surrendered by its exponents in the seventeenth century. Here, one suspects, his reading of Scottish theology may be more creative and constructive than he claims. The textual evidence for placing Calvin and Knox on one side of a binary division against the Reformed orthodoxy of Rutherford, Dickson, and the Westminster

---

[33] J. McLeod Campbell, *The Nature of the Atonement* (Cambridge: Macmillan, 1856).

[34] James M. Gordon, *James Denney (1856–1917): An Intellectual and Contextual Biography* (Milton Keynes: Paternoster, 2006), 223.

[35] Torrance, *Scottish Theology*, 40.

[36] Ibid., 23.

[37] Karl Barth, *The Knowledge of God and the Service of God According to the Teaching of the Reformation* (London: Hodder and Stoughton, 1938), 68–79.

Confession is at best slender.[38] The doctrine of double predestination seems structurally the same, even if later iterations adopted more nuanced expressions under the pressure of fresh problems and controversies. Torrance's startling claim that election is determined Christologically to the extent that even reprobation is caused by the love of God merits attention.[39] But, as a reading of Calvin and Knox, it seems egregious.

3. Union with Christ

Again much of the material bears a striking resemblance to the survey of Scottish theology which Torrance had presented to the General Assembly of the Church of Scotland in the late 1950s. In describing this union, he appeals to the twofold form it takes in John Craig's Catechism, a text that he had published earlier in *The School of Faith* (1959).[40] In the introduction to this work, Torrance provides one of the clearest summaries of his own theology by way of exposition of the Reformed catechisms. Most of this is repeated almost forty years later. The "carnal" union of the incarnation in which Christ takes our human condition is the foundation of the "spiritual" union by which we are engrafted into the church through Word and Sacrament. As a result of the prior carnal union, the subsequent spiritual union has a universal reference. The being and action of Christ determine all people, whether they know this or not. "All are involved already objectively in [Christ's] human life and His work in life and death, i.e. not only on judicial and transactional grounds, but on the ground of the constitution of His Person as Mediator."[41] As a reading of Craig, this tends to lose something of the sixteenth-century context, particularly Craig's remark that without spiritual union, the carnal union avails us for nothing.[42] More explicitly universalist and set within a stronger Christological realism, Torrance's theology strikes a different note.

4. Assurance

A lack of assurance has surfaced at several moments in Scottish Reformed Christianity. The *Marrow of Modern Divinity* resonated with many in the late seventeenth and early eighteenth centuries in part because of its stress upon the assuring nature of faith in Christ. Instead of ruminating on the possibility of one's election or turning inwards to seek evidence of its fruits, the Christian is counseled to look outward to Christ and his gospel. In laying hold of this, a proper sense of assurance will arise. In the early nineteenth century, McLeod Campbell's pastoral difficulties in Rhu arose when he detected an uncertainty among his parishioners as to whether they could count themselves among the elect. This lack of assurance troubled him and generated fresh emphases in his preaching which led eventually to his deposition from the ministry in 1831. Torrance champions McLeod Campbell at every turn of the way, regarding his theological work as a decisive recovery of the older Reformed tradition, especially with regard to the controlling place assigned to an integrated account of incarnation and atonement. Campbell was convicted of teaching that assurance is of the essence of faith, as were the "Marrow men" more than a century earlier.

---

[38]Donald Macleod, "Dr T. F. Torrance and Scottish Theology: A Review Article," *Evangelical Quarterly* 72, no. 1 (2000): 58–60.

[39]Torrance, *Scottish Theology*, 16.

[40]Thomas F. Torrance, *The School of Faith: The Catechisms of the Reformed Church* (London: James Clarke, 1959).

[41]Ibid., cxiii.

[42]Ibid., 113.

But is it right simply to say that assurance is an essential component of Christian faith? Here a distinction may be needed between the content of faith which assures us of our redemption and the act of faith which is always assuring. Somewhat ironically to demand that assurance always accompany the act of faith as an essential ingredient may be to set the bar too high and so to reintroduce a measure of uncertainty among those who struggle with difficulty and doubt. If psychological assurance is lacking, it may be pastorally counterproductive to insist that it is essential to a genuine faith. "If assurance is of the essence of the faith, what are we to say to those who lack it? That they are unbelievers?"[43] Torrance's exposition of the matter however can accommodate a contrast between the objective ground of assurance in Christ and the subjective awareness of one's salvation by contemplating the strength of one's faith or the purity of one's works.[44] A distinction needs to be maintained between the assuring object and the subjective act. If assurance attaches essentially to one's self-awareness, then the psychologizing tendencies that Torrance generally deplores will simply reassert themselves.

5. Limited Atonement

Much of Torrance's invective is directed toward the theory of limited or particular atonement which he regards as a post-Dort corruption of the Reformed tradition. The standard mediating formula that Christ's death was sufficient for all but efficient only for some (i.e., the elect) is judged unacceptable, and he claims, somewhat controversially in light of the textual evidence, that Calvin had entirely eschewed this notion.[45] For Torrance, the person and work of Christ are for all—since all humanity is determined by the history of the incarnation. Any gap between sufficiency and efficiency makes no sense on this model, though Torrance remains anxious to distance himself for any commitment to a universal salvation (*apokatastasis*). The tendency of federal orthodoxy to postulate a limited atonement results in a God who is not wholly invested in the work of Christ. Behind Christ's atoning action, there lurks an inscrutable divine will that is moved by something other than love. Though recognizing that the Westminster Confession is a temperate expression of this theology, he judges that it suffers from the same root problem. "The rigidly contractual concept of God as lawgiver together with a necessitarian concept of immutable divine activity allied to double predestination, with its inescapable implication of a doctrine of limited atonement, set the Church with a serious problem as to its interpretation of biblical statements about the offer of the Gospel freely to all people."[46]

6. The Significance of Mission

The problems are compounded by the failure of this theology to generate an adequate missionary impulse—this is a further animating theme in Torrance's reading of Scottish theology. His repeated conviction is that the theory of limited atonement inhibited the free offer of the gospel throughout the world. While there is some evidence for this, particularly in the nineteenth century,[47] it is less clear that preaching was ever restricted in its scope in Scotland. Indeed, the maintenance of a national territorial church, coupled

---

[43] Macleod, "Dr T. F. Torrance and Scottish Theology," 66.
[44] Torrance, *Scottish Theology*, 218–20.
[45] Macleod, "Dr T. F. Torrance and Scottish Theology," 60–1.
[46] Torrance, *Scottish Theology*, 137.
[47] A. C. Cheyne, *The Transforming of the Kirk* (Edinburgh: St Andrew Press, 1983), 82.

with a comprehensive approach to infant baptism, suggests that the Reformed church was able to resolve these tensions by reference to the distinction between the visible and invisible church. Moreover, the problems experienced in Reformed theology were here generated by the foregrounding of an Augustinian doctrine of double predestination. And to claim that Calvin taught an entirely different doctrine is not borne out by the textual evidence. In this respect, Torrance's attempt to drive a wedge between Calvin and later Calvinism has proved largely unsuccessful as an historical exercise. But his complaint nevertheless has some theological traction. If a controlling function is assigned to the doctrine of predestination, as in the third chapter of the Westminster Confession, problems surrounding the love of God, assurance of salvation, a restriction of the atonement, and the terms in which the gospel is to be offered will inevitably arise.

THEOLOGICAL SCIENCE

By the mid-1960s Torrance was intensely engaged with his theological science, a project that explored the methodological relations between the natural sciences and Christian theology. In many ways, this took him beyond anything that Barth attempted, although Torrance remained anxious to show the continuity of this work with that of his Basel teacher. In other respects, his work in theological science develops earlier convictions that owe something to the influence of Daniel Lamont, another of his teachers. For Lamont, there was important apologetic work to be done in showing the consistency of Christian faith with the best insights of other disciplines. Yet this work took place from within faith—he uses the analogy of viewing the stained glass windows from inside rather than outside the cathedral walls—and it proceeded from the revelation of God in Jesus Christ.[48] In this respect, the subjectivity and initiative of God had to be respected. Some of this adumbrates Torrance's later work and continues a Scottish tradition of maintaining a constructive relationship of theology with the natural sciences. The 1935 Statement of Faith that was approved by the united Church of Scotland devotes an opening section to the consistency of Christian faith with scientific discoveries. "The Church welcomes the knowledge brought to light by scientific inquiry into all the facts of nature and history, in the assurance that all true understanding of these facts will serve to show forth the glory of God."[49] Alister McGrath has shown how Torrance's early lectures in Auburn reflect this same spirit, particularly as mediated by Lamont's teaching. Here he argues that naturalism and revelation are complementary; they should neither be placed in opposition nor reduced one to the other. Torrance's more mature work on theological science may thus be considered a return to interests and convictions that can already be discerned in his student years.[50]

A later if minor influence on Torrance's mature work on theological science was the philosophy of John Macmurray, his colleague in Edinburgh. Torrance seems an unlikely ally of Macmurray whose theological views remained somewhat opaque. Yet Torrance's writings during the 1960s are punctuated with references to his older philosophical

---

[48]Daniel Lamont, *Christ and the World of Thought* (Edinburgh: T&T Clark, 1934).

[49]J. G. Riddell, *What We Believe* (Edinburgh: Church of Scotland Publications, 1937), 6.

[50]Alister McGrath, *Thomas F. Torrance: An Intellectual Biography* (Edinburgh: T&T Clark, 1999), 199–204; and Myk Habets, *Theology in Transposition: A Constructive Appraisal of T. F. Torrance* (Minneapolis, MN: Fortress, 2013), 27–66.

colleague. These reveal a borrowing from Macmurray's work that is particularly evident in his 1969 publication on *Theological Science*. The constant tilting at the deleterious patterns of dualist thought is redolent of Macmurray's philosophy, particularly the subject–object split. The claim, presented tirelessly, that the mode of knowledge must be appropriate to the nature of the object as it discloses itself to us is again reminiscent of Macmurray albeit with significant input from Michael Polanyi. Torrance writes, "It is Professor Macmurray's contention that knowledge in action is our primary knowledge, for the knowing Self is an agent having his existence in time where he is active both in pre-scientific and in scientific knowledge."[51]

Torrance goes on to assert that a new logical form of personal activity "may be developed in which the theory of knowledge occupies a subordinate place within actual knowledge, and in which verification involves commitment in action."[52] In theological terms, what this means for Torrance is that the knowledge of God is always and only shaped in a life of faith and obedience to the divine Word that becomes incarnate. The strongly realist cast of this theology is here reinforced by epistemological arguments that drew from Macmurray. It is also linked to an anthropology that insists upon the embodiedness and sociality of human life, themes that are strongly Hebraic and that also find support in Macmurray's writings.

Commentators on Torrance have often stressed the influence upon his thought of Patristic writers, especially Athanasius, of John Calvin and the other Reformers, and of modern scientific thinkers such as Clerk Maxwell and Einstein. But if this reading of his writings on theological science is correct, then we have again to reckon with more local influences, including that of John Macmurray. Torrance himself offered a glowing eulogy to Macmurray after his death in 1975, describing him as the "quiet giant of modern philosophy, the most original and creative of savants and social thinkers in the English-speaking world."[53]

CONCLUSION

The institutional shaping and proximate influences upon Torrance's work will require to be taken into account by scholars seeking to place him better in historical context. This is not merely a matter of the location and place of his work nor an attempt to discern a partisan national identity which he himself would have deplored—the currency of theological ideas must surely be ecumenical and international. The influence of Barth and the wider Patristic and ecumenical traditions of the church is everywhere present in Torrance's major writings. Nevertheless, a reading of his output in its Scottish context offers a significant critical opportunity for the following reasons. Partly as a result of its sheer erudition, Torrance's work often presents as a somewhat timeless reading of the Christian tradition with allusions gathered from early and modern sources. At times, it is as if Athanasius, Scotus, Calvin, and Barth were all affirming and denying the same things by being transported into twentieth-century conversations. His reading of Scottish theology runs the same risk. And partly as a result of its comprehensive scope, Torrance's

---

[51] Thomas F. Torrance, *Theological Science* (Oxford: Oxford University Press, 1969), 3–4.
[52] Ibid., 4.
[53] John S. J. Costello, "The Life and Thought of John Macmurray," in *John Macmurray: Critical Perspectives*, ed. David Fergusson and Nigel Dower (New York: Peter Lang, 2002), 34.

theology comes as a complete package that is difficult to unwrap and sift. Students often remarked on this. His theology was so powerful, systematic, and wide-ranging that one was confronted with a stark choice of either to submit to it in its entirety or to be cast out as a radical dissident unable to subscribe to its fundamental tenets. This could make it harder to assimilate critically, to revise and adapt, and to reach an understanding of its strengths and weaknesses. The force of Torrance's personality coupled with the magisterial quality of his work at times made it difficult for students to be appreciative while also maintaining a critical distance that enabled them to develop their own lines of enquiry and distinctive contributions to the problems and challenges facing the church in their day and generation. But a more contextual reading of his work—the originating impulses, the influential figures, the formative movements, the particular controversies in which he was embroiled—might help us to see better those ways in which his work can be challenged, criticized, and appropriated. None of this is intended to diminish his significance. He ranks among the great theologians of the Scottish Reformed tradition. Indeed, it is hard to think of another theologian in the history of New College whose work rivals the spiritual force, intellectual erudition, and theological energy of Tom Torrance.

CHAPTER FOUR

Thomas F. Torrance and Ecumenism

JOEL SCANDRETT

AN ECUMENICAL THEOLOGIAN

Thomas F. Torrance was born to be an ecumenical theologian—or so it would seem from a study of his life. Torrance was born in China in 1913 to a Presbyterian father and Anglican mother, missionaries whose marriage was brought about in part through the Edinburgh World Missionary Conference of 1910.[1] Though raised a Scottish Presbyterian, Torrance was deeply influenced by his Anglican mother, Annie Elizabeth (Sharpe) Torrance. Annie was a member of both the Churches of England and Scotland and was counted by Torrance as the "theologian of the family." Torrance's father, Thomas Torrance senior, held to an evangelical Church of Scotland piety that had little time for a sectarian "hyper-Calvinism"—a view which his son fully shared. T. F. Torrance himself also married an Anglican, Margaret Edith Spear, who too was a member of both churches. He endeavored with her "to be really ecumenical in living out the relations between the two churches." Thus, it was the evangelical and ecumenical ethos modeled by Torrance's own parents—his "first and best teachers in theology"—that laid the pattern for his own life and vocation.[2]

The 1910 Edinburgh World Missionary Conference brought about the marriage of Torrance's parents, not to mention his birth. However, it was also a catalyst in the emerging ecumenical movement that would shape Torrance's career as a theologian. Widely recognized as a catalytic ecumenical event, the Conference contributed directly to formation of the World Council of Churches (WCC). This came principally through the work of the Faith and Order Movement, which was founded out of the Conference that same year.[3] The Faith and Order Movement merged with the Life and Work Movement in 1948 to form the WCC and continues today as the Commission on Faith and Order. It was to this Commission that Torrance was later appointed.

Ecumenical efforts were on the rise between the two world wars, years during which Torrance studied philosophy and theology at the University of Edinburgh, and

---

[1] Alister E. McGrath, *T. F. Torrance: An Intellectual Biography* (Edinburgh: T&T Clark, 1999), 10.
[2] John I. Hesselink, "A Pilgrimage in the School of Christ—An Interview with T. F. Torrance," *Reformed Review* 38 (1984): 49-50.
[3] Founded by Episcopal Bishop Charles H. Brent, who attended the 1910 Conference. See Ruth Rouse and Stephen Neill, eds., *A History of the Ecumenical Movement 1517-1948* (London: SPCK, 1954).

undertook his doctoral thesis on the Apostolic Fathers while studying with Karl Barth in Basel.[4] During this time Torrance's interest in historical theology and especially Greek Patristic theology was growing, the latter of which would have a profound impact upon his thought.[5] However, it was following the Second World War that the ecumenical movement and Torrance's career would converge. Torrance's interest in ecumenical matters began to appear in his publications from the late 1940s while still a parish minister.[6] His subsequent appointment in 1950 to the Chair of Church History at New College, Edinburgh, and then to the Chair of Christian Dogmatics, paved the way for his major contributions to ecumenics.

The 1950s were a period of remarkable ecumenical engagement for Torrance.[7] From 1950 to 1958, he participated in dialogues between the Churches of England and Scotland. From 1952 to 1962, he served on the WCC Faith and Order Commission and "was heavily involved in theological dialogue every year."[8] In 1954 alone, he took part in the WCC Conference in Evanston, Illinois, the Faith and Order Conference in Chicago, Illinois, and the World Alliance of Reformed Churches General Council in Princeton, New Jersey. This period of intensive participation pressed Torrance both to identify key points of challenge to ecumenical relations and to work constructively through fundamental questions of ecclesiology and sacramental theology. Much of the fruit of that work is evident in his 1955 *Royal Priesthood*[9] and his two-volume *Conflict and Agreement in the Church*.[10]

This period of ecumenical endeavor also established Torrance as a first-order ecumenical theologian. Though he withdrew from WCC and other dialogues in the 1960s, he never ceased his work in ecumenical theology nor withdrew from relationships he had formed with other theologians.[11] He contributed, for example, to some of the key issues that led to *Lumen Gentium*,[12] served on the 1974 Reformed-Roman Catholic Study Commission on the Eucharist, and led a 1975 colloquy on the ecumenical significance of Karl Rahner.[13] And even as his focus was turning to matters of science and hermeneutics, he continued to produce a steady stream of ecumenical essays throughout the 1960s and 1970s.[14]

---

[4]Thomas F. Torrance, *The Doctrine of Grace in the Apostolic Fathers* (Edinburgh: Oliver & Boyd, 1946).

[5]Torrance's first choice of thesis topics was "the scientific structure of Christian dogmatics," but Barth thought him too young and encouraged his interest in Patristic theology. See McGrath, *T. F. Torrance*, 42–6. See also Jason R. Radcliff, *Thomas F. Torrance and the Church Fathers* (Eugene, OR: Pickwick Publications, 2014), 58 n. 7.

[6]Most notably his response to the WCC's Preparatory Studies: "Concerning Amsterdam, I: The Nature and Mission of the Church; A Discussion of Volumes I and II of the Preparatory Studies," *Scottish Journal of Theology* 2, no. 3 (1949): 241–70.

[7]See McGrath, *T. F. Torrance*, 94–102. See also Elmer M. Colyer, *How to Read T.F. Torrance: Understanding His Trinitarian & Scientific Theology* (Downers Grove, IL: InterVarsity Press, 2001), 46–7.

[8]Hesselink, "A Pilgrimage in the School of Christ," 58.

[9]First edition: *Royal Priesthood*, Scottish Journal of Theology Occasional Papers, no. 3 (Edinburgh: Oliver & Boyd, 1955); Second edition: *Royal Priesthood: A Theology of Ordained Ministry* (Edinburgh: T&T Clark, 1993).

[10]Thomas F. Torrance, *Conflict and Agreement in the Church, I: Order and Disorder* (London: Lutterworth Press, 1959); *Conflict and Agreement in the Church, II: The Ministry and the Sacraments of the Gospel* (London: Lutterworth Press, 1960).

[11]For example, Yves Congar, Georges Florovsky, and Gerard Phillips.

[12]Hesselink, "A Pilgrimage in the School of Christ," 59.

[13]See Torrance, "Toward an Ecumenical Consensus on the Trinity," *Theologische Zeitschrift* 31 (1975): 337–50.

[14]For example, Thomas F. Torrance, *Theology in Reconciliation: Essays towards Evangelical and Catholic Unity in East and West* (London: Geoffrey Chapman, 1975). See also McGrath, *T. F. Torrance*, 260–75, and the invaluable digital bibliography on the T. F. Torrance Theological Fellowship website (https://www.tftorrance.org/bibTFT).

It was near the time of his 1979 retirement from the Chair of Christian Dogmatics that Torrance embarked upon possibly his most important ecumenical endeavor. From his early days as a student Torrance had been influenced by the pro-Nicene theology of the Greek Fathers.[15] In the course of his ecumenical endeavors he had formed close relationships with a number of leading Orthodox theologians.[16] These came to fruition in 1977, while Torrance was serving as Moderator of the General Assembly of the Church of Scotland. On behalf of the World Alliance of Reformed Churches, Torrance proposed to the Ecumenical Patriarch of Constantinople and other Orthodox leaders a theological dialogue on the doctrine of the Trinity. This proposal was accepted and led to a long-running series of dialogues that culminated in two volumes of essays and the 1992 "Agreed Statement on the Holy Trinity."[17]

Though influenced by Greek Patristic theology from the outset, we see in this period a more explicit focus by Torrance upon the Greek Fathers than in earlier decades.[18] This bore fruit in some of Torrance's most significant theological works, especially *The Trinitarian Faith: The Evangelical Theology of the Ancient Catholic Church* (1991) and *The Christian Doctrine of God, One Being Three Persons* (1996). While constructive and synthetic in argument, both works—and indeed, virtually all of Torrance's work throughout this final period—draw deeply upon the Greek Patristic corpus and are thoroughly ecumenical in outlook.

In sum, we see in the course of Torrance's life and work an abiding commitment to the whole οἰκουμένη, a commitment which appears first as ecumenical endeavor among Western Christians, but expands to include—indeed, to prize—theological discourse with the Orthodox tradition. Ever faithful to his own Reformed theological heritage, his unceasing efforts to further Christian unity through theological discourse and collaboration place Torrance among the most important ecumenical theologians of the twentieth century. We turn now to consider key aspects of his ecumenical theology, which remained consistent throughout the latter half of the twentieth century.[19]

A NICENE ECUMENISM

As evinced by his magisterial *The Trinitarian Faith*, the theology articulated in the Nicene-Constantinopolitan Creed represents for Torrance a high-water mark of Christian theological consensus. Torrance robustly upholds the time-honored status of the Nicene

---

[15] So, Torrance, "The Greek Fathers remain my main love and I repair to them all the time, and learn from them more than from any other period or set of theologians in Church history," 1973 letter to Georges Florovsky in Matthew Baker and Todd Speidell, eds., *T. F. Torrance and Eastern Orthodoxy: Theology in Reconciliation* (Eugene, OR: Wipf & Stock, 2015), 323. Re. "pro-Nicene," see Myk Habets, "'The Essence of Evangelical Theology': Critical Introduction," in Torrance's, *The Trinitarian Faith: The Evangelical Theology of the Ancient Catholic Church*, Cornerstones edition (London: T&T Clark, 2016).

[16] Most notably Georges Florovsky, Chrysostom Constantinides, George D. Dragas, Archbishop Methodios Fouyas, Angelos J. Philippou, and John Zizioulas. See Baker and Speidell, *T. F. Torrance and Eastern Orthodoxy*.

[17] In Thomas F. Torrance, ed., *Theological Dialogue between Orthodox and Reformed Churches*, vol. 2 (Edinburgh: Scottish Academic Press, 1993). See also https://ecumenism.net/archive/docu/1992_orth_warc_trinity.pdf

[18] For example, Thomas F. Torrance, ed., *The Incarnation: Ecumenical Studies in the Nicene-Constantinopolitan Creed A.D. 381* (Edinburgh: Handsel Press, 1981); and Thomas F. Torrance, *Divine Meaning: Studies in Greek Patristic Hermeneutics* (Edinburgh: T&T Clark, 1992). See also McGrath, *T. F. Torrance*, 280–93.

[19] Many of Torrance's earlier essays are either reprinted verbatim in later collections or substantially incorporated in later works.

Creed as a touchstone for all ecumenical endeavors. He affirms the Creed as a normative articulation of the Rule of Faith to which Christians of all traditions should ascribe. In this respect, Torrance is in step with much mainstream ecumenical practice of his day.

However, for Torrance, the value of the Nicene Creed lies not only in its normative status as a theological statement. The Creed also represents an achievement of profound theological insight into the Being, Persons, and constitutive relations of the triune God. Nicaea's fixing of the *homoousion* as the theological lynchpin of Christology and Trinitarian theology established the Creed as both a normative declaration and a theological heuristic for subsequent generations.[20] Thus, while the Creed is the *sine qua non* and theological touchstone for all Christian theological reflection, it is also a means by which we may gain real knowledge of the living God.

> The basic decision taken at Nicaea made it clear that the eternal relation between the Father and the Son in the Godhead was regarded in the Church as the supreme truth upon which everything else in the Gospel depends. Jesus Christ is himself the content of God's unique self-revelation to mankind .... It is only when we know God the Father in and through his Son who belongs to his own being as God that we may know him in any true and accurate way.[21]

Vital to Torrance's ecumenical theology is his understanding of the relation between Nicene Trinitarian theology and Nicene ecclesiology. For this real knowledge of Jesus Christ as the content of God's unique self-revelation *is itself constitutive of the Church's existence*. The knowledge of God stated in the Creed is not merely a discursive knowledge of theological propositions. Rather, it is a faithful apprehension through the Holy Spirit of the reality of "Christ clothed with his Gospel," who is ever present in his Church. This is the Deposit of Faith—the kerygmatic foundation of the Church's existence in time and space, the continuous, constitutive relation of the Church's existence as the Body of Christ.

> When, with the pouring out of the Holy Spirit upon the Church, Christ thus clothed with his Gospel indwelt the Church and united it to himself as his Body, the Word and Truth of the Gospel embodied uniquely in Christ also became embodied in a subsidiary way in the apostolic foundation of the Church .... Thus, the New Testament *kerygma* referred not merely to the proclamation about Christ but to the *reality* proclaimed, Jesus Christ who continues to be savingly at work through the *kerygma*. That is surely how the original Christians understood the deposit of faith.[22]

In Torrance's view, this realist Christocentric ecclesiology is the ecclesiology of the Nicene faith and prerequisite to all attempts at ecumenism. Without such a shared apprehension of the reality of Jesus Christ as the ontological ground of the Church, all ecumenical endeavor is compromised from the outset. However, when such a shared apprehension is present, Christian unity is attainable because it is rooted in real knowledge of God and his incarnate Word, who is the ground and source of the Church's life.

---

[20]See Torrance's "Introduction" to *The Incarnation: Ecumenical Studies in the Nicene-Constantinopolitan Creed*, xi–xxii.

[21]Torrance, *The Trinitarian Faith*, 3.

[22]Ibid., 258–9. See Thomas F. Torrance, "The Deposit of Faith," *Scottish Journal of Theology* 36, no. 1 (1983): 1–28.

A CHRISTOCENTRIC ECUMENISM

Thus, "the Church is grounded in the Being and Life of God, and rooted in the eternal purpose of the Father to send his Son, Jesus Christ, to be the Head and Saviour of all things."[23] This essentially Pauline[24] understanding of the Church, Torrance argues, must be the starting point for ecumenical theology. For it is the eternal purpose of God to save alienated and dying humanity by first uniting to himself, through his Incarnate Word and Holy Spirit, a covenant people conformed to his will and purposes.

God's eschatological purposes for the Church are therefore bound up with God's purposes for the whole human race and indeed the whole of creation. Given the fundamental problem of human alienation from God and the resultant alienation we experience within ourselves and in relation to one another, the reconciliation effected by God in human history must eventuate in the reconciliation of human beings with one another. The result is a new humanity grounded in God's saving union with humanity in Jesus Christ. The Church of Jesus Christ is God's chosen means and proleptic realization of this eschatological purpose:

> What has been fulfilled intensively in the Church through the operation of the Spirit must be fulfilled extensively in all mankind and in all creation. As such, the Church is to be regarded as the new humanity within the world, the provisional manifestation of the new creation within the old. At its heart lies the mystery of the union between Christ and His Church, which presses out toward universal fullness.[25]

However, continues Torrance:

> The Church cannot share the life of Christ to the full, and cannot embody in itself the reconciliation He bestows, without fulfilling its mission to all mankind, in bearing the Gospel of reconciliation to all for whom He died, without seeking to embody in the midst of the world's divisions the oneness of the fellowship of reconciliation.[26]

Thus, the question of the unity of the Church in Torrance's thought is inextricably related to the larger question of the eschatological reconciliation and unity of humanity with and in God.

For Torrance, the germ and matrix of this reunion of humanity is the Incarnation of the eternal Word and Son of God as Jesus Christ. In his assumption of human nature in and through the economy of his earthly ministry, Christ the incarnate Son binds alienated and dying humanity to himself, reestablishing the ground of human being in the life of God and forging a way within himself for human beings to be reconciled and united to God. In the union of his divine nature with human nature, Jesus Christ is established as the Head of the Church. Indeed, says Torrance:

> *Christ is the Church,* for the Church is Church only in Him. Christ the Incarnate Son of God is the Church because He embodied Himself in our humanity and as such gathered our humanity in Him into oneness with God. He identified Himself with us, made Himself one with us, and on that ground claims us as His own, lays hold of us,

---

[23] Thomas F. Torrance, "The Foundation of the Church," *Scottish Journal of Theology* 16, no. 2 (1963): 113.
[24] For example, Ephesians 1:22.
[25] Thomas F. Torrance, "The Mission of the Church," *Scottish Journal of Theology* 19, no. 2 (1966): 138.
[26] Ibid., 140.

and assumes us into union and communion with Him, so that as Church we find our essential being and life not in ourselves but in Him alone.[27]

While Christ is the Church, Torrance simultaneously avers that the Church is *not* Christ. For the source and dynamic vitality of the Church's existence lies not within the Church but beyond itself in its ascended and reigning head, to whom the Church is united through the Gospel by His Word and Spirit. This point is vital to Torrance's ecumenism. Rejecting all suggestions that the Church is somehow a continuation of the Incarnation, Torrance insists that the Church exists only by virtue of its union and participation in Christ through the Holy Spirit. As such, *the Church is the Body of Christ*, but only through a relation of union and communion with Christ its Head. As the Body of Christ, united and conformed to Christ in its cruciform life, the Church is far more than just another human community. Indeed, it is nothing less than "the earthly-historical form of the existence of Jesus Christ."[28] Nonetheless, the sole real, constitutive relation that grants the Church its existence, vocation, and vitality is its union and communion with Christ. So Torrance:

> That is what we need to learn again today … that when we think of the Church our eyes must travel at once to Christ the Lord Himself, for it is He who is the essence of the Church; it is only in Him that the Church is Church, only in Him that it coheres and has its principle of being and unity, and only in and through Him does it have its function and mission in the Gospel.[29]

AN ECCLESIOCENTRIC ECUMENISM

As mentioned above, Torrance proffers this Christocentric ecclesiology as representative of the apostolic and Patristic legacy of the Church leading up to and finding expression at Nicaea.[30] As with other aspects of his theology, he employs this line of argument in both a positive and negative manner. Positively, he uses it to articulate and flesh out the relations and structures of his own neo-Patristic[31] ecclesiology. Negatively, he uses it as a means of critiquing later ecclesiological developments in the history of the Church that he deems deficient.

In regard to ecumenism, Torrance employs this strategy to affirm the Church's union with Christ through the Holy Spirit as the sole, sufficient ground of Christian unity, while rejecting any attempt to appeal for Christian unity on the basis of a social or juridical understanding of the Church. In this regard, he is especially critical of Tertullian, Cyprian of Carthage, and Augustine for what became the dominant "Latin" understanding of the Church as a closed community under the authority of the bishop, which was "clearly influenced by Roman conceptions of society and law." This development played a determinative role in the Roman Catholic understanding of the Church as "a divinely instituted society in the world under the universal headship of the bishop of Rome, and

---

[27] Thomas F. Torrance, "What Is the Church?" *The Ecumenical Review* 11 (1958): 9. Emphasis is his.
[28] Torrance, quoting Karl Barth (CD 4/1) in *The Trinitarian Faith*, 276.
[29] Torrance, "What Is the Church?" 7.
[30] See especially the chapter "The One Church," in *The Trinitarian Faith*, 252–301.
[31] See Radcliff, *Thomas F. Torrance and the Church Fathers*.

with canonically defined structures of unity, continuity and authority."³² By contrast, church authority and government in the East, while ordered according to conciliar canons and bishops, "were construed in terms of κοινωνία rather than in terms of hierarchical structure," and the episcopate "was held to be subordinate to the apostolic foundation of the Church, as well as to the Lord Jesus Christ the one Head of the Church."³³ Torrance clearly sees the Eastern tradition as preferable to the West in this respect.

Torrance is likewise opposed to any ecclesiology that would construe the unity of the Church as an essentially moral or rational unity. Such ecclesiologies presuppose that the Church's chief mode of relation to Christ is moral or rational, not a real, personal, and spiritual union. Whether in regard to ancient Arianism, doctrinaire confessionalism, or modern ecclesiologies that relegate Jesus Christ to the status of moral exemplar, Torrance's response is the same: the Church is not a community formed through the external, voluntary association of like-minded people. Rather, the Church is constituted by a dynamic, internal ontological relation to Jesus Christ "through the reconciling and incorporating activity of the incarnate Son and the communion of the Holy Spirit."³⁴

The vital implication to underscore here is Torrance's insistence that the ground of the Church's unity in Jesus Christ *is ontologically prior to its ecclesial structures*. Such structures are necessary, but they are secondary to the real, transcendent ground of the unity of all Christians as the Body of Christ united to its living Head, who is continually establishing and extending his Church throughout the world. While required for the order, discipline, and ministry of the Church in its various sociohistorical contexts, all ecclesial structures and their distinctives are relativized by the Church's fundamental unity with and in Christ, who is himself the Church's *Esse*.³⁵ Moreover, in light of the eschatological destiny of the Church, such structures are provisional. So, says Paul Molnar, "Torrance's view of the church ... is at once ecumenically and theologically grounded in such a way that he is able to stress how the church is the visible presence of Christ on earth and in history, while at the same time avoiding any idea which would reduce the church's reality to its institutional structures."³⁶

Thus, for Torrance, the ground of the Church's unity is nothing other than the very relation of union with Christ through the Holy Spirit that constitutes its existence in the first place. Just as the Church is really one in Christ, so all churches are really united with one another in Christ. Christian unity is possible because Christians *are already one in Christ*. Says Torrance:

> Jesus Christ alone is the ground of the Church's unity and the Holy Spirit establishes the Church upon that ground, gives it unity through union with Christ and continues to maintain and uphold the unity in the midst of diversity. There is only one Mediator between God and Man who makes all who believe in Him one Body with Him. There is only one incarnation and one atonement. There is only one Spirit, and therefore there is only one Body of Christ and one Church in Him .... Oneness thus belongs to

---

³²Torrance, *The Trinitarian Faith*, 271.

³³Ibid., 272.

³⁴Ibid., 278.

³⁵"Christ is Himself the essence of the Church, its *Esse*. That fact immediately relativizes and makes ultimately unimportant these endless and tiresome discussions about what is of the *esse* or the *bene esse* or the *piene esse* of the Church," Torrance, "What Is the Church?" 7.

³⁶Paul D. Molnar, *Thomas F. Torrance: Theologian of the Trinity* (Farnham and Burlington, VT: Ashgate, 2009), 265.

the very nature of the Church in its inner and outer life …. As it is one in the Spirit, so it must live out that oneness in the Body.[37]

In sum, Torrance's approach to Christian unity calls for the mutual apprehension by all churches of the one Church as the visible Body of Christ, ontologically established beyond itself in the Incarnate Word of God and persisting through human history. Church doctrines and canons necessarily outline and describe church faith and order and are therefore required, but they cannot serve as a basis for unity—in part because they cannot agree on which are primary and which secondary. Rather, in Torrance's view, the singular basis and starting point for Christian unity must be *the mutual recognition among each of the churches of the one Church and Body of Christ subsisting within the others*. Thus, says Torrance:

> If we ourselves are in Christ we cannot fail to discern His Body in others whom He is pleased to call His own and whose Sacrament He is pleased to honour with His own real Presence and Spirit. If we fail to discern it in others the first question we must ask is whether we have ourselves learned to regard the Church as Christ's very own Body, as the Body of which He is the Head and Lord and Saviour and Husband.[38]

A SACRAMENTAL ECUMENISM

In light of his elevation of the Church's ontological union with Jesus Christ as the singular basis and criterion for the unity of the Church, it stands to reason that Torrance also elevates Baptism and Communion as the sacramental correlates of that union and unity. In keeping with his Christocentric realism, he upholds Jesus Christ as the singular μυστήριον from whom Baptism and Communion derive and in whom they participate (κοινωνία). Christ is "not only the agent or instrument of our salvation but its very substance, so the matter of the Sacrament is to be found in the substance of Christ Himself."[39]

Torrance therefore insists that the sacraments have no reality apart from the Word. For "to make them self-sufficient and independent of the Word would be to take away their sacramental character, for it would deny to them their element of mystery, or infinite recession in the Word that is in the bosom of God and is God."[40] However, because they *are* God-given means of participating in the mystery of the incarnate Word, their reality and efficacy are upheld and sustained by that Word.

Thus, Baptism and Eucharist are the "sacraments of the Gospel" because they participate in the mystery of Jesus Christ's whole vicarious saving life and work as the incarnate Word of God. As such, they are means of κοινωνία with Christ and with all those who are in Christ. Baptism is the Christ-appointed means by which all believers are united to him by the Holy Spirit, in his baptism at the Jordan River, in the baptism of his death and resurrection, and in the whole of his vicarious reconciliation of humanity to God. And if Baptism is the sacramental means of our union with Christ, then it is also the means of our union with one another in Christ.[41]

---

[37]Torrance, "The Mission of the Church," 141.

[38]Torrance, "What Is the Church?" 8.

[39]Torrance, *Conflict and Agreement in the Church, II*, 142.

[40]Ibid., 164.

[41]See Torrance, *The Trinitarian Faith*, 290–2. See also Torrance, "The One Baptism Common to Christ and His Church," in *Theology in Reconciliation*, 82–105.

As Baptism is Christ's sacramental means of the Church's union with him, so Holy Communion (or Eucharist) is his means of the continual renewal and strengthening of that union. In its repeated practice of participation through Communion in the life of the risen Christ through the Holy Spirit, the Church continually receives into itself His indwelling presence and is renewed as His Body. Like Baptism, if Communion is the sacramental means of renewing our union with Christ, then it is also the sacramental means of renewing our union with one another in Christ. How the application of the ecumenical practice of Communion is to be undertaken is a difficult question, as we will see below. However, it is clear that Torrance sees it as a necessary sacramental dimension of the unity of the Church.

Thus, for Torrance, Baptism and Communion are Jesus's own appointed sacramental signs and means by which the unity of his Church is established, persists, and is made manifest within the life of the Church in the world. While Baptism is the sacramental entry point into union with Christ and the ground of the Church's unity in Christ, it is Communion that especially stands as the visible sign of that unity. Baptism is inherently and unavoidably individual. Communion, by contrast, is the inherently corporate sacrament of union with Christ that most visibly manifests the unity of the Church in the world. Says Torrance, "It is in the Eucharist ... that the Church becomes visible as the Body of Christ in history, for it is there that it becomes a membered Body under the Headship of Christ."[42]

THE FRUIT OF ECUMENISM—A COMMUNION OF LOVE

The ultimate outcome of all ecumenical endeavor should be Christian love. However, Torrance is consistent in asserting that the ground of Christian love is nothing other than the eternal love of God poured into the world in and through Jesus Christ by the Holy Spirit. As Christ's Body, the earthly historical form of his existence, the Church is the principal place in which that love is to be found:

> This Church is a communion of love .... In the Christian Church there dwells the personal presence of Jesus Christ and it is His love that masters the community and binds them into unity, and this love was such a new and masterful thing, divine love in its overflow into the lives of men, that a rare word had to be used to describe it—*agape*.[43]

Thus, love among Christians is the "overflow" of Christ's love for the Church and begins with the love they receive and share in Jesus Christ.

This overflow of divine love among Christians in the Church means that the Church is also a community of reconciliation, "a fellowship of those who have been reconciled to God in Christ and those who have therefore been reconciled with one another."[44] This reconciling love is not limited to the interior life of the Church but is an ever-expanding center of the reconciling love of God in the world, coextensive with the proclamation of the Gospel and the Church's embodiment of the Kingdom of Christ in the world.[45] Sin has

---

[42]Torrance, *Conflict and Agreement in the Church*, II, 194.
[43]Torrance, "What Is the Church?" 16–17.
[44]Ibid., 17.
[45]Torrance, "The Mission of the Church," 138–40.

corrupted the natural diversities of the world, distorting them into destructive divisions, but Jesus has sent his Body into the world "to overcome the power and divisiveness of sin, and so to provide healing for mankind, reconciling man to God and man to man in Himself."[46]

It is therefore within the frame of the Church as a communion of love and reconciliation that Torrance locates an embodied Christian unity, the nucleus of the eschatological unity of humanity. Tragically, however, sin has also invaded the Church, bringing division where there should be unity and presenting a divided Church to the world. While God graciously continues to use the Church to draw people to himself, this does not negate the "sin of division."[47] In Torrance's view, the place at which the Church's division is to be overcome is the Lord's Table. Thus:

> The discipline of the Lord teaches us that because the Holy Supper witnesses to our unity in Christ, we must first be reconciled with our brother before we bring our gift to the altar, but it also teaches us that it is here above all that we are renewed in our reconciliation with our Lord, and therefore that it is by this renewal that we can be reconciled to one another.[48]

Consequently, Torrance insists that intercommunion between churches should not be the result of their reconciliation but its starting point. If Communion is the matrix of Christian reconciliation, then it must be so not only among individuals, nor only within a given church or denomination, but also between separated ecclesial bodies. For the real, ontological union and unity we already share as the one Church of Jesus Christ precedes not only all ecclesial structures but their divisions as well. Thus, concludes Torrance:

> If we are really ready to seek reconciliation in Christ we cannot but enter upon Intercommunion as soon as possible, and, in and through the forgiven and healed relation to Christ which it mediates, work together towards *fullness* of Communion between the Churches.[49]

In sum, for Torrance, the locus of Christian unity is already objectively inherent, and therefore principally present, in the relation between Christ and the Church before it is realized among churches. It is therefore principally a corporate unity, which cannot be reduced to matters of particular relations though it necessarily includes them. Moreover, it is a unity that is objectively real prior to any rational apprehension thereof or mutual affection among those who share in that apprehension—though such should be its outcome. Finally, it is in and through the shared ecclesial practice of Holy Communion that, for Torrance, Christian unity should be undertaken and effected.

THE CHALLENGE OF ECUMENISM

In his preparatory work for the 1954 WCC conference in Evanston, Torrance was the principal drafter, with input from Georges Florovsky, of a statement entitled, "Towards Evanston: Our Oneness in Christ and Our Disunity as Churches."[50] As indicated by

---

[46] Torrance, "What Is the Church?" 17.
[47] Ibid., 18.
[48] Torrance, "The Mission of the Church," 143.
[49] Torrance, *Conflict and Agreement in the Churches*, II, 10–11. Emphasis his.
[50] Torrance, *Conflict and Agreement in the Churches*, I, 263–83.

the title, this statement acknowledged both the unity of the Church in Jesus Christ and divisions inherited and perpetuated by the churches. The statement also included a summary outline of its purpose, which provides a helpful distillation of Torrance's thought found throughout his ecumenical corpus:

In the following statement we seek:

(i) to speak of the oneness of the Church (a) as enduring reality grounded in the oneness of Christ and His Church once and for all wrought out in His incarnation, death, and resurrection; (b) as eschatological growth and fulfilment in the Church, for in spite of the divisions of the world in which it is involved the Church is ever renewed through communion in the death and resurrection of Christ and grows up in the unity of the faith into the fulness of Christ;

(ii) to speak of the oneness of the Church in the face of our actual disunity in the Church on earth, acknowledging that though there are God-given diversities in creation and in the gifts of the Spirit which are to be honoured, it is ultimately sin that divides, but believing that He who by the death of Jesus Christ has overcome the contradiction of sin will not allow the oneness of the Church to see corruption, for by the death and resurrection of Christ He triumphs over our sin and division, and gives us already an anticipation of our unity in the one Body of the one Lord;

(iii) to speak of the oneness of the Church as the commanding reality of the Church in Christ to which we must respond in the obedience of faith: (a) listening together in the midst of our disunity to the voice of the one Lord, that we may be compacted together and grow up together into Him who is the Head of the Body; (b) being ready to let the mind of Christ be in us, so that as He was obedient unto the death of the Cross, we may follow Him in denial of ourselves, even as "churches", and in taking up our cross; (c) learning to speak the truth in love with one another, and to discern in others the one Body of which we are members; (d) bearing joint witness in the Gospel, pointing away from our dividedness to the One Lord who has reconciled the world to Himself and has put all our divisions under the judgment of His Cross. In this obedience of faith we believe we shall be changed, although wherein we shall be changed we can know only in the act of faith and self-denial.[51]

Several points in this summary are worthy of note. First, we see Torrance's now-familiar insistence upon the real ontological unity of the Church in Jesus Christ. However, we also note the eschatologically conditioned character of the visible manifestation of that unity among the churches. While the Church is already truly one in Christ, the diverse and sin-conditioned character of the Church's existence in this age of the world means that the full realization of that unity will only be achieved at the Eschaton, when the Church is reunited with its Lord. "Until that promise is fulfilled the Church continues to be a pilgrim people in a strange land (cf. Heb. 11:13) so that all its life and work on earth are incomplete, although it has already become one Body with the coming Christ."[52]

At the same time, the statement points to the problem of real obstacles of sinful division that are perpetuated in the churches of the οἰκουμένη. While the "God-given diversities"

---

[51]Ibid., 263–4.
[52]Ibid., 268.

that derive both from creation and the distinctive charisms of the Holy Spirit are to be treasured, they have also become occasions for sinful "divisions of the world to penetrate back into [the Church] so that its own unity in mind and body has been damaged, and its mission of reconciliation in the world has been seriously injured."[53] This is a scandal, in respect both to the realization of God's love within the Church and to the credibility of the Church's proclamation of the Gospel in the world.

Thus, while the goal of ecumenism is to realize and visibly embody the unity of the Church in human society, Torrance's principal concern is to address the scandalous problem of sinful divisions and to restore the credibility of the Gospel. He does not emphasize ideas of institutional reunification, which would contradict both his insistence upon the priority the church's ontology over its ecclesial structures and his understanding of the eschatologically conditioned character of the Church's diverse existence in this age. Rather, his emphasis is upon overcoming sinful divisions toward the goal of mutual recognition of the Body of Christ, shared Eucharistic participation, and joint witness to the Gospel for the sake of the world.

In its final point, the above summary emphasizes the need for churches (a) to listen and learn from one another, (b) to be open to "the mind of Christ" in obedient self-denial of themselves "even as churches," (c) to "speak the truth in love" as they discern the one Body of Christ in other churches, and (d) to join as churches in common witness to the Gospel in word and deed. Together these imperatives call for an attitude of openness to the real unitive and corrective agency of the incarnate Word of Christ in the midst of the churches.

Sadly, says the statement, "we deny the sole Lordship of Christ over the Church by usurping it, by claiming the vineyard for our own, by possessing our 'church' for ourselves, by regarding our theology, order, history, nationality, etc., as our own 'valued treasures.'"[54] In this regard, Torrance identifies elsewhere in his corpus some of the difficult challenges that persist as obstacles to the realization and embodiment of Christian unity. These fall broadly into three ecclesial categories: Roman Catholic, Reformation, and Orthodox, each of which in its own way has failed to apprehend and submit to the ontological reality of Jesus Christ as the unitive ground and head of the Church.

While acknowledging its massive achievement in the religious and social development of Western society, Torrance is critical of the captivity of the Roman Catholic Church to a dualistic understanding of itself as, on the one hand, an external juridical body governed by extrinsic legal structures—which understanding it received and accommodated during in its emergence in the Roman imperial world—and on the other hand, an internal mystical body of the church as a spiritual reality. This dualism has been both the occasion for the Reformation itself and an ongoing barrier to unity between Roman Catholic and Reformation Churches.

However, Torrance is deeply encouraged by the recovery of Greek Patristic theology by the Roman church in the twentieth century, which led to the profound breakthroughs of the Second Vatican Council in the 1960s.[55] Among these, Torrance especially identifies the following:

---

[53] Torrance, *Theology in Reconciliation*, 7.

[54] Torrance, *Conflict and Agreement in the Churches*, I, 277.

[55] Torrance, *Theology in Reconciliation*, 52–70.

> One of the immense gains of the Second Vatican Council was the recovery of the Greek patristic insight that the Church is grounded beyond itself in the divine-human nature of Christ and through Christ in the transcendent communion of the Holy Trinity, from which it derives its essential intelligible structure to which all its visible institutional structures in this world are subordinate.[56]

This achievement indicates a genuine turning point in Roman Catholic ecclesiology, one that is in clear accordance with the realist Christocentric ecclesiology of Torrance's ecumenical theology. As such, it continues to hold profound importance for ecumenical relations between the Roman Catholic Church and other churches. However, Torrance also identifies tendencies toward Roman Catholic retrenchment in response to Vatican II along the same lines of extrinsic juridical identity that has stood as an historic obstacle to unity. As long as the extrinsic emphasis upon the precedent of canon law is not also open to reform, this will continue to be a temptation for the Roman Catholic Church.[57]

Among Reformation churches, Torrance identifies the problem of the impetus of an historic reaction to Rome—especially crystallized by the Council of Trent—which took various forms of sectarian confessional extrinsicism. What began as a genuine breakthrough of renewal and reform collapsed into an analogous Protestant form of doctrinaire extrinsicism, which was fueled by the rise of independent European states and their respective churches. This post-Reformation sectarian fragmentation rendered the Reformation churches especially vulnerable to the secularizing forces of modern rationalism and deistic naturalism. Consequently, Protestantism became increasingly characterized by "a dualism between a world of inward spiritual experience evoked by 'existential' relation to an utterly transcendent God and an external world of material experience governed by rigid laws of cause and effect in a mechanistic universe."[58] Especially in relation to matters of ecclesiology and ecumenism, these continue to pose challenges to the Reformation traditions.

Torrance sums up the particular challenge of Protestant-Catholic relations in the Western churches as follows:

> The concrete structure of the Church in history is consistent only if ... it is completed from beyond itself as through the Spirit it participates in the mystery of Christ .... If the Catholic Churches need to learn the supreme importance of this meta-canonical ingredient in the structures of the Church, the Evangelical Churches certainly need to learn the necessary place of the canonical ingredient in the inner coherence and structured continuity of the Church, if they are to escape from the damaging dualism between theological and historical continuity, or between the invisible and visible Church.[59]

Not surprisingly, Torrance is least openly critical of the Orthodox tradition, for which he holds immense esteem and a debt of gratitude. Nonetheless, he acknowledges that the Orthodox tradition, like the Roman, can be captive to its own canonical traditions in a way that stand as an obstacle to ecumenism. As evinced in his correspondence with George Florovsky over the question of intercommunion, Orthodox ecclesiology and

---

[56] Ibid., 64.

[57] Torrance, "Ecumenism and Rome," *Scottish Journal of Theology* 37, no. 1 (1984): 59–64.

[58] Torrance, *Theology in Reconciliation*, 46.

[59] Ibid., 68.

sacramental theology present a difficult counterargument to Torrance's understanding of the unity of the Church.[60]

Ironically, the organization of which Torrance is most critical regarding challenges to ecumenism is the World Council of Churches. Torrance identifies a shift in the WCC's ecumenical orientation throughout the later twentieth century that resulted in the undermining of its own evangelical and Christological foundation—a foundation without which Torrance is convinced it will fail. Abandoning its earlier commitments to the evangelical mission of the Church, the WCC has opted for a social justice agenda predicated not on the agency of God's Word and Spirit but upon the agency of secular political power. Says Torrance:

> So far as the World Council of Churches is concerned, or at least the Evangelical Churches represented by it are concerned, the centre of gravity has shifted away from the evangelical mission of the Church to one in which it is not justification by grace that seems to predominate but justification by social righteousness. Protestant Churches have become infected by sociological trends, and the clamour to give a "political" slant to ecumenical activity, in such a way that the authentic notes of ecumenism have been severely dulled. This is evident in the way the World Council of Churches tends to take its agenda from the public media and to be intent on deploying secular power-structures for spiritual ends.[61]

In light of these developments, Torrance places greater hope for the future of authentic Christian ecumenism in dialogue and cooperation between churches, rather than in the ideologically driven platforms of much of modern ecumenism.

ASSESSING TORRANCE'S ECUMENISM

While a comprehensive assessment of Torrance's significance for ecumenism is beyond the scope of this chapter, the following concluding observations and questions may identify points for further consideration.

Torrance's ecumenical theology was clearly of import in the early days of the WCC, and there is no question that the ecumenical movement as a whole has grown and spread. In this regard, we may recognize Torrance's important contribution to ecumenism. However, Torrance's own ecumenical theology appears not to have had lasting impact in those circles. Insofar as Torrance's assessment of the ecumenical movement is accurate, it seems that his realist Christocentric ecclesiology was swimming against the tide of a sociopolitically construed ecumenism which has since passed over and beyond him. However, there are indications of late that Torrance is gaining a new hearing elsewhere. Several of the authors appearing in this volume stand as a case in point: Both Orthodox theologian Matthew Baker and Anglican theologian Jason Radcliff endorse Torrance's work as bridge for Protestant–Orthodox relations.[62] Baptist theologian Myk Habets appropriates Torrance's thought in his consideration of the doctrine of *theosis*.[63]

---

[60] See Matthew Baker, "The Correspondence between T. F. Torrance and Georges Florovsky (1950–1973)," *Participatio* 4 (2013) "T. F. Torrance and Eastern Orthodoxy," 287–323.

[61] Torrance, "Ecumenism and Rome," 61.

[62] Baker, *T. F. Torrance and Eastern Orthodoxy*, xi; Radcliff, *Thomas F. Torrance and the Church Fathers*.

[63] Myk Habets, *Theosis in the Theology of Thomas Torrance* (Farnham: Ashgate, 2009).

Reformed theologian George Hunsinger demonstrates Torrance's continuing ecumenical relevance in his appropriation of Torrance's eucharistic theology.[64] And Roman Catholic theologian Paul Molnar elevates the ecumenical potential of Torrance's sacramental theology.[65] Insofar as these treatments and others indicate a new season of engagement with Torrance's work, his ecumenical theology may yet be of service to the task of Christian unity.

In regard to the substance of Torrance's ecumenical theology, at least three major questions are worth considering. The first, and most obvious, concerns Torrance's commitment to intercommunion as a *means* to ecumenical *rapprochement*, rather than merely a desired outcome. Though his emphasis upon intercommunion is not as prominent in his later work, there is no indication that he abandoned it. As such, it stands as one of the distinctive aspects of his ecumenical theology and therefore one of the most contested. As his disagreement with Florovsky indicates, Torrance's approach to intercommunion (which should in no way be confused with "open communion") entails an ecclesiologic that most Orthodox and Roman Catholics will encounter as an ecumenical impasse, rather than a bridge. While this may prove Torrance's point regarding the controverted relation between the living Christ and historically conditioned ecclesial structures, the impasse remains.

Second, and related, is the larger question of Torrance's understanding of sacramental unity as either a basis or criterion for Christian unity. For many churches in the Anabaptist, Pietist, and Pentecostal traditions, sacramental theology is not a principal feature of ecclesial identity and practice, nor does it inform their approach to ecumenical engagement. There is a clear preference, if not prejudice, in Torrance's thought in this regard. While his retrieval of the Patristic legacy grants clear and important gains for relations between Orthodox, Roman Catholics, and the Magisterial Reformation Churches, it stands at odds with many Protestant traditions coming out of the Radical Reformation or later. Torrance's approach appears to support George Lindbeck's observation of two distinct types of ecumenism, which he characterizes as "unitive" and "interdenominational." Like Torrance, unitive ecumenists ground their efforts in sacramental theology and Patristic *ressourcement*. By contrast, interdenominational ecumenists are less interested in matters of ecclesial identity and practice, and instead ground their efforts in common experiences of encounter with Jesus Christ in various modalities.[66] Whether or not we accept Lindbeck's analysis, the question of how Torrance's theology might be accessible to non-sacramental traditions remains.

Third, and proceeding from the previous two questions, it seems that Torrance was overly optimistic about what he initially thought the ecumenical movement could achieve. There is a decidedly optimistic tone in Torrance's early discussions about the changes taking place in the twentieth century and their significance for ecumenical relations. Despite the catastrophes of the twentieth century, Torrance seems to have remarkable confidence both in the promise of Patristic theology for ecumenical *rapprochement* and in the promise of scientific breakthroughs in physics and cosmology, to overcome divisions in human thought and society. In light of his own later critiques of the obstacles facing

---

[64]George Hunsinger, *The Eucharist and Ecumenism: Let Us Keep the Feast* (Cambridge: Cambridge University Press, 2008).

[65]Molnar, *Thomas F. Torrance: Theologian of the Trinity*, 265–323.

[66]George A. Lindbeck, "Two Kinds of Ecumenism: Unitive and Interdenominational," *Gregorianum* 70, no. 4 (1989): 647–60.

the ecumenical project, not to mention society as a whole, it seems that ecumenism today merits a more modest approach. Ecumenical strategies that appear to be bearing fruit in recent years tend to focus on practical ecumenism as a grassroots movement, with less attention to theological dialogue. Whether this is an entirely positive development merits critical consideration. In what ways might Torrance's realist Christology offer both corrective insight and constructive resources for a more chastened ecumenism in the twenty-first century?

These critical questions notwithstanding, it is clear that Torrance's ecumenical theology remains an invaluable contribution to the cause of Christian unity, especially from the standpoint of those in the Reformation traditions. The implications of his constructive retrieval of Greek Patristic thought for the renewal of Protestant ecclesiology are especially profound and in many circles are only beginning to be recognized.

CHAPTER FIVE

Thomas F. Torrance and Karl Barth

Similarities and Differences

PAUL D. MOLNAR

In this chapter I will compare Thomas F. Torrance and Karl Barth by discussing their approach to knowledge of God; their understanding of the Trinity as the driving force of Christian theology; and their belief that the resurrection is the starting point of theology, but it is so only to the extent that the incarnation is taken seriously as the "ontological ground of our knowledge of God" such that it is "allowed to occupy its controlling centre" while also taking the activity of the Holy Spirit seriously by allowing "both divine revelation and our understanding of it" to be conceptualized in "*dynamic* and not in static terms."[1]

KNOWLEDGE OF GOD

It is revealing that when Torrance began to study Barth seriously, what most impressed him was that "any rigorous scientific approach to Christian theology must allow actual knowledge of God, reached through his self-revelation to us in Christ and in his Spirit, to call into question all alien presuppositions and antecedently reached conceptual systems, for form and subject-matter, structure and material content, must not be separated from each other."[2] Torrance's own understanding of Scripture was deepened because he was able to see that both fundamentalism and liberalism[3] were "but rationalising variations on the ancient adoptionist and docetic heresies, which kept passing over into each other in their betrayal of the Gospel."[4] This remark suggests that Torrance likely had in mind Barth's rejection of what he labeled Ebionite and Docetic Christology as two approaches to Jesus Christ in his uniqueness as the incarnate Word which clearly did not allow Christ

---

[1] Thomas F. Torrance, *Karl Barth, Biblical and Evangelical Theologian* (Edinburgh: T&T Clark, 1990), 122.
[2] Ibid.
[3] For Torrance's concise and important rejection of fundamentalism and liberalism as approaches that failed to take the incarnation seriously in different ways, see his *Reality and Evangelical Theology* (Philadelphia, PA: The Westminster Press, 1982), 15–19.
[4] Torrance, *Karl Barth*, 122.

himself as God's self-revelation to be the sole criterion of truth. In fact they could not do so, since the former began with the adoptionist presupposition that Jesus was called God only because of the impression he made on his followers and not because he *was* the eternal Son of the Father; thus at best, such a Christology could only allow Christ to be an extraordinary human being, but not the unique revelation of God in history—not the one Mediator who acted and acts as our reconciler and redeemer. The latter began with the docetic presupposition that Jesus was called God only because and to the extent that he was thought to embody the idea of divinity the community embraced on grounds other than those disclosed by Jesus himself. In other words, it was thought that knowledge of God could be had without allowing one's thought to be shaped by Jesus himself in his human history as the incarnate Word.

Torrance went on to say that the first part of *Church Dogmatics* I/1, which discussed dogmatics as "a critical science" in a rigorous way, "fell somewhat short" of what he was "looking for,"[5] but he found what he was looking for in the second chapter of that volume in Barth's treatment of the "revelation of the Triune God."[6] He was most impressed by the importance of the hypostatic union, the "*consubstantial communion* between the Persons of the Holy Trinity" and especially what he called "Barth's very impressive account of the doctrine of the Holy Spirit as the distinctive Freedom of God to be present to the creature and to realise the relation of the creature to himself as its true end."[7]

Enough has been said here to conclude that Barth and Torrance were very close theologically in allowing their thinking about God to begin and end with Jesus Christ as the revelation of God in history. Put another way, they both began with God's economic trinitarian self-revelation. There is no doubt that Torrance and Barth both believed that the doctrine of the Trinity which was not to be found directly in the Bible, but which was an accurate development of doctrine from the biblical witness,[8] was the central doctrine of the Christian faith and thus the controlling center for all dogmatics. That is why Torrance could say that if any doctrine was held apart from the doctrine of the Trinity it would be seriously malformed[9] and that the doctrine of the Trinity is indeed the "ground and grammar of theology."[10] Barth held a similar view as he began his treatment of the doctrine of the Trinity saying that "in giving this doctrine a place of prominence our concern cannot be merely that it have this place externally but rather that its content be decisive and controlling for the whole of dogmatics."[11] For Barth "The doctrine of the Trinity is what basically distinguishes the Christian doctrine of God as Christian, and therefore what already distinguishes the Christian concept of revelation as Christian, in contrast to all other possible doctrines of God or concepts of revelation."[12]

---

[5] Ibid., 123.

[6] Ibid.

[7] Ibid.

[8] Thomas F. Torrance, *The Christian Doctrine of God, One Being Three Persons* (Edinburgh: T&T Clark, 1996; reissued in Cornerstones edition by Bloomsbury T&T Clark, 2016), 49; and Karl Barth, *Church Dogmatics*, 4 vols. in 13 pts., vol. I, *The Doctrine of the Word of God*, pt. 1, ed. G. W. Bromiley and T. F. Torrance, trans. by G. W. Bromiley (hereafter: *CD*) (Edinburgh: T&T Clark, 1975), 308.

[9] Torrance, *Christian Doctrine of God*, 31.

[10] Thomas F. Torrance, *The Ground and Grammar of Theology* (Charlottesville: University Press of Virginia, 1980), xi, 158–9; Paul D. Molnar, *Thomas F. Torrance: Theologian of the Trinity* (Farnham and Burlington, VT: Ashgate, 2009), 31–72.

[11] Barth, *CD* I/1, 303.

[12] Ibid., 301.

BEING AND ACT

Both theologians held this view precisely because they believed that God's being and act were one. Thus, Barth insisted that "if we really want to understand revelation in terms of its subject, i.e., God, then the first thing we have to realise is that this subject, God, the Revealer, is identical with His act in revelation and also identical with its effect."[13] This is a pivotal insight because what Barth means is that since Jesus Christ is the incarnation of the Word of God, therefore there is no way to acquire true knowledge of God apart from the act of God in that unique history of Jesus himself as attested in Scripture. Further, since the Holy Spirit is God himself in the unity of being of the Father, Son, and Holy Spirit, our ability to hear that Word and understand it comes to us only as the Holy Spirit enables that understanding as what he called the "subjective reality of revelation."[14]

It would be a major misunderstanding of Barth and of Torrance who followed him in this, to assume that when they emphasize the fact that God's being and act are one, they mean to reduce God to his actions *ad extra*. They both insist that God is the one who loves in freedom. Therefore, God is eternally one in his actions of knowledge and love within the immanent Trinity and had no need to love us. Nevertheless, God eternally chose to love us and to have us as his covenant partners and so God freely decided to create, reconcile, and redeem us without becoming dependent on us. Barth thus opposed the ideas that "God becomes a predicate of man, or ... that man becomes a requisite in God's nature ... [since] we must not think away the free basis that this correlation [between God and us] has in God."[15] Accordingly,

> If we will not listen to the fact that Christ is antecedently God in Himself in order that *in this way* and *on this basis* He may be our God, then we turn the latter, His being God for us, into a necessary attribute of God. God's being is then essentially limited and conditioned as a being revealed, i.e., as a relation of God to man. Man is thus thought of as indispensable to God. But this destroys God's freedom in the act of revelation and reconciliation.[16]

For his part, Torrance frequently says, in thinking about God in faith, "we can never think or speak of him truly apart from his revealing and saving acts or behind the back of Jesus Christ, for there is no other God."[17] But, like Barth, Torrance also insists that while "God *is* Love" that "does not mean that God is Love in virtue of his love for us, but that God is in himself the fullness and perfection of Love in loving and being loved which out of sheer love overflows freely toward others."[18] Indeed, Torrance consistently held that "we do not say that God is Father, Son, and Holy Spirit, because he becomes Father, Son and Holy Spirit to us, but while we only know him because he becomes so to us, he only becomes Father, Son and Holy Spirit to us precisely because he *is* first and eternally Father, Son and Holy Spirit in himself alone."[19] Like Barth, Torrance held that

---

[13] Ibid., 296.

[14] Barth, CD I/2, 242. Thus, "Man is free for God by the Holy Spirit of the Father and the Son. In that consists the reality of revelation," 243. This act of the Spirit has a "strictly negative meaning" as well since we are free for God "in the Holy Spirit," but "we are not free for God except in the Holy Spirit," ibid.

[15] Barth, CD I/1 172.

[16] Ibid., 420–1, emphasis mine.

[17] Torrance, *Christian Doctrine of God*, 5.

[18] Ibid.

[19] Thomas F. Torrance, *The Doctrine of Jesus Christ* (Eugene, OR: Wipf & Stock, 2002), 107.

the "doctrine of the Trinity which involves the very root and ground of Christian truth all in itself is the guard of truth here" so that without the dogma of Christ's preexistence, "there can be no Trinity: and the central basis of Christianity would then be cut out. The Trinity and Pre-existence of Christ are tenets of faith that stand or fall together."[20]

Like Barth, then, Torrance was very consistent in recognizing and maintaining God's freedom in himself and for us without introducing logical necessities into the divine being as happens so frequently today. Thus, Torrance held that "the incarnation was not necessary for God to be God and live as God: it flowed freely, unreservedly and unconditionally from the eternal movement of Love in God."[21] The incarnation was a new act, new even for God, Torrance says, following Athanasius, just as creation was something new, even for God. This, Torrance says, "warns us that we cannot think of the ontological Trinity as if it were constituted by or dependent on the economic Trinity." So, while there is a "oneness between the ontological and the economic Trinity" we must nonetheless distinguish and delimit the economic from the immanent or ontological Trinity since there are "elements in the incarnate economy such as the time pattern of human life in this world which we may not read back into the eternal Life of God."[22]

FURTHER POINTS OF AGREEMENT AND ASPECTS OF DIFFERENCE

While Torrance and Barth certainly were one in these important matters, there were differences between them as well. Whereas both agreed on the importance of distinguishing without separating the immanent and economic Trinity, Torrance thought that there was an element of subordination in Barth's doctrine of the Trinity.[23] And while both theologians applied the doctrine of justification by faith to our knowledge of God, insisting that there are no analogies that are true in themselves and that the truth had to come to us through an act of the Holy Spirit actualizing atoning reconciliation within our minds by uniting us with Christ, Torrance pursued what he called a "new natural theology" while Barth would not lend his little finger in the service of natural theology.[24] Furthermore, Torrance was never happy with Barth's choice to speak of the persons of the Trinity as "modes of being."[25] He also moved beyond Barth's view of the *Filioque* as well as the traditional view of the doctrine of appropriation which he nevertheless thought Barth properly reconceptualized.[26] Torrance further criticized Barth for not specifically

---

[20] Ibid. See also Barth, *CD* I/2, 878–9.

[21] Torrance, *Christian Doctrine of God*, 108.

[22] Ibid., 109.

[23] Regarding the element of subordination, see Molnar, "The importance of the doctrine of justification in the theology of Thomas F. Torrance and of Karl Barth," *Scottish Journal of Theology* 70, no. 2 (2017): 198–226; and "The obedience of the Son in the theology of Karl Barth and of Thomas F. Torrance," *Scottish Journal of Theology* 67, no. 1 (2014): 50–69.

[24] Thus Barth, "Even if we only lend our little finger to natural theology, there necessarily follows the denial of the revelation of God in Jesus Christ. A natural theology that does not strive to be the only master is not a natural theology," *CD* II/1, 173.

[25] See George Hunsinger, *Evangelical, Catholic and Reformed: Doctrinal Essays on Barth and Related Themes* (Grand Rapids, MI: Eerdmans, 2015), 27–8.

[26] Regarding the *Filioque*, see Paul D. Molnar, "Theological Issues Involved in the *Filioque*," in *Ecumenical Perspectives on the Filioque for the 21st Century*, ed. Myk Habets (London: Bloomsbury T&T Clark, 2014), 24–34. Regarding Torrance's view of the doctrine of appropriation, see *Christian Doctrine of God*, 200.

focusing on the humanity of the risen and ascended Lord in CD IV/3 by speaking more generally of the humanity of God.[27] Still, there is no doubt that they were at one in holding to the importance of the incarnation and resurrection as decisive events in history that led to a proper understanding of the Trinity and thus of all other doctrines, especially the doctrines of creation and atonement. Let us briefly explore some differences between Barth and Torrance as it relates to knowledge of God.

While both Torrance and Barth believed that there was no place for the doctrine of justification on its own, they both believed that, as Torrance held, it belonged "to the inner texture of the Gospel and becomes evident as its cutting edge."[28] In connection with knowledge of God, Torrance regularly maintained that we must think from a center in God and not from a center in ourselves just because justification means "a perpetual living in Christ, from a centre and source beyond us" so that "to be justified is to be lifted up above and beyond ourselves to live out of the risen and ascended Christ, and not out of ourselves."[29] Above all, this meant that our faith in and through which we know God as he truly is rests not on our faith but on "the faith of Christ alone" so that in faith we "flee from our own acts of repentance, confession, trust and response, and take refuge in the obedience and faithfulness of Christ."[30] In sum Torrance held:

> Far from looking for justification on the ground of our "orthodoxy," we can only serve the Truth faithfully or truthfully if we point away from ourselves and our statements to Christ himself. He who boasts of his orthodoxy sins against justification by Christ alone, for he justifies himself by appeal to the truth of his own beliefs or formulations of belief and thereby sets himself in conflict with the Truth and Grace of Christ.[31]

Torrance believed that justification forced the Reformers to realize that "they had to reject the idea that the criterion of truth is lodged in the subject of the knower or the interpreter" of Scripture since any proper interpretation of Scripture means that "we are thrown back upon the Truth of the Word of God."[32] For them, Torrance rightly held that "the centre of authority" was transferred from "the subjectivity of man or the Church to the objectivity of the Truth itself." In this connection Torrance firmly stressed that "no one since the Reformation has applied justification by God's grace alone so radically and daringly to human theologizing as Karl Barth. It means, as he has shown us, that we can never look for the truth in ourselves but must look for it beyond ourselves in God."[33] Torrance thus agreed with Barth that "we can never claim the truth of our own

---

[27] Torrance, *Karl Barth*, 134. See also Paul D. Molnar, Introduction to the Cornerstones edition of Thomas F. Torrance's *Space, Time and Resurrection* (London: T&T Clark, 2018).

[28] Thomas F. Torrance, *Theology in Reconstruction* (London: SCM, 1965), 150.

[29] Ibid., 152.

[30] Ibid., 160.

[31] Torrance, *Reality and Evangelical Theology*, 149.

[32] Thomas F. Torrance, *God and Rationality* (Edinburgh: T&T Clark, 1997), 67–8. See also "Truth and Authority: Theses on Truth," *Irish Theological Quarterly* 39, no. 3 (1972): 217. Importantly, Torrance held that Schleiermacher, Bultmann, and Heidegger, each in their own way did finally operate with a criterion of truth lodged in us. This took a "radical form" in Kant, ibid., 220; also, *Transformation & Convergence in the Frame of Knowledge: Explorations in the Interrelations of Scientific and Theological Enterprise* (Grand Rapids, MI: Eerdmans, 1984), 38–40. Torrance opposed any form of "non-conceptual knowledge" as it always places the criterion of truth finally in us, see Torrance, "Truth and Authority," 226–7; and Molnar, *Torrance: Theologian of the Trinity*, 33–6, 124–5, 172–4.

[33] Ibid., 68. See also Torrance, *Theology in Reconstruction*, 163.

statements, but must rather think of our statements as pointing away to Christ who alone is the Truth. Theological statements do not carry their truth in themselves."[34]

Barth and Torrance are one in this. In speaking of our knowledge of God, Barth held that "our views and concepts and words are of themselves too narrow to apprehend God" but that God could "take up his dwelling in this narrowness."[35] A person can be:

> Taken up by the grace of God and determined to participation in the veracity of the revelation of God ... As a sinner he is justified ... The veracity of the revelation of God, which justifies the sinner in His Word by His Spirit, makes his knowledge of God true without him, against him—and yet as his own knowledge and to that extent through him.[36]

DIFFERENCES

Nevertheless, there are some differences between them. Torrance held that there was a place for natural theology and it is sometimes said that this distinguishes him from Barth since by finding this place his thinking was in line in some sense with the long tradition of natural theology. Yet, that is not quite accurate since Torrance argued that the proper place for natural theology in Christian theology is exclusively within revealed theology. Thus, natural theology or what he calls his "new" natural theology can only exist in a transformed situation in which it never operates independently of revelation. The problem with that assertion, however, is that once natural theology is transformed by its function within revelation, it ceases to be natural theology, that is, a theology that is based on nature, history, or conscience. Before discussing the disagreement between Barth and Torrance on this issue, let us first explore one recent critique of Torrance's theory of knowledge.

Barth, Torrance, and Critical Realism

Paul La Montagne has argued that Torrance "recognizes and describes Barth's critical realism in a manner that *almost* captures its character. But because he accepts and adopts von Balthasar's thesis about the turn from dialectic to analogy in Barth's work he continually speaks as though being a critical realist entitled Barth to be a positive realist without further dialectical reservation."[37] Accordingly, Torrance failed to realize that for Barth "the dialectic of certainty and uncertainty which is our part in this event" continues in our knowing God. In this way La Montagne believes Torrance neglected the fact that the certainty of our knowledge is "controlled from the side of the event which is God's part" such that "certainty inheres in revelation, and not in our theology."[38] Thus, for Barth, "the dialectic still remains on our part."[39]

---

[34] Ibid. See also Torrance, *Christian Doctrine of God*, 76.

[35] *CD* II/1, 212.

[36] Ibid., 213.

[37] D. Paul La Montagne, *Barth and Rationality: Critical Realism in Theology* (Eugene, OR: Cascade, 2012), 173, referring to Thomas F. Torrance, *Karl Barth: An Introduction to His Early Theology 1910–1931* (Edinburgh: T&T Clark, 2000), 85.

[38] Ibid., 175–6.

[39] Ibid., 176, referring to *CD* II/1, 75. Importantly, Barth finished his statement that dialectic still remains on our part saying: "Yet not in such a way that we are still in the grip of that dialectic" but that it is "controlled from the side of the event which is God's part," *CD* II/1, 75. Thus God's truth stands before us, Barth says, "in all its divine certainty, and it can genuinely be apprehended by us," ibid.

La Montagne provides an example of Torrance not quite getting Barth right. Torrance wrote: "Christology, therefore, has for Barth a supreme *critical* significance, for it is through Christology that theology is enabled to break through subjectivism, in its romantic-idealist or its existentialist forms, to the sheer reality of God. And it is through radically Christo-centric thinking that pure *theology* can arise and be preserved from all corruption from the side of anthropocentric thinking."[40] La Montagne notes that, while it is true that for Barth, Christology has a critical significance, "it is revelation itself that is the source of our self-criticism; doctrines are only an attempt to theorize that critique. Moreover, the continuing presence of dialectic in Barth's thinking means that theology *never* breaks through to the sheer reality of God. God breaks through to us. Our theology is *not* pure and is *not* preserved from all corruption."[41] Torrance is said to have side-stepped Barth's point that "anthropocentric corruption, especially in the form of natural theology, is endemic to us as human beings" because Torrance wrote that "when our statements are simply and formally identical with statements of the text of Scripture in which Christ speaks his Word to us, they are directly authoritative."[42] Such a remark, according to La Montagne, neglects Barth's emphasis on the hiddenness of God such that even "the language of ecclesiastical dogma and that of the Bible is not exempt from this crisis. It is not the case, then, that we have only, say, to rediscover the world of the biblical view and concept or to adopt the biblical language, in order to make the viewing and conceiving and language of truth our own."[43] In sum, Torrance fails to maintain the fact that "a reservation" must be "held against all human thinking about God," including "dialectical thinking."[44] In what follows I would like to show that on each of these points, La Montagne has *almost* gotten Torrance right, but that he misses key nuances in Torrance's thought that considerably mitigate his criticisms and place Torrance much closer to Barth than La Montagne is willing or able to admit. Even in their different views of natural theology, as we shall see, there is some basic agreement despite the fact that Torrance wishes to pursue a "new" natural theology and Barth refused to pursue any sort of natural theology.

KNOWING THE WORD OF GOD

La Montagne has argued that for Barth a realist and objective knowledge of God is "a consequence of the Word of God" and thus it is not "a presupposition by virtue of which" one could "claim that we have the word of God in hand in our theology or interpretation of Scripture."[45] The implication of this criticism clearly is that for Torrance, following Balthasar, Barth was misunderstood as a "positive realist without further dialectical reservation." Is this true? On the one hand, Torrance does make occasional statements

---

[40]Ibid., referring to Torrance, *Karl Barth: An Introduction*, 143.
[41]Ibid.
[42]Ibid., referring to Torrance, *Karl Barth: An Introduction*, 188.
[43]Ibid., 176–7.
[44]Ibid., 177.
[45]Ibid., 174.

that make it seem so.⁴⁶ On the other hand, even in Torrance's book introducing Barth's early theology, Torrance does not deny but affirms the fact that dialectic continues in Barth's thought. What he does claim is that dialectic is no longer employed by Barth in an exaggerated way as Barth himself noted in his own self-criticism by speaking of God's supposed "tangential relation" with the world. Rather, in his later thinking within the *Church Dogmatics* Barth also stressed that because God actually became incarnate in Jesus Christ to reconcile the world to himself, we must also speak of God acting for us within the world in his Word and Spirit from both the divine and human side as our representative and substitute.⁴⁷ In his early "dialectical period" Barth is said to have allowed his thinking to be

> a correlate of justification by grace alone, in its epistemological reference … it is a form of thinking which acknowledges that the only legitimate justification or demonstration of Christian truth is that which is in accordance with its nature, as truth and grace of God … Dialectical thinking, therefore, as Barth employed it, is to be considered a form of combining statement and inquiry with the intention of letting the Truth declare itself to us.⁴⁸

Contrary to La Montagne's claim that Torrance held that Barth moved *from* dialectic *to* analogy (leaving dialectic behind), Torrance maintained that the struggle involved in Barth's early dialectic period "is clearly a struggle that has gone on ever since, and must go on if theological terms are not to become debased."⁴⁹ Torrance thinks there was a breakthrough for Barth, but it was from a "severely dialectical form" of thinking such that "a less austere and more positive and reconciling form of thinking could be taken up in its place."⁵⁰ It is a misreading of what Torrance actually says to claim that he was substituting analogy for dialectics in his understanding of Barth because Torrance argued: "To be sure, the dialectic continues, but now it is rather the movement of inquiry which penetrates into the interior dialectic of the subject-matter, into the logic of the Logos."⁵¹

---

⁴⁶Thus, Torrance sometimes speaks as though we can relate ourselves to God's truth by developing the capacity to do so. Therefore, as we "learn to act toward God in accordance with his nature as Lord, and develop the capacity to relate ourselves objectively to him" we come to know "what true rationality and true objectivity are," *Theology in Reconstruction*, 233. Yet, Torrance immediately modifies this implication by arguing that for us to genuinely think objectively and rationally, we must "allow God in the sheer majesty and transcendence of his divine Being and Act to press upon us within the structured objectivities of things and other persons … and open us up for truly objective relation toward himself, in which we are reconciled to him and healed of our mental alienation and estrangement … This is not something we can achieve, but we can let it happen" (ibid.). And this can happen only as we pray for and rely on the Holy Spirit to place us under the determination of God's saving grace. Additionally, Torrance argued that when Peter answered Jesus's question: "Who do you say that I am?" with his statement "'Thou art the Christ, the Son of the living God' … Jesus pointed out that this was not an answer that could be given from the side of man, but from the side of God. It was from God himself that this revelation had come to them, for the Reality of God is not to be discerned through natural insight," ibid., 118–19.

⁴⁷Torrance, *Karl Barth: An Introduction*, 85, 88–9.

⁴⁸Ibid., 88.

⁴⁹Ibid., 89.

⁵⁰Ibid.

⁵¹Ibid. Torrance thought Barth moved on from an idealist dialectic with his view of analogy since that was grounded exclusively in God's actions in Jesus Christ himself, ibid., 194. That indeed allowed Barth to claim that God is knowable to us only in Christ and that if we follow that rule "which is the basic rule of all sound doctrine" then "the statement that God is knowable to man can and must be made with the strictest possible certainty, with an apodictic certainty … freed from any dialectic and ambiguity, with all the certainty of the statement 'the Word was made flesh,'" *CD* II/1, 162.

TORRANCE/BARTH AND THE KNOWLEDGE OF GOD

What about La Montagne's assertion implying that for Torrance we have a realist theology that differs from Barth's because it offers "pure" theology as a "presupposition by virtue of which to claim that we have the word of God in hand in our theology or interpretation of Scripture"?[52] It must be said that Torrance never held such a view and in fact rejected this very thinking on numerous occasions. That is precisely why Torrance insisted that no statements about God or the Word of God are true in themselves. Like Barth, in his pursuit of "pure doctrine,"[53] Torrance held that the "truths of statement are what they ought to be when they serve the truth of being, and the truths of created being are what they ought to be when they serve the Supreme Truth."[54] Thus, for Torrance, as for Barth:

> We ourselves are rightly related to God only as we serve his divine majesty, freedom and authority, in the absolute prerogative of his own truth, in the divine power of his own self-evidence, and in the pure light of his own being—that is in such a way as never to transfer the centre of authority from the objective revelation of God to ourselves.[55]

Indeed, when Torrance referred to Christology's critical significance, he certainly never meant to substitute Christology for Christ himself as the only one who enables us to think rightly about him through the power of his Holy Spirit. Thus:

> Materially considered, the verification of theological statements is found only in the Grace of God in Jesus Christ, as He actively gives Himself in His own Being through the power of the Spirit to be the object of our knowledge (*per modum entis*) and the justification of our human modes of knowing and speaking of Him as we seek to act in conformity to His Word and Truth in Jesus Christ.[56]

Therefore, "justification by putting us in the right with the Truth of God calls in question all that claims to be knowledge of the truth on our part and calls into question our theoretical statements in so far as they claim to have truth in themselves, and directs them away from themselves to Christ as the one Truth of God."[57]

So on the very same page where Torrance spoke of pure theology and of Christology's critical significance, he meant to stress that "Christological thinking carries within it a thinking from out of the concrete act of God's grace in atonement" and thus provides theology "with its critical criterion by means of which it can distinguish objective theological thinking from all mythological objectification."[58] Torrance could not have meant that this criterion was in our hand as he constantly insisted that we must think from a center in God and not from a center in ourselves and also stressed that true

---

[52] La Montagne, *Barth and Rationality*, 174.

[53] See Barth, *CD* I/2, 764–6.

[54] Torrance, "Truth and Authority," 240.

[55] Ibid.

[56] Thomas F. Torrance, *Theological Science* (Oxford: Oxford University Press, 1978), 200.

[57] Ibid., 201.

[58] Torrance, *Karl Barth: An Introduction*, 143. By pure theology Torrance clearly referred to the doctrine of the Trinity and thus to theology grounded in and determined by "the final Reality of God himself ... in the ultimate relations intrinsic to God's own [triune] Being," *Ground and Grammar of Theology*, 158–9.

knowledge of Christ could only come to us as an act of Christ himself through his Spirit and not at all through us trying to work our way toward him.[59]

Let us explore a bit more how close Torrance's thinking about this matter truly is to Barth's approach. Torrance directly embraces Barth's important insight that we may only know God because and as God knows us. Hence, "Faith is the relation of our minds to the Object who through His unconditional claims upon us establishes the centre of our knowing in Himself and not in us, so that the whole epistemological relation is turned round—we know God in that we are known by Him."[60] Indeed, Torrance claims "it is precisely in knowing us, in making us the objects of His knowledge, that He constitutes us subjects over against Him, the lordly Subject, and therefore gives us freedom to know Him even while in our knowing we are unconditionally bound to him as the Object of our knowledge."[61] Just as in Barth's thinking, Torrance maintains that God enables us to know him in our existing "subject-object relationship" in which "we are involved in a whole complex of ideas and conceptions and categories and analogies." However, when God gives himself to be known by us "far from throwing us back upon ourselves, upon our frailty and inadequacy and incapacity, to accredit Him, He comes in Grace to draw us out of our frailty, to lift us above ourselves, and create within us the capacity to know Him."[62]

Yet this capacity does not become ours in the sense that knowledge of God is now under our control, because Torrance argues that in this event God "acts critically and creatively upon our ideas, conceptions, categories, analogies, giving them an orientation and a possibility beyond any power they have in themselves."[63] And he strongly opposes any idea of infused grace which would open the door to "an authoritarian exercise of the magisterium" instead of allowing its proper exercise of authority to serve "the inherent and ultimate authority of the truth itself [in its identity with God acting in history for us]."[64] This means that in knowing us and enabling us to know himself through our union with Christ in the Holy Spirit our actual knowledge of God takes place through "a radical conversion of all our analogies"; thus, we cannot use them "as archetypal analogies" but only as "ectypal" analogies since they must find their power outside themselves and only in God's grace as the one who enables such knowledge in faith all along the line.[65]

TRUTH ACTING IN PERSON

Torrance explicitly relied on Barth's distinction between God's primary objectivity and secondary objectivity which was so crucial to Barth's own understanding in *CD* II/1.[66] God is self-sufficient as the one who knows and loves in himself (primary objectivity)

---

[59] Thomas F. Torrance, *Incarnation: The Person and Life of Christ*, ed. Robert T. Walker (Downers Grove, IL: IVP Academic/Milton Keynes: Paternoster, 2008), 1–5. Thus "We cannot earn knowledge of Christ, we cannot achieve it, or build up to it. We have no capacity or power in ourselves giving us the ability to have mastery over this fact. In the very act of our knowing Christ he is the master, we are the mastered. He manifests himself and gives himself to us by his own power and agency, by his Holy Spirit, and in the very act of knowing him we ascribe all the possibility of our knowing him to Christ alone, and none of it to ourselves," 2.

[60] Torrance, *Theological Science*, 132.

[61] Ibid.

[62] Ibid., 132–3.

[63] Ibid., 133.

[64] Torrance, "Truth and Authority," 241. For how this might affect one's view of analogy, see Torrance, *Theology in Reconstruction*, 114.

[65] Torrance, *Theological Science*, 133.

[66] See Barth, *CD* II/1, 16–18, 21–2, 48–52.

and God makes himself knowable to us in a mediated way precisely through his covenant relations with us and uniquely in Jesus Christ himself (secondary objectivity). That is why Torrance can say:

> God's Truth is His Person turning to us and condescending to become one with us that He may turn us to God in revelation and reconciliation. God does not have to do this. He is entirely free to live His own Life apart from us, but in His freedom he chooses to turn to us and give Himself to us to be known and loved.[67]

Knowledge of God in truth therefore takes place precisely because "it is out of pure Grace that He gives Himself to us to know and think as the Truth, so that our knowing and thinking Him presuppose and repose upon His prior decision or movement in Grace to be the object of our knowing and thinking."[68] Consequently, "He gives Himself to be our Truth and so to be Truth for us. This is the Truth from beyond us, Truth upon which we have no claim, but Truth nevertheless which in sheer Grace gives himself to us and establishes us in fellowship with the Ultimate Truth beyond ourselves."[69]

Again, in a manner quite similar to Barth, Torrance insists that "the Truth reveals that we are not in the Truth and delivers us from the vicious circle of our own untruth, reconciling us to the Truth and putting us in the right with it beyond us."[70] Hence, revelation discloses to us that we are sinners who have no capacity to know God in truth, but who can do so only on the basis of grace, only because God empowers us to do so in all our incapacity. That is one reason Torrance repeatedly stresses that even in our best theology that aims to be pure theology, we are and remain unprofitable servants who are utterly dependent on the grace of God "which is the ultimate secret of the truth of our knowledge of God."[71] Therefore, "It is because the Truth of God is His Grace that justification by Grace alone belongs to true knowledge of God—that is to say, the verification of theological statements is to be undertaken in terms of justification by Grace alone."[72]

All of this then means that Torrance does not presuppose a scientific way of our getting to God via Christology or any other set of presuppositions under our control. Rather, in a manner very similar to Barth, he insists:

> We do not only look at Jesus Christ as the Way, the Truth and the Life, but that through assimilation to Him we look *with* Him, so that *by* Him and *through* Him we are directed to the Father. Jesus is not the Way, the Truth and the Life in abstraction from the Father, but is the Way, the Truth and the Life who brings us to the *Father*. Therefore our knowing has to be assimilated to Jesus' knowing of the Father ... our statements have to be conformed to His statements of the Father.[73]

---

[67]Torrance, *Theological Science*, 157.

[68]Ibid.

[69]Ibid.

[70]Ibid., 158.

[71]Ibid. See also Torrance, *Theology in Reconstruction*, 161.

[72]Ibid.

[73]Ibid., 160. Assimilated here as elsewhere in Torrance's thought does not mean being confused with Jesus or the Holy Spirit; it means to be brought into conformity with Christ in knowledge and love through union with Christ in his true humanity and true deity.

These are crucial remarks because they clearly indicate that it is precisely through our union with Jesus Christ in and through the power of his Holy Spirit and thus also the power of the resurrection itself that we can, here and now, know God in truth without projecting our ideas onto God. So, when Torrance refers to Christology, he clearly means that we can only know God as he is in himself, that is, in his internal relations as Father, Son, and Holy Spirit as we share in Jesus's human knowledge of God which is enabled by Christ himself in the power of his Spirit as a miracle. That is why he flatly insists:

> Theological statements by their very nature cannot be abstracted from the Life and History of Jesus, and therefore they are truly theological in so far as they are faithfully Christological, that is, in so far as they take their living shape from assimilation to the obedience and prayer, the praise and adoration of Jesus which He offered to the Glory of the heavenly Father. Theological truth, therefore, has its essential *form* in the Life of Jesus in which He laid hold upon our mind and will and bent them back in Himself to perfect love and confidence in the Father, to joyful acquiescence in the Truth and glad submission to the will of God.[74]

The power of these remarks can only be grasped when one realizes that for Torrance, God acts for us uniquely in and through the power of what occurred in the hypostatic union of humanity with God in the union of natures which took place in Jesus Christ for our benefit. Because nothing really can separate us from the love of God disclosed in the fact that Jesus himself remained at one with the Father in his whole incarnate life, through temptation and death itself, we, in him through baptism share in his knowledge of the truth and in his living the truth in his obedient life even to death on the cross. This is where Torrance's important understanding of the Holy Spirit acting as God for us illuminates just how important it is to realize that in Jesus Christ, God has acted once and for all and even now both from the divine and from the human side in his vicarious substitution for us. Thus, the freedom of the Spirit may be understood

> as the freedom of God to actualise his relation with us and the freedom of God to actualise our relation with himself … He does this not only from the side of the Creator to the creature but from the side of the creature toward the Creator by bringing its relations to the Creator to their proper end in him, and thereby establishing the creature in an enduring ontological relation to God.[75]

Importantly, however, Torrance does not ascribe this ontological relation in some sense to us. Rather, he insists that while "the creature does not have any continuity in relation to God that belongs to the creature in itself, it does have a relation to God which is continuously given and unceasingly sustained by the presence of the Holy Spirit."[76]

TORRANCE AND BARTH ON SACRAMENTS

This thinking, one might say, also separates Barth and Torrance because while Barth followed his son Markus and famously rejected applying the term "sacrament" to the church's actions in Baptism and the Eucharist, Torrance directly criticized Barth for

---

[74]Ibid., 161.

[75]Torrance, *Christian Doctrine of God*, 152.

[76]Ibid.

reverting to a previously rejected form of "dualistic" thinking.⁷⁷ It is vital to see why Torrance criticized Barth here. He believed that Barth too sharply distinguished between Baptism with the Holy Spirit and Baptism with water. Torrance's own view of the matter was that Jesus Christ vicariously was baptized in the Jordan not because he needed to repent and believe but because he was living his incarnate life in our sinful flesh in perfect obedience to the Father for our benefit, that is, in order to represent us as our high priest and mediator. It is precisely at this point where Torrance's stress upon Christ's high-priestly mediation in his human actions of baptism, prayer, and sacrifice that Torrance differed from Barth. Torrance was able to hold together the church's present actions in Baptism and the Lord's Supper with these historical actions of Jesus as mediator and high priest there and then, and here and now in the Spirit, in a way that Barth did not, with his rejection of the term "sacrament."⁷⁸ In conversation with Barth over these matters and in suggesting to Barth that some of his students ended up with a rather docetic view of the resurrection, Torrance suggested that if Barth had sufficiently emphasized Christ's continued high-priestly activity from both the divine and human side after the ascension, then the sacraments of Baptism and the Eucharist could be seen as the church's acting together with and through and in Christ's present human and divine actions uniting Christians to him and therefore with and through him to the Father.

It must be admitted that Torrance's understanding of these matters is more consistently accurate than Barth's. Torrance brilliantly explained exactly how crucial it was to maintain the importance of Christ's human representation of us. He stressed that it was through Christ's actions here and now in the power of his resurrection and through the action of his Holy Spirit that he really unites us to his "new humanity" and thus also to a genuine sharing in the knowledge and love of the eternal Father and Son through faith and hope. This union of God and us is what will be disclosed at the redemption when Christ returns to judge the living and the dead. Among contemporary theologians, George Hunsinger has offered a compelling view of the Lord's Supper that builds on Torrance's view.⁷⁹ Interestingly, Barth's response to Torrance was to ask him to rewrite the problematic sections of his doctrine of reconciliation.

TORRANCE'S NEW NATURAL THEOLOGY

We now introduce one other area of disagreement or difference between Barth and Torrance, namely, the issue of natural theology. It is complicated because even though Torrance argued for his "new" natural theology especially when pursuing dialogue between

---

⁷⁷See Paul D. Molnar, *Karl Barth and the Theology of the Lord's Supper: A Systematic Investigation* (New York: Peter Lang, 1996), 303.

⁷⁸For a fine illustration of what Torrance means, see *Theology in Reconciliation: Essays towards Evangelical and Catholic Unity in East and West* (London: Geoffrey Chapman, 1975), 208–14, where he insists we must learn "to worship God through and with and in the mind of Christ … the presence of his Spirit in us means that Christ's prayer and worship of the Father are made to echo in us and issue out of our life to the Father as our own prayer and worship. While it is we who pray, we pray not in our own name but in the name of Christ," ibid., 208–9.

⁷⁹George Hunsinger, *The Eucharist and Ecumenism* (Cambridge: Cambridge University Press, 2008), writes: "The full contemporaneity of Christ's person in his work here and now, and of his work in his person, would have to take place, for Barth, primarily through Word and Sacrament. Yet it fell to T. F. Torrance, Barth's student, to make the connection that his mentor never quite managed to carry through," 17. He made the connection by arguing that the action of the church in the Lord's Supper was "not another action than that which Christ has already accomplished on our behalf, and which is proclaimed in the Gospel," ibid.

theology and science, his dogmatic theology, as already noted, is quite consistently rooted in God's economic trinitarian self-revelation in harmony with Barth's approach. So, while he rejected natural theology as traditionally understood and while he never attempted to move from an analysis of nature to knowledge of God by "throwing a logical bridge between the world and God,"[80] there remain ambiguities in his argument. In his last conversation with Barth, Torrance proposed to Barth a way of explaining exactly why Barth rejected natural theology as traditionally understood by not rejecting it completely but by bringing it into the sphere of revelation in a transformed way as the infrastructure or "intrastructure" of human knowledge of God which takes place in faith, by grace, and through revelation.

THEOLOGICAL GEOMETRY

Torrance's analogy is one that he repeated many times. It was the analogy from geometry. This is where Torrance sees a kind of overlap between modern science, following Einstein, and modern theology which is faithful to the union of God and humanity which took place in the incarnation, life, ministry, death, resurrection, and ascension of Jesus Christ himself. Both science and theology, Torrance held, should think in a way that holds together concept and reality, the theoretical and the empirical. Indeed, it is only by holding these together that one can truly think theologically in a way that avoids the kinds of dualism and subjectivism evident in the thinking of Schleiermacher and Bultmann for instance. Thus, for Torrance, Schleiermacher's great error was to embrace in his thinking "the old Hellenic distinction between the *sensuous* and the *spiritual*, that is, between the realm of physical events and the realm of consciousness, and the idealist resolve to transcend the distinction through a co-ordinating principle drawn from the realm of the spirit and consciousness."[81] That was the realm that was regarded by Schleiermacher as "ultimately real."

Torrance, however, opposed this because he held that for the Christian tradition:

> The spiritual is presented in forms that are bound up with the physical and the sensuous, which applies not only to cultic and sacramental acts but to the historic tenets and dogmas of the faith. To the purified self-consciousness these are mythological forms thrown up by sensuous thinking, but since they are expressions of man's inner life and spirit they must be retranslated and made understandable as determinations of the religious consciousness.[82]

In sum, Torrance was saying here, as he did in his various criticisms of Bultmann, that Schleiermacher and Bultmann had detached their ideas of Christianity, including incarnation and resurrection from the empirical events in space and time in which the Word actually became incarnate and rose from the dead, and located their view of truth in the feeling of absolute dependence and Jesus's God-consciousness (subjectivism) as in Schleiermacher and in our existential decisions of faith (subjectivism) as in Bultmann. Thus, any real incarnation or any genuine bodily resurrection and ascension of Jesus had to be regarded as mythological projections from us rather than as distinct acts of

---

[80]Torrance, *Reality and Evangelical Theology*, 32.
[81]Thomas F. Torrance, "Hermeneutics According to F. D. E. Schleiermacher," *Scottish Journal of Theology* 21, no. 3 (1968): 257.
[82]Ibid., 257–8.

God's revelation in identity with these sensuous events within history. Just such thinking embodied the dualism overcome by God himself for us in the hypostatic union and outpouring of the Spirit at Pentecost.

So, Torrance's "new" natural theology was meant to affirm that humanity can indeed know God in himself as he really exists in his own unique objectivity as the eternal Father, Son, and Holy Spirit, but that this knowledge could never occur as long as it expressed only the subjective or idealist projections of the human spirit or human religious consciousness. This was the basis for Torrance's statement to Barth that Barth was only rejecting natural theology insofar as it operated *independently* of revelation as a kind of prolegomenon to revelation. To explain this, he gave his example of geometry explaining that when geometry is detached from physics it is *incomplete* and must be completed beyond itself in physics for it to operate properly as four-dimensional geometry.[83] The problem here concerns the fact that for Barth, once natural theology is transformed in the way advocated by Torrance, it ceases to be natural theology because in its transformed condition or action it now functions solely within faith and by grace and revelation. So, to call this a "new" natural theology, from Barth's perspective, would be a major mistake since what Torrance actually intends to describe is quite obviously a theology of human nature as reconciled by God in Christ. The fact that this is his intention is underscored by his own frequent assertion that "we must let all preconceived forms or frameworks of thought be called into question by those which arise on the ground of actual empirical knowledge of God."[84]

The discrepancy here then is that Barth consistently insisted that he would never support natural theology[85] and that natural theology provides no service to the church,[86] because *either* one lived by faith and by grace and came to know God truly through his own self-revelation *or* one relied upon nature and thus advanced some form of self-justification which both Torrance and Barth adamantly and consistently opposed. There is therefore a difficulty regarding Torrance's analogy here, even according to his own theological presuppositions. It concerns the fact that he believed that for us to know God in truth, our "diseased," "twisted," and "in-turned" minds need to be healed through union with the mind of Christ and thus as the Holy Spirit actualizes in us the reconciliation achieved for us in the life, death, and resurrection of Jesus Christ *before* we could know God in truth.[87] When this happens then we can plainly see that natural theology is not simply *incomplete* as geometry might be without physics. That is the limit and weakness of such an analogy. It cannot simply be carried over into theology because theology never

---

[83]See Torrance, *Reality and Evangelical Theology*, 34, *Transformation & Convergence*, 281–2 and *Reality and Scientific Theology* (Eugene, OR: Wipf & Stock, 2001), 42.

[84]Ibid., 33–4. This is precisely why Torrance can meaningfully say that "the resurrection is therefore our pledge that statements about God in Jesus Christ have an objective reference in God, and are not just projections of the human heart and imagination, objectifying forms of thought in which we fashion a God in terms of the creaturely content of our own ideas," *Space, Time and Resurrection* (Edinburgh: T&T Clark, 1998), 72–3. This makes sense because unless the Word actually became flesh in Jesus Christ and unless Jesus Christ actually rose bodily from the dead, then our speech about God would only be symbolic since "our cognition does not rest upon any objective ground in God and our statements about him do not terminate upon his reality, but are to be regarded as detached expressions in the realm of myth and ritual," ibid., 72.

[85]See Barth, *CD* II/1, 172–3.

[86]"Christian theology," Barth says, "has no use at all for the offer of natural theology, however it may be expressed," *CD* II/1, 168.

[87]Torrance, *Theological Science*, 310; *Atonement: The Person and Work of Christ*, ed. Robert T. Walker (Downers Grove, IL: IVP Academic/Milton Keynes: Paternoster, 2009), 441; *Christian Doctrine of God*, 152–4; and *Theology in Reconstruction*, 231, 238–9.

moves from the realm of history without faith, but in faith always recognizes that human sin is what led to the cross. Even now, it could lead to the idea that there is a seamless movement from one form of thinking (geometry) to another (theology) with the idea of an *incomplete* geometry. However, it must be stressed here that natural theology is the product of sinful human beings who do not yet or no longer know God on the basis of his grace as he has enabled such knowledge in and through Jesus Christ and our union with him in faith. So it is not a matter of our natural theology simply *becoming complete* as with geometry; it is a matter of repentant rethinking of all we know or think we know in light of revelation, as Torrance frequently insisted. How then should we think about this significant difference between Barth and Torrance?

My suggestion is to drop the idea that there is such a thing as "new" natural theology because one may either think of God in faith and by grace or one may attempt to know God by relying on nature or what Barth termed "man as such."[88] When the latter approach is attempted, that *always* means that theologians are either unwilling or unable to make this clear-cut decision for or against the truth as it comes to us in revelation in the power of the Holy Spirit. According to Torrance, natural theology could only function as transformed in such a way that it operated solely within revelation "on the ground of actual empirical knowledge of God." Hence it is "in relation to these forms of thought, which press themselves upon our minds when we seek to know God in accordance with his nature and the steps he takes in making himself known to us, that natural theology can fulfill its proper function" as the "epistemological intrastructure of our knowledge of God."[89] Here Torrance's thinking simply nullifies his own important stress on the need for the Holy Spirit to actualize atoning reconciliation in us so that our minds are healed of what he called the serious mental disease of not thinking objectively about God.[90] That failure to take account of his own view of sin disclosed in revelation at this point explains why there are remnants of the old natural theology Torrance rejected resident in his own thinking.[91] And his search for a "new" natural theology has caused confusion for those

---

[88] Barth, *CD* II/1, 165.

[89] Torrance, *Reality and Evangelical Theology*, 34.

[90] Torrance, *Theology in Reconstruction*, 233. Torrance's explicit idea that "a closer relation must be established between natural theology and revealed theology," *Transformation & Convergence*, 281, has misled some to try to find a place for natural theology in relation to revealed theology in ways that subvert how we know God on the basis of grace, faith, and revelation. See, for example, Molnar, "Response to Alexander J. D. Irving. Natural Theology: An Impossible Possibility?," 148–84 in *Participatio:* The Journal of the Thomas F. Torrance Theological Fellowship Vol. 4 (2018). What Torrance actually meant by this was that a theology based on revelation had to take seriously events in space and time in and through which God has encountered us such as in the incarnation and resurrection and still encounters us as the risen, ascended, and coming Lord in and through the sacraments and in the church. He also meant to stress that theology operating within faith could not be fideistic but had to employ human reason in obedience to revelation here and now.

[91] It is on this point that La Montagne's critique of Torrance has some relevance. In a thorough, helpful, and thought-provoking treatment of Torrance's reflections on natural theology Myk Habets noticed this problem, as well as the problem of Torrance calling our epistemological understanding of God in faith natural theology at all, *Theology in Transposition: A Constructive Appraisal of T.F. Torrance* (Minneapolis, MN: Fortress Press, 2013), 84–5, 91. Habets thinks that Torrance, following Calvin, wanted "to develop a consistent and appropriate way of coordinating but not confusing natural revelation, natural theology, and a theology of nature so that natural science can be used by theologians, and also theology can be instructive to natural scientists," 85. While I think Habets is right in saying this, and while we agree that Torrance was really offering a theology of nature as reconciled in Christ, his analysis does not sufficiently address the question I am raising, namely, whether this thinking within revelation is natural theology at all. According to Barth natural theology's proper function is to give way to a theology that is faithful to the revelation of God in Christ as understood through the power of the Holy Spirit. The problem here is that even according to Torrance's own presuppositions, the only way natural theology can function is when it ceases to be natural theology, that is, a theology based on human nature and reason and becomes a theology employing reason on the basis of faith, grace, and revelation.

who claim to follow his thinking.[92] Torrance never intended to argue for a theology that could function by assuming that natural science could investigate God's actions within history. He could easily have maintained what he calls the "epistemological intrastructure of our knowledge of God" without natural theology since the fact that we actually know God with our human views and concepts is not due to anything we possess, but only to the gift of God's grace in Christ enabling such knowledge. Thus:

> Apart from that act [the incarnation] there is no possibility for men and women to know him [God] … In themselves men and women are not free toward God, to know him, believe in him and love him … God in Christ really comes to us in his love and grace … Jesus Christ is in himself the objective ground and the possibility for human faith in God. In faith man is wholly dependent on what he receives, and must surrender himself … [even this surrender] cannot be achieved by man in his own strength; it is not even a human possibility at all, that is subjectively speaking—and here we have to do with the reality and presence of the Holy Spirit who makes valid this objective actuality and objective possibility provided for us in the saving Humanity of Christ which is united to the Eternal Word of God.[93]

With these statements Barth and Torrance are wholeheartedly in agreement.

We have seen that Karl Barth and Thomas F. Torrance are in substantial agreement with regard to human knowledge of God since both theologians hold that no human views or concepts are true in themselves. They only become true in our human acts of faith as we obey the Word of God in the power of his Holy Spirit; the fact that this happens at all is a miracle since it is an act begun, upheld, and completed by the hidden grace of God and therefore never comes under our control even though we know God with what Barth called an "apodictic certainty" as long as our thinking takes place from a center in God and not from a center in ourselves as Torrance repeatedly asserted.[94] Methodologically and theologically Torrance and Barth were united in applying the doctrine of justification by grace and by faith to all aspects of theology. While they disagreed about the precise function of natural theology, they also agreed that proper knowledge of God could only take place in faith and by grace as it began and ended with Christ in the power of the

---

[92]In a paper available online, https://www.academia.edu/31648728/A_Trinitarian_Theology_of_Nature, entitled "Advancing the Dialogue: A Trinitarian Theology of Nature," Lisanne-D'Andrea Winslow and Walter Schultz make the following remarks which I think Torrance would flatly reject on theological grounds. They ask, "How can we learn what God has embedded therein [in nature] for us to know about himself?" and they conclude that since God is embedded in nature God's *"eternal power, and divine Trinitarian nature, as understood by scientific discovery, placed in the creation by God"* are not only accessible to ordinary scientific investigation [thus confusing science and theology] but that *"science itself* [natural science] *becomes an investigation of God's divine action and self-disclosure"* (ibid., 5). Thus, "The language of nature … holds in its mysteries the self-communication of the Divine" (ibid.). This thinking overlooks Torrance's insistence that science cannot use theology to investigate nature any more than theology can use natural science to speak about the God who creatively acts within nature. Torrance's scientific theology was meant to operate in accordance with the unique nature of God recognized through faith in God's revelation which meets us within nature.

[93]Torrance, *The Doctrine of Jesus Christ*, 138.

[94]See Barth, *CD* II/1, 162. That center of course is provided in the incarnate Word so that "Jesus Christ is the first and last word of Christian faith and the Christian Church." In Jesus Christ and not apart from him there is a human readiness for God. For Barth "because in eternity He intercedes for us; and because in the Holy Spirit the unity of the Father and the Son becomes effectual among and in us too in the twofold form of faith and the Church" one can say that "the statement that God is knowable to man can and must be made with the strictest possible certainty, with an apodictic certainty, with a certainty freed from any dialectic and ambiguity," *CD* II/1, 161–2.

Holy Spirit. And while they disagreed about the function of sacraments within the church partially because Torrance held to a strong sense of Christ's continued high-priestly mediation between God the Father and us and Barth spoke more generally about the humanity of God, there is little doubt that Barth himself did not wish to advance a docetic view of ecclesiology and certainly also wished to uphold Christ's continued high-priestly mediation. Thus, while there was some inconsistency on Torrance's part with respect to natural theology, there was also some inconsistency on Barth's part with respect to the sacraments. Nonetheless, it seems entirely feasible that if they were both to discuss these issues today, they might well agree that a more consistent focus on the grace of God in Christ, the giver of grace, is and should be the main focus of both sacramental theology and systematic theology itself.

CHAPTER SIX

Thomas F. Torrance's Influence upon Ray Anderson's Paradigm of a Practical Theology of Ministry

TODD SPEIDELL

Certain critics have charged that Thomas F. Torrance's cardinal doctrine of the vicarious humanity of Christ evacuates humans of their agency and thus of their humanity. John Webster, for example, claims that "the vigorous affirmation of *solus Christus* may well threaten rather than validate man." For Webster, "The question poses itself: does Christ's fraternity with the human race validate or invalidate our humanity?"[1] He thinks that Karl Barth's theology more adequately emphasizes moral agency, "which is obscured in Torrance's exclusive stress upon the vicarious character of Jesus' being and act in relation to humanity. In Torrance's account of the matter, Jesus' humanity threatens to absorb that of others; in Barth's account, Jesus' humanity graciously evokes corresponding patterns of being and doing on the part of those whom it constitutes."[2] David Fergusson agrees when he complains that for Torrance, "the divine-human relation tends to be largely a private one," with only occasional hints of a "wider sociopolitical significance ... Yet the important relations and movements in Torrance are, as it were, vertical rather than horizontal."[3]

Contrary to these critics, I will demonstrate how Ray Anderson perceived and developed Torrance's emphasis on the vicarious humanity of Christ as a foundation for

---

[1]*Eberhard Jüngel: An Introduction to his Theology* (Cambridge: Cambridge University Press, 1986), 102–3; see n. 49, which extends his critique of Jüngel to Torrance.

[2]*Barth's Ethics of Reconciliation* (Cambridge: Cambridge University Press, 1995), 171.

[3]David Fergusson, "The Ascension of Christ: Its Significance in the Theology of T. F. Torrance," *Participatio* 3 (2012): 106. All of vol. 3 is devoted to Torrance's basic and central emphasis on the *interrelationship* of incarnation and atonement. Also see *Participatio* 5 (2015) on the vicarious humanity of Christ and ethics in Torrance's theology. I have developed a Torrancian social ethic in my *Fully Human in Christ: The Incarnation as the End of Ethics* (Eugene, OR: Wipf & Stock, 2016).

a practical theology of ministry that integrated the so-called private and social or alleged vertical versus horizontal. Anderson more fundamentally read Torrance as a trinitarian–incarnational churchman with a non-dualistic and praxis-oriented theology. Christ's vicarious humanity does not threaten or invalidate our humanity, both for Torrance and for Anderson, but precisely the opposite (as TF was fond to say): Christ affirms and redeems us so that we may be and become fully human in him. In the words of Torrance:

> Jesus Christ is God's self-address to man, but this self-address in order to achieve its end had to penetrate, take form and domicile itself within the address of man to man, as the Word of Christ abiding among men. *The reciprocity established between God and man in Jesus Christ had to create room for itself within the reciprocities of human society, and the Word of God which had come "plumb down from above" had to deploy itself in the horizontal dimensions of human existence in order to continue its speaking and acting throughout history.*[4]

PASTOR RAY ANDERSON

Six years before Ray Anderson left his pastoral position in Covina, CA, to study with Thomas F. Torrance in New College, Edinburgh, he published his first book, *Like Living Stones*. One can see there, prior to his studies with Torrance, early sentiments of Torrance's later, decisive, and systematic theological influence on Anderson's publications.[5] For example, Anderson says that "'revelation' is much more than what we have discovered about God—it is what God has chosen to give to you concerning Himself; and if we use the word 'revelation' in that sense, we will have a wonderful key to what the Bible is."[6] Also, anticipating Torrance's central emphasis on the *interrelationship* of incarnation and atonement, Anderson writes: "We often think of redemption as being solely limited to the cross and Christ's death, but it was in God's heart from the beginning to redeem man."[7] He also affirms in this early work Christ's assumption of fallen human nature:

> Notice that in the death of Christ or in His life His primary purpose was not that he should live a life of example, but that He should be born into the human predicament …. Christ was born *into* the human predicament, and when He was born He became part of the sin of the human race. He took upon Himself the nature of humanity. The fact that He had no personal sin does not mean that He did not accept the human predicament.[8]

---

[4]Thomas F. Torrance, "The Word of God and the Response of Man," in *God and Rationality* (Oxford: Oxford University Press, 1971), 151–2. Emphasis added to underscore key counterevidence to the Webster–Fergusson thesis.

[5]Most books by or about Anderson may be found in The Ray S. Anderson Collection, Gen. ed. Todd H. Speidell (Eugene, OR: Wipf & Stock). See especially Christian D. Kettler's *Reading Ray S. Anderson: Theology as Ministry, Ministry as Theology* (Eugene, OR: Pickwick, 2010). Kettler, however, is not a mere commentator on Anderson but has penned his own contributions to a practical theology based on Anderson and Torrance. See especially his *The God Who Believes: Faith, Doubt, and the Vicarious Humanity of Christ* (Eugene, OR: Cascade, 2005); and *The God Who Rejoices: Joy, Despair, and the Vicarious Humanity of Christ* (Eugene, OR: Cascade, 2010).

[6]Ray S. Anderson, *Like Living Stones* (1964; reprint. Eugene, OR: Wipf & Stock, 2010), 15.

[7]Ibid., 63.

[8]Ibid., 67.

The other book that Anderson wrote while in pastoral ministry was *Soulprints*, a Kierkegaardian diary as a published form of his journal entries (1962–70) on personal, pastoral, and theological reflections. These Kierkegaardian musings (under the influence of his former Fuller Seminary professor Edward John Carnell but also showing an early affinity with Torrance, who read Kierkegaard as an incarnational realist) suggested early on how Anderson understood ministry as a theological endeavor, just as he likewise viewed theology as a pastoral affair. This early book also prefigured his later work on theological anthropology, for example:

> It must be that Christ is involved if there is reality of change into the good. If, instead of the righteousness of Christ as a mental substitute for my own reality as a person, I acknowledge the existence of God in the inner movements of my own awareness, and this I claim with assurance in that Christ did send the Holy Spirit, his own spirit into my life, so that the estrangement of myself from myself and from God could be bridged; if then I acknowledge the presence of God in my movements, those who become a part of me through that perilous exchange of selves involved with genuine relationship, cannot escape being involved in the reality of God in a redemptive way.[9]

Preparing for the commencement of his doctoral work with Torrance, Anderson resigned his position as pastor of the Covina Evangelical Free Church on February 28, 1970 (which he had held in this church he founded in 1959).[10] He continued his journaling, including a section of poetry and one on theological reflections that indicated the early influence of Torrance on him, including the related impact of Michael Polanyi.[11] He boldly states his theology of incarnational ministry: "If there are two sides to humanity, Jesus will often be found on the wrong side. This is a scandal to the righteous, but pleasing to God."[12] It is clear why he viewed the focus of his ministry as "exploration into God," a phrase he adopted from the English playwright Christopher Fry. His emphasis on Christian community as a place of Christ's healing presence attracted many "seekers," who experienced the reality of what Anderson liked to quote from Polanyi: "Our believing is conditioned at its source by our belonging."[13]

While these two early books indicate Anderson's pre-Torrance theological sensibilities, his church ministry context profoundly informed his nascent theology. He recounts his experience as a young pastor who had just graduated from Fuller Theological Seminary. Armed with his typed notes from systematic theology (he took the course from Paul King Jewett), he expounded from the pulpit an academic account of the doctrine of God, philosophically based with the support of proof-texts from Scripture. After a few

---

[9] Ray S. Anderson, *Soulprints: Personal Reflections on Faith, Hope and Love* (1996; reprint. Eugene, OR: Wipf & Stock, 2011).

[10] Ibid., 93.

[11] Ibid., 152, 161, 195.

[12] Ibid., 153.

[13] For a brief biographical account of Ray's life and career, see the Introduction to *On Being Christian ... and Human: Essays in Celebration of Ray S. Anderson*, ed. Todd H. Speidell (Eugene, OR: Wipf & Stock, 2002), 10–12. Also see David Allan Hubbard's "Foreword: An Appreciation," in the earlier *Festschrift* for Anderson: *Incarnational Ministry: The Presence of Christ in Church, Society, and Family*, ed. Christian D. Kettler and Todd H. Speidell (Eugene, Or: Wipf & Stock, 2009), in which Hubbard writes of the very large file folder he had of Anderson's many suggestions for running Fuller Theological Seminary for "the consideration of innovation, if not revolution." Hubbard concluded: "No faculty could handle a whole crew of Ray Andersons. But any faculty would be poorer without at least one," ibid., xi.

months of his doctrinal preaching, a parishioner suggested to him that he preach with the concrete lives and actual concerns of his congregation in mind! They already believed that God was all-powerful and could do *everything*, but could he do *anything for them?* While God knows everything, does he know them and their needs? Anderson then began to develop a trinitarian–incarnational theology of ministry, which theology nourished the souls of his congregation and his own as well.[14] His experience as a pastor paved the way for his work with Torrance and helped him understand that Torrance was no mere academic theologian, as critics have misunderstood him, for Anderson mined Torrance's pastoral, ecclesial, and missional theology in his lifelong vocation to articulate and develop a practical theology of ministry.

STUDIES IN SCOTLAND: DOCTORAL DISSERTATION WITH T. F. TORRANCE

Anderson began his doctoral study with Torrance at age forty five. He completed his dissertation in two years (1970–72), which was published as *Historical Transcendence and the Reality of God*.[15] Its primary theological influences were Dietrich Bonhoeffer, first and foremost, as well as Karl Barth, John Macmurray, Kornelis Miskotte, Ronald Gregor Smith, and Torrance. Torrance's colleagues in New College, James B. Torrance, John Zizioulas, and Roland Walls, were also theological and personal guides for Anderson.[16]

Anderson later recalled that reading two of Torrance's early books, *Theology in Reconstruction* (1965) and *Theological Science* (1969),[17] attracted him to Torrance and gave him his "first introduction to an incarnational theology presented with scientific rigor, and grounded in a trinitarian epistemology of the self-revealing act of God .... It was his emphasis on the vicarious humanity of Christ by which we are given participation in the ongoing intra-trinitarian relations between the Son and the Father that drew me to study under him."[18]

Torrance's scientific theology was "non-dualistic" and "praxis-oriented," two key ideas that would eventually serve as a basis for Anderson's practical theology, for it postulated "an interaction between theory and praxis, grounded in the humanity of Christ as the

---

[14]Anderson describes his experience as a young pastor in *The Soul of God: A Theological Memoir* (Eugene, OR: Wipf & Stock, 2004), 19–24, and declares "A Manifesto for Christian Ministry" based on "the humanity of Christ" in ibid., 24–30, and *The Soul of Ministry* (Eugene, OR: Wipf & Stock, 1997), 90–6.

[15]Ray S. Anderson, *Historical Transcendence and the Reality of God* (Grand Rapids, MI: Eerdmans, 1975).

[16]Zizioulas's essay "Human Capacity and Human Incapacity," originally an unpublished essay presented at the Society for the Study of Theology (Oxford University, April 1972), as cited in Anderson, *Historical Transcendence and the Reality of God*, 239–40, 243, 250, 296, 304; and James B. Torrance's essay "The Place of Jesus Christ in Worship," *Church Service Society Annual* 40 (May 1970): 41–62, also cited in *Historical Transcendence and the Reality of God*, 246–7, were influential for Anderson. Roland Walls, who had not published when Anderson studied in Edinburgh, had a strong personal impact upon him.

[17]Thomas F. Torrance, *Theology in Reconstruction* (London: SCM, 1965); and *Theological Science* (London: Oxford University Press, 1969; 2nd edition, Edinburgh: T&T Clark, 1996).

[18]Ray S. Anderson, "The Practical Theology of Thomas F. Torrance," *Participatio* 1 (2009): 49. Anderson comments, in what was his last published statement, that "despite the often rather obscure syntax and concepts in his writing, the theology of Thomas Torrance was deeply rooted in the church, its ministry and its mission in the world .... Torrance can be understood as a practical theologian offering a non-dualistic and praxis-oriented theology based on the selfrevealing God in Jesus Christ," ibid.

actualization of divine self-revelation which makes possible not only our true knowledge of God but also knowledge of our own humanity."[19] Anderson would discover:

> Torrance has gone beyond Barth in demonstrating how the self-revealing Word of God through Christ (dogma) also becomes the basis for the ongoing priestly ministry of Christ (praxis) .... Thus, the Christological foundations for Torrance's theology are as significant for the practical theologian as for the dogmatic theologian. In this way, I will argue, Torrance has anticipated and created a positive theological foundation for what has become a new direction in practical theology, moving beyond mere methods or application of truth as theory into practice, into the discovery of truth through praxis.[20]

Torrance's influence on Anderson is evident throughout his dissertation and foundational for his later work in theology of ministry. Citing Torrance's *God and Rationality*,[21] he writes of the "inner logic" and "intelligible rationale" of the reality and transcendence of God in the incarnation, which grasps "our whole person by the inescapable reality of truth as it confronts us." Such "axiomatic thinking" discloses "the intrinsic structure of reality itself," which penetrates "to the inner intelligibility of things, in nature or in God" and reveals "the humanity of God."[22] A "fatal dualism" (from the Augustinian tradition, according to Torrance), however, has created a cultural split in modern theology, which separates "social science" from "pure science" and "theological and scientific knowledge." "The very core of rationality (that is, a cognitive relation to reality)," building upon both Torrance and John Macmurray, "is the capacity to respond appropriately to the nature of that which objectifies itself to us."[23] Anderson seized upon these Torrancian theological axioms and wrote a dissertation as a foundation for his vocation as a practical theologian.

Torrance's essay "The Word of God and the Response of Man"[24] would provide a fundamental paradigm for Anderson and a decisive influence upon his theology of ministry. Jesus was *both* the Word of God to humanity *and* the perfect human response to God, thus upholding and fulfilling God's covenant with Israel on "both sides" (which would become a favorite phrase of Anderson's) of the incarnation: that is, both God's revelation to us and his reconciliation of us to himself.[25] The transcendent God reveals himself in history, the space–time structure of human existence, by his Spirit and through Scripture as "a process of inscripturation in Israel's history with God."[26]

Anderson's chapter, "The Incarnational Christian,"[27] begins to lay a foundation for his practical and ecclesiological theology. In it he writes in his characteristically kerygmatic style:

---

[19] Ibid., 51.

[20] Ibid., 52.

[21] Torrance, *God and Rationality*.

[22] Anderson, *Historical Transcendence*, xv n. 6, 11–13 n. 34 & 43, 105 n. 6.

[23] Ibid., 49–50 n. 40 & 43, 54–7 n. 56, 58, 60, & 66, 116 n. 23. Anderson also begins to draw upon Torrance's *Theological Science*.

[24] Torrance, *God and Rationality*, 137–64.

[25] Anderson, *Historical Transcendence*, 172 n. 80, 120–3 n. 39, 43, & 47, 135 n. 82, 140–3 n. 95, 98, & 99. Anderson also begins to cite Torrance's *Space, Time and Incarnation* (London: Oxford University Press, 1969).

[26] Anderson, *Historical Transcendence*, 180 n. 97, 182–3 n. 106, 200 n. 39, 213–4 n. 70 & 71, 220 n. 85, 234 n. 8. Anderson also cites Torrance's *Theology in Reconstruction*.

[27] Ibid., 252–66.

[Christ] was not a religious man in the way that men think of the religious "side of life." He did not have access into the privileged sanctuaries of the priests. In the midst of a religious culture that prized appearance and cultivated form, he appeared among men clothed simply in grace and truth. He refused to recognize as spiritual that which was artificial and affected. He valued the truth of being and doing over right-sounding words and beautiful prayers. He stated divine realities in terms of human experience. His life-style was that of a man who lived among men; where distinctions were made between the sacred and profane which tended to be inhuman, he openly "profaned" the sanctity of even the law to give dignity to man (Luke 6:6–11). He appeared in the world, as Bonhoeffer said, "incognito as a beggar among beggars, as an outcast among the outcasts, despairing among the despairing, dying among the dying."[28]

Christ established "solidarity" between God and humanity "at the level of *actual* humanity, not idealized humanity," and thus "the relation of the kenotic community to the world" also has a solidarity and an equal share in "the common humanity of Christ." "The kenotic community," he continues in a way that evidences his own creativity beyond that of his mentor,

> does not merely penetrate the world as a privileged community which maintains its own distinctive boundaries and identity—a form of "spiritual colonialism"—but the penetration can only be one which bears the "incognito" of the Incarnation itself; not in a "cunning masquerade," as Barth again reminds us, but … accepting the fact that it must be honestly and unreservedly among them and with them.[29]

Therefore, "the Christian dare not break the 'incognito' by setting the sacred over against the secular and the supernatural over against the natural." Rather, "the 'new people of God' who received the Spirit and thus were recognized as 'belonging' to God, operated with no fixed boundaries."[30] He cites the words of Torrance:

> Thus through the Incarnation it is revealed to us that God in His own Being is not closed to us, for He has come to share with us the deepest movement of His divine heart, and so to participate in our human nature that the heart of God beats within it. We know that in the springs of his own eternal life God is ever open and ready and eager to share the weakness and sorrow and affliction of others and to spend Himself in going to their relief and in saving them.[31]

---

[28]Ibid., 252. He cites Bonhoeffer's *Christology*.

[29]Ibid., 253–4. Anderson cites Barth's *Church Dogmatics*, IV/3.

[30]Ibid., 255, 268.

[31]Ibid. 275. Anderson cites Torrance's essay "Service in Christ," in *Service in Christ: Essays Presented to Karl Barth on His 80th Birthday*, ed. James I. McCord and T. H. L. Parker (London: Epworth Press, 1966), 4–5, which is a key essay to dispute the Webster–Fergusson charge that Torrance was not so concerned with practical affairs. Consider the more recent book by Nathan Hieb, *Christ Crucified in a Suffering World: The Unity of Atonement and Liberation* (Minneapolis, MN: Fortress, 2013), which likewise repeats the misinformed criticism that the "spiritual" overshadows the "sociopolitical" in Torrance's theology. In his words: "In a mirrored one-sidedness [to Sobrino's liberation Christology], Torrance rarely refers to liberation but speaks of the salvific effects achieved by Christ in overwhelmingly eternal and spiritual terms that cause him to miss the direct relevance of the cross to the temporal, material dimension of human life. Torrance employs a two-level view of reality in which the eternal, spiritual dimension trumps temporal, material reality, rendering insignificant the daily struggles of sociopolitical life," ibid., 241. It is telling that Hieb's bibliography includes *none* of Torrance's explicit essays on ethics, such as "Service in Jesus Christ," while he uncritically perpetuates the Webster critique.

While a doctoral student, Anderson was beginning to develop his incarnational and ecclesial theology under Torrance's influence. The following passage indicates how Anderson understood how the vicarious humanity of Christ affirms our humanity and thereby provides a foundation for practical theology, and it is worth quoting at length:

> It is Christ himself who has taken *our* weakness upon himself, who has borne our sorrows and our sins, who has absorbed our pain and tasted our death. He is the *diakonos*, the servant who provided in his own person the ground and the source of all such service .... The church is not and cannot become the "servant to the world" and thus distinguish herself as incarnational. For the church is also the kenotic community, and only *knows* that Christ's *diakonia* takes all human weaknesses and needs upon himself. But the world does not know this until the Christian closes the circle of transcendence through *diakonia* in fellowship with Christ and gives material and physical substance[32] to the spiritual reality of this grace. The church is the place where Christ, clothed with his gospel, meets the Christ clothed with the desperate needs and the human hopes of the world.
>
> The church, therefore, does not heal and help the physical and social needs of man as a kindly physician or a benevolent case worker, but struggles as the kenotic community to bind its own members into the body of Christ, sharing the battle against the forces of evil and exposing itself to the pain and anguish of emotional as well as physical suffering .... The service of the Word brings to man a transcendent power of liberation from bondage and participation in the life of God. But this Word is itself the response, and thus the service of response has its ground in the historical transcendence of the divine Word made flesh.[33]

Anderson's practical theology, still in nascent form, suggests a "caring" based not on human "capacity" but on "the transcendence of God's love," which humans possess only as "incapacity." Therefore, "the concrete level of human existence has its own real participation in the life of God," especially when humans experience a "negation," such as physical disease or emotional illness. "But we are speaking of more than merely the treatment of sickness," Anderson insists, "for the condition of sickness represents a threshold for the eschaton to overcome the negation of the good" that deals with "total 'sickness'" in "the radical way in which Jesus brought healing."[34] There were no "failures of healing on the part of Jesus," he continues, "for the hope brought by a restored body was a limited hope; we can assume that even Lazarus had to face a second death and burial. The eschaton brings man into the reality of a total deliverance from that which negates man's true fulfillment in God, and this means forgiveness of sin. Salvation (*soteria*) is health and wholeness."[35]

The body of Christ, then, is "a refugee with the refugees, with no outer wall to separate saint from sinner, with no inner sanctuary to be guarded against profanation"; it is

---

[32] Perhaps "presence" would have been a more suitable word choice than "substance."

[33] Ibid., 275–6.

[34] Ibid., 297–300. The language of human "capacity" and "incapacity" indicates the influence of John Zizioulas, as previously noted.

[35] Ibid., 301.

"nonetheless the place which is also the presence of the living God ... for its place is bound up with the humanity of Christ and is therefore the place of the kenotic community."[36] Anderson pens his theology in a way that reflects his own pastoral experience, both before and after his PhD work with Torrance.

RAY ANDERSON AS PRACTICAL THEOLOGIAN

Anderson's doctoral dissertation thus indicated the early influence of Torrance. Torrance's theology would have an enduring influence on Anderson, who went on to become professor of Theology and Ministry and director of the Doctor of Ministry program at Fuller Theological Seminary, and the author of twenty-seven books. While at Fuller, he also served as pastor of Harbour Fellowship in Huntington Beach, CA, which both provided mission outreach to the unchurched and a ministry context that he felt vital for any seminary professor or administrator. He would eventually develop his approach to practical theology as his distinctive contribution to the legacy of Torrance and which made a larger impact on the field and direction of practical theology itself.[37] As he later summarized his pastorally oriented theology it is clear that it was built upon the foundation of what he learned from Torrance:

> The church, as the body of Christ, participates in Christ's ongoing ministry of revelation and reconciliation. In the Incarnation, the Son of God penetrated into the ontological structures of fallen humanity in order to restore humanity to its proper and divinely purposed existence through the reconciling ministry of Christ, which continues[38] as the ministry of the church. This is the incarnational basis for a practical theology of the church's life and existence.[39]

In Torrance, Anderson found a unitary epistemology that could overcome the dualistic gap that had separated the foolish divide between "academic theology" and "practical skills," which had plagued Anderson himself as a young pastor until at least one parishioner confronted him about using his systematic theology notes from seminary

---

[36] Ibid., 304–5. He would later cite (in his *On Being Human: Essays in Theological Anthropology* [Grand Rapids, MI: Eerdmans, 1982], 129, 205) a lecture by Torrance on the "eschatological reserve" for the disorder of this world to learn of God's grace and truth as he "creates space and time for faith and repentance," especially in the context of authentic Christian community that presents Jesus Christ in Word and Sacrament to "all of us disordered human creatures" in need of the curing ministry of Christ existing as community.

[37] As Andrew Purves commented on The Ray S. Anderson Collection (Eugene, OR: Wipf & Stock Publishers): "Ray Anderson pioneered a path that changed the direction of pastoral theology. At a time when ministry studies were Christologically anemic, he brought to bear a rigorous Trinitarian doctrine of God on the ground of a thoroughgoing understanding of Jesus Christ as a basis for a theology of ministry that was singular and groundbreaking. His opening essay on theology of ministry in his edited volume, *Theological Foundations for Ministry*, is arguably the most important essay on ministry in the last fifty years. Anderson went on to write extensively on pastoral theology, covering an astonishing range of topics, including theological anthropology, death and dying, family, psychology and counseling. I am delighted that Anderson's legacy in print will be available to a new generation of men and women who seek to ground their practice of ministry in conversation with a godly theologian, pastor, and teacher." Also, Deborah van Deusen Hunsinger similarly noted that Anderson's contribution to the field of pastoral theology was "incomparable" and "unparalleled" in his ability to go "unerringly to the theological heart of pastoral dilemmas" (comments also found on the back cover of The Ray S. Anderson Collection).

[38] Perhaps "by the Spirit through the church" would be more precise, especially in light of Torrance's rejection of the church as the continuation of the incarnation.

[39] Anderson, "Practical Theology," 58–9.

as a basis for his dull preaching! Such an unhappy dualism between theory and practice could only leave pastoral ministry cut off from theology or awaiting the "application" of theology to ministry. Torrance's non-dualistic approach provided for Anderson a heuristic exploration of his mentor's theology as a basis for revisioning practical theology in a way that reconceived both theology and ministry.[40] As he saw it:

> The knowledge of God which results from the historical act of God's self-revelation in Christ is not only revealed knowledge of God's inner being as grounded in the eternal relations of Father, Son and Holy Spirit, but is also a vicarious participation of humanity in that intradivine relation as the basis for a saving knowledge of God. This has far-reaching implications for practical theology. The mediatorial role of Christ works from both sides of the revelatory event in such a way that our knowledge of God through Christ is not only saving knowledge, that is, it is a subjective reality, but it also brings the objective reality of God's Word into our contemporary situation in such a way that the praxis of the Spirit is actually the praxis of Christ occurring through the praxis of the church.[41]

The church, suggests Anderson, "participates in Christ's ongoing ministry of revelation and reconciliation." For Christ had "penetrated into the ontological structures of fallen humanity in order to restore humanity to its proper and divinely purposed existence," which is the sole basis for the church's ministry to fellow broken people. He concludes:

> What is supremely needed, therefore, in all the churches today, is a far more profound understanding of the Incarnation, the coming of God himself into the structures of creaturely and human being, in order to restore the creation to its unity and harmony in himself—that is, a Christology with genuine substance in it once more, the theology of the incarnate Son of God, the one Lord Jesus Christ, "being of one substance with the Father, by whom all things were made." And then, in intimate correlation with such a Christology, what is supremely needed also is a far more profound understanding of the Church as a divine creation within the ontological structures of the universe, entrusted with the mission of healing and reconciliation in the depth of being.[42]

Anderson perceived in Torrance's scientific theology a distinctively theological approach to pastoral ministry. "That is the living God who still acts here and now through Jesus Christ in the Spirit," Anderson quotes Torrance for his own purposes as a practical theologian, "but in the Spirit means in God's own distinctive way and with God's own distinctive kind of power, and therefore beyond any realm of human control and manipulation." "Correspondingly," he continues with another axiomatic insight from Torrance, "the church constitutes the social coefficient of our knowledge of God, for in the nature of the case we are unable to know God in any ontorelational way without knowing him in the togetherness of our personal relations with one another." Anderson found this kind of "living theology" providing a transformation of practical theology beyond pragmatic techniques and psychological methods to an understanding

---

[40] Ibid., 53–6.
[41] Ibid., 57–8.
[42] Ibid., 58–9.

of the "social structures" of ministry having "a coefficient value as a hermeneutic of the Word of God."[43]

Anderson, as a pastor who had decided to pursue rigorous academic study with Torrance, now discovered key insights to overcoming "the dualism of setting theory apart from practice by viewing the word of Christ and the work of Christ as two aspects of the one event of the Word of God." He also appreciated that his mentor's "insistence on the ecclesial context, where prayer, worship and obedient response to the Word of God take place, fits well within the scope of practical theology as we now understand it."[44]

After studying with Torrance, Anderson developed a trinitarian–incarnational theology of ministry, which he practiced as a professor and pastor alike throughout his career. One ought to recall that Torrance himself was a pastor in Alyth and Aberdeen.[45] Anderson summarizes what he saw in Torrance as a foundation for revolutionizing the field of pastoral theology:

> We can now understand why the practical theology of T. F. Torrance leads to a theology of pastoral care. The vicarious humanity of Christ overcomes the epistemological dualism with regard to the self-revelation of God and provides a unitary basis for understanding the relation of theory and practice. The vicarious humanity of Christ also overcomes the dualism between theological and psychological approaches to the healing of persons. For Torrance, the atonement is thus grounded in the Incarnation in such a way that Christ's assumption of our humanity under physical, psychological and spiritual distress not only provides an objective basis for the forgiveness of sin but also for the healing of humanity.[46]

Anderson would spend his career in spelling out the significant implications for practical theology. Pastors should not be pseudo-psychologists but should be advocates of people in need of the care and cure of Christ, through whom "God has entered into the 'godforsaken' place (Matthew 27:46) where the absence of God's supernatural power is countered by the presence of God's suffering love."[47] For Christ clothed with his Gospel "has a counterpart in the Christ clothed with the needs of the world." Anderson comments that the missiological emphasis of Torrance's theology is not surprising because he was born and raised in a missionary family in China. "Beyond that family heritage," however,

> his vision of God's purpose in assuming humanity in the person of Jesus Christ is understood to be a mission to all humanity already completed in Christ. Mission is not to be understood as a way of actualizing a gospel imperative through practical

---

[43] Ibid., 60. Citations are from Thomas F. Torrance, *Theology in Reconciliation*, 291; and *Reality and Evangelical Theology*, 46.

[44] Ibid., 61.

[45] To quote Torrance: "Actually I myself learned more about those truths in my own pastoral ministry than through reading books. Again and again as I wrote a lecture or delivered it, I said to myself that is something I learned in Alyth or Aberdeen, and remembered the situation when that truth of the Gospel really came home to me when I was engaged on a pastoral visit, and read a passage of the Bible and prayed with people in their homes." He especially learned of the vicarious humanity of Christ in his pastoral ministry: "That truth has always been a source of strength to me in my understanding of the Gospel and attempts to speak to others about it, for in and through all my stumbling words and acts, I rely on the crucified and risen Lord Jesus himself who is present fulfilling his own ministry, undergirding mine in his name from below and above." Both quotations are from his reply to Ray Anderson in *The Promise of Trinitarian Theology: Theologians in Dialogue with T. F. Torrance*, ed. Elmer M. Colyer (Lanham, MD: Rowman & Littlefield, 2001), 322.

[46] Anderson, "Practical Theology," 61.

[47] Ibid., 62.

methods and means. On the contrary, the actuality of God's reconciliation of Christ (2 Cor. 5:19) is itself the dogmatic basis for a practical theology of mission. Practical theology, as envisioned by Torrance, therefore calls theology and the church back to its roots as a fundamentally missionary church with a particular vision and a specific task to perform in the world. As a missionary church it is crucial that it remains faithful to its missiological task and vision. One of the primary tasks of the practical theologian is to ensure that the church is challenged and enabled to achieve this task faithfully.[48]

CONCLUDING SELECTIONS AND NOTATIONS OF ANDERSON'S WORKS

Of Anderson's twenty-seven published books, I will conclude with selective choices and comments about how he developed what he learned from his two years of doctoral study with Torrance, whom he considered both a dogmatic and a practical theologian, again contrary to dualistic critique from a few critics, who had provided him with a unitary vision of theology and ministry of what he called Christopraxis.

As director of Fuller Seminary's DMin program, he edited a published volume, *Theological Foundations for Ministry*, which presented a theological paradigm or coherent understanding of ministry based especially on T. F. and J. B. Torrance, Barth, and Bonhoeffer. He wrote the foundational essay "A Theology for Ministry"[49] for this volume of nearly 800 pages. In it, he decried the dualism of "pure" versus "applied" theology or dogmatic versus pragmatic concerns. He insisted instead "that ministry precedes and produces theology, not the reverse" and yet "ministry is determined and set forth by God's own ministry of revelation and reconciliation in the world, beginning with Israel and culminating in Jesus Christ and the Church." He continued his dialectic: "Ministry cannot be construed solely as the practical application (or technique) which makes theological knowledge relevant and effective. Theological activity must emerge out of ministry and for the sake of ministry …. The 'practice' of ministry … is itself a theological activity."[50]

God is on "both sides" of revelation and reconciliation, as Anderson was fond to say, for the one ministry of Christ is to reveal God to us and to reconcile us to God in his vicarious humanity. In his words:

> Christ's primary ministry is to the Father for the sake of the world, not to the world for the sake of the Father. This means that the world does not set the agenda for ministry, but the Father, who loves the world and seeks its good, sets this agenda. This Christological, and actually Trinitarian, basis for ministry rules out both utilitarianism

---

[48]Ibid., 64. Anderson quotes Torrance again: "In one of his most eloquent missiological utterances, Torrance says: 'The Church cannot be in Christ without being in Him as He is proclaimed to men in their need and without being in Him as He encounters us in and behind the existence of every man in his need. Nor can the Church be recognized as His except in that meeting of Christ with Himself in the depth of human misery, where Christ clothed with His gospel meets Christ clothed with the desperate need and plight of men.'" From "Service in Jesus Christ," in *Theological Foundations for Ministry*, ed. Ray S. Anderson (Grand Rapids, MI: Eerdmans, 1979), 724.

[49]Ray S. Anderson, "A Theology for Ministry," in *Theological Foundations for Ministry: Selected Readings for a Theology of the Church in Ministry*, ed. Ray S. Anderson (Edinburgh: T&T Clark, 1979), 6–21.

[50]Ibid., 7.

which tends to create ministry out of needs, and pragmatism, which transforms ministry into marketing strategy.[51]

Note well this exhortation pastors and DMin students but also academic professors of theology!

As professor of Theology and Ministry, Anderson taught a theology sequence that he called "Theological Anthropology and the Revelation of God," "Divine Reconciliation and the Incarnation of God," and "Christian Community and the Kingdom of God." For the first course, he published his book on theological anthropology.[52] He largely relied on Barth's theology to sketch a basis for pastoral ministry and care, but he also drew on Torrance's concept of "eschatological reserve":

> In a lecture on grace and the Word of God, Thomas F. Torrance once identified the interval between the declaration to the paralytic (Mark 2) of the Word of forgiveness and the Word of physical restoration as the "eschatological reserve" by which God creates space and time for faith and repentance .... Before that final Word comes in its absolute transforming power, the paralytic is held fast by the Word of forgiveness, which is the same Word.[53]

"The cure of souls must be exercised under this eschatological critique," he warns, "in order that we might be delivered from either 'playing God' with presumed omnipotence or copping out altogether and resorting to caring as a substitute for curing."[54] The church, Anderson continues, "is responsible to know the difference between order and disorder, but wise enough to contextualize disorder with grace and truth." He concludes:

> Through skilled psychotherapy from a Christian orientation, through authentic community in which love is shared in practice as well as in pronouncement, through the presence of Jesus Christ in Word and Sacrament, all of us disordered human creatures can discover the wisdom and truth of God's order. Sexual disorders are not of a different kind. They are first of all human disorders, and there is a place for being and becoming human in the space and time of God's Word.[55]

He co-taught "Theology of the Family" with Dennis Guernsey and coedited a sequel volume to *On Being Human* entitled *On Being Family*.[56] At the same time he wrote another sequel on a theology of death, which Blackwell published as *Theology, Death and Dying*.[57] (When I asked Ray why he didn't entitle this third book, *On Being Dead*, he said he'd preferred

---

[51] Ibid., 8–9. *Theological Foundations for Ministry*, in fact, has a trinitarian outline, especially Parts Two and Three: "Jesus' Ministry to the Father on Behalf of the World"; and "Jesus' Ministry in the Spirit for the Sake of the Church." Anderson would later expand on the theme that all ministry is God's ministry in *The Soul of Ministry: Forming Leaders for God's People* (Louisville, KY: John Knox, 1997), and *The Soul of God*, the latter being a summary statement through theological autobiography of the vicarious humanity and priesthood of Christ for ministry.

[52] Anderson, *On Being Human*.

[53] Ibid., 129.

[54] Ibid., 205.

[55] Ibid., 129.

[56] *On Being Family: A Social Theology of the Family*, ed. Ray S. Anderson and Dennis B. Guernsey (Grand Rapids, MI: Eerdmans, 1986). Years later he also wrote *Something Old, Something New: Marriage and Family Ministry in a Postmodern Culture* (Eugene, OR: Wipf & Stock, 2007).

[57] Ray S. Anderson, *Theology, Death and Dying* (Oxford: Blackwell, 1986).

to include some ethics and go with: *On Being Good and Dead!* But alas, that was too much pizzazz for the publisher.) In this latter book, he compares the church to a hospice with a vicarious role to uphold the weak and dying, which also indicates the sacramental emphasis of the Scottish Presbyterian Torrance upon the Free Evangelical heritage of Anderson:

> There is a human ecology which upholds our human dignity ... There is an ecology of faith as well. There is a "hospice" for Christian faith; it is the community of those who uphold the truth and promise of baptism on our behalf when we are too ignorant or too weak or too confused to call ourselves "child of God." This "hospice of Christian community" enfolds us through the eucharistic celebration of forgiveness, healing and hope in Jesus Christ. So, when our own faith shatters over the sharp edges of unrelenting pain and incurable sickness, faith itself is not destroyed for we are upheld even in our unfaith, by the arms of faith. This community of love and faith is the "hospice" in which all are prepared for the "way of the Lord."[58]

He also cotaught courses in Fuller's School of Psychology, for which he wrote *Christians Who Counsel*.[59] He would later write *Self-Care*[60] and *Spiritual Caregiving as Secular Sacrament*.[61] When the Society for Christian Psychology started its journal *Edification*, they chose Ray Anderson's theology as a focus for one of its two foundational volumes.[62] They appreciated his holistic view of human beings as fundamentally embodied as social, psychological, sexual, and spiritual, such as he argued in his essay "The Social Ecology of Human Personhood: Implications of Dietrich Bonhoeffer's Theology for Psychology."[63] Anderson labored as a theologian in the human and social sciences as his mentor did in the arena of physical science.

While Anderson wrote many other books too, especially for a more semipopular audience, my final comments will focus on his *The Shape of Practical Theology*.[64] In this mature work, he defines "practical theology as truly a theological enterprise rather than mere mastery of skills and methods," with "the praxis of practical theology as critical engagement with the interface between the word of God as revealed through Scripture and the work of God taking place in and through the church in the world."[65] If theory takes precedence over practice, as in the modernist view, "then practice tends to be concerned primarily with methods, techniques and strategies for ministry, lacking

---

[58]Ibid., 157.

[59]Ray S. Anderson, *Christians Who Counsel: The Vocation of Wholistic Therapy* (Grand Rapids, MI: Zondervan, 1990).

[60]Ray S. Anderson, *Self-Care: A Theology of Personal Empowerment and Spiritual Healing* (Wheaton, IL: Bridgepoint, 1995).

[61]Ray S. Anderson, *Spiritual Caregiving as Secular Sacrament: A Practical Theology for Professional Caregivers* (New York: Jessica Kingsley, 2003).

[62]"Special Issue: The Work of Ray S. Anderson," Guest editor Todd Speidell, *Edification: Journal of the Society for Christian Psychology* 1, no. 2 (2007), which later became part of The Ray S. Anderson Collection (Eugene, OR: Wipf & Stock).

[63]Ray S. Anderson, "The Social Ecology of Human Personhood: Implications of Dietrich Bonhoeffer's Theology for Psychology," in *On Being a Person: A Multidisciplinary Approach to Personality Theories*, ed. Todd H. Speidell (Eugene, OR: Wipf & Stock, 2002), 146–73.

[64]Ray S. Anderson, *The Shape of Practical Theology: Empowering Ministry with Theological Praxis* (Downers Grove, IL: IVP, 2001).

[65]Ibid., 8.

theological substance," but if practice trumps theory, "ministry tends to be based on pragmatic results rather than prophetic revelation."[66] Instead, for Anderson:

> Practical theology is a dynamic process of reflective, critical inquiry into the praxis of the church in the world and God's purposes for humanity, carried out in the light of Christian Scripture and tradition, and in critical dialogue with other sources of knowledge. As a theological discipline its primary purpose is to ensure that the church's public proclamations and praxis in the world faithfully reflect the nature and purpose of God's continuing mission to the world and in so doing authentically addresses the contemporary context into which the church seeks to minister.[67]

Anderson helpfully outlines the modern development of practical theology beginning with Friedrich Schleiermacher and a focus on the theory of church practice, developing with Eduard Thurneysen's more Reformed emphasis on pastoral theology, and concluding with the postmodernist model of Don Browning's understanding of practical theology.[68] Anderson's contribution to the contemporary development of the field is "Christopraxis": providing a "christological concentration at the core and a trinitarian theology at the foundation." "Christopraxis," he continues, "is the continuing ministry of Christ through the power and presence of the Holy Spirit."[69] Anderson's model has both an ecclesial and a missional focus with a primary focus on church praxis but "not simply the internal workings of the church community" since its boundaries "are defined by the boundaries of God's continuing mission" to redeem the world.[70] He proclaims:

> The incarnational community is not merely the "practical theology" department of the church, where truths learned in seminary are put into practice. Rather the praxis of ministry is itself the context in which both the authority and true order of theology is grounded.[71] The theological task is that of interpreting the praxis of Christ, both in its revealed sense as the "dogma' of the gospel of Christ and in its contemporary form as divine *latreia*, or reconciliation, as the ministry of the church. It is noteworthy that the primary theological documents of the New Testament were produced by the apostle Paul from the itinerant centers of his own praxis of ministry. Theologians who are first of all recognized as academic scholars and technicians may not be the theologians that the church needs in carrying out its own theological task as the *latreia* of Christ.[72]

"The praxis of the Spirit of the risen Christ," announces Anderson, constitutes a "new school of theology."[73] The word "praxis," he notes, does not simply mean "action" or "practice" since it is "value-directed and theory-laden" action driven by *meaning*. It is reflective "action that not only seeks to achieve particular ends but also reflects on the means and the ends of such action in order to assess the validity of both in the light of its

---

[66]Ibid., 14.

[67]Ibid., 22.

[68]See ibid., 24–9.

[69]Ibid., 29.

[70]Ibid., 31–2.

[71]To be clear, for Anderson the authority and true order of theology is grounded in grace in its identity with the Giver of grace, who establishes and maintains the context.

[72]Ibid., 128.

[73]Ibid., 39.

guiding vision." It is "reflective action that is laden with belief."[74] "Christopraxis," then, "is itself the continuation of Christ's own ministry of revelation and reconciliation" in and through the church.[75] In Torrance's words, "As the incarnate presence of the living God in space and time, he presents himself to our faith as its living dynamic Object," which calls for a way of thinking and living based on "the life-giving acts of Christ in the depths of human being" with radical implications for one's "daily life and activity."[76]

Anderson moves from the foundational shape of practical theology to the praxis-oriented theology with the risen Jesus as hermeneutical criterion: "The resurrection of Jesus to be the living Lord of the church constitutes a continuing hermeneutical criterion for the church's understanding of itself as under the authority of Scripture."[77] For example, he makes a case for sexual parity in pastoral ministry.[78] Despite the exegetical ambiguity of relevant New Testament texts, "we must remember that the living Christ is Lord of Scripture as well as Lord of the church," and "he is the hermeneutical criterion for interpreting Scripture in such a way that his present work of creating a new humanity fulfills the promise of Scripture," which includes his calling for and the participation of "both women and men into the task of co-creating the new humanity through pastoral ministry by the gift of his Holy Spirit."[79] Torrance similarly defended women's ordination when he wrote:

> In Jesus Christ the order of redemption has intersected the order or creation and set it upon a new basis altogether. Henceforth the full equality of man and woman is a divine ordinance that applies to all the behaviour and activity of the "new man" in Christ, and so to the entire life and mission of the Church as the Body of Christ in the world.[80]

---

[74]Ibid., 47–8.

[75]Ibid., 54.

[76]Ibid., 24, quoting from Torrance's *Reality and Evangelical Theology*. To be clear, for Torrance the church's ministry is a service of Christ the reconciler who actualizes that reconciliation in us through the Spirit here and now.

[77]Ibid., 79.

[78]See ibid., 87, 90–101.

[79]Ibid., 101, though perhaps Anderson should have emphasized that the Spirit enables us to live as part of Christ's new humanity through union with the risen Lord. Also see 112, where Anderson considers "biblical antecedent" as a component of his hermeneutic and as a counter-balancing factor to "exegetical ambiguity." Also see 282, where "biblical antecedents" exist for supporting women in pastoral ministry and leadership roles but not for ordaining practicing homosexuals. In chapter 16 (266–83), Anderson argues for theological and pastoral considerations that go beyond "the few texts that condemn specific homosexual acts" (271) to foundational biblical texts (especially Gen. 1:26-7) and theological affirmations (especially as understood by Karl Barth) that view "human sexuality as an 'ordered ontology' of personal and biological differentiation" (275). Pastorally, one must also acknowledge "an element of the tragic in the sexual arena of life … of the brokenness and tragic aspects of the human sexual experience as well as of the divine intention regarding it," which he believes affects those who are single, impotent, and of homosexual orientation (279–80). While "God's preference" for human sexuality is male–female differentiation, "God's presence" includes all who need his forgiveness, mercy, and grace, which the church must reflect to all. "Inclusion on the basis of God's presence," however, "does not grant anyone in the body of Christ the right to ordination. Whether or not a person with a homosexual orientation should be excluded from consideration for ordination is a matter for the church to decide" (281); and "those who argue for the normalization of homosexual relationships and full acceptance by the church must do so on other [than biblical] grounds" (112).

[80]Thomas F. Torrance, "The Ministry of Women," in *Gospel, Church, and Ministry: Thomas F. Torrance Collected Studies I*, ed. Jock Stein (Eugene, OR: Wipf & Stock, 2012), 207–8. This essay was originally published in 1992.

I conclude with a few quotations from "The Little Man on the Cross: Where Is God When We Suffer?," where Anderson lays a theological foundation for social justice and Christian morality based on the redeeming presence and advocacy of God himself. His poetic and kerygmatic words express the heart and humanity of his theological convictions, as they demonstrate the interconnections of his wide-ranging practical theology:

> Social justice is not an abstract principle, nor is it an ideal to be pursued. Social justice is the core of human experience. It is bread and water; it is blood and bones; it is brothers and sisters who unlearn the knowledge of how to hurt and how to kill and who learn to live in the power, the freedom and the hope with which God intended that we should live.
>
> If there is any theological basis for social justice, it lies between us, within our humanity; it is anthropological. Social justice is the divinely ordained order of human existence .... Social justice is a divinely endowed gift of human freedom. Freedom for the other is a divine gift, a calling to be human .... Human rights and social justice argued on the basis of the individual, natural right to live will ultimately be impersonal, tyrannical and destructive. I will eventually fight you for my natural right to live. Being with and for the other is the core of being human. It is an expression of a freedom to be human, accepting the responsibility of being human. Recognizing one's self in another is an affirmation of the divine gift of freedom. Where there is not that freedom, there will not be social justice.
>
> But the truth of the gospel is not that humanity has been put on the cross; it is rather that the cross has been sunk deep into humanity .... To be with our brothers and sisters into whose flesh and bones the cross has been sunk is to be part of the meeting of Christ with himself, where Christ-clothed-with-his-gospel meets Christ clothed with the needs and the hurts of his brothers and sisters.[81]

---

[81]Ray S. Anderson, "The Little Man on the Cross: Where Is God When We Suffer?," in *The Shape of Practical Theology*, 311–2. The expression of Christ "clothed with his gospel" is from Calvin.

CHAPTER SEVEN

Thomas F. Torrance

Historian of Dogma

JASON R. RADCLIFF

KARL BARTH ON CALVIN, TORRANCE ON BARTH

In his book *The Theology of John Calvin*, Karl Barth introduces his exposition of Calvin's theology by discussing the Reformer's distinction between "history" and "sacred history."[1] Barth goes on to examine what Calvin meant when he discussed the importance of sacred history (by which Calvin meant biblical history, but which Barth extended to church history) for Christians, an importance which moves beyond the historical–critical work of an historian as traditionally understood. Barth proceeds, then, to examine what he understands Calvin to mean, listing three meanings and extending them to his own interpretation of Calvin, who for Barth is a part of the aforementioned "sacred history."

First, says Barth, "the historical Calvin is the living Calvin."[2] For Barth this means that establishing that Calvin said something in a particular way—and this can be established by examining the history of Calvin's ideas, it can be established through a study of the French and Latin of Calvin, or through a variety of other historical means—is only at the surface of the "historical Calvin." So, says Barth, "the historical Calvin is the living Calvin who, as he did say this or that, wanted to say something specific, one thing, and who, insofar as his works are preserved, still wants to say it, perhaps in a way that he could not do in his lifetime and to earlier readers of his works."[3] Barth argues that this is, of course, because Calvin's ideas are not simply Calvin's ideas but because the Holy Spirit is working in and through Calvin. Thus, says Barth, "Calvin's theology is historical because, through every transparency and means of communication, it is teaching by the immortal Spirit of God."[4]

Second, says Barth, one who wishes to understand Calvin must do more than read and make Calvin's ideas their own. Rather, argues Barth, Calvin was a teacher and those desirous of being "Calvinists" must sit at his feet, listen to him as a teacher, and dialogue with him. In Barth's words, "Being taught by Calvin means entering into dialogue with him, with Calvin as the teacher and ourselves as the students, he speaking, we doing our

---

[1] Karl Barth, *The Theology of John Calvin* (Grand Rapids, MI: Eerdmans, 1995), 1. Calvin's discussion of the subject is itself based upon Cicero's *De Oratore* 2.36: "history is life's teacher."
[2] Barth, *The Theology of John Calvin*, 4.
[3] Ibid.
[4] Ibid.

best to follow him and then—this is the crux of the matter—making our own response to what he says."[5] An historical dialogue with Calvin of this form, says Barth, "may end with the taught saying something very different from what Calvin said but that they learned from, or better, through him."[6] However, Barth also warns about moving too far beyond what Calvin actually said; or, at least, warns that one must start with Calvin's actual written words. Barth, says Calvin, "like Paul … is dead, and the only deposit of what he said in his writings and recorded sermons is the only form in which he can speak to us today."[7] Barth says someone wishing to think with the historical Calvin must begin first with Calvin himself.

Third, therefore, argues Barth, any truly "historical" study is as much about the "historian" as the historical figure being examined. Barth states: "All study of history is above all itself history, the living, speaking, and working past, and thus itself the present as well. No historian can be detached and not seriously seek and find himself or herself in history. Have you ever found a historical book that is not above all else a mirror of its author's soul?"[8]

Barth's brief *apologia* of history as "living history" which is ultimately a "mirror" into the historian's soul paves the way for Barth to discuss in the rest of his book a Calvin and a Calvinism which many would argue looks a lot like Barth and Barthian theology. To this accusation one might imagine Barth responding with a resounding "Yes, that is precisely the point!" That is, Barth understood his task as an historian of Calvin's theology to be to not only tell his readers what Calvin said (this was certainly his starting point), but even more so to synthesize it, make it his own, and create something of his own Barthian variety out of it. For Barth, this was real "Calvinism."

One need not wonder how much Torrance learned from his beloved teacher Barth on this approach to history for Torrance's reading of historical theological figures followed this model precisely. For Torrance, reading the great theologians of church history must move beyond what they say on the page, for they are living figures and Torrance clearly wishes to sit at their feet, learn from them, and apply them directly to the issues he sees in theology and in the church in his day, an exercise that oftentimes exposes more about Torrance and his theological convictions than the figures themselves; or, if Barth is right, perhaps it in fact exposes as much about Torrance as it does the historical figures, which is to say, a lot! The present chapter seeks to examine Torrance as an historian of dogma and examine his methodology of doing "history of dogma." The chapter will argue that Torrance, at least in his approach to historical theological figures (particularly the Church Fathers), is neither a systematic theologian, nor an historian, and is not an historical theologian but is rather a Christocentric (or "dogmatic" in the traditional sense) theologian approaching the Fathers as living historical figures ("saints" might be the traditional term), sitting at their feet and thinking with them. The chapter will argue this by first articulating what Torrance is not doing, then exploring what he is doing, and then by offering an illustrative case study, namely, Torrance's Athanasius of Alexandria as a fourth-century Barth and Barth as a twentieth-century Athanasius.

---

[5]Ibid.
[6]Ibid.
[7]Ibid., 5.
[8]Ibid., 8.

WHAT TORRANCE IS NOT: A SYSTEMATIC THEOLOGIAN, AN HISTORIAN, AN HISTORICAL THEOLOGIAN

Before exploring what Torrance is doing as an historian of dogma, it is important to first examine what he is not doing nor attempting to do. In his approach to the history of theology Torrance is neither a systematic theologian, nor an historian, nor an historical theologian. In order to unpack why Torrance is not each of these, this chapter will examine critiques leveled at Torrance in each vein.

First, Torrance is not approaching theological history as a systematic theologian in the traditional sense. Torrance is often misunderstood in this realm and thus often critiqued for doing just this. For example, in his book *The Bible in Athanasius of Alexandria*, Ernest critiques Torrance for approaching Athanasius and the Fathers as a theologian.[9] Many critics of Torrance, most notably Colin Gunton, have leveled the accusation against him of reading the Church Fathers, particularly Athanasius, through an unfair Western, Reformed, or Barthian theological lens.[10] Yet, as shall be seen, these accusations fail to grasp precisely what Torrance is aiming to do. Torrance is indeed approaching church history theologically. He is indeed approaching church history from his own Reformed, evangelical, and Western standpoint,[11] but he is doing so because he views the theological ideas he finds in church history less as "historical artifacts" (to use Ip's helpful phrasing)[12] and more as living sources from sacred history (to use Barth's phrasing as above).

Second, Torrance is not approaching theological history as an historian. It is true that Torrance's first post at the University of Edinburgh was to a position in Church History. Nonetheless, he never claimed that his work in his approach to theological history was in the realm of Church History. For this reason, perhaps, Torrance's arguably exceptional work in Patristics is generally ignored by Patristics scholars. John Behr, a scholar at the forefront of patrology today, laments the fact that contemporary patrology has largely become a study of the history of late antiquity, rather than theology.[13] For this reason, it would seem, patrologists often do not take Torrance's work in the history of theology seriously.[14] Torrance is rarely utilized by scholars in the Patristics and pretty much never by historians, even when his work speaks directly into an area they are writing about.[15]

---

[9] James D. Ernest, *The Bible in Athanasius of Alexandria* (Leiden: Brill, 2004), 13.

[10] See, for example, ibid., 17; Colin E. Gunton, *Father, Son, and Holy Spirit: Essays toward a Fully Trinitarian Theology* (London: T&T Clark, 2003), 44–52; Donald Fairbairn, "Review: Jason Radcliff, *Thomas F. Torrance and the Church Fathers*," Participatio 5 (2015): 117–8.

[11] See Jason R. Radcliff, *Thomas F. Torrance and the Church Fathers* (Eugene, OR: Pickwick, 2014), for an elaboration upon this.

[12] Pui Him Ip, "'Back to the Fathers': The Nature of Historical Understanding in 20th Century Patristic Ressourcement," Reviews in Religion and Theology 23, no. 1 (2016): 5.

[13] John Behr, *The Mystery of Christ: Life in Death* (Crestwood: St Vladimir's Seminary Press, 2006), 18. Notably Behr and Anatolios, who does similar patrological work, both write appreciatively of Torrance. See, for example, John Behr, "Review: *Divine Meaning: Studies in Patristic Hermeneutics*, by T. F. Torrance," St. Vladimir's Theological Quarterly 42, no. 1 (1998): 104–5; and Khaled Anatolios, *Athanasius: The Coherence of His Thought* (New York: Routledge, 2004), 23–4.

[14] See my *Thomas F. Torrance and the Orthodox–Reformed Dialogue* (Eugene, OR: Pickwick, 2018), for an exploration of Torrance's hugely problematic absence in contemporary discussion of the Patristic doctrine of the Trinity.

[15] Again, see ibid., for a discussion of Torrance's work on the Greek Patristic doctrine of the Trinity wherein he basically came to the same conclusions as scholars today are making, but he came to them nearly twenty years prior!

Third, Torrance is not approaching theological history as an historical theologian. His great works on theological history such as *The Trinitarian Faith* and *The Christian Doctrine of God* are clearly doing far more than tracing the development of the doctrine of the Trinity, which is more broadly illustrative of Torrance's approach to theological history. When Torrance approaches theological history, he is not seeking to trace out the development of doctrine on its own terms. Rather, as exhibited in the two aforementioned books, Torrance "imaginatively reconstructs [the Fathers] in light of Reformed and evangelical theology … [and the Nicene] theme of the [*homoousion*]."[16] The figures and ideas Torrance encounters in theological history are not immovably dead on the page. Rather, they are living and still speaking to Torrance and his time as a part of the *communio sanctorum* and thus he is able to reconstruct them (to use the language of his book *Theology in Reconstruction*) in light of the living Christ, of whose Body they are a part.

WHAT TORRANCE IS: AN HISTORIAN OF DOGMA, A RESSOURCEMENT THEOLOGIAN

Torrance is, at the core, a "ressourcement" theologian "returning to the Fathers." In his article "'Back to the Fathers': The Nature of Historical Understanding in 20th Century Patristic *Ressourcement*," Ip helpfully summarizes the task of "patristic ressourcement" in which Torrance was a part when he states:

> When theologians set out to "return to the Fathers", it is rarely out of pure historical curiosity. Very often, patristic ressourcement is motivated by a conviction that an intense engagement with the classical sources is necessary for theological renewal in the present. There is a sense that something valuable in these sources needs to be retrieved, remembered, and re-appropriated for today.[17]

In other words, theologians who "return to the Fathers" are not simply reading them historically, if they are reading them historically at all. Even more so, ressourcement theologians returning to the Fathers are doing so out of a strong belief that the Fathers are living texts, indeed living members of the Body of Christ; in other words, "saints." An approach to the Fathers as "saints" rather than, in Ip's language, as "historical artifacts"[18] entails a vastly different approach than the purely historical or historical–critical.

WHY CAN TORRANCE "RESSOURCE" THE FATHERS?

Torrance held that the Reformed tradition in which he was a part was inherently ecumenical and, as such, very much rooted in the Greek Fathers. In Torrance's *Memorandum A* published in *Theological Dialogue Between Orthodox and Reformed Churches,* vol. 1, he stresses how the Reformed tradition has never sought to be a "new" church but rather sees itself as a prophetic movement of reform within the Western church.[19] Torrance

---

[16] See Radcliff, *Thomas F. Torrance and the Church Fathers,* 113.

[17] Ip, "Back to the Fathers," 5.

[18] Ibid.

[19] See also the 1979 Minutes from the Orthodox–Reformed Dialogue in Thomas F. Torrance Manuscript Collection. Special Collections, Princeton Theological Seminary Library. Box 170.

argues that "the Reformed Church is the Church reformed according to the Word of God so as to restore to it the face of the ancient Catholic and Apostolic Church."[20] The Reformed tradition, says Torrance, "does not set out to be a new or another Church but to be a movement of reform within the One Holy Catholic and Apostolic Church of Jesus Christ."[21] Torrance explains that the Reformed Churches have always been guided by "classical Greek theology," the "great Alexandrian and Cappadocian theologians," the Augustinian doctrine of grace, and the Trinitarian theology of the Greek Fathers.[22]

In light of this, in Torrance's thorough introduction to his collection of Reformed catechisms, *The School of Faith*,[23] he contends, "it belongs to the nature of theology to be *catholic*," which he sees as involving both historicity and ecumenicity.[24] Torrance believes that theology is inherently "dialogical" meaning that it is conversational, a conversation between God and his people.[25] Thus, for Torrance, theology is necessarily historical and ecumenical: historical "because it is historical dialogue with God" and ecumenical because "the exposition of theology as hearing of the Word and understanding of the Truth cannot be private to one particular Church."[26] Torrance understood "ecumenical" to mean not only in his own time but throughout history, very much paralleling Barth's approach to sacred history as outlined above.

All of that is to say, when Torrance turns to theological history he is not doing so as simply an academic exercise of examining historical artifacts. Rather, Torrance turns to theological history as a member of the Body of Christ himself, sitting at the feet of other members of the *communio sanctorum* who are living and still speaking into Torrance's own time and context. Thus, Torrance feels he can read, for example, the Nicene Fathers in light of the Reformers and in turn read them both in light of Barth while also feeling free to raise questions where appropriate. For, each is a living member of the Body of Christ speaking by the power of the same Holy Spirit.

---

[20]Thomas F. Torrance, *Conflict and Agreement in the Church*: vol. 1: *Order & Disorder* (London: Lutterworth Press, 1959), 76.

[21]Thomas F. Torrance, "Memoranda on Orthodox/Reformed Relations," in *Theological Dialogue between Orthodox & Reformed Churches*, vol. 1, ed. Thomas F. Torrance (Edinburgh: Scottish Academic Press, 1985), 3. As Lukas Vischer states during the Third Consultation, "the Reformed Churches see themselves as *within* the Christian tradition which seeks ancient catholicity, rather than as a separate tradition." Joe McLelland adds to this that this also is "a spirit of movement," that is, one of many movements of reform within the Western church, not simply *the* Reformation. He states "we Reformed tend to overemphasize the uniqueness of the 16th century Reformation." See The Thomas F. Torrance Manuscript Collection. Special Collections, Princeton Seminary. Box 170.

[22]Torrance, "Memoranda on Orthodox/Reformed Relations," 4. He understands John Calvin as particularly indebted to Gregory Nazianzen. See, for example, Thomas F. Torrance, *Trinitarian Perspectives: Toward Doctrinal Agreement* (London: T&T Clark, 1994), 21–40.

[23]Thomas F. Torrance, "Introduction," in *The School of Faith: The Catechisms of the Reformed Church* (London: James Clarke/New York: Harper & Row, 1959; reprint. Eugene, OR: Wipf & Stock, 1996), xi–cxxvi. Torrance clearly valued this text as illustrative of his approach to theology for, according to Robert Walker and Tom Noble, two former students of Torrance's, Torrance used to recommend this introduction to his students as preparatory reading for his dogmatics lectures. See Robert T. Walker, "Editor's Introduction" to Thomas F. Torrance, *Atonement: The Person and Work of* Christ, ed. Robert T. Walker (Downers Grove, IL: IVP Academic/Milton Keynes: Paternoster, 2009), lxxxiv.

[24]Torrance, "Introduction," lxv.

[25]Ibid., lxv–lxvii.

[26]Ibid., lxvii–lxviii.

TORRANCE'S APPROACH TO THE HISTORY OF THEOLOGY AS SEEN IN HIS APPROACH TO THE CHURCH FATHERS

Whereas Torrance's understanding of the catholicity and Greek Patristic rootedness of the Reformed tradition in many ways allowed him to return to the Church Fathers very naturally, it is also obvious that his use of the Church Fathers was unique. As has been argued in *Thomas F. Torrance and the Church Fathers,* Torrance's reading of the Fathers was creative and imaginative, consisting of catholic themes and figures, centered around the fulcrum of the Nicene *homoousion*, that central assertion that Jesus Christ, as the incarnate Word, is of the same essence as the Father in his divinity and with us in our humanity by virtue of the incarnation. In other words, Torrance's approach to the Fathers was Christocentric in a creatively synthesized Reformed–Patristic theology.[27] As Robert Walker helpfully puts it, Torrance is a "dogmatician, concerned to listen to the Fathers and think out with them the evangelical faith. He looks through their eyes to know the same realities of God and faith as he sees through Reformed eyes."[28] Indeed, Torrance approached the Fathers from a Reformed and ecumenical perspective, and Dragas elucidates that Torrance "seeks to build up his theology on the one, historical common ground ... he is prepared at the same time to confess in full modesty and sincerity their historical particularities and fortify himself only with their positive forces."[29]

Synthesizing the Church Fathers in catholic and evangelical themes, Torrance extrapolates what he sees as best of the Patristics, the best of the Reformation, and the best of the modern eras of the theological tradition and synthetically combines them, recentering them upon Jesus Christ and his Gospel of grace. In Walker's words, Torrance's "theology is highly original, which does not mean first and foremost that he developed new concepts, although he did, but that he made new connections between known theological ideas and concepts. For him, originality was not necessarily thinking new thoughts but making new connections."[30]

---

[27] However, more deeply this approach was central to Torrance's understanding of himself as a theologian and churchman. As Torrance says in his introduction to *The School of Faith*, theology is inherently catholic. By this Torrance means theology is "dialogical" both vertically between God and his people and horizontally between God's people, which is why, as he says, "the exposition of theology as hearing of the Word and understanding of the Truth cannot be private to one particular church." See Torrance, "Introduction," lxv. Torrance was ecumenical from his childhood. He reflects in his unpublished intellectual autobiography, *Itinerarium Mentis in Deum*, that he recalls an ecumenical atmosphere in his home life, which began as a missionary child in China, instilled into his family by a Presbyterian father and Anglican mother. Thomas F. Torrance, *Itinerarium Mentis in Deum: T. F. Torrance—My Theological Development*. The Thomas F. Torrance Manuscript Collection. Special Collections. Princeton Theological Seminary Library, Series II, Box 10. Ecclesiologically, Torrance understood himself to be part of the Scottish evangelical tradition, standing in a line of theological succession from the Patristic era through John Calvin and brought into Scotland by figures such as Robert Bruce, Robert Boyd, and John Forbes of Corse, and states as such not only in his published works but also in correspondence with George Dragas about the connection between the Scottish church and the ancient Greek church. Thomas F. Torrance, *Preaching Christ Today: The Gospel and Scientific Thinking* (Grand Rapids, MI: Eerdmans, 1994), 18–19; *Theology in Reconciliation: Essays towards Evangelical and Catholic Unity in East and West* (London: Geoffrey Chapman, 1975; reprint. Eugene, OR: Wipf & Stock, 1996), 83–4; "Introduction," in *The Mystery of the Lord's Supper: Sermons on the Sacrament Preached in the Kirk of Edinburgh by Robert Bruce in AD 1589*, ed. Thomas F. Torrance (London: James Clarke, 1958), 32. So, it must be said at the start that Torrance's approach to the Fathers was a part of an ecumenical approach instilled in him from his birth.

[28] Robert T. Walker, "Review of *Thomas F. Torrance and the Church Fathers: A Reformed, Evangelical, and Ecumenical Reconstruction of the Patristic Tradition*," *Theology in Scotland* 23, no. 2 (2016): 67–9.

[29] George Dion Dragas, "The Significance for the Church of Professor Torrance's Election as Moderator of the General Assembly of the Church of Scotland," *ΕΚΚΛΗΣΙΑΣΤΙΚΟΣ ΦΑΡΟΣ* LVIII, no. III–IV (1976): 226.

[30] Robert Walker, "Recollections and Reflections," *Participatio* 1 (2009): 43.

Torrance then reconstructs the Patristic tradition around the *homoousion* into "streams" or "threads" in theological history. As such, Torrance believes that certain eras of theological history captured the inner structure of the Gospel best. [31] Torrance sees these eras connected to one another in an evangelical stream which is a sort of "golden thread" running throughout theological history. Within the evangelical stream, the three instances that best captured this inner structure are Nicaea (particularly Athanasius), the Reformation (particularly Calvin), and contemporary evangelical theology (particularly Karl Barth).[32]

Torrance sees the Fathers and the Reformers as complementary to one another. Furthermore, he says that the Reformation emphasis on grace is complementary to the Nicene emphasis on the oneness in essence between the Father and the Son, bringing Nicene theology to its logical end.[33] For Torrance, Barth is ultimately the funnel through which the Nicene theology of the *homoousion* of Christ and the Reformation theology of the *homoousion* of grace are dynamically combined and filtered into contemporary theology.

It is in this imaginative synthesis of the Church Fathers with the issues of his own day that Torrance offers perhaps his greatest, or at least most creative, contribution to the study of theological history. Like Newman before him, Torrance reads the Church Fathers into contemporary debates and reads contemporary debates back into the Church Fathers.[34] In "Karl Barth and the Latin Heresy," Arius's division of the divine Logos from the human Jesus sheds light on nineteenth-century liberalism's division of the Christ of faith from the Christ of history. In Torrance's "Memoranda on Orthodox/Reformed Relations," Nestorian dualism between the human and divine Jesus sheds light on Federal Calvinism's doctrine of Limited Atonement. In *The Trinitarian Faith,* the problem with the Cappadocian Fathers' emphasis on the Person of the Father as *arché* of the Trinity sounds just like John Zizioulas's work in Social Trinitarianism. In *Preaching Christ Today,* Augustine's implicit pagan dualism sounds almost exactly like the critiques Karl Rahner had of post-Scholastic Roman Catholicism, critiques which Torrance greatly appreciates. In "The Legacy of Karl Barth" Torrance even states that both Barth and Athanasius were fighting "*Contra Mundum*" for the evangelical and catholic faith of the *homoousion* against forms of liberal dualism in their day.[35] Torrance's amalgamation of contemporary theological debate with Patristic debate is, perhaps, his greatest strength inasmuch as

---

[31] See also Elmer M. Colyer, *How to Read T.F.Torrance: Understanding His Trinitarian and Scientific Theology* (Downers Grove, IL: InterVarsity Press, 2001), 360.

[32] Thomas F. Torrance, *Reality and Evangelical Theology* (Philadelphia, PA: Westminster Press, 1982; reprint. Eugene, OR: Wipf & Stock, 1999), 14–15; *Preaching Christ Today,* 20; *Theology in Reconciliation,* 235–7, 285; *Theology in Reconstruction* (London: SCM, 1965; reprint. Eugene, OR: Wipf & Stock, 1996), 267.

[33] Torrance, *Theology in Reconstruction,* 225. Furthermore, Torrance states: "[It is] when Greek Patristic Theology is studied and interpreted in the strong biblical perspective restored through the Reformation of the Church in the West that its permanent place in the foundations of Evangelical Theology may be appreciated in a new way ... [and] when Reformed Theology is reassessed and interpreted in light of its ancient roots in the evangelical theology of the early centuries that its essential catholicity and its unifying force are to be understood," Torrance, *Trinitarian Perspectives,* 21–2. The Reformers, argues Torrance, attempted "to carry through a Christological correction of the whole life and thought of the Church. It was an attempt to put Christ and his Gospel once again into the very centre and to carry through extensive reform by bringing everything into conformity to him and his Gospel." See Torrance, *Theology in Reconstruction,* 265.

[34] See in particular Thomas F. Torrance, *Space, Time and Incarnation* (London: Oxford University Press, 1969); "Karl Barth and the Latin Heresy," *Scottish Journal of Theology* 39, no. 4 (1986): 461–82.

[35] Thomas F. Torrance, "The Legacy of Karl Barth, 1886–1986" in *Karl Barth, Biblical and Evangelical Theologian* (Edinburgh: T&T Clark, 1990), 160–1.

he applies the Fathers to his own context. Torrance has a very dynamic way of using historical texts and he jumps from the fourth century to the sixteenth century to the twentieth century, often in one sentence. He uses fifth-century heresies to critique much later theological problems. This can be an extremely helpful application of the Fathers to contemporary problems and a successful attempt at what Georges Florovsky has called a Neopatristic synthesis; yet it can also be highly confusing. Here, Torrance's greatest strength may have also been his greatest weakness. He made the Fathers highly relevant to his contemporary time by, for example, viewing the ways that Athanasius's attack on Arianism overlapped with his own contemporary battle with liberal theology. However, this was somewhat oversimplified simply because Arianism, though similar, was not the same as nineteenth-century liberal theology. Despite the strong similarities between Barth/Athanasius and Arianism/nineteen-century liberal theology, the two surely had their differences. For example, in "Karl Barth and the Latin Heresy," Torrance paints a picture of Athanasius and Barth as both fighting the same perennial battle against dualism. In many ways, this is typical of Torrance and his favorites throughout church history tend to sound very similar to one another in their commitments and in the theological battles they fought. Therefore, to conclude its examination of Torrance's approach to the history of dogma, this chapter will now examine Torrance's connection of Barth to Athanasius as something of a case study of what Torrance is doing when he turns to theological history.

CASE STUDY: TORRANCE ON KARL BARTH AND ATHANASIUS

Torrance's approach to theological history was primarily driven by drawing connections. Torrance draws connections between the great movements and figures in church history, stating that the Reformation is parallel to Nicaea,[36] Calvin is parallel to Gregory Nazianzen,[37] Athanasius is parallel to Anselm and Kierkegaard,[38] and the Scottish tradition inherits the Greek Patristic tradition.[39] Similar to his heroes, Torrance's villains have their own parallels. For example, the nineteenth-century liberals are Arian, and the Westminster Calvinists are Nestorian.

Most illustrative of Torrance's approach to theological history, however, is his connection of Karl Barth to Athanasius in his essays "Karl Barth and Patristic Theology"[40]

---

[36]See, for example, Torrance, *Theology in Reconstruction*, 265. Torrance states: "When Greek Patristic Theology is studied and interpreted in the strong Biblical perspective restored through the Reformation of the Church in the West that its permanent place in the foundations of Evangelical Theology may be appreciated in a new way ... [and] when Reformed Theology is reassessed and interpreted in light of its ancient roots in the evangelical theology of the early centuries that its essential catholicity and its unifying force are to be understood." See Torrance, *Trinitarian Perspectives*, 21–2. Torrance also asserts that there were three stages/instances of theology that affirmed the notion that divine revelation is God revealing his οὐσία to humankind: Patristic (the *homoousion*), Reformation ("the immediate act of God in the presence of he Being as revealed"), and Karl Barth (bringing the two together; being-in-act and act-in-being). See Torrance, *Reality & Evangelical Theology*, 14–15. See also *Preaching Christ Today*, 20, and *Theology in Reconciliation*, 235–7 and 285.

[37]Torrance, *Trinitarian Perspectives*, 21–76.

[38]Thomas F. Torrance, *Reality and Scientific Theology* (Eugene, OR: Wipf & Stock, 2001), 86–93.

[39]Torrance, *Scottish Theology: From John Knox to John McCleod Campbell* (Edinburgh: T&T Clark, 1996). See especially 1–45, 49–90, 93, 125–53.

[40]See, for example, Thomas F. Torrance, "Karl Barth and Patristic Theology," in *Theology beyond Christendom. Essays on the Centenary of the Birth of Karl Barth*, ed. John Thomson (Allison Park, PA: Pickwick, 1986), 215–39.

and "Karl Barth and the Latin Heresy." In these two pieces Torrance discusses his viewpoint that Karl Barth, following in the classical tradition of the church, was attacking Augustinian, Cartesian, and Newtonian dualism which had been running rampant in the church.[41] Even more so, Torrance sees Barth as inheriting both the Greek Patristic and Reformation tradition and combining their best qualities. Torrance then argues that Barth combines the Nicene emphasis on Jesus's oneness with the Father (the *homoousion* of Jesus, the incarnate Word) and the Reformation emphasis on salvation being an act entirely of God (the *homoousion* of grace) and filters them into twentieth-century theology in his battle against dualism in an attempt at preserving the oneness between God-to-us and God-in-himself.[42]

Torrance sees this dualism problematically undergirding Western theological doctrines of revelation[43] and reconciliation.[44] In "Karl Barth and the Latin Heresy" Torrance argues that this dualism is indeed the "Latin Heresy" prevalent throughout much of theological history in the West and is evident in such theologians as Leo the Great, Anselm, Peter Lombard, Aquinas, and, more generally, Roman Catholic and Reformed theology. Torrance sees "obvious connections" between Karl Barth and Athanasius in their battle against this type of dualism.[45] Sometimes, however, instead of "obvious connections" between Athanasius and Barth (as Torrance puts it), Athanasius begins to look nearly identical to Barth and Barth to Athanasius. However, this is not problematic in light of what Torrance is doing; again, he is not attempting a traditional church history or systematic theology, rather his agenda is one of constructive theological history and thus connections between figures can legitimately be made in light of their similar theological emphases in different contexts.

For Torrance, then, Barth is a twentieth-century Athanasius fighting anew the Gospel battle against dualism that separates God-to-us from God-in-himself. In his words:

> [Barth] saw that the rationalistic dualism which he found in the liberal framework of thought was essentially the same as the gnostic dualism that had been analysed and exposed so acutely by Irenaeus the acknowledged Father of early Church theology, and the epistemological and moralistic dualism no less acutely analysed and rejected by Athanasius and the Nicene theologians in the Arian controversy.[46]

For Torrance, Barth fought against this problematic theological dualism using the same battleax as Athanasius before him: the Nicene *homoousion*. As Torrance states, "It was certainly one of Karl Barth's greatest contributions to the development of dogmatic theology that he set himself to think out the profound implications of the *homoousion* for the doctrine of God, Father, Son and Holy Spirit."[47]

Torrance goes on to argue throughout his essay on "Barth and Patristic Theology" that Barth essentially applies the Nicene *homoousion* to epistemology, Christology, the

---

[41]Torrance, "Karl Barth and the Latin Heresy," 463.

[42]See Thomas F. Torrance, *The Christian Doctrine of God, One Being Three Persons* (Edinburgh: T&T Clark, 1996), 7–10; Torrance, "Karl Barth and the Latin Heresy," 462; Torrance, *Karl Barth* 146; and Torrance, *The Christian Doctrine of God*, 4.

[43]Torrance, "Karl Barth and the Latin Heresy," 463–73.

[44]Ibid., 473–9.

[45]Ibid., 476.

[46]Torrance, "Karl Barth and Patristic Theology," 190.

[47]Ibid., 191.

doctrine of the Trinity, and soteriology, creatively extending Athanasius's own use of the theological concept.[48] For Torrance it was the Nicene *homoousion* that drew the connection between Barth and Athanasius, making them theological parallels to one another, parallels that draw out the best of each, in Torrance's mind.

CONCLUSION: TORRANCE, THE HISTORIAN OF DOGMA

This chapter has argued that Torrance approaches theological history as an historian of dogma in an absolutely unique way. He imaginatively and creatively reconstructs the theological tradition in light of itself, reshaping the Fathers in light of the Reformation, reshaping the Reformers in light of the Fathers, and using Barth to reshape them both. Torrance views the ideas and figures he encounters in the history of dogma as living members of the *communio sanctorum* empowered by the same Holy Spirit to witness to the same God through the same Jesus Christ of whose Body they are a part. It is regrettable that Torrance's history of dogma is, perhaps because of this unusual method of appropriation, under (and often entirely un) utilized by scholars who would in fact greatly benefit from Torrance's conclusions.[49]

---

[48]Ibid., 189–201.

[49]See my *Thomas F. Torrance and the Reformed-Orthodox Dialogue* for an argument in this regard about Torrance's work in the history of the doctrine of the Trinity.

CHAPTER EIGHT

Theological Science Then and Now

TRAVIS STEVICK

When one encounters the writings of Thomas F. Torrance for the first time, it does not take long to notice that he has a deep and abiding interest in science, even advocating for something he calls "Theological Science." For the reader who does not already know what Torrance intends to express by this, its meaning may not be immediately obvious. It is clear that Torrance believes that theologians can learn (or be reminded of) much from natural science. Even in the midst of his most explicitly theological reflections, the insights of natural scientists arise to illuminate either the point at hand or the issues at stake.[1] It is also clear that Torrance believes that theology has to, and should, speak to the development of natural science, not as a way of influencing the material content of those sciences but to point out potential blind spots and to offer alternative ways of viewing the world that may prove more fruitful.[2]

As interesting as those lines of thought may be, and while Torrance spends significant time pursuing each of them, they are not primarily what he means by "Theological Science." For Torrance, the key defining characteristic of all authentically scientific activity is that it seeks to gain knowledge of its object according to its nature. That is, science attempts to understand things as they really are and not according to some foreign framework of thought we bring *to* the object. As such, Torrance believes that it is possible to have scientific knowledge of God and that theology can, in fact, be a science.

> In scientific theology we begin with the actual knowledge of God, and seek to test and clarify this knowledge by inquiring carefully into the relation between our knowing of God and God Himself in His being and nature. Then in the light of this clarification we

---

[1] For some examples of this, see Thomas F. Torrance, *Theological Science* (Oxford: Oxford University Press, 1969), 116; *Christian Theology and Scientific Culture* (Oxford: Oxford University Press, 1980), 8; *Reality and Scientific Theology* (Edinburgh: Scottish Academic Press, 1985), 39; *Reality and Evangelical Theology* (Philadelphia, PA: Westminster, 1982), 53; *Transformation and Convergence in the Frame of Knowledge* (Grand Rapids, MI: Eerdmans, 1984), 249–50.

[2] Some examples of this are Torrance's conviction that the Reformation influenced the development of natural science. See Torrance, *Theology in Reconstruction* (Grand Rapids, MI: Eerdmans, 1965), 14–15, 63, 67, 69, 91–2; *Theological Science*, 60–1, 75, 85; *Divine and Contingent Order* (Oxford: Oxford University Press, 1981), 32; John Philoponos's remarkably prescient theory of light, *Christian Theology and Scientific Culture*, 89; *The Trinitarian Faith: The Evangelical Theology of the Ancient Catholic Church* (Edinburgh: T&T Clark, 1988), 108; and the return of natural science to the conviction that nature is contingent rather than necessary, *Theology in Reconstruction*, 63; *Divine and Contingent Order*, viii, 31–2; *Reality and Scientific Theology*, 12.

seek to be more and more open and ready for God, so that we may respond faithfully and truly to all that He declares and discloses to us of Himself.[3]

Torrance calls this kind of knowledge, which is faithful to the nature of the thing known, knowledge *kata physin*, or *kataphysic* knowledge.[4] This definition is seemingly uncontroversial, for it is unlikely someone would say that *real* knowledge seeks to know something in terms foreign to it. However, this key insight has far-reaching implications and has been called the "fundamental axiom of Torrance's theology."[5] It is difficult to overstate the importance of this central conviction to the length and breadth of Torrance's thinking.

To be clear, Torrance roots the nature of science not in the exactitude of our calculations, the accuracy of our predictions, or the completeness of our theories.[6] All of those may be helpful in science and scientific investigation may produce many of those things along the way, but that is not the *nature* of science, as Torrance understands it. For Torrance, science is primarily marked by its commitment to the object of our knowledge and our willingness to question ourselves and everything about ourselves in light of what we come to know. Indeed, it can be understood as the scientist being questioned by the object they seek to know.[7]

> As we direct our questions to our chosen field we allow it to disclose itself to our inquiry, and as that takes place we proceed to question our initial questions, and then we pose our revised questions to the field and in the light of what further becomes disclosed we re-question our prior questioning, and so on. Thus scientific inquiry operates in such a way that it cuts back constantly into ourselves the questioners, in order to invert the determining factor from ourselves to what we seek to know. This is why rigorous scientific inquiry far from being some sort of impersonal progression of induction is a highly distinctive movement of interaction of the inquirer with the object, in which acts of personal self-criticism and personal judgment are called for all through the process of distinguishing what we know from ourselves and of checking the illegitimate projection of ourselves, our subjective states and conditions, into what we seek to know.[8]

This stress on the priority of our actual knowledge over epistemological considerations brings Torrance into close relation to Albert Einstein, one of his favorite scientists.

> However, no sooner has the epistemologist, who is seeking a clear system, fought his way through to such a system, than he is inclined to interpret the thought-content of

---

[3] Torrance, *Theological Science*, 9.

[4] Torrance, *Divine Meaning: Studies in Patristic Hermeneutics* (Edinburgh: T&T Clark, 1995), 141, 211; *God and Rationality* (Oxford: Oxford University Press, 1971), 52–3, 89–95, 114–16; *Reality and Scientific Theology*, 50; *The Christian Frame of Mind* (Colorado Springs, CO: Helmers and Howard, 1989), 72; *The Ground and Grammar of Theology* (Charlottesville: The University Press of Virginia, 1981), 8–10, 33; *The Mediation of Christ*, revised ed. (Colorado Springs, CO: Helmers and Howard, 1992), 2–5; *Theological Science*, 25–6, 198; *Transformation and Convergence*, 221. Torrance sees this epistemological conviction at work in the theology of the early church (Torrance, *Trinitarian Faith*, 20, 51).

[5] Elmer M. Colyer, *The Nature of Doctrine in T. F. Torrance's Theology* (Eugene, OR: Wipf & Stock, 2001), 15.

[6] See Travis M. Stevick, *Encountering Reality* (Minneapolis, MN: Fortress Press, 2016), 137–44.

[7] This is most clearly evident when the "object" under investigation is God. See, for example, "Questioning in Christ," in *Theology in Reconstruction* (Grand Rapids, MI: Eerdmans, 1965), 121.

[8] Torrance, *Reality and Scientific Theology*, 26–7.

science in the sense of his system and to reject whatever does not fit into his system. The scientist, however, cannot afford to carry his striving for epistemological systematic that far. He accepts gratefully the epistemological conceptual analysis; but the external conditions, which are set for him by the facts of experience, do not permit him to let himself be too much restricted in the construction of his conceptual world by the adherence to an epistemological system. He therefore must appear to the systematic epistemologist as a type of unscrupulous opportunist.[9]

There are those who would be skeptical of any definition of science that would allow Christian theology to qualify as a science. Such people may demand that the theologian demonstrate, on nontheological grounds, the legitimacy of their discipline. That is to say, before a theologian can get on with their work of engaging with God and articulating their findings, some would argue that they must prove, to the satisfaction of the skeptic, that there even *is* a God to be engaged with, and they must do this without recourse to theological appeals, which would be seen as begging the question.

However intuitive and reasonable such a demand may seem to those who would doubt the legitimacy of theology as a science it would, if applied to any other science, prevent *any* science from getting off the ground. "Each special science, starting within the field of pre-scientific knowledge, presupposes the reality and accessibility of its own proper object and the possibility of knowing it further, and refuses to justify itself as a science by stepping outside of its own actuality, but leaves the question of its justification to be answered by its own positive content and inner rationality."[10] We do not insist that physicists demonstrate, on nonphysical grounds, the reality of physical entities, nor do we insist that biologists demonstrate, on nonbiological grounds, the reality of biological entities.

In every one of the special sciences, we do not begin with epistemology and then move on to the actuality of knowledge, but begin with the knowledge we have actually gained and, only *a posteriori*, attempt to explain how it is that we have arrived at this knowledge.[11]

> It must be admitted that we operate with an inchoate epistemology as soon as we begin to engage in theological inquiry, that is with a tacit understanding of how we know God, although it can yield a proper epistemology only as we advance in the knowledge of God and submit our actual knowing to criticism and control in accordance with the nature of the object of our knowledge. This means that all the way through theological inquiry we must operate with an *open* epistemology in which we allow the way of our knowing to be clarified and modified *pari passu* with advance in deeper and fuller knowledge of the object, and that we will be unable to set forth an account of that way of knowing in advance but only by looking back from what has been established as knowledge.[12]

---

[9] Albert Einstein, "Remarks to the Essays Appearing in This Collective Volume," in *Albert Einstein: Philosopher-Scientist*, ed. Paul Arthur Schilpp (La Salle, IL: Open Court, 1970), 684.

[10] Torrance, *Theological Science*, 3. With regard to theological science in particular, Torrance argues that one cannot reason one's way to ultimate truth. "There is no way to demonstrate this Truth outside of the Truth; the only way for the ultimate Truth to prove Himself is to be the Truth, and the only way for us to prove the ultimate Truth is to let Him be what He is before us, in His αὐτουσια and αὐτεξουσια," *Theological Science*, 144.

[11] For the importance of dealing with the actuality of knowledge before worrying about the possibility of knowledge, see Torrance, *Theological Science*, 25–43.

[12] *Theological Science*, 10. Original emphases.

The practical implications of this is that, while it is true that theology presupposes the reality of God and God's accessibility to human beings, this is not inherently a liability, as every science presupposes the reality and accessibility of their own subjects of inquiry. What this *does* do, however, is make it clear that all science rests on ultimate beliefs which, for the purposes of the science, are accepted without proof.

TORRANCE AND ULTIMATE BELIEFS

One crucial implication of Torrance's key scientific conviction, that we know things truly only when we know them according to their natures, is that there is an irreducible fiduciary component to all our knowledge. That there exists a given object of our knowledge (i.e., it is not a construction of our minds or society) and that it is accessible to us are not things we *prove* before engaging in scientific investigation, but things that are either confirmed or disconfirmed based on our ongoing engagement. Torrance calls these convictions, which shape our engagement with reality and exert a controlling influence on how we make sense of our experiences, "ultimate beliefs," since they rely upon nothing other than, in Einstein's words, "intuition, resting on sympathetic understanding of experience."[13]

> The controlling statements with which we operate in science are both unfalsifiable and unverifiable. They are statements which express what we have called ultimate beliefs, beliefs without which there would be no science at all, beliefs which play a normative role in the gaining and developing of all scientific knowledge. Yet these ultimate beliefs are by their very nature irrefutable and unprovable. They are irrefutable and unprovable on two grounds: (1) because they have to be assumed in any attempt at rational proof or disproof; and (2) because they involve a relation of thought to being which cannot be put into logical or demonstrable form. Ultimate beliefs, then, are to be understood as expressing the fundamental commitment of the mind to reality, which rational knowledge presupposes and on which the reason relies in any authentic thrust toward the truth. Far from being irrational or non-rational, these ultimate beliefs have to do with the ontological reference of the reason to the nature and structure of things, which all explicit forms of reasoning are intended to serve, and without which they are blind and impotent. It is indeed not finally through formal reasoning that knowledge and understanding are advanced, but through the responsible commitment to reality in which our minds fall under its intelligible nature and power, and thereby gain the normative insights or ultimate beliefs which prompt and guide our inquiries, which enable us to interpret our experiences and observations, and which direct the reasoning operations of our inquiries to their true ends.[14]

One question that presses forward with the acknowledgment of such beliefs is over how one can tell whether a belief is truly ultimate or else is in some way deficient and so, at best, penultimate. This is parallel to the question in some branches of epistemology as to what beliefs can justly be called "properly basic." Can *any* belief qualify as an unquestionable ultimate belief, such as the belief in the yearly return of the Great Pumpkin?[15] A concern

---

[13] Albert Einstein, "Principles of Scientific Research," in *The World as I See It* (New York: Covici Publishing Company, 1934), 125–6.

[14] Torrance, *Transformation and Convergence*, 194.

[15] Alvin Plantinga, "Reason and Belief in God," in *The Analytical Theist*, ed. James F. Sennett (Grand Rapids, MI: Eerdmans, 1998), 149.

might be that acknowledging the necessity of ultimate beliefs nurtures fideism and a retreat from rationality. That is to say, does the admission of such ultimate beliefs mean that Torrance is guilty of *fideism*?[16]

This is not the case for Torrance's theological science. Treating inaccurate convictions as if they are ultimate need not result in endless self-blinding. To cite one well-known example from the history of science, the treating of phlogiston as an ultimate belief in the study of combustion did not make it irreformable but resulted in its abandonment. In the same way, while ultimate beliefs may not rationally be criticized directly from within the framework they define, it is possible that such frameworks, if not properly rooted in reality, will crumble under their own weight.

Beyond this, in Torrance's actual usage of the term, ultimate beliefs are not concepts that we, at least in practice, multiply without restriction. Torrance uses the term in both a narrower and wider sense. In the narrower sense of the term, ultimate beliefs are simply the things we *must* believe if we are going to behave appropriately, relative to reality. It is an ultimate belief of any scientist that what they are investigating exists. Without that existential belief, science could not get started and would make no sense. In his wider usage of the term, Torrance uses the term in a way that is not far removed from other concepts in the philosophy of science, such as Thomas S. Kuhn's *paradigms*.[17] They are convictions we adopt, without proof, and attempt to understand reality in light of them until it becomes clear they need to be revised and replaced.

Perhaps the most troubling implication of Torrance's insistence that *all* true knowledge has a fiduciary component and that our knowledge is always built on our ultimate and penultimate beliefs, where the latter can be falsified, though only indirectly, and the former can be neither verified nor falsified,[18] is what such a position will do to our ideal of *objective* knowledge. If one is not able to get behind, or stand outside, their ultimate beliefs (in the wider sense), how can one ever hope to achieve objective knowledge of an object? It seems that, even if we were to purify our knowledge of distorting elements, we would not be able to *know* that this was so. As such, we seem to be in a situation where our knowledge is distorted in one way or another, or else undistorted, but with no way to test it to verify its non-distortion.

TORRANCE AND OBJECTIVITY

Within the context of our cultural discussion of science and its value, when people speak of the value of "objective" knowledge, it seems as if it is used to say that objective knowledge is knowledge that we would have if we could step outside the relationship of commitment to the object and encounter it from any arbitrary point of view. Perhaps the paradigm case of such objective knowledge is embodied in the shift from a geocentric to a heliocentric view of the solar system. With such a shift, we no longer consider the cosmos

---

[16]For an analysis of whether Torrance's convictions are fideistic, see Stevick, *Encountering Reality*, 61–4. For a discussion on the charge that Torrance's position is guilty of Foundationalism, see 65–71.

[17]Thomas S. Kuhn, *The Structure of Scientific Revolutions*, 3rd ed. (Chicago, IL: University of Chicago Press, 1996).

[18]For Torrance on ultimate beliefs, see his chapter in *Belief in Science and in Christian Life: The Relevance of Michael Polanyi's Thought for Christian Faith and Life*, ed. Thomas F. Torrance (Eugene, OR: Wipf & Stock, 1998), 1–27; *Transformation and Convergence*, 191–214.

simply from our own limited perspective, we consider it as we would if we could observe the solar system as a whole.

However, this way of conceiving of objective knowledge as our epistemological ideal, which conjures up images of being able to manipulate and handle an object until it yields to our scrutiny, seems utterly inappropriate when applied to our knowledge of God. A God who makes an absolute prohibition on the creation of idols and requires our need for revelation to have true knowledge of God cannot be manipulated by human beings.[19]

For Torrance, the idea that our knowledge can be detached from the fact that it is *we* who know it is not authentic objectivity but a distorting object*ivism*.[20]

> Whenever we operate, as we have been tempted to do regularly in post-Cartesian thought, with a subject/object relation in which the object is regarded as standing opposed to the subject, and therefore with an impersonal model of thought, we become trapped in detached, objectivist relations to what is other than ourselves. Thus the very model of thought which we use inevitably tends to exclude the place of personal agency in our knowing and in the nature of what we seek to know.[21]

For Torrance, the goal is not that our *knowledge* will be objective but that *we* will be properly objective, which we achieve when we allow the object of our knowledge to truly be objective to us, which means allowing it to *object* to us when we try to overlay it with ways of thought derived from elsewhere.[22] Torrance gives succinct expression to this conviction when he writes, "Our questions are genuine, truthful questions when they are rooted in this basic question, that is, when they are controlled by the sheer pressure which the objective reality exerts upon us."[23]

Objectivity, then, is not something that we *have* but something that describes our way of *being* and *doing*. It characterizes the relationship between the personal knowing subject and the object of investigation. As Relativity and Quantum physics have demonstrated, it is not possible to transcend the subject–object relationship. However, this does not mean that we are hopelessly trapped within our limited subjectivity, because our subject–object relations are kept in check and controlled by other relations.

One kind of such relations are what Torrance calls "subject-subject-object relations," what might also be called "intersubjectivity."[24]

> The really objective is that which is shareable, what we can experience together or in common, and which is transcendent to each of us and therefore also to all of us. Hence in all objective knowledge we try to eliminate those features which we cannot

---

[19]This is revealed in Torrance's distaste for traditional natural theology.

[20]For Torrance's condemnations of objectivism, see *God and Rationality*, 188–9; *Reality and Scientific Theology*, 14–15, 189; *Theology in Reconstruction*, 232; *Theological Science*, 38–9, 93, 296 n. 1; *Transformation and Convergence*, 153.

[21]Torrance, *Reality and Scientific Theology*, 132–3.

[22]For such accounts of objectivity, see Torrance, *God and Rationality*, 92; *Transformation and Convergence*, 75; *Theological Science*, xv–xvi, 36, 295–6; *Reality and Scientific Theology*, 14. In the field of theology, this manifests itself in the conviction that we do not come to know God through our own efforts because it is only by grace that we come to know him. Indeed, it is only by means of revelation and reconciliation that we may have any authentic knowledge of God. See Torrance, *Theological Science*, 41; *Christian Theology and Scientific Culture*, 93; and *The Mediation of Christ*, 101–2.

[23]Torrance, *Theological Science*, 124.

[24]Ibid., 210.

share together or cannot have in common with others, and which are relative only to this or that person in this or that particular situation. It is the closed mind, the autistic individual, the detached person, who is incapable of communicating with others, who is obstructed in the pursuit of knowledge or in the prosecution of scientific inquiry. This also applies to a society or community that has become inbred in its own ideological development and uses its own objectified self-consciousness as the criterion for reality or authenticity.[25]

Because of this, different subjects, each engaging with a common object of study, can bring their differing experiences of that object into dialogue with one another with the hope that they can engage in a kind of epistemological triangulation. In this case, it is precisely the nonidentity of those experiences that can lead to a deeper knowledge of reality. Torrance described this kind of engagement as being like a stereoscope, where two pictures, different at every point, combine together for a greater and more realistic experience of the reality pictured.[26]

The other relations which serve as a check on our subjectivity are what Torrance calls "subject-object-object relations."[27]

> In genuinely scientific thinking, however, while symbolic representation retains an essential place, we are concerned to penetrate into the objective coherences and structured interrelations of things in themselves—that is, into object-object relations in which our subject-object relations are transcended and controlled from beyond themselves by reference to the ontological structure of the realities being investigated. This transition from primitive to scientific thinking is one in which we move from mythos to logos, from image to inner logic, from subjectivity to objectivity.[28]

Whereas subject–subject–object relations allow us to consider a kind of scientific relativity where different subjects experience the same object in different, but complimentary, ways, subject–object–object relations tap into the fact that the objects of our knowledge do not only interact with thinking and speaking subjects but also interact with non-personal objects. This kind of engagement has been the mainstay of the harder sciences for hundreds of years to one degree or another. Its centrality is evident in such landmark experiments as the Michelson–Morley experiment where the hypothetical luminiferous ether's characteristics could be evaluated based on how it affected the speed of light

---

[25]Torrance, *Reality and Scientific Theology*, 112.

[26]Torrance, *Transformation and Convergence*, 119. For a discussion on subject–subject–object relations, see Stevick, *Encountering Reality*, 86–7.

[27]Torrance does not speak of these kinds of relations often, but it is in the background of much of his thought, especially the need to break out of a way of thinking dominated by vision. Torrance, *Transformation and Convergence*, 252; *Theology in Reconstruction*, 14–15, 170; *Juridical Law and Physical Law*, 2nd edition (Eugene, OR: Wipf & Stock, 1997), 34; and *The Christian Frame of Mind*, 37–41. It should also be noted that, though Torrance speaks here, as elsewhere, in terms of "object–object" relations, he has not forgotten that the knowing subject is always involved. It is also assumed in Torrance's discussions of what he calls "onto-relations." *Reality and Evangelical Theology*, 42–51; *Mediation of Christ*, 47; *Transformation and Convergence*, 230; *Space, Time and Resurrection* (Grand Rapids, MI: Eerdmans, 1976), 185; *Christian Doctrine of God, One Being Three Persons* (Edinburgh: T&T Clark, 1996), 102–3; *Christian Theology and Scientific Culture*, 26–7, 51; *Divine and Contingent Order*, 109–10; *Juridical Law and Physical Law*, 43–4; and *Ground and Grammar of Theology*, 174. For a discussion on subject–object–object relations, see Stevick, *Encountering Reality*, 93–7.

[28]Torrance, *Transformation and Convergence*, 252.

traveling through it.[29] It is also crucial in Young's "double slit" experiment, where properties of quanta were discerned not so much by manipulating the quanta directly but by manipulating objects with which they interacted.[30] Subject–object–object relations are perhaps less readily available in the field of theology, but they are not nonexistent. It is precisely Christian doctrines of creation and Christ's Lordship over the forces of nature that fuels some of the engagement between theology and natural science.[31]

This practical upshot for our knowledge is that while it is not possible to escape the subject–object relation, acknowledging this is not tantamount to rejecting any meaningful claim to objectivity in the traditional sense. While we may never be able to achieve knowledge of objects such that they do not rely upon any particular point of view, this does not eliminate the possibility of authentic, scientific knowledge. Even the hardest of the natural sciences have had to come to terms with this and have continued to press for ever more faithful knowledge.

TRUTH

Just as Torrance's insistence on the inescapability of ultimate beliefs requires a shift in our understanding of objectivity, so this latter shift requires a similar readjustment over how we understand the notion of truth. Since the days of Aristotle, Western thought has conceived of truth primarily as a relation between our statements and reality. In Aristotle's words:

> Falsehood consists in saying of that which is that it is not, or of that which is not that it is. Truth consists in saying of that which is that it is, or of that which is not that it is not. Therefore he who says of anything that it is (or that it is not) says what is either true or false.[32]

Such a theory of truth locates truth within *statements* made by *persons*. In light of Torrance's understanding of the role of ultimate beliefs and objectivity, it would seem that such an understanding of truth is insufficient.

---

[29]For an accessible introduction regarding the problem leading to the development of the Michelson–Morley experiment, see Albert Einstein and Leopold Infeld, *The Evolution of Physics: The Growth of Ideas from the Early Concepts to Relativity and Quanta* (Cambridge: Cambridge University Press, 1938), 164–77. For a particularly helpful introduction for beginners to the experiment itself, see Robert H. March, *Physics for Poets* (New York: McGraw-Hill Inc., 1970), 115–23. Note that while today it is felt that the Michelson–Morley experiment falsified belief in the ether, the significance of the 1887 experiment (as well as the earlier version by Michelson in 1881) was stated to be that it refuted a *particular theory* of the ether, namely, that of Fresnel. It was only "twenty-five years later that the Michelson–Morley experiment came to be seen as 'the greatest negative experiment in the history of science.'" Imre Lakatos, "Falsification and the Methodology of Scientific Research Programmes," in *Criticism and the Growth of Knowledge: Proceedings of the International Colloquium in the Philosophy of Science, London, 1965*, vol. 4, ed. Imre Lakatos and Alan Musgrave (Cambridge: Cambridge University Press, 1970), 159–65.

[30]One of the more accessible introductions to the "double slit" experiment can be found in Richard Feynman, *The Character of Physical Law* (London: Cox and Wyman, 1965), 121–42. See also March, *Physics for Poets*, 109–12.

[31]For example, see the recent two-volume publication: Andrew B. Torrance and Thomas H. McCall, eds., *Knowing Creation: Perspectives from Theology, Philosophy, and Science* (Grand Rapids, MI: Zondervan, 2018) and *Christ and the Created Order: Perspectives from Theology, Philosophy, and Science* (Grand Rapids, MI: Zondervan, 2018).

[32]Aristotle, *Aristotle's Metaphysics*. Everyman's Library. Trans. John Warrington (London: J. M. Dent & Sons, 1956), book IV, chapter 7, section 1.

The reason it seems insufficient is because it assumes that we are always in a position to decide whether something "is the case" or not. As we have seen, Torrance believes that the beliefs we bring to our investigation may cloud our ability to understand what truly is the case. If we are operating with a "penultimate" belief, one that seems reasonable to hold, but which has alternatives that may also be reasonably held,[33] it is possible we are operating with the wrong belief which will incline us to assign truth or falsity in light of those inadequate beliefs rather than in light of reality itself. If we define truth primarily in terms of statements, we will be inclined toward either tacitly substituting "what is the case according to my theoretical convictions" for "what is the case" or else rendering the overwhelming majority of statements as being, strictly speaking, false.

Both courses of action have proven to be tempting in modern philosophy of science. On the one side, Thomas S. Kuhn, who introduced the idea of "paradigms" into the understanding of science once wrote, "if I am right, then 'truth' may, like 'proof,' be a term with only intra-theoretic applications."[34] On the other side, there has been the question over whether we can use the word "true" to describe our scientific statements, since our understanding of "what is the case" has changed so radically over the years. One way to deal with this is to say that our scientific theories may not be "true," but we seek for them to be "approximately true." One definition of this is provided by Stathis Psillos. "A theory is approximately true if it describes a world which is similar to the actual world in its most central or relevant features."[35] Another result has been a certain skepticism that our scientific theories identify or name truth at all.[36]

Torrance is not happy with either of these alternatives and avoids a choice between them by developing a different theory of truth. At the root of Torrance's theory of truth we find a discussion of Anselm's work *De Veritate*, permutations of which can be found in several places in Torrance's writings.[37] In his discussion of Anselm,[38] Torrance discusses three senses in which something may be true. First, there are two truths of statement, one where a statement makes grammatical sense within itself, regardless of whether it accurately describes any particular state of affairs. While this is not what most people mean when they speak of a statement being "true,"[39] it has value in that it must have this truth of statement before it can have truth in any other sense.

---

[33]For Torrance on penultimate beliefs, see *Transformation and Convergence*, 203–12. For a discussion on penultimate beliefs, see Stevick, *Encountering Reality*, 48–54.

[34]Kuhn, "Reflections on My Critics," in Lakatos and Musgrave, *Criticism and the Growth of Knowledge*, ed. Lakatos and Musgrave, 266.

[35]Stathis Psillos, *Scientific Realism: How Science Tracks Truth. Philosophical Issues in Science*, ed. W. H. Newton-Smith (New York: Rutledge, 1999), 103.

[36]One line of thought along these lines is the "disastrous meta-induction," put forward by Hilary Putnam. Hilary Putnam, "What Is Realism," in *Scientific Realism*, ed. Jarrett Leplin (Berkeley: University of California Press, 1984), 146.

[37]Torrance's major discussions on Anselm's treatment of truth can be found on *Reality and Evangelical Theology*, 126–37; *Reality and Scientific Theology*, 143–7; "The Place of Word and Truth in Theological Inquiry According to St. Anselm," in *Studia Medievalia Et Mariologica*, P. Carolo Balic OFM Septvagesium Explendi Annum Dicta, ed. P. Zavalloni (Rome: Antonianum, 1971), 142–7; and "Ethical Implications of Anselm's De Veritate," *Theologische Zeitschrift* 24, no. 5 (1968): 309–13.

[38]It could be questioned whether Torrance is simply analyzing Anselm's own position or whether he is perhaps pressing Anselm's discussion beyond its original intent. As such, while Torrance clearly sees his theory of truth as coming from Anselm, it is not the intent of this chapter to discuss the truth or falsity of that. Let it suffice at this point that this is Torrance's own position, whatever Anselm believed.

[39]It could be argued that this is the kind of "truth" that is implied in a coherence theory of truth.

The second truth of statement is when a statement not only makes grammatical sense within itself but faithfully refers to a state of affairs in the world, such as when the statement "the sky is clear today" is made on a day when there are no clouds. It must be noted that this, or something very much like it, is what most people throughout history have considered to be the main way we use the term "truth,"[40] that a statement is true when it states what is the case, independent of the statement. Torrance affirms this usage but feels it is not the highest sense in which something may be "true."

The third sense in which something may be true, and the highest which may be ascribed of creaturely reality, is "the truth of being." This is the fact that some particular being is what it is and not something else. While it may seem unnecessary to say that everything that exists is what it is and isn't what it isn't, this undergirds Torrance's stress that it is inappropriate to overlay reality with our false beliefs about reality. Ontology carries with it a moral imperative to think of things according to what they are and not as we may desire them to be.[41]

Torrance continues following Anselm in naming a fourth sense in which something is true, the "supreme truth of God." While the affirmation of this truth cements the contingent character of all other truth and seems demanded by traditional Christian convictions, its primary relevance for this discussion is that it emphasizes that "truth," for Torrance, is to be understood as something that refers primarily to *being* and only secondarily to statements.[42]

This emphasis illuminates an element of Torrance's thought that differentiates him from others who would seem, at first glance, to hold similar positions. When Torrance describes himself as a "realist," or as a "critical realist," he is highlighting his radical commitment to reality rather than any particular explanation or articulation of reality. Within the philosophy of science, to be a "realist" usually implies a commitment to the idea that the goal of our statements is that they should "give us ... a literally true story of what the world is like: and acceptance of a scientific theory involves the belief that this is true."[43] In such a view, "realism" is meant to describe our theories (at least our ideal theories) and how we interpret them. For Torrance, it is meant to describe a commitment that is articulated well in the words of Roy Bhaskar, "epistemological relativism ... is the handmaiden of ontological realism and must be accepted."[44] That is to say, if our ultimate commitment is to reality, it cannot also be to a particular explanation of that reality, however ideal. This conviction is put particularly clearly when looking at how we use the word "truth" in different contexts.

> Now if we think of Jesus Christ in this way as the Truth in his own Person, our statements about him, biblical and theological statements, cannot be true in the same sense as Jesus Christ is true, for they do not have their truth in themselves but in their

---

[40] Indeed, it could be said that this is exactly what is meant by a correspondence theory of truth.

[41] On the moral imperative of ontology and its relation to Torrance's epistemology, see Travis M. Stevick, "The Unitary Relationship between Ethics and Epistemology in the Thought of T. F. Torrance," *Participatio* 5 (2015): 91–106.

[42] Torrance's use of "truth" in this way is somewhat idiosyncratic. For a discussion of how Torrance uses phrases like "God is truth" differently than Aquinas, see Stevick, *Encountering Reality*, 125–7.

[43] Bas C. Van Fraassen, *The Scientific Image* (Oxford: Oxford University Press, 1980), 8.

[44] Roy Bhaskar, *A Realist Theory of Science*. 3rd ed. (London: Verso, 2008), 249. For Torrance, it is not that truth is relative but that statements about the truth necessarily are. "Provisional" might be a term he would be more comfortable with.

reference to him away from themselves, and they are true insofar as that reference is truthful and appropriate. By referring to him away from themselves, they both subordinate themselves to him and discriminate themselves from him. A semantic relation of this kind holds good, as we have seen, in any realist relation between statements and realities to which they refer. But if Jesus Christ is the ultimate Truth of God, as we believe him to be, then our statements about him, insofar as they are true, must refer to him accordingly, subjecting themselves to him and discriminating themselves from him in their utter difference from him as creaturely and contingent.[45]

DISCLOSURE MODELS

If we insist that our quest for knowledge is rooted primarily in knowing something as it is and not in terms we project upon it, and that we are seeking knowledge of the reality we are studying and not a series of factually true statements, it has consequences for the construction of our scientific theories. We must take our theoretical constructions seriously, because there is no way to engage with reality without bringing presuppositions to the task. By the time any of us begin a scientific engagement, we are shaped by ideas about the subject or object of our study, either by our own experience, or those we have inherited from our society, even if it is just in the language we use to describe reality.

Torrance describes the development of our scientific theories as the ascending of a series of conceptual levels, probing ever more deeply into the object of our study. At the first level, we begin with our basic, nonscientific encounter with reality and our natural description of it. At this level, what Torrance calls the evangelical–doxological level in the field of Christian Theology, but which could be called the empirico-theoretical level in the natural sciences, we are not explicitly engaging in scientific reflection or in resolving apparent tensions within our experience.[46] That does not mean, however, that our descriptions have not been impacted by inchoate theoretical considerations.[47] We find this level of description, for example, in the biblical witness to God's revelation and in the collection and collation of observational data, such as the astronomical data gathered by Tycho Brahe.

It is important to note that it is at this level where most of our deepest theological convictions take their root.

> We may speak of this level as that of *incipient theology* on which, as we would expect, empirical and conceptual, historical and theological, factors are naturally and spontaneously interwoven with one another. From the very start of our believing experience and knowledge of the incarnate economy of redemption undertaken by Jesus Christ for our sakes, form and content are found fused together both in what we are given to know and in our experience and knowing of it. A child by the age of five has learned, we are told, an astonishing amount about the physical world to which he or she has become spontaneously and intuitively adapted—far more than the child could ever understand if he or she turned out to be the most brilliant of physicists.

---

[45]Torrance, *Reality and Evangelical Theology*, 124.

[46]Torrance's discussions of this level can be found in *Ground and Grammar of Theology*, 156–7; *Christian Doctrine of God*, 83–4, 88–91.

[47]Bas Van Fraassen puts this idea particularly vividly: "I am immersed in a language which is thoroughly theory-infected, living in a world my ancestors of two centuries ago could not enter," *The Scientific Image*, 81.

> Likewise, I believe, we learn far more about God as Father, Son, and Holy Spirit, into whose Name we have been baptized, within the family and fellowship and living tradition of the Church than we can ever say: it becomes built into the structure of our souls and minds, and we know much more than we can ever tell.[48]

While Torrance considers this to be the first level of our scientific engagement, it is not yet what many would describe as "scientific." For this we move to the second level, the "first theoretical/theological level."[49] This name is not to imply that it is only at this point where theoretical considerations come into play. Rather, it is here that we *explicitly* engage in theoretical reflection. At this level, we attempt to organize our experience in such a way that attempts to provide a consistent theoretical framework that shows how the experiences hang together in a coherent way. It is hoped that this level will also give some account of the reality that gave rise to those experiences. The account at this level is not considered to be final. Rather, it is the fashioning of a tool to facilitate further engagement with reality. "The purpose of such a theory is to enable us to penetrate into the intelligible connections latent in reality that ground and control our basic experiences and cognitions, and illuminate them for us."[50]

> At the fundamental level of our evangelical and experiential apprehension and worship of God arising out of the incarnate economy of his saving love in Jesus Christ, we learn that the Person of Christ as Lord and Savior, his saving acts and his message of salvation are ultimately one and the same … Our concern at this secondary level, however, while distinctly theological, is not primarily with the organic body of theological knowledge, but with penetrating through it to apprehend more fully the economic and ontological and Trinitarian structure of God's revealing and saving acts in Jesus Christ as they are presented to us in the Gospel.[51]

It is entirely possible, if not highly probable, that the first attempts to generate a theory at this level will turn out to be inadequate to reality upon further investigation. This is not a problem in Torrance's view because the purpose of our theories is not to generate a literally true account of what reality is like but to facilitate our contact with reality to reach ever more appropriate knowledge according to the reality's nature. As such, when an attempt results in an inadequate result, it is not seen as having failed to produce a true theory; rather it is seen as having succeeded in bringing us into contact with reality in such a way that reality could stand in judgment over our theory and force us to think it through again. If the theory had failed to bring us into contact with reality, we would have learned nothing new. It is precisely because we *do* learn something new that we know our theory has succeeded, in however a limited way.[52]

---

[48]Torrance, *Christian Doctrine of God*, 89.

[49]Torrance's discussions of this level can be found in *Ground and Grammar of Theology*, 157; *Christian Doctrine of God*, 84–5, 91–8.

[50]Torrance, *Christian Doctrine of God*, 84.

[51]Ibid., 91.

[52]For Torrance's use of the phrase "limiting case," see *Divine and Contingent Order*, 27–8; *Transformation and Convergence*, 45, 180, 321–2; *Ground and Grammar of Theology*, 103, 171–2; *Christian Doctrine of God*, 85–6; and *Space, Time and Resurrection*, 16–17. Torrance claims the term comes from Von Weizsäcker in *Theological Science*, 265–6. It should be noted once again that this knowledge is not ultimately something that we generate by our human intelligence but it is knowledge that must be "justified" by the "grace" of reality. This is especially clear when it comes to our knowledge of God, which is only ever the result of grace. *Transformation and Convergence in the Frame of Knowledge*, 211–12.

For Torrance, science is about more than simply providing a more or less coherent account of our experience of reality. Truly kataphysic knowledge involves probing behind mere appearances to elucidate the source of those appearances. That is to say, it is not enough to give a coherent account of our experience of reality, but we must explain *why* those appearances are thus and so.

This brings us to the third level of our scientific theories, what Torrance calls the "second theological level" for theology, but could be called the "second theoretical level" for natural sciences.[53] Here we try to probe into the concepts developed at the first theoretical level with the goal of determining which are central and which are peripheral, and to develop a theoretical account of reality that utilizes the fewest concepts, and covers the widest range of experiences, as possible.[54]

> Through this stratification of concepts and levels scientific theology penetrates into the primordial unity constituting the "natural" intelligible basis of our knowledge of God, which results in an immense clarification and simplification of its whole structure. In proportion as that basis comes to view in its ultimate economic simplicity, it becomes apparent that some intermediate levels are only of a methodological nature, and that many of the conceptions they carry, necessary as they may have been in the process of theological development, must eventually disappear as temporarily expedient but ultimately irrelevant abstractions. Thus the profundity and richness of our theological understanding is proportionate to the economic simplicity or paucity of its foundational concepts and the universality of their range of enlightenment.[55]

Torrance's favorite example is the Christian Doctrine of the Trinity. While this third-level theory does not explicitly deal with many Christian concerns, it aims to articulate the reality of God upon which all other theological considerations must be built if they are to be faithful and with which they must be consistent.[56] If such a third-level theory can be reached, it functions as a means of purifying and focusing discussions at the second level of our theories. It also aids us in making judgments as to which of seemingly equally valid interpretations of data at the first level are appropriate. To give an example from natural science, the shift to a heliocentric cosmology helps us to decide between alternative explanations of the "tower experiment."[57] It provides a theoretical account of why it is that data that seems to point away from heliocentrism arises in the first place.

---

[53]Torrance's discussions of this level can be found in *Ground and Grammar of Theology*, 157-9; *Christian Doctrine of God*, 85, 98-101.

[54]For a discussion on this stratification of our theories and its implications, see Stevick, *Encountering Reality*, 163-87.

[55]Torrance, *Transformation and Convergence*, 305.

[56]This is not to say that the doctrine of the Trinity is in any way unimportant or impractical, but simply that, at this higher level, we are not explicitly concerned with its practical implications. Such implications are explored in the lower level doctrines that relate to this one higher level doctrine.

[57]The "tower experiment" was an experiment, whether actually performed or merely in thought, that argued that since a rock, when dropped from a tower, moves straight down to the ground, the earth must be stationary. If it were in motion, as suggested by the advocates of heliocentrism, the rock "would travel many yards to the east in the time the rock would consume in its fall, and the rock ought to strike the earth that distance away from the base of the tower." Galileo Galilei, *Dialogue concerning the Two Chief World Systems* (Berkeley: University of California Press, 1953), 126, cited in Paul K. Feyerabend, *Against Method*. 3rd edn. (London: Verso, 1993), 56. While a geocentric view interprets the phenomenon that objects fall straight down as evidence that the earth does not move, a heliocentric view would claim that the earth brings its atmosphere with it as it moves through space and so the two are empirically equivalent at that point.

This ability to show not only that previous explanations were wrong but how intelligent and reasonable people could believe them is helpful whenever possible.

The practical upshot of these levels of our scientific engagement is that it means that no single level contains all the relevant data. It means that if we wish to provide a consistent account of our experience or of our theological convictions, we must seek their completion beyond themselves at a higher level.[58] It means that we must take our theories as seriously as possible, for we can make no progress without them, but we must also hold them loosely, because the truth of statement is never to be confused or equated with the truth of being. We also know that there may indeed come a day when we find we must revise our theories or doctrines, but that need not be because they were *false* in the traditional sense of "saying what is not the case," but because they were inadequate to the task of articulating the depth of the truth of being. When the truth of reality outstrips our theoretical resources and we find we must put our theories aside and search for new ones, we may often treat the old theories as a kind of "limiting case," where they remain useful, so long as we are considering reality in carefully controlled circumstances.[59]

CONCLUSION

Thomas F. Torrance was a theologian who was concerned with epistemological considerations and such concerns permeated his writing on every topic. Given the nature of his writings, many of which are collections of essays on common themes rather than systematic expositions, it may not be immediately clear to the one encountering Torrance's work for the first time, especially if those first experiences are via his more explicitly theological works, that Torrance's epistemological insights, taken as a coherent whole, provide a robust and carefully nuanced scientific and theological method. Indeed, it performs admirably, even when compared with the main positions in the philosophy of science contemporary with Torrance's career.[60]

Torrance's treatments of important topics are frequently scattered throughout several volumes. This is perhaps even more true of his epistemological and scientific discussions. It is hoped that this summary will clarify Torrance's scientific procedure and that the resources cited in the footnotes will orient the new student of Torrance to the relevant discussions and lead to increased understanding and appreciation of what he has to offer the church and philosophy.

---

[58]This is the major insight Torrance appropriates from Kurt Gödel. For Torrance's description of Gödel's incompleteness theorem, see *Transformation and Convergence*, 135–48. See also *Juridical Law and Physical Law*, 17; *Reality and Evangelical Theology*, 73–4; *Reality and Scientific Theology*, 123–4; *Ground and Grammar of Theology*, 70; *Theological Science*, 243, 255, 257; *Theology in Reconstruction*, 60, 97–8; *Divine and Contingent Order*, 157 n. 55.

[59]Perhaps the greatest example of this use of a limiting case is with the remaining usefulness of Newtonian physics. Strictly speaking, every statement of Newtonian physics that involves concepts like mass, energy, velocity, and time is "false" because we realize they are, at best, first approximations to Einsteinian physics. However, that does not mean they are not useful. While Torrance never discusses the possibility that Nicene Trinitarianism could ever become a "limiting case" of a deeper and richer theological development, he does entertain some thoughts along these lines with regard to the Nicene *homoousion*. See Torrance, *The Trinitarian Faith*, 144. See also Stevick, *Encountering Reality*, 184–7.

[60]For a survey of these major philosophical positions and an evaluation of Torrance in light of them, see my essay "The Function of Scientific Theory in the Thought of T. F. Torrance," *Participatio* 7 (2017): 49–70.

PART TWO

Dogmatics

CHAPTER NINE

Thomas F. Torrance on the Doctrine of Revelation

JOHN C. MCDOWELL

INTRODUCTION

In the Preface to the published version of his Warfield Lectures, Colin Gunton claims that "the doctrine of revelation has been in recent times at once neglected and overused."[1] The neglect, he declares, is the fruit of certain criticisms of the doctrine and its subsequent dislocation from claims to rational inquiry. Any repair of this involves the theologian in an apologetic task: to engage in a set of conversations with cultured despisers to unpack the rational framing of the reality of revelation. The overuse he speaks of is potentially more dogmatically interesting, however. Gunton implies that it has had a detrimental effect on the nature and function of the doctrine. He explains that in reaction of the dissipation of the doctrine in modernity theologians (and here he specifically names Karl Barth) sought to "overcome the epistemological challenges" by means of it, resulting in "an overemployment ... an imbalance in the systemic structure" of theological thought. Gunton's worry at this point seems to be that an inordinate amount of time is devoted to a single doctrine in order to counter epistemic pressure. Over recent centuries, the doctrine has become associated with epistemic conditions and grounds for theological speech, part of theology's prolegomena. That reduces the doctrine to matters of noetics, and this is itself the product of the modern preoccupation with epistemology or reflections on how we know what we claim to know. John Webster, on the other hand, offers a more substantial critique at this point. The shifting locus for the doctrine's use had less to do with a simple overdetermination of its intellectual importance, or its undue capture of the theological imagination, than with the very "distortions of its shape."[2] According to Webster, what emerged was a reconstruction of the concept of revelation within a cultural metaphysic "in which the guiding hand was very often philosophical rather than dogmatic." This is not an insignificant reconstruction, since "these reduced accounts of revelation were seriously under-determined by Christian content of Christian teaching about God. 'Revelation', that is, was transposed rather readily into a feature of generally 'theistic' metaphysical outlooks." Even if revelation has to do with the very conditions of theological speech, its possibility as a rational activity, the reduction of the concept to

---

[1] Colin Gunton, *A Brief Theology of Revelation*. The 1993 Warfield Lectures (London and New York: T&T Clark, 1995), ix.

[2] John Webster, *Holy Scripture: A Dogmatic Sketch* (Cambridge: Cambridge University Press, 2003), 11.

its location as an epistemic prolegomenon has involved a significant loss and distortion. Therefore, to speak of this, rather than "the life-giving and loving presence of … God," as "revelation" can actually be misleading.[3]

In crucial ways, the appeal to revelation became not that of the description of the *Self-givingness of God* in God's freedom (or God's Self-presentation as grace) but rather of the manner in which the *knowing subject grasps* God and does so on grounds either that are specifiable without reference to the material content of Christian dogmatic claims or that bypass normal knowing processes in some non- or prerational givenness. What happens, among other things, Webster observes, is a strict identification of revelation and Scripture so that "Scripture precedes and warrants all other Christian doctrines as the formal principle from which those other doctrines are deduced."[4]

These broadly overlapping concerns of Gunton and Webster are, to varying degrees, concerns also of Thomas F. Torrance, and such pervade his postcritically realist account of revelation that has remained remarkably consistent over several decades of publication. First, there is an apologetic locus to his reflections on this by way of explicating the intelligible order of the doctrine of revelation and doing so through indicating the parallels and overlaps with other accounts of knowing. "If theology is to survive the crisis of these times, it must move out into the full light of day, engage in critical revision of its own theoretic framework, and go on to fresh scientific construction under the pressure and determination of its own object."[5] This is Torrance's heavily burdened construal of *theological science*, and here the critic might want to press whether he is occasionally prone to a determinative epistemic reduction. Second, and crucially in this regard, to speak of Torrance as *explicating* the intrinsic intelligibility or rationality of the order of revelation is decisive since it is only in and through the reality or actuality of God's revelatory act that theology is possible. This is a statement that is dogmatically asymmetrical and irreversible. Revelatory-talk does not function to ground the possibility of the subject's knowing of God, as if God is an Object and end of human knowing, an idle Thing who is discovered by the inquisitive human subject. It is noticeable that Torrance does not provide any substantial work specifically focused on "revelation," but rather divine disclosure-talk pervades his theological corpus as something dogmatically substantial and therefore not as formally reducible to a doctrinally independent and pre-dogmatic prolegomenon. As Webster argues, and Torrance would undoubtedly agree, "The doctrinal under-determination and mislocation of the idea of revelation can only be overcome by its reintegration into the comprehensive structure of Christian doctrine, and most especially the Christian doctrine of God."[6]

The doctrine of revelation is the condition both of human knowing, not merely of God but of anything, and of creaturely existing as it is given by the Self-communicating presencing of God. It has to do with what grounds all things, or "reality in its depth," so that our claims to the knowledge of reality are not "artificially cut short at appearances."[7] The scope of what is meant by "revelation," then, is considerably broader than that of

---

[3] Webster, *Holy Scripture*, 12.

[4] Ibid., 13.

[5] Thomas F. Torrance, *God and Rationality* (London: Oxford University Press, 1971), 5.

[6] Webster, *Holy Scripture*, 13.

[7] Thomas F. Torrance, *The Ground and Grammar of Theology: Consonance between Theology and Science* (Edinburgh: T&T Clark, 1980), 35; *The Mediation of Christ* (Exeter: The Paternoster Press, 1983), 11, respectively.

noetic conceptuality. It has to do with more than the conditions for theological talk since it is ontologically the very *content* of what theology speaks of—the Self-disclosure of the *God* who *gives* God's very *Self* to be known. What this means is that it has to do with *disclosive presence*, the presence of God to all things. As Torrance declares, "There is only one grace ... for God himself in the fullness of his triune being is present in all his acts of creating, revealing, healing, enlightening and sanctifying."[8] In this mode of thinking, dogmatic theology functions for the "edification of the Church in hearing and appropriating the Word of God, and as the discipline of the Church in assimilating all its thinking and speaking to the Mind of Christ, that it may continue to become what it is, the One Body of the One Lord."[9]

THEOLOGICAL SCIENCE AND THE OBJECTIVE SUBJECTIVITY OF GOD

Given the ample attention Torrance pays to methodological issues one could be forgiven for imagining that he has succumbed to the tendency that was criticized above by Gunton and Webster. Nonetheless, in a number of ways, Torrance amplifies Barth's reflections on theology as *Wissenschaftliche*, as well—or fittingly ordered or rational reflection, "a disciplined penetration into the inner intelligibility of the faith."[10] What is most crucial is that theology methodologically should refuse any imposition of what is improper on its reflective activity "by schematising it to an external or alien framework of thought."[11] Accordingly, properly disciplined thinking "lays itself open to the nature and reality of the object in order to take its shape from the structure of the object and not to impose upon it a structure of its own prescription."[12]

Torrance names this well-ordered thinking "theological science," and he spends considerable, indeed an inordinate, amount of time across a plethora of publications unpacking the parallels between the flow of a disciplined theology and of natural scientific study which "is only the rigorous extension of that [same] basic way of thinking and behaving."[13] Torrance claims "that theology and science have both critical and constructive contributions to make to each other."[14] Yet what is crucial here is the manner of the comparison which this affords Torrance, since it must be admitted, there is only slight *material* conceptual benefit that permits him to claim little more than a *formal* or methodological overlap with a "disclosure model."[15] After all, theology's "object" is *sui generis*. God is not an "object" of our knowing that can be inspected in the way that matters of creaturely reality can by the methods of proper to the natural sciences and

---

[8]Thomas F. Torrance, *The Trinitarian Faith: The Evangelical Theology of the Ancient Catholic Church* (Edinburgh: T&T Clark, 1988), 328–9.

[9]Thomas F. Torrance, "Introduction: The Place of Christology in Biblical and Dogmatic Theology," in *Essays in Christology for Karl Barth*, ed. T. H. L. Parker (London: Lutterworth Press, 1956), 28.

[10]Torrance, *God and Rationality*, 6.

[11]Torrance, *The Mediation of Christ*, 13.

[12]Torrance, *God and Rationality*, 9.

[13]Torrance, *The Ground and Grammar of Theology*, 8.

[14]Thomas F. Torrance, *The Christian Frame of Mind* (Edinburgh: The Handsell Press, 1985), 3.

[15]Torrance, *The Ground and Grammar of Theology*, 125.

therefore cannot be appealed to "as a stopgap in the formation of some hypothesis to explain a set of physical connections in nature."[16]

The nature of theology's subject matter as "no-object" demands a conceptual unfolding of the mode of articulation and rationality "appropriate to it, one which it suggests to us out of its own inherent constitutive relations and which we are rationally constrained to adopt in faithful understanding and interpretation of it."[17] From this claim, Torrance advances that theology and science, while rationally overlapping in their mode of rationality, nonetheless are distinctive. It is true that the doctrine of creation permits Torrance to entertain theology as speaking of the very conditions for the rational order, that order of "objective rationality of the universe" without which there can be no scientific investigation.[18] In other words, this account of the prevenience of divine action enables a refusal of "secularization" through any straightforward displacement of God as the ground and grammar of the very intelligibility of the world and everything in it and negating that which the sciences seek to describe as contingent. Creation, therefore, "must be regarded not only as having taken place through the Logos but *in* the Logos which nevertheless remains utterly transcendent over it all."[19] Science cannot return the favor by grounding or positioning theology. The point of "theological science," then, is not to gesture toward a pre-theological ground for theological reflection and speech, a factor that would determine the very nature of theological claims and set a bar against which they would need to be measured. Rather, it provides a sense of overlapping rationalities and rational methods. Even so, Torrance appeals to the unpacking of a quite different subject–object dialectic, and he conceptually draws on a theme prominent in Barth's work to make sense of the "unique nature of its [viz., theology's] own proper Object."[20] By this, Torrance articulates that "God is at once the Subject and the Object of revelation, and never the Object without also being the Subject."[21] In fact, operating from such a conceptuality Torrance explains that "an *epistemological inversion* takes place in our knowing of God, for what is primary is his knowing of us, not our knowing of him."[22] Whatever else one can say about it, it is crucial in any attempt to draw Torrance into conversation between theology and the sciences to recognize that the former actually involves "an *epistemological inversion* of our ordinary knowing relation."[23] Among other things, this encourages Torrance to be concerned with redirecting modern thinking with its problematic grounding of knowing in human subjectivity.

Talk of revelation is only well-ordered talk when it is theological: in other words, when it is primarily a way of speaking about the activity of God and nothing less than God. Concomitantly, it is only talk of God if it reflectively follows with integrity "the ground of our actual knowledge of God" that is ordered by, and is appropriate to, the nature of

---

[16] Ibid., 9.

[17] Torrance, *The Mediation of Christ*, 13–14.

[18] Thomas F. Torrance, *Christian Theology and Scientific Culture* (Belfast: Christian Journals Ltd., 1980), 7.

[19] Thomas F. Torrance, *Theology in Reconciliation: Essays towards Evangelical and Catholic Unity in East and West* (London: Geoffrey Chapman, 1975), 219.

[20] Torrance, *Theological Science* (Oxford: Oxford University Press, 1978), 25.

[21] Thomas F. Torrance, *The Christian Doctrine of God, One Being Three Persons* (Edinburgh: T&T Clark, 1996), 22.

[22] Ibid., 105.

[23] Thomas F. Torrance, *Preaching Christ Today: The Gospel and Scientific Thinking* (Grand Rapids. MI: Eerdmans, 1994), 47.

the subject matter itself.[24] Theology cannot claim to be theological knowledge unless it follows and is disciplined by the logic of the reality or objectivity of God's own being-in-act as the Triune Lord, a Triunity that constitutes "the *ultimate ground* of theological knowledge of God, the *basic grammar* of theology."[25] Put otherwise, "How God can be known must be determined from first to last by the way in which He actually is known."[26] Unpacking what is involved in this leads Torrance into specifying the regulative centrality or the hermeneutical function of Christology.

> Theology, therefore, involves a knowledge which is determined and controlled in its content by what is given in Jesus Christ, and operates with a mode of rational activity which corresponds to the nature of the object of this knowledge in Jesus Christ. It is the incarnation of the Word which prescribes to dogmatic theology both its matter and its method, so that whether in its activity as a whole or in the formulation of a doctrine in any part, it is the Christological pattern that will be made to appear.[27]

The concept of a "Christological pattern" certainly allows Torrance to emphasize the Christological contours of all well-ordered dogmatic work, although he does have a tendency to treat Christology with little reference to its historicality, both as a doctrinal claim in its own right by the historically embedded church and as a claim about the history of God as incarnate. As shall be seen in other contexts regulating his account of revelation, Torrance has a rather attenuated sense of the historically contingent and its contributing role in our knowing of God, even though he does provide statements that nod toward something that requires more consistent fleshing out: "In Jesus Christ all theological statements are made within the concrete forms of space and time, within the medium of historical thinking and action, where they involve commitment to the Truth in historical life and action and an appropriate mode of verification."[28]

Any concern in this area should be cognizant also of Torrance's awkward dependence on the concept of creaturely response as *conformity*. At its best, this concept depicts the asymmetry of God's givingness, of the Self-presencing of God as God's Self-manifestation that is *received*. Moreover, it does describe the *consequent shape* of the receptivity as being *formed by, through, and in* this divinely initiated communicative action. Dogmatics, in this mode, is tasked with bringing "the mind of the Church to ever renewed conformity to the work and activity of God in His Word."[29] It involves the bringing of "our belief and knowledge of God to expression in the patterns of thought and speech which we gain under the impact of God's creation upon us."[30] This is why Torrance contends for the *objectivity* of God in God's Self-revelation. It is *God* who is known in God's giving and the "scientific knowledge" appropriate to the objectivity that this possesses.[31]

---

[24]Torrance, *God and Rationality*, 165.
[25]Torrance, *The Ground and Grammar of Theology*, 158–9.
[26]Torrance, *Theological Science*, 9.
[27]Torrance, "Introduction: The Place of Christology in Biblical and Dogmatic Theology," 13.
[28]Torrance, *Theological Science*, 177.
[29]Torrance, "Introduction: The Place of Christology in Biblical and Dogmatic Theology," 14.
[30]Thomas F. Torrance, "Introduction," in *Belief in Science and in Christian Life: The Relevance of Michael Polanyi's Thought for Christian Faith and Life*, ed. Thomas F. Torrance (Edinburgh: The Handsel Press, 1980), xvii.
[31]Torrance, *Theological Science*, 295.

Another way of saying this is to claim that revelation is about the relations of creatures to God established *by grace* or the free activity of God to be God for the plenitudinous beneficence of God's presence to creatures. "It is only out of pure Grace that God gives Himself to be the object of our knowing and thinking."[32] Torrance never develops theologically away from the contouring of theological activity announced in his early study on the Apostolic Fathers: grace "has to do with the divine act of intervention ... [C]*haris* is now the presupposition of all man's relations with God and constitutive of the whole Christian life."[33] Torrance insists that grace remains a pure act of God in God's free Self-giving in Christ and through the Spirit, and therefore it cannot be handled, and cannot be subjected instrumentally to the power of human control, protection, or dispensing, as if a form of "magic [that] could conjure up and manipulate 'the divine.'"[34] Accordingly, he is at pains to insist that the Self-revelation of God brings with it concomitant conditions for its reception. Here Torrance unpacks the themes of the uncontrollability of grace (since it is *God's* giving); the universality of grace (as God's Self-giving to *all things*); the proper dependency of creatures on grace (as the condition and proper end of *their flourishing*); and of the reality of grace not as "a *datum* handed over to the control and manipulation of our thought" but as "a *dandum* that must ever be given anew, for the Gift and the Giver are identical."[35]

Torrance's interest in ensuring that theology is grounded in, and is always attentive to following the movements of, divine grace clearly expresses his concern to prevent the distorting effects on the intelligibility of theology's "object" or subject matter through the *a priori* imposition of "a *preconceived* metaphysics."[36] His interrogative voice is pressed into the attempt to unmask occasions when just such distortions occur. For instance, he worries about "forms of thought not taken from the realities themselves but from contemporary philosophies," those that have been shaped by the Hellenistic dualistic philosophies that informed "the radical dualism between the *cosmos noetos* and the *cosmos aisthetos*, and between God and the creation, that lay at the heart of Arian theology," and through to "the new formalistic Aristotelianism and then in the light of the Cartesian mode of questioning the self-understanding."[37] The dogmatic conditions for these claims are Christological, and Torrance is at pains to indicate the substantive presence of God as incarnated, for Jesus Christ "is the embodiment of the Word and Truth of God in his own personal Being."[38]

Following Barth's apprehension over the form that the hiddenness of God takes in the Reformed and Lutheran predestinarian traditions, separating economic and immanent Trinities or revelation's divine form and content, Torrance for his part proclaims that "what Jesus Christ is toward us ... he is inherently in himself in his own divine Being."[39] The radicality of the claim of the hypostatic union, "the indissoluble union of God and man in the one Person of Christ," is that God is Self-revealed in Jesus Christ, that what God is in Christ God is antecedently and eternally in God's in God's Self and therefore

---

[32]Ibid., 299.
[33]Thomas F. Torrance, *The Doctrine of Grace in the Apostolic Fathers* (Eugene, OR: Wipf & Stock, 1996), 29.
[34]Torrance, *Theological Science*, 299.
[35]Ibid., 344.
[36]Ibid., 288.
[37]Torrance, *Theology in Reconciliation*, 224; *Theological Science*, 340.
[38]Thomas F. Torrance, "The Deposit of Faith," *Scottish Journal of Theology* 36, no. 1 (1983): 2.
[39]Torrance, *The Christian Doctrine of God*, 99.

not hidden behind the back of as if utterly different in character and motivation from (and, for instance, free to withdraw God's gracious presence from creatures) Christ.[40] The aim of these claims is the protection of the integrity of revelation as revelation *of God*, of God's own *Self*, and the refusal to entertain the prospect of God turning God's back on what God does in Christ. That means that the doctrine of God can only have "its material content" with regard to Christ.[41]

Athanasius's theology of the *homoousion* is frequently appealed to in order to articulate a theology of God's Self-communicative "being-for-others" as the creative overflow of the eternal communion of the Triune "being-who-loves."[42] While Torrance admits the limitations and the relativity of the Nicene Creed, he does recognize that the Christological and pneumatic *homoousion* lends itself appropriately to reading the mutual coinherence, or perichoretic activity, of Son and Spirit eternally within the life of the irreducible relations of the mutual knowing of the three persons of the divine communion. In fact, "the *homoousion* is the ontological and epistemological linchpin of Christian theology."[43] Jesus Christ, then, cannot be envisaged as a moment in God's ways with the world, as one of several instruments. Rather, the *homoousion* allows Torrance to specify the ontological substance or content of revelation as the God-human life of Jesus Christ who sums up and fulfils all God's activities in the economy and thereby expresses the *a posteriori* move from the human performance of Jesus Christ to the ontological substructure that is meant by theology as discourse grounded in the God whose being is in God's action. Consequently, Torrance reasons, "what God communicates to us is not something of himself but his very Self, true God from true God. In him the Revealer and the Revealed, the Giver and the Gift are of one and the same Being."[44] For this reason, Torrance speaks of Jesus Christ as being "the complete revelation of God to man."[45] By this is not meant an eschatological realization that has no excessiveness, no plenitude that remains to be grasped and responded to. Rather, the concept here serves as a way of providing a theological location—that *God*, without ceasing to be God, is in Christ irrevocably in such a way that Giver and Gift are one. Consequently, Torrance continues, Christ as the Word assuming flesh has "become the final Word of God to man and the one Mediator between God and man."[46]

Torrance, therefore, aims to identify and resist "the damage which dichotomous ways of thinking have done to our knowledge of God, not least to our knowledge of God in Jesus Christ. Their effect has been to detach Jesus Christ from God, to detach Jesus Christ from Israel, and to detach Christianity from Christ himself."[47] What Torrance calls "dualism," and rather too neatly and cavalierly sees as *the* difficulty underlying all that he theologically objects to, detaches the singularity of the simple and immanent God from God's economic Triune relationality; the love of the crucified Lord from the hidden God; the material from the spiritual so that modern thinking becomes naturalistically materialist in a mechanistic sense, and "the spiritual" takes on the private form of "a merely subjective

---

[40] Citation from Torrance, *The Ground and Grammar of Theology*, 160.
[41] Torrance, *The Christian Doctrine of God*, 110.
[42] Ibid., 104.
[43] Torrance, *The Ground and Grammar of Theology*, 160–1.
[44] Torrance, *The Christian Doctrine of God*, 21.
[45] Torrance, "Introduction: The Place of Christology in Biblical and Dogmatic Theology," 15.
[46] Ibid.
[47] Torrance, *The Mediation of Christ*, 11.

state of affairs"; God from the world so that God becomes at best a deistic idol and is regarded as an object over against all other objects by the subject of human knowing; "science and faith, [thereby] depriving faith of any objective or ontological reference and emptying it of any real cognitive content"; subject from object so that "the observing and thinking subject was thrown back upon himself as the one centre of certainty in a sea of doubt"; "thought and life, reason and behaviour, law and nature."[48] Put simply, such dualistic modes of thinking disrupt the movement of faithful thinking regarding the reality of the "very different biblical distinction between the Creator and the creature, and the freedom of the Creator to be present and active in his creation."[49]

As the ground and grammar of the created order itself, God's presence to the creature in Christ through the Spirit is what makes anything and everything articulatable, knowable, and rational. Consequently, Torrance develops a theological account of created nature and the natural knowledge of God, of thinking appropriately *kata phusin* (according to nature), "for the reality of God presses upon us everywhere in nature," even if Torrance consistently retains Barth's critical concerns about a distorted version of methodological "natural theology."[50] A problematic form of natural theology "came to the fore and flourished during periods in which dualist modes of thought prevailed in science and philosophy," and in which there was a significant "deistic breach between God and the world ... which made it all the more imperative for natural theology, if it was to exist at all, to throw a logical bridge across the gap to God."[51] By this, Torrance has in mind any *praeambula fidei* or efforts to reason to the divine object from rational self-reflection or cosmological-reflection that have not been reordered in and by grace, or presuppositions of theology that are "independent of or antecedent to its own operations."[52] It is clear from his account that "nature after all is dumb; she cannot talk back to us."[53] Only an unsophisticated reading of Torrance alongside Barth would set them against each other on "natural theology." For neither theologian can the natural order speak of God or be itself a transparent window onto divine things. Torrance insists:

> Such a logical bridge between God and the world, and indeed between being and statement, has now been comprehensively demolished, not just by the rigorous theology of Karl Barth, but by the profound revolution in logic that has taken place, in which it has been made clear that it is impossible to state in statements how statements relate to being, without resolving everything into statements.[54]

For Torrance, just as for Barth, the key is to put to nature questions that are appropriate to her, that the humble following of her answers refuses "to force our own patterns upon it" and "determine the shape and pattern of the universe," and those questions are formed through the creativity of God in and through the eternal Son manifest in the incarnate presence of the Word.[55] This is something the so-called natural theology cannot do,

---

[48] Citations from Torrance, "The Framework of Belief," in Torrance, *Belief in Science and in Christian Life*, 3; *The Ground and Grammar of Theology*, 27; *God and Rationality*, 8 and 4, respectively.

[49] Thomas F. Torrance, *Theology in Reconstruction* (London: SCM, 1965), 211.

[50] Torrance, *Theological Science*, 103.

[51] Torrance, *The Ground and Grammar of Theology*, 76, 85.

[52] Ibid., 90.

[53] Torrance, *God and Rationality*, 41.

[54] Torrance, *Preaching Christ Today*, 44.

[55] Citations from Torrance, *Theology in Reconstruction*, 15, 16.

however, and accordingly it is called into question by the very substance of the doctrine of justification by faith. The reordering of the knowing subject in God's reconciling act implies that "justification puts us in the right and truth of God and therefore tells us that we are in untruth."[56] Without this, the attempt to know God through the natural order begins in a problematic subjectivity and ends in a form of obfuscation.

CREATURELY RESPONSIBILITY

A further and simultaneous feature of Torrance's account of divine Self-manifestation is that not only is God manifest in Christ to the creature, but the creature is exalted into communicative engagement with God so "that authentic knowledge of God is embodied in our humanity."[57] As Torrance urges—somewhat echoing the observations of Barth that Revelation involves the triadic logic of revelation as the coinherence of Revealer, Revelation, and Revealedness—"In the Hebrew idiom revelation implies not only the uncovering of God but the uncovering of the ear and heart of man to receive revelation."[58] Jesus Christ is at once the complete revelation of God to humanity and the correspondence on the latter's part to that revelation required by it for the fulfilment of its own revealing moment. In other words, in Christ is the gift of the giving God and the human reception he "adapts ... to receive and apprehend" in obedience, creating "in us the capacity to hear, recognize and apprehend Him, and evokes from us the consent and understanding of faith in His self-revelation."[59]

Crucial to this scheme is the hypostatic union, the Chalcedonian refusal to confuse the natures so as to confess the integrity and inseparability of Jesus Christ as simultaneously God's accommodating Self-manifestation and the concretely perfect human response. The Son is the manifestation of God by "living out his divine life within our human life as a real human life," "creating communion between man and God."[60] In him, in the Head who has gathered up and embodied all things, creatures have responded with obedience to God.

It is into his humanity, and his eternal filial relation with the Father enfleshed in human form, that the Spirit of Christ unites human beings and that is properly what is meant by being *human*. Thus, Torrance maintains with Calvin, "there can be no true knowledge of man except within our knowledge of God" and specifically in the action of God in establishing humanity for communion with God.[61] The Self-giving of God entails an unreserved gift of "entry into the inner fellowship of his divine Life by allowing us to share in God's own eternal Spirit."[62] For this reason, Torrance operates with Athanasius's theo-logic of in the Spirit, through the Son, to the Father, and with the Nicene determination to accord full *homoousial* deity to the Spirit while refusing to separate the Spirit's agency from that of the Son's (even if they are appropriately distinctive in the nature of their operations). Accordingly, he opposes the "spiritualization" of the Spirit, a subjecting of the Spirit to

---

[56]Ibid., 162.
[57]Torrance, *The Christian Doctrine of God*, 1.
[58]Torrance, *The Mediation of Christ*, 20.
[59]Ibid., 22; *God and Rationality*, 21.
[60]Torrance, *Trinitarian Faith*, 55; "Introduction: The Place of Christology in Biblical and Dogmatic Theology," 13.
[61]Torrance, *Theology in Reconstruction*, 99.
[62]Torrance, *The Christian Doctrine of God*, 2; and especially *The Trinitarian Faith*, 54–6.

the human spirit so that pneumatic language becomes a way of speaking of subjective states and affections in religious self-understanding. The Spirit, no less than the Father or the Word, "cannot be interpreted in terms of immanent principles or norms within the creaturely processes."[63] Rather, Christology is the criterion by which the work of the Spirit is identified as being those of *God's* Spirit, and not the misreading of the identification of Spirit and church performance or the immediate interiority of the subjective individual, of "our own creative spirituality," and of "inward moral and religious states."[64] Consequently, Torrance provides a nod toward the controversial *Filioque* as, when properly interpreted, protecting the Christological shape of the non-independent Spirit whose "special function is thus to bring to completion the creative purpose of God."[65]

The direction Torrance's thinking takes here offsets to some degree any concern that he has construed theology through an epistemological overdetermination. For him, "knowledge of God" is not a formal epistemic matter to be addressed prior to the material demands of doctrine. Rather, it is entirely one with God's reconciliatory acts and is in fact their purpose. "Revelation does not achieve its end as revelation apart from reconciliation, for only through reconciliation can revelation complete its own movement within man, bringing out of our humanity the obedient reception of revelation which is an essential part of its very substance."[66] This set of claims indicates that for Torrance, revelation is itself more than epistemic, and he is able to draw on Michael Polanyi's account of participatory indwelling in order to support his claims concerning the participation of the knower in scientific knowledge, and on the operation of fiduciary frameworks of "tradition of convictions in which we participate" in the epistemic process. Revelation has to do with the disclosure of the loving presence of the triune God to that which God has freely created in order to unite it with God's communal life.[67] Any criticism of Torrance as reducing the theologic of the revelatory act and knowledge of God overextends itself and would require a more nuanced revision.

What might such a revised version of a concern with the epistemic sense of Torrance's account look like? One thing it might do is ask a question: What role does human agency have given the emphasis on the substitutionary nature of the vicarious humanity of Jesus Christ; on the human being who creatively forms, and under the conditions of sin remodels, human life as hearing and responding to God's Self-disclosure; and on the God who draws humanity into the divine communion in the Spirit? Language of *imposition* is particularly unfortunate in this regard: "We have to allow the Word in its obedient humanity to impose itself upon us, and allow ourselves to go along with it, to be led and guided and corrected in all our thinking and speaking so that it becomes our own."[68] The conjunction of "imposition" with "permission" language here suggests that the action of God through Christ in the Spirit is not coercive and therefore does involve human agency

---

[63] Thomas F. Torrance, *The School of Faith: The Catechisms of the Reformed Church* (London: James Clarke/New York: Harper & Row, 1959), xcvii.

[64] Citation from Torrance, *Theology in Reconstruction*, 242.

[65] Torrance, *God and Rationality*, 171. On Torrance's use of the *Filioque*, see John C. McDowell, "On Not Being Spirited Away: Pneumatology and Critical Presence," in *Ecumenical Perspectives on the Filioque for the 21st Century*, ed. Myk Habets (London: Bloomsbury T&T Clark, 2014), 167–84.

[66] Torrance, "Introduction: The Place of Christology in Biblical and Dogmatic Theology," 18.

[67] Citation from Torrance, "The Framework of Belief," 23.

[68] Torrance, "Introduction: The Place of Christology in Biblical and Dogmatic Theology," 31.

of judgment and willing. Just what an account that articulates more fully the material integrity of human agency looks like Torrance does not venture to say.

One way in which the integrity of real human agency is articulated is in terms of the use of imagery of noetic *discovery* and what he calls "respect for the objectivity of facts."[69] On one occasion he uses an oddly petrified geological image of a "stratified structure" in order to understand the levels of depth perception in the act of knowing God.[70] The point he attempts to make with this otherwise troubling image that he takes from Einstein and Polanyi is that the biblical and other creaturely witnesses really do speak of God in such a way as to resist reducing God's Self-revelation to "the spatio-temporal processes of this world."[71] Yet to conceive of this in terms of *strata* would be particularly and deeply problematic, something of a foundationalist image in its referential scope. In fact, this is a strange move for one educated by Barth, since for the latter the notion of the *event* of revelation was so theologically determinative. Torrance's talk of *structures* only serves to intensify the difficulty, and against this one needs to hear his critical caution that "theological dogmatics is not a closed, logico-deductive system of knowledge, but an open science, disciplined and controlled by a logic beyond our own minds, and therefore never relieved of the need for critical and positive reconstruction in the light of the truth as our minds become progressively open to it through appropriate inquiry."[72] The knowledge of God is not only dynamic, but each "level" does not sit sequentially on top of any other since they overlap with, and indeed interpenetrate, the others. A theology of the revelatory act of God's through creatureliness cannot result in any "level" being left behind at any stage of the process of knowing, otherwise the highest level of the speakability of the knowing of God becomes a naked knowing of an ultimately unmediated revelation. If God gives God's Self to be communed with, that occurs in and through the constant creaturely mediation of God. The difficulty is that Torrance appears to slip into trying to solve epistemic problems set by the terms of divine-creaturely distance, and in so doing resorts to using ladder-level concepts to fill in the perceived epistemic gap while ensuring the clear authority of God's speech. "The outstanding characteristic of theology is that it operates with a direct act of cognition in *hearing* God and engages in the act of conception through *audition*."[73] Language of "directness" serves to ensure that it is *God* who is present, although it is less clear that Torrance actually consistently envisages this directness as being bound up with mediateness. As Rowan Williams warns, theology should not "be seduced by the prospect of bypassing the question of how it *learns* its own language."[74] Without a vigorous sense of the creaturely mode of the generation of revelatory reception, and the complexity of what that entails, theology slips into operating from robust modes of unchallengeable authority.

A further critical issue opens up here. On occasions Torrance actually bypasses this rather conceptually flat imagery by speaking not of looking deeper into, but rather of the *transparency* of the media of God's revelation, and therefore of the "intuitive knowledge" or "immediate experience of his personal presence."[75] This language functions to enact a

---

[69]Torrance, *Theological Science*, 288.

[70]Torrance, *The Christian Doctrine of God*, 83.

[71]Ibid., 82.

[72]Torrance, *God and Rationality*, 90.

[73]Torrance, *Theological Science*, 23.

[74]Rowan Williams, *On Christian Theology* (Oxford: Blackwell, 2000), 131.

[75]Torrance, *Theology in Reconstruction*, 84.

theology of witness, to pointing away from oneself. "We are not concerned ... with the human speech of the Bible as an independent theme of study, that is, with the humanity of the original witnesses in themselves, all of whom without exception point away from themselves to the Word of the Lord which has laid hold upon them and drawn them within its saving operation."[76] And yet, without significant qualification, this discourse is also problematic. It can too easily slip into construing the divine-creature relation competitively or in inverse proportion—that the creature decreases rather than increases in the context of the Self-presencing of God for faithful creaturely flourishing. If the creaturely media become transparent, then there is a danger of a kind of revelatory Docetism, a clothing that can be penetrated or that is, in the end, incidental to the divine manifestation. For this reason, Torrance has been accused of operating with an epistemically "frail concept of intuition."[77] Consequently, without explaining that it is the *sinful* self that has to be denied, Torrance declares that "to listen and deny ourselves, to listen and repent of what we want to make the Bible say, to listen in such a way as to let the Bible speak against ourselves, that is to listen indeed to the Word of God."[78] At least here the *metanoic* reference does suggest a context for the kind of self that has to be denied. But there is too little sense of the reconfiguration of the self here that self-denial involves a reordering of self with and for others. Does this imperil Torrance's account of human agency by rendering human beings as "the passive recipients of a self-evident truth"?[79] Certainly talk of God "bearing upon my experience and thought so powerfully that I cannot but be convinced of His overwhelming reality and rationality" can start to sound like it does.[80]

The problem is more evident in the conceptuality used in the following assertion: "Our great problem is that we are unable really to listen to the Word of God speaking in our own speaking, and it is our own speaking which is usually uppermost."[81] Here Torrance simply sets divine and human speaking over against each other, so that divine activity occurs through a non-corrupting transparency of human receptivity that is predicated on the non-constructiveness of human passivity. Moreover, this way of framing the relation of divine and human activity in the revelatory act does not pay sufficient rhetorical attention to the difficulty involved in failing to recognize that the biblical witnesses are themselves speakers so that there is no simple hermeneutical transparency involved in reading the texts. Pressing the rhetoric any harder will slip into a form of revelatory Docetism and that would undermine the very conceptual gain Torrance has made through the *homoousion*.

At least one way in which Torrance's account can theologically circumvent some of the concerns that it is prone to an unwitting competitiveness, setting two objects over against each other that displace each other from a circumscribed space, is in terms of the occasional apophatic reminder that refuses to objectify God. Despite all the revealing discourse and the imagery of transparency and of the church's need to be conformed to the form of the Word made flesh, as well as the coinherence of Father, Son, and Spirit,

---

[76]Torrance, "Introduction: The Place of Christology in Biblical and Dogmatic Theology," 29.

[77]Ronald F. Thiemann, *Revelation and Theology: The Gospel as Narrated Promise* (Notre Dame, IN: University of Notre Dame, 1985), 40.

[78]Torrance, "Introduction: The Place of Christology in Biblical and Dogmatic Theology," 30.

[79]Thiemann, *Revelation and Theology*, 40.

[80]Torrance, *Theological Science*, v.

[81]Torrance, "Introduction: The Place of Christology in Biblical and Dogmatic Theology," 30.

Torrance is convinced that there is an apophatic dimension to well-ordered theology, an inexhaustibility to theological "discovery." By this notion of divine inscrutability is not intended an absence of knowledge of God at the end of nature or reason's limits, as with Immanuel Kant, or a divine hiddenness that depends on separating the content of revelation from God's Being, but rather an excessiveness of divine presence that overflows the boundaries of the creaturely form and capacity. Therefore, he argues, "Apprehension is a grasping of God which does not exhaust His transcendent reality and mystery."[82] God's "inexhaustible Nature infinitely transcends all our thoughts and words about him."[83] Likewise, from a different direction, Torrance warns against an inappropriate Christic mythology or anthropomorphism which allows "us indiscriminately to read back into God all that we know of Jesus in the flesh," even if he does not offer reading rules for learning "how to distinguish what is properly anthropomorphic from what is improperly anthropomorphic in our knowledge of him."[84] The question has to be put, nonetheless, as to whether this element is given appropriate weighting in his doctrine of God. There is a robust confidence in Torrance's talk of God but is it sufficiently hesitant for a theology that recognizes the non-objectifiability of the eternally "unfathomable depths of the riches of and wisdom of God"?[85] He does recognize that dogmatics articulates the *eventfulness* of divine agency, and the free or gracious giving of God, and he also notes that in the revelatory act knowers "are summoned to repentance and are forced into ruthless self-criticism."[86] Yet the *continual* stammering of the theologian before the divine event is minimized or tacked on as something of an appendicized caution to his exposition.

Torrance, at least on occasion, admits the difficulty involved in recognizing the divine discourse, the complexity of providing a *faithful* interpretation. "The *lalia* of Jesus, His human speech, is ambiguous, and is not to be understood except in terms of the *logos* that utters it and stands behind it, but on the other hand there is no revelation of the *logos* apart from the human *lalia*."[87] Such a claim, however, appears less frequently than should be expected for one attentive to the subtleties of human perception as exhibited in the history of the debates over Christian belief. Likewise, Torrance admits that "we acknowledge that in itself, in its human expression, the Bible is word of man with all the limitations and imperfections of human flesh, in order to allow the human expression to point us beyond itself, to what it is not in itself, but to what God marvellously makes it to be in the adoption of His grace."[88] Even so, without substantive attention to matters of history and hermeneutics, it is not altogether clear how the Word speaks through the words, and in what ways, if any, the creaturely clothing actually *continues* problematically to shape the community of readers' hearing and judgment. The rhetoric is assertive in a way that flattens the complexities of creaturely realities "within the realm of contingent objectivity" and weakens the pole of the contingency in his talk of revelation's contemporaneousness in and through the "corporeality" of "earthen vessels."[89]

---

[82] Torrance, *God and Rationality*, 22.
[83] Torrance, *The Christian Doctrine of God*, 4. See also ibid., 108–9.
[84] Torrance, *The Ground and Grammar of Theology*, 163.
[85] Torrance, *The Christian Doctrine of God*, 74.
[86] Torrance, "Introduction: The Place of Christology in Biblical and Dogmatic Theology," 30.
[87] Ibid., 28.
[88] Ibid., 26.
[89] Torrance, *Theological Science*, 288; *Karl Barth, Biblical and Evangelical Theologian* (Edinburgh: T&T Clark, 1990), 105.

This concern is not abetted by other categories he tends to heavy-handedly adopt without significantly subtle description. Given the way that Torrance speaks of the Christological grounding of all things, that all things have their form in the God of Jesus Christ, and therefore are communicative products of God's Triune relations, his heavy dependence on interventionist, inbreaking, condescending, "downward motion," and revelatory or "epistemic bridge" concepts to describe revelation can disrupt the continuity and indivisibility of God's creative and revelatory work.[90] Of course the context for this least problematic rendering of these images is as ways of protecting the initiative of God's sovereign freedom, of the ontic distinction of God and creature, and of the forced discontinuities manufactured by the distorting operations of sin (in a kind of distorted nature against grace scheme). Even so, in the context of modern tendencies to objectify God and to therefore separate God and creature in such a way as to require bridging concepts, this approach requires particularly judicious handling. This is not helped by speaking of "the epistemological relevance of the Spirit."[91]

A second way for offsetting some of the potential for inversely construing the God-creature relation occurs in Torrance's account of God's revelation (since one of the prime dogmatic locations for appropriately construing the nature of the relations is in the doctrine of creation) as taking place through the "instrument conveying" revelation, or the "vessels bearing the treasure of revelation"—as the media for God in Christ's mediatorial action.[92] "Here revelation assumes certain men and incorporates them in revelation from their own side and incorporates them not as co-revealers nor as co-redeemers, but as recipients of revelation and as ambassadors of reconciliation."[93] This talk, of course, needs to pay attention to what is appropriate about these media, what it is that makes them media from their side, what characterizes them and their performance as "constituting ... a creaturely correspondence to His own Word"—otherwise the decisionistic co-opting talk sounds arbitrary and occasionalistic. The answer has to do with their obedience—"Just as we speak of His life in terms of obedience, so we must speak of the Bible as obedience to the Divine self-revelation, in which the human word of Holy Scripture bows under the divine judgment just because it is part of His redemptive and reconciling work."[94]

Consequently, he proclaims, "Dogmatic theology acknowledges that all our hearing and thinking of the Word of God is conditioned by our place in the Church."[95] In that regard, knowing is a communal and not an individualistically describable activity. Torrance is aware of the inheritance that shapes perception or hearing, and it is here that he advocates for dogmatics' critically interrogative role in the life and witness of the church.

> In all this, dogmatics is the instrument whereby the Church inquires whether its traditional teaching is in conformity with Christ, and is the means whereby as far as possible it is emancipated from the *Zeitgeist* which always threatens the thinking and teaching of the Church with historical relativity, and is the discipline whereby the

---

[90] Citations from Torrance, *Theology in Reconstruction*, 99; *The Ground and Grammar of Theology*, 165.
[91] Torrance, *God and Rationality*, 165.
[92] Torrance, "Introduction: The Place of Christology in Biblical and Dogmatic Theology," 25, 22.
[93] Ibid., 21.
[94] Ibid., 25.
[95] Ibid., 34.

Church is prevented from imprisoning the Truth in definitive dogmatic formulations of any age. Thus, the Church is kept ever open to the renewed understanding of Christ the Truth.[96]

Nonetheless, his sense of the history of doctrine to the Nicene Creed can appear too glibly progressivistic and therefore assertive rather than carefully argued. In fact, when he does appeal to the history of exegesis, he does so in the context of approving the Reformers' genealogical primitivism:

> The method pursued by the Reformers ... instead of adopting the Roman [Catholic] view of tradition that the truth of a thing is what has actually become of it in history, they traced the understanding of a thing back through history, and claimed to understand the errors of the present by seeing the actual steps taken in arriving at it.[97]

CONCLUSION

Even at their most rhetorically dense, Torrance's theological writings are shaped by an account of the knowledge of God that is remarkably consistent throughout and which manifests itself in a coherent flow from the confronting priority of the divine Subject manifesting God's Self to, and creating the conditions for the reciprocity and subjectivity from, the creature. It is this presence of God as free and sovereign lord to the creature in and through the mediatory earthen vessels that provides "the objective depth or the ontological density of dogma."[98]

Torrance is certainly concerned to ensure that dogmatics does not lose its moorings as a *creative* activity, a creaturely response to divine Self-revelation. In fact, when providing an account of the similarities of theology and other sciences he assures that "perhaps the first thing to be said is that theological science shares with the special sciences in being a *human inquiry*."[99] The emphasis he wants to provide here is not so much about the intelligibility of "its object" as about the integrity of the "rational investigation." Any account of the Self-giving of God in Christ, by the Spirit, as Self-objectifying object—subject of human knowing

> forces dogmatics to be a highly critical science in which all theological statements are to be severely tested to determine whether, in their correlation with the subject and in their claim to speak of God, Father, Son and Holy Spirit, they really do intend God, whether it really is Christ that they mean, and whether they really do distinguish the Holy Spirit from the human spirit.[100]

Whether Torrance has been successful here is not entirely clear.

---

[96]Ibid.
[97]Torrance, *Theology in Reconstruction*, 23.
[98]Torrance, *Theological Science*, 348.
[99]Ibid., 286.
[100]Torrance, *Theological Science*, 352.

CHAPTER TEN

The Importance of the Personal in the Onto-relational Theology of Thomas F. Torrance

GARY W. DEDDO

The most fundamental and critical elements of Thomas F. Torrance's theological understanding involve grasping the connection between the ontological, relational, and personal dimensions of revelation. Torrance is convinced that faithful Christian theology requires that the personal, biblically and theologically defined, qualifies every other theological term and concept. The personal characterizes the Christian apprehension of reality out of its Living Center, namely, the triune God revealed in Jesus Christ. For Torrance the personal, as disclosed in this Center, is central, regulative, and more fundamental than other key theological terms such as "being," "act" or "action," "ontic," and "relations." Thus, Torrance frequently uses the word "personal" to qualify these very terms. Overlooking this configuration of Torrance's thought will undermine full appreciation for what he has to offer and has led to confusion and misunderstanding among academics and those in pastoral ministry.

Furthermore, since so much Western theology works within frameworks in which these and other key theological terms and meanings are either disintegrated or understood in nonpersonal or impersonal ways, Torrance's theological synthesis centered in the personal constitutes a profound critique of both academic and pastoral theology.

No matter the current context, grasping Torrance's agenda and appreciating the depth of his critique and the scope of promise, whether within academic setting or church context, requires giving full play to the issue and significance of the personal, both divine and human.

PREREQUISITES FOR FOLLOWING TORRANCE'S THOUGHT

Following Torrance's flow of thought is demanding for several reasons—reasons not always appreciated and taken into consideration. First, it requires a comprehensive grasp of the whole of biblical material, that is, of what Torrance regards as the personal achievement of revelation accomplished by a personal God.

Second, following Torrance demands a willingness to critique both theological traditions and those of Western intellectual history. His critique, under biblical and theological constraint, searches deep into the foundations of Western habits of mind, both ancient and modern. Torrance does not just offer new ideas to think, but rather believes the biblical content and the reality to which it bears witness demand a certain frame of mind to apprehend. That frame of mind calls for critiquing and reformulating not only what we think but how we think, reflecting on the conceptual tools we use to think and talk about God or humankind.

Third, the challenge is even more demanding when one's own mode of theological reflection turns out to be dependent upon the conceptual framework that comes under Torrance's biblical and theological critique. It is never easy or simple to face the prospect of theological *metanoia*.

KEY RECONFIGURATIONS OF OTHER THEOLOGICAL TERMS

Torrance's consideration of the personal, as biblically and theologically disclosed, takes place at the center of a constellation of other theological terms such that it catalyzes their reconfigurations. That constellation of theological terms with the personal at the core characterizes the foundations of his thought. Within that larger constellation, the most important and challenging reconfiguration is Torrance's thinking together the ontic and relational. In Western philosophical or theological tradition being and relationship are assumed to be unrelated or even in opposition to one another.

Torrance's understanding of a proper theological synthesis requires us to regard relationships as essential to being, to what things are. Things would not be what they are apart from the actual relationships in which they exist. Relations are not accidental to what things are but are essential. In Torrance's words, the being of everything is "constituted by" the relations within which they exist. So, actual and particular relationships must be accounted for in order to know or understand what something or someone is and how, then, to rightly relate to what is. So, Torrance's theological framework is not simply relational, concerned about the quality of relationships things or persons have (e.g., ethics). Biblical revelation requires that we think "onto-relationally" to use the term Torrance had to coin to better communicate what he was meaning.

But if we are to grasp and follow Torrance, even onto-relationship must be further qualified. First, those "being-constituting" relationships are dynamic or interactive. What something is cannot be well understood and very easily could be misunderstood and mistreated if assumed to be static, fixed, or equated with timeless states of being. Rather, the interaction that takes place over time contributes essentially to what it is. What things are, in theological understanding, involves particular dynamic relationships, interaction, between things that are in some way ontologically distinct, or other. These relational dynamics *can* be transformative of the things or individuals depending upon what things are interacting.[1] For Torrance, assuming fixed, static, inert, mechanical,

---

[1] The uncreated immanent relations within the triune God must be differentiated from God's relationship with created things and from relations between created things. The nature of the things relating have to be accounted for in the interaction. So, the relationships are all dynamic and interactive and are comparable but not identical. The relationships are then analogical to each other. The ontic cannot simply be reduced to the relationship. The ontic aspect bears upon the relationship and the relationship bears upon the ontic. Both the onto and relational aspects must be preserved and not transmuted or dissolved by the other.

and causal relationships within the being of God, between God and God's creation, or between human beings, has a distorting effect upon Christian theological understanding and biblical interpretation.

Although the onto-relations must be grasped in a dynamic and interactive way, a further qualification is called for by biblical revelation and theological synthesis. The dynamic, interactive onto-relations must be regarded as involving *personal* dynamics and *interpersonal* interactions when referring to God and/or human persons. These onto-relations are inherently interpersonal. This personal framework then rules out understanding God and persons, their being, acting, relating, and interacting, in impersonal ways. This reconfiguration has enormous implications for academic theology as well as pastoral ministry and the Christian life and mission.

With this introduction we will now explore in more detail the personal aspect of Torrance's Christian onto-relational theology.

THE NORM OF THE PERSONAL, JESUS CHRIST, HIMSELF

The norm that regulates and orders Torrance's understanding and articulation of what it means to be a person or to be personal is the revelation of God in the incarnate Son of God, Jesus Christ. So, the norm is not an *a priori* definition, not even a theological definition, but the reality of the living God present, active, and revealed in Jesus Christ. The Incarnation and Trinity provide the ultimate foundations for Torrance's theological understanding. So, Torrance repeats throughout his writings that the triune God revealed in Jesus Christ is alone truly personal. Discovering what a person is takes place by knowing, having fellowship with, being in real relationship with this God. When we are in active relationship with this God we are coming to know the truly and ultimately personal. Torrance puts his conviction succinctly: "In the strictest sense God alone is Person, for he is a fullness of personal Being, and as such is the creative Source of all other personal being."[2] And perhaps even more sharply Torrance avers: "The one Being ... of God must be understood as intrinsically and intensely personal."[3]

How we come to know God as being personal is not through speculation or subjective intuition, religious or mystical experience, but most directly through the person of Jesus Christ, which would include his teaching about himself. "By drawing near to us in Jesus Christ who took our human nature upon himself and lived out his divine life within it as a human life, God has opened up to us knowledge of his innermost Self as a fullness of personal being and brought us into intimate personal communion with himself as Father, Son and Holy Spirit."[4]

Giving full consideration to the revelation that took place through the personal presence of Jesus and his self-interpretation leads to the discovery of the ultimate source of what is truly personal, namely, the Persons of the Trinity. "If the one Being of God is identical with the Communion of the three Divine Persons and the Communion of the

---

[2] Thomas F. Torrance, "The Soul and Person, in Theological Perspective," in *Religion, Reason and the Self: Essays in Honour of Hywel D. Lewis*, ed. Stewart R. Sutherland and T. A. Roberts (Cardiff: University of Wales Press, 1989), 116.

[3] Thomas F. Torrance, *The Christian Doctrine of God, One Being Three Persons* (Edinburgh: T&T Clark, 1996), 121. Cf. Thomas F. Torrance, *The Trinitarian Faith: The Evangelical Theology of the Ancient Catholic Church* (Edinburgh: T&T Clark, 1995), 230.

[4] Torrance, *The Trinitarian Faith*, 65–6.

three divine Persons is identical with the one Being of God, then we must think of the one God as a fullness of personal being in himself."[5] Torrance presents the full picture when he brings three terms together: "Hence it may be said that the Being of God is to be understood as essentially *personal, dynamic and relational Being.*"[6]

Torrance readily recognizes that the Reality of God will always exceed what we can say about God in creaturely words, concepts, ideas, metaphors, poetry, narrative, and so forth. So, if the church is to articulate a doctrinal norm for its preaching, proclamation, teaching, counseling, and public witness, then its aim will be to find and use words that most faithfully point to the same reality as does the irreplaceable norm of the words of biblical revelation which bear witness to the truth and reality embodied in Jesus and his word to us.

EARLY CHURCH THEOLOGIANS AND THE PERSONAL

Torrance alerts us to the fact that the early church had to take up this very task as it sought to offer a faithful articulation of apostolic revelation in its own cultural, intellectual, and religious context. As a result, according to Torrance and a host of others, most notably Greek Orthodox theologian John Zizioulas, a radically new understanding of persons, divine and human, entered the stream of human history.[7]

The focus of the early church's wrestling was in finding words and concepts that had adequate meaning when used to refer to the person of Jesus Christ and his relationship to God. His absolutely unique relationship to God as a human person/being eventually led to an astounding apprehension of God being personal, rather than being impersonal, immobile, abstract, or merely conceptual. This understanding was in great contrast to all Hellenic philosophical notions, often echoing Aristotle's notion of the Unmoved Mover.

> On the other hand, the doctrine that in Jesus Christ God's own eternal Logos had personally become man within space and time shattered all forms of cosmological dualism, whether Platonic, Aristotelian or Stoic, which did not allow for any interaction of God with the empirical world. It undermined the impersonal or merely quasi-personal modes of thought that had characterized Hellenic religion, philosophy and culture, and gave rise to the distinctive category of the person which had hitherto not been reached even within the Hebraic world of thought.[8]

HEBRAIC ROOTS OF THE GOD WHO IS PERSONAL

The revelation of God in Jesus Christ indelibly confirmed that the one and only God of the universe worshipped by the Hebrew people was in being, personal being. Ultimate being and source of all being was disclosed as personal.

---

[5] Torrance, *Christian Doctrine of God*, 161.

[6] Ibid., 124. Emphasis in original.

[7] See John D. Zizioulas, *Being as Communion: Studies in Personhood and the Church*. Contemporary Greek Theologians Series Number 4 (New York: St Vladimir's Seminary Press/London: Darton, Longman and Todd, 1985). While Torrance did not agree with Zizioulas on all matters, such as the essences/energies distinction and his ecclesiology, they did both affirm the personal nature of God being brought out by key Patristic theologians in great contrast to prevalent Hellenistic notions.

[8] Torrance, "The Soul and Person, in Theological Perspective," 103–4.

This affirmation was not of course alien to Hebrew understanding. The entire account of Israel's relationship to their God, the God of all Creation, involved a history of interactive relationship. Yahweh's interaction with his people, while not at all identical to them, still most closely resembled the personal, dynamic, and interactive character of human relationships, even of the most intense, intimate, and so personal kinds of relationships that human beings can have with one another. The height of this revelation before the advent of Jesus Christ was God's interaction with Moses, when the God of Abraham, Isaac, and Jacob named and gave the self-description and self-identification as "I am who I am" as recorded in Exodus 3:14. Torrance also notes that we find this also in Isaiah.[9] This event itself represents an intensive personal interaction of God with a human person in personal terms, concerning the sharing of God's unique personal identity.

Indeed, Jesus himself made use of this self-same self-identity with his "I am he" and "I am" declarations.[10] Taken together these revelations solidified the church's approach to this God as a personal Subject, a Who, an "I." These defining interactions point to a God who is a Self, who is self-determining, and who is self-existing. They also cohere with the fact of God's self-revealing and self-giving character demonstrated throughout Israel's history.

So Torrance summarizes:

> This emphatic reiteration of the "I am" of Yahweh found not only in these citations from Isaiah but throughout the Old Testament Scriptures, reinforces for us the fact that the one Being (μια οὐσία) of God must be understood as intrinsically and intensely personal—even, it may be said, apart from the "I am" of the Lord Jesus, although the oneness between the "I am" of Yahweh and the "I am" of the Lord Jesus makes it quite impossible for us to think otherwise of the Christian use of *ousia* than as essentially personal. The Being or "I am" (οὐσία or Ἐγώ εἰμι) of the Lord God is the ultimate divine Source of all his personal and personalizing activity through Jesus Christ and in the Spirit, God himself acting personally in the Lord Jesus and God himself acting personally in the Lord the Spirit.[11]

Torrance notes other key elements in the Hebrew apprehension of God that anticipate the final and most personal element of God's self-revelation in Jesus Christ. A whole constellation of Hebrew terms indicate the personal characteristics of God's relationship to Israel and through Israel to all the nations: *hesed* (love), *berith* (covenant), and *tsedeq* (righteousness). These characterizations of relationship found throughout the Hebrew Scriptures are often brought into correspondence with one another and so mutually condition their respective meanings, ones that ultimately point to the God who is "I am who I am," or, alternatively translated, "I am who I will be." Because they apply to God specifically they also are applied to Israel and to human relationships because God and his people are bound together in his covenant love.[12] Hebrew life is intrinsically life in personal relationship.

---

[9]Isa 43:3, 11.

[10]Some examples are "I am the way, the truth and the life." "I am the resurrection and the life." "Before Abraham was, I am."

[11]Torrance, *Christian Doctrine of God,* 120–1.

[12]Thomas F. Torrance, "The Doctrine of Grace in the Old Testament," *Scottish Journal of Theology* 1, no. 1 (1948): 58, 62.

NEW TESTAMENT INTENSIFICATION OF THE PERSONAL

In the New Testament writings, Torrance identified a corresponding indicator of God's personal involvement with human persons. Key to the mission and ministry of Jesus Christ is the work of his person identified by the verb *katallasso* and the noun *katallage*. These are usually translated "to reconcile" and "reconciliation." Reconciliation is what characterizes in the most personal way what Christ has done for us. Torrance notes that this word is exclusively reserved for the particular interaction that takes place between human persons and between God and his human creatures. It involves peace and love and also justification or atonement in the sense of being reunited (becoming at-one).[13] A seemingly more intensive expression builds on that key term, namely, *apokatallasso* found in Ephesians 2:13-16 and Colossians 1:19-22.[14] Torrance summarizes:

> Reconciliation thus concerns the personal relation between God and man. It is a two-sided relationship but in this, the side of man is subordinated to the side of God. It is God himself who forms anew the relation between himself and humanity—the human part is to accept this reinstatement, this reconciliation, and so Paul in Romans speaks of "receiving atonement or reconciliation (*katallagen*)."[15]

Another fascinating indicator of God's personal relationship with his people is the Hebraism "face to face" (פָּנִים אֶל־פָּנִים). This image is also picked up and carried forward in the New Testament writings using the Greek word *prosopon* (προσοπων). For example, "The LORD would speak to Moses face to face, as one speaks to a friend" (Exod. 33:11); "And there has not arisen a prophet since in Israel like Moses, whom the LORD knew face to face" (Deut. 34:10); and "For now we see in a mirror dimly, but then face to face. Now I know in part; then I shall know fully, even as I have been fully known" (1 Cor. 13:12).

All these personal–relational descriptions coalesce and find their fulfillment, their source, and their embodiment in the incarnation of the Son of God, Jesus Christ. Here we have the most personal, intense, and direct revelation of the nature and character of God that is not a projection of the human, but sets a norm above it and for it; a *sui generis* revelation. "He who has seen me has seen the Father," declares Jesus (Jn. 14:9). Jesus is "Emmanuel, God with us" (Mt. 1:23). The Father is working and so is the Son (Jn. 5:17). To know the Son is to know the Father (Jn. 14:7). To believe in the Father is to believe in the Son whom he sent (Jn. 12:44). He is "from above," we are "from below" (Jn. 8:23). He is Lord, we are not (Jn. 13:13). The Father has life in himself and the Son also has life in himself (Jn. 5:26). He, Jesus, alone has the Spirit without measure (Jn. 3:34). He is the one through whom all things came into existence and through whom all things are upheld (Heb. 1:2). He is the one mediator between God and humankind (1 Tim. 2:5). He alone knows the Father and makes him known (Mt. 11:27). He is our life, our wisdom, righteousness, sanctification, and salvation (1 Cor. 1:30). We only come to the Father through him (Jn. 14:6). He has and sends us God's Holy Spirit in the name of the Father (Jn. 15:26). Torrance rehearses all these pronouncements made by Jesus himself, and

---

[13] Thomas F. Torrance, *Atonement: The Person and Work of Christ*, ed. Robert T. Walker (Downers Grove, IL: IVP Academic/Milton Keynes: Paternoster, 2009), 142–4. Torrance references Romans 5:8-11 and 2 Corinthians 5:14-21.

[14] Ibid., 144.

[15] Ibid., 142. Cf., Rom. 5:11.

more, and goes on to incorporate teaching by the New Testament writers who bear him authoritative witness to the distinct and personal aspect of Jesus's relations to us.

An additional aspect of the intensively personal presence and activity of God in Jesus that Torrance returns to again and again is that the Word of the Lord of Israel is Jesus himself, the Logos or Word of God. The God revealed in Jesus Christ is a speaking, communicating, and self-disclosing God. Such revelatory speaking manifests intensely personal elements of interactive and interpersonal relationship. Jesus is the "eloquence"[16] of God through whom God creates and through whom God redeems. Such redemption and reconciliation then necessarily involve true revelation, the communication of the truth about God, the faithfulness of God. Salvation means reconciliation *and* revelation, not one without the other. But both of these involve in-depth personal interaction and self-disclosure.

Torrance sums up the acutely personal nature of the Incarnation:

> In him as the incarnate *Ego Eimi* of God himself, Person, Word and Act are uniquely and indivisibly one, interpenetrating and coinhering in one another. Thus, Jesus Christ meets us as One whose Word and whose Act coincide with the living reality of his Person, and whose Person is not other than his Word or his Act, for his Person is intrinsically Word and Act, while his Word and Act are never impersonal but always intrinsically personal. He is in Person identical with his Word, his Word is itself his Act, and his Act is the power of his Person.[17]

Not only in Word and Act has God related to humanity, but in and through a particular, individual person, rather than through a book, through magic, subjective experiences, aesthetic imagination, realizations achieved through contemplation of impersonal features of nature, mathematics, or philosophizing. There is no greater personal means for God to meet humanity.

> In the Incarnation the Son of God became one particular and individual Man, for that was the way in which He entered into relation with all men in the flesh. Hence in the new economy of the Covenant determined by the Incarnation the relations of God with all men are relations through this one Man, Jesus. That is to say, the relationship of God with every man is acutely personalised through personal and historical relation to Jesus.[18]

GOD'S PERSONAL RELATING HAS A PARTICULAR PERSONALIZING EFFECT

As in Jesus we have the acute personalisation of all God's ways and works with mankind, so in Jesus we must think of the *autoexousia* of God incarnate operating in an intensely personal and personalising way, that is, never by impersonal command or detached

---

[16]Torrance, *The Trinitarian Faith*, 131.

[17]Thomas F. Torrance, "The Trinitarian Foundation and Character of Faith and Authority in the Church," in *Theological Dialogue between Orthodox and Reformed Churches*, 2 vols., ed. Thomas F. Torrance (Edinburgh: Scottish Academic Press, 1985), 1, 90–1.

[18]Thomas F. Torrance, "The Mission of the Church," *Scottish Journal of Theology* 19, no. 2 (1966): 134.

deed, but always and only in such a way that he is immediately and personally present in his word and act with the undiminished *Ego Eimi* of his divine-human Being.[19]

Jesus Christ was sent by the Father in the Spirit to bring about both a reconciliation of mind and a reconciliation of persons in relationship. The alienation of human beings from God affects both, so both must be renewed and redeemed from the captivity of the deceptive and relationship-distorting power of sin. So, the ministry of Christ, as Torrance typically frames it, involves both revelation and reconciliation. Not only are bodies (so to speak) disobedient but so are minds. While some distinction can be made, they are not separated. Persons are whole and spiritual regeneration involves whole persons—mind, soul, and body. So, receiving the revelation of God in Christ affects the whole person. A person cannot stand apart from the revelation since the revelation comes in a personal form, Jesus Christ, with the intent of reconstituting the person addressed. This dynamic can be seen in Jesus's encounters with particular persons and groups in the New Testament. Torrance sums this dynamic up:

> Moreover, since as Father, Son and Holy Spirit God is a fullness of personal Being in himself and the transcendent Source of all personal being, all his actions toward us in making himself known are intensely personal …. God interacts personally and intelligibly with us and communicates himself to us in such a personalising way or person-constituting way that he establishes relations of intimate reciprocity between us and himself within which our knowing of God becomes interlocked with God's knowing of himself. Thus, unlike anything that is found in natural science, there is a two-way relation between the different levels that obtain in theological knowledge, initiated by God, informed by his personal address to us in his Word and sustained through the presence of his Spirit in our personal response to his Word.[20]

GOD'S ADDRESS OF LOVE IN JESUS CALLS FOR PERSONAL RESPONSE

The core of Jesus's teaching is about himself and about his unique relationship to the Father and so about his unique place in the redemptive work of the Father. This work expresses not only his heart but the personal purposes of the Father and the personal mission of the Spirit. Behaviors that Jesus addresses serve as signals indicating the direction of a person's personal relationship with God. In this way none of Jesus's actions, whether doing or speaking, are impersonal. This is why Torrance often calls Jesus's interactions "encounters." They set up a personal crisis—as to how persons will respond to the encounter—by receiving what Jesus is offering or by rejecting it and him. No one is the same after being addressed by Jesus.

While the personal is multifaceted, Torrance is clear that what is centrally personal about God and about God's dealings with his human creatures is that it is characterized by God's own kind of love. This is a love that creates, sustains, and renews relationships in what is true and good. God's love is never separated from what is true and what is good for life as God knows or judges. God's love is for his creatures, but that means it is against

---

[19] Torrance, "The Trinitarian Foundation and Character of Faith and Authority in the Church," 80.

[20] Torrance, *Christian Doctrine of God*, 88.

what is against them with the same intensity. Jesus judges what does and doesn't lead to right relationship and life according to the good purposes of God. He judges or discerns or sorts out what-is-what in order for those he loves to not enter into condemnation, the consequences of the sin and evil that destroys life and hates the truth.

So, the New Testament writers, Torrance points out, had to find a word and fill it with particular meaning to make it serve as an adequate pointer to God's kind of love. Our love is not the norm or standard, but God's love is. And that love is shown us not only in Jesus's relationship with us but most profoundly and clearly in Jesus's relationship to the Father (and the Spirit), who has loved him from before the foundations of the creation. And that word was *agape*.

Here is a snippet of what Torrance has to say on the topic of love being personal.

> At the same time, the perfect oneness of the Being of God with his Loving, and the fact that the reciprocal relations between the Father, the Son and the Holy Spirit are the onto-relations in virtue of which they are who they are, mean that loving activity and personal being must be understood to qualify and define one another. This has the effect of deepening and reinforcing the theological concept of "person", and "personal", not only in respect of our understanding of the Father, the Son and the Holy Spirit as Persons in relation to one another, but in respect of our understanding of the Triune God as a fullness of personal and loving Being in Himself. In the Communion of the Holy Trinity the Father is Father in his loving the Son and the Spirit, and the Son is Son in his loving of the Father and the Spirit, and the Spirit is the Spirit in his loving of the Father and the Son. It is as such that the love that flows between the Father, the Son and the Spirit, freely flows in an outward movement of loving activity toward us with whom God creates a communion of love corresponding to the Communion of Love which he ever is in himself.[21]

Further:

> It is only in the light of the unsparing self-giving and the intimate self-revelation of God to us in Jesus Christ his beloved Son that we come to know the Nature of God the Father as Love, the transcendent Love with which he loves himself and which is the inner movement of his eternal Being, the Love with which he loves the Son and the Son loves the Father, out of which his love flows freely and unstintingly toward us. We do not think of God as the eternal Being who also loves, but of God's very Being as Being who loves and of God as he who is Love. It is in terms of that eternal unoriginated fatherly Love that we are taught to think of God the Father as the Almighty or Omnipotent Creator.[22]

And the nature, quality of that love is paradigmatically demonstrated and enacted in the atoning work of God in Christ:

> And, what is more, it is only in the light of the atoning sacrifice of Christ on the Cross and of his triumphant resurrection from the dead for our sakes, that we may really begin to understand what it means for God to be Lord of our existence, as the Lord over life and death, over being and non-being, and over the future as well as over the

---

[21] Ibid., 166.
[22] Ibid., 139.

past and the present. The one eternal God and Father of our Lord Jesus Christ, is our God and our Father through him.[23]

The Love of God is a threefold love originating in the very being of God among the Triune Persons, extended to us in Jesus Christ, and then lived out among his people for the sake of the world as a witness to the glory of the Trinity. Full weight can be given, then, to John's witness that "God is love" (1 Jn. 4:16).[24]

THE PERSONAL ELEMENT IN EARLY CHURCH CREEDS

Torrance gives significant consideration to the development of doctrine, especially in the early church. His aim is not so much to engage in historical theology but to retrieve for the benefit of the church today the best the early church had to offer. So, Torrance's treatment is critical, selective, and nuanced. The doctrines and pivotal terms Torrance traces out were central to some of the most influential theological writings of the first six centuries, prominent in early church debate, and are found in the early ecumenical creeds. Torrance demonstrates that the eventual consensus achieved around several of these pivotal theological terms all bring to the fore the personal aspects of God's onto-relational nature and corresponding personal and interactive relationship with creation and human persons.

The first and central term is *homoousios*.[25] Through a tumultuous and long process, the consensus indicated that Jesus was both of identical being with God, the Father, the uncreated Creator of all and of identical being with us, created human beings—the double *homoousios* (as per Chalcedon). This term captured the idea that Son of God remained what he was in his very divine and uncreated being (*ousia*) while assuming the created being (*ousia*) of human creatures.

The fact that God's redemptive purposes, both revelational and reconciling, took this personal form revealed that the very *being* of God was compatible with personal human being. They can exist and be personally related in the very direct and personal form of Jesus. God's being, although uncreated and the source of all being, is, then, not antithetical to personal-created being.

But this coexistence of divine and human being in the Son incarnate, crucified, resurrected, and ascended also meant that human being could have an abiding reality, an ontological status that mirrored or shared in God's real being. Real relations are intrinsic to the essential being of the uncreated triune God and to the created human being. This revelation disclosed God to be more personal than previously imagined in any recognized religion or philosophy and that humans have a far greater abiding ontological existence and reality than previously assumed, especially in contrast to Hellenistic religion or philosophy. In Aristotelian, Platonic, or Gnostic frameworks that which is mortal, changeable has no abiding reality, like the interchangeable masks worn by Greek actors (*prosopa*, persons) representing different characters. Under the impress of the Incarnation, crucifixion, resurrection, and ascension of Jesus the Son of God, the very notion of the personal was transfigured, gaining a sense of an abiding reality, having ontological status.

---

[23]Ibid., 139–40.

[24]Although we cannot switch the subject and predicate and say that "love is God," for that is an entirely different claim, a rather impersonal and abstract one.

[25]Torrance, *Trinitarian Faith*, 215, and the Nicene-Constantinopolitan Creed.

But the double *homoousios* was not worked out independently nor did it serve alone. It became a keystone, but not the whole bridge, in the early church's thinking. The term *hypostasis* and its adopted cousin, *prosopon,* were incorporated into the norm of the church's faith (as per Chalcedon). We now translate these with the English word "person." The real being of the Son was best regarded as having real personal (hypostatic) subsistence in relationship to the Father from all eternity. Father and Son were to be regarded as distinct in their personhood, that is, in their hypostatic nature (*hypostaseis*) and united in their being (*ousia*). This was summed up in the consensus statement that eventuated: God is one in Being (*ousia*) and three in Person (hypostasis). They were not three beings nor was God rightly understood to be one Person. But the fact that the Being of God was regarded as being constituted by three "persons" indicated and backed up what was revealed in the Son. God is truly personal. The being of God was not less personal than the Persons.[26] The ontic unity of God was a triunity of three Persons. The Father was personal in the way the Son was and the Son was personal in the way the Father was. Later it was explicitly elucidated that the Spirit was eternally real, distinct, and personal as well.

That the eternal Son of God could assume a created human personal existence as well in the incarnation called for further clarification about his eternal personhood. The consensus came to be that the Son's person, *hypostasis*, was best understood as having two natures, a divine nature and a human nature. The ontological and personal nature of the Son was thereby further recognized and secured.

When speaking of the Son's Person (*hypostasis*) in connection with the incarnation, an alternative term often used was *prosopon*. In its ordinary nontheological context *prosopon* (person) meant the mask worn by an actor in Greek theater that indicated a temporary role taken on in the drama. The mask had no abiding reality. In growing recognition that the Person of the Son constituted a real being standing out (*hypo-stasis*) in relationship to the Father, a radical degree of abiding reality had to be granted the meaning of *prosopon* that was absent in the regular use of the word.

The eternal Person of the Son who had from eternity his personhood while sharing in the one divine nature along with the other Divine Persons had also taken on or assumed a human nature, the nature common to all human beings. The Son was truly and originally Person in relationship to the Father and also in relationship to human nature or being. And that relation extends, in Torrance's view, to the assumption of not only our fallen condition, but also to assuming to himself our fallen natures so as to rescue it from evil and sanctify it in himself.[27]

The consensual way to put this all together was to say that the Son remained what he was while also adding to his Person human nature in such a way that there was only one Person, the eternal Son of God, who had two natures. In this way the personal nature of the Son was thereby protected but was also reinforced. The Personhood of the Son was real and abiding and eternally possessing the shared divine nature. And by the incarnation human being was affirmed as being of abiding and real personal significance. Neither divinity and personhood nor humanity and personhood were opposed or incompatible.

The relationships between two natures were also clarified. The two natures, divine and human, should be regarded as unconfused, undivided, not separated, nor changed

---

[26]Torrance, *Christian Doctrine of God*, 161.
[27]Thomas F. Torrance, *Incarnation: The Person and Life of Christ*, ed. Robert T. Walker (Downers Grove, IL: IVP Academic/Milton Keynes: Paternoster, 2008), 208.

(as stipulated by Chalcedon). In this way the two natures were joined in the one Person while remaining truly distinct. There is an abiding difference between the being of God and human beings, but there is a compatibility in that both are rightly identified as being personal and so able to engage in interpersonal relationship. God is personal in a divine or uncreated way and humans are personal in a human or created way. But both are able to somehow be together in the one Person of the Son.

Further than this the early church did not take the formal debate. How this could all be, in the eternal being of the Trinity and in the person of the Son, was regarded as a mystery that could not be rationalized especially in terms of human-created realities. The formal doctrines were upheld in part because they protected the mystery. They went far enough to feed the understanding faith sought and to guard against the erosion of trusting faith and worship by contrary teaching. But some questions remained.

Torrance believes that other terms that became available but which were never incorporated into any ecumenical creeds could be vitally helpful—in particular, the *anhypostatsis* and *enhypostasis* couplet.[28] Notice that it involves the *hypostasis*, the person, of the Son. Torrance takes this up and refines it from its original early church use to bring out even more fully the personal nature of the onto-relations of God with human persons in the Person of the Son.

Torrance believed that further advance could be made by making more explicit what is implicit in much of the early church's consensual understanding of the personal nature of the divine and human person. A term circulating in Christian teaching that had this potential was *perichoresis*. This term was first used to elucidate the relationship between the two natures in the one person of the Son incarnate. But it was later brought over into the discussion of the relations between the divine Persons. What comes to the fore with the incorporation of this term into the larger constellation of concepts is the dynamic nature of the relationship between the trinitarian Persons. The root meaning is "to envelop each other" or "to make room for each other." More commonly *perichoresis* is translated "mutual indwelling" or "co-inhering" and sometimes "interpenetrating." This word best elucidates the "I am in the Father and the Father in me" expression of Jesus (Jn. 14:10-11). It also brings together the interactive, dynamic, and reciprocal nature of persons in relationship. This captures well the revelation given by Jesus that there is true personal interaction within the triune life and being, namely, a knowing, glorifying, and loving before there ever was a creation.[29] *Perichoresis* points to the absolutely unique kind of unity with plurality that the Trinity is. It serves as an interpersonal onto-relational concept in the doctrine of God.

Torrance recognized the significant overlap of the theological meaning of *perichoresis* with the biblical emphasis on "union" with Christ brought about by the fellowship and communion (*koinonia*) of the Spirit. They both expressed a personal and dynamic interaction between God and persons that brings about a fruitful harmony in relationship. This kind of interpersonal relationship is most concretely demonstrated in the biblical understanding of the nature of the Body of Christ. Through baptism by the Spirit into Christ, individual members are incorporated into the Body of Christ. United with Christ, the individuals do not become the Head of the Body, and the Head of the Body does not become members. The distinction of persons is maintained in the *koinonia* of the Spirit.

---

[28] Ibid., 228–32.

[29] See Jn. 17:14; Mt. 11:27; and Jn. 17:15.

Like *perichoresis*, union with Christ neither fragments members' real unity with Christ nor dissolves their real personal distinction.

PERICHORESIS AND TORRANCE'S TERM "ONTO-RELATIONAL"

Torrance's synthesizing the foundational and normative biblical material with subsequent theological reflection, which reached a high point in *perichoresis,* brought Torrance to the place where he needed to find a more adequate way to refer to the unique union and communion of the Triune Persons which would also counter misleading non-dynamic and/or non-relational ways of understanding of God's being. Referring foremost to the intra-trinitarian relations, he coined the word "onto-relational."[30] Since the divine Persons have their being by being in relationship with one another, being and relationship must be brought together to refer adequately to the eternal being of God which consists of eternal relations. The triune relations, at least, must be given ontic status since they are intrinsic to the kind of being that the Trinity has. The being of God is not without relations and the relations of the Trinity are "being-constituting relations."

Torrance recognized that so often the connotation of "being" is static and not dynamic nor interactive. And the connotation of "relationship" is arbitrary, accidental or non-essential, subjective, and transient or ephemeral. Uncorrected habits of mind operating in this framework most often promote an understanding of "being" held apart from relationship and of relationship held apart from being. Such a non-relational understanding of God's being has never been completely eradicated from much of standard church teaching down through the ages. So, the more standard or default understanding of the being of God has remained largely non-dynamic, static, and fixed in the theology of the church. God's interaction with his creation is often conceived as establishing or even causing states of being rather than fostering a dynamic, interactive, personal relationship. This remained the case even while the church continued to proclaim as orthodox the abiding reality of the three divine Persons and of the one Person of the Son who assumed also a human nature to himself. In Torrance's view this problem had to be addressed. Its understanding of the one triune God fell short of the reality to which the biblical revelation pointed and also had a detrimental effect upon every church doctrine and the church's lived faith, worship, and mission.

Torrance's "solution" was to bring together and coordinate or synthesize on a biblical basis the theological understanding captured by the terms *ousia, hypostasis, persona,* and *perichoresis.*[31] With help from his concept of onto-relations, Torrance brings together the ontic, interactive, relational, and personal dimensions of the triune God and the Trinity's relationship to creation. But the central element of his constructive work is the personal nature of the onto-relations of the Trinity and between the Trinity and humanity. Persons,

---

[30]See Gary Deddo, "The Realist and Onto-Relational Frame of T. F. Torrance's Incarnational and Trinitarian Theology," *Theology in Scotland* XVI Special Issue (2011): 105–33, and "T. F. Torrance: The Onto-Relational Frame of His Theology," *Princeton Theological Review* XIV, no. 2 (2008): 35–47.

[31]He saw Calvin taking some steps in this direction but not fully or even consistently working it out. Karl Barth's work was the next notable breakthrough that Torrance also drew upon although the impetus he gained from his teacher H.R. Mackintosh is notable. Torrance critically engaged and borrowed from an astounding range of Christian thought found throughout its history, although he gave primary consideration to the biblical foundations and those formulations of early church teaching that built on them.

divine and human, have their being not just by being in a relationship but by being in a *personal* relationship. Human life is to mirror divine life and even ultimately share in it by having its being in interpersonal communion.

THE PERSONAL AND ONTO-RELATIONAL GOD–WORLD RELATIONSHIP CONTRA DEISM, PANTHEISM, PANENTHEISM

Torrance recognized that these positive theological developments exerted particular resistance against both deistic and pantheistic/panentheistic ways of understanding the God–world relationship. Both deism and panentheism assume a rather impersonal, mechanical, and generic relationship between God and the world.

A deistic approach regards God's relationship being indirect and mediated by what is not God, for example, natural laws, evolutionary principles. God may be assumed to be of a personal sort, but is not personally present and active, remaining transcendently separated. Creation is viewed as a largely autonomous mechanism of independent cause and effect interactions. There is no need for personal divine interaction, whether or not there is such a Personal God. In this frame, such direct and personal interaction has been construed as a violation of creation!

A deistic framework fosters or manifests many impersonal ways of relating to God. It may express itself through attempts to bargain with God. Such bargaining often involves looking for contractual arrangements that can mediate the relationship with God including legally defined ways. Relationship with God is thereby managed through mutually agreed conditions or legally described mutual obligations. "If I do this for you God, then I can count on you to do that for me? Right?" It can also foster a relationship where God is approached as a means to human ends. The first and last question is, then, what's in it for me? or, how can I get the most out of a relationship with God? God, if useful at all, is treated as a means to help humans realize their own independently conceived ideals or ends.

THE PERSONAL, ONTO-RELATIONAL GOD–WORLD RELATIONSHIP CONTRA CAUSAL DETERMINISM

Impersonal approaches can also take the form of assuming that God does interact with creation—by being the cause of everything, by exercising meticulous control. This can lead to a kind of Christian determinism or fatalism. Some welcome this impersonal view, while others react against it. Doctrinal expressions can range from causal notions of the election of individuals to the imposition of a "blanket" universalism.

Torrance counters both these forms of determinism largely on the basis of their involving causal and impersonal relations that set aside the true nature of God revealed in the person and personal work of reconciliation that calls for personal response.

Contrary to deistic assumptions, the God of the Gospel does not remain at a distance, uninvolved, disinterested, untouched by his creation—only interacting with it indirectly through the use of tools, instruments, means that don't involve God's own self. Rather, God is involved in a history of relationship that reaches back to creation itself, through the history of Israel that culminates in the incarnation and will reach its ultimate fulfillment in the consummation of the Kingdom of God with Christ's personal return. God has taken a personal interest in the history of the world but also in each and every individual person.

Contrary to deistic assumptions, the God of Jesus Christ is personally and directly involved with his creation without ceasing to be God. God, as God, is personally present to his creation through the Son and by the personal presence of the Spirit. The full meaning and intensity of that interpersonal relationship is fostered within a proper personal-onto-relational understanding not only of the Incarnation but of the subsequent presence of the Holy Spirit as depicted in the New Testament.

On the other hand, Torrance's personal-onto-relational understanding resists being subordinated to the assumptions of a pantheistic or even a panentheist understanding that amounts to an identity or fusion of creation with God. In those cases what is personal and particular is largely lost in the ontic overlap of divine and created being. There is little if any room for any personal interaction with God, since interaction is concentrated within the general, generic, impersonal, and automatic mechanisms embedded in Creation, although attributed to or identified with God.[32] While providing a universal framework for the God–world relationship, it is one that is relatively impersonal, abstract, generic, and deterministic. Some will find security in such an assumption, but the cost is great and in Torrance's view incompatible with Christian faith and worship.

THE PERSONAL, ONTO-RELATIONAL GOD–WORLD RELATIONSHIP AND GRACE

The ultimate loss even in the panentheistic framework is the dissipation of God's real, actual, personal, particular, free, dynamic, and unconditioned *grace*. Without ceasing to be God, the God of grace relates with and interacts with his creation, personally and particularly. This is the significance of God's anointing and electing purpose. The God of covenant grace relates to particular persons and peoples that in the end does reach out to all—but not by means of generic tools, instruments, or on the basis of universal principles. The personal God of Israel and the Church chooses, decides, acts, and interacts in a personal way with particular persons and peoples at particular times and places establishing reciprocal personal communication and ongoing relationships.

When God's grace is amalgamated into nature and the outworking of its intrinsic potentials (its *entelechy*), then the personal, deliberate, liberating, freeing, and transforming nature of God's grace is lost. Creation then doesn't require a personal intervention of a deliberate action that creation itself couldn't accomplish itself, given its inbuilt potentialities—perhaps operating by the infusion of God's spirit generally present throughout it. Creation then is self-redeeming. No costly grace is needed; no alien righteousness need be given. The decisive, personal, particular relationship of covenantal grace is unnecessary. The personal and particular and responsive dimensions of relationship are lost—and in the end God's grace has evaporated.

---

[32]The personal and particular aspects of relationship between God and creation are lost in both pantheism and panentheism, even if in the latter view God and creation is said not to be coterminous.

EVIL, SUFFERING, AND THE PERSONAL, ONTO-RELATIONAL GOD–WORLD RELATIONSHIP

Assuming an ontological continuity of creation with God also has great implications for how evil and suffering will be understood. In this scheme, evil and suffering will be viewed and resolved by the affirmation of universal impersonal principles operating generically throughout creation. This, as Torrance notes, is a form of determinism and constitutes a rationalization of evil.[33] Suffering and evil will be regarded as a "natural" aspect of the development of creation and/or human freedom and so be to some degree intrinsic and necessary to God's purpose and nature. Evil and suffering, although perhaps in the end left behind, will be a necessary means to the end of that potential perfection of a developing creation and in some views an evolving God. The ideal end of the universe self-justifies the evil and suffering experienced along the way.

Evil as well as suffering becomes to some degree rationalized and self-justifying. The future may hold out a better ideal, but the past remains bloody and broken. In the pantheist or panentheistic view there is no need for a personal inbreaking of God to undo, rework, and redeem creation making all things new. The past remains what it was, serving at best as a justified means to a possible greater final end.

SALVATION IN JESUS CHRIST IS PERSONAL, SELF-GIVING, AND SELF-REVEALING

The Gospel of grace is a very different story because it involves a personal and particular God interacting personally and particularly with his creation, through personal and particular relationships, individual and corporate. It is not a story of self-salvation, self-justification, or of the ends justifying the means, potentially or actually. The personal element of the onto-relational story is highlighted for Torrance in the saving work achieved by the Person of the Son incarnate. For this saving work involves a personal self-revelation and a personal self-giving. God himself in the person of the Son is our Lord and Savior. God did not send someone or something else to accomplish that work. The New Testament brings out the personal nature of God's saving relationship with his creation and creatures by speaking of this self-giving.[34] The early church acknowledged this with the Nicene *homoousion*. God is our savior, not a creature. A favorite way Torrance likes to express this truth is that the Gift of God is God the Giver. The Gift and the Giver are identical. God does not give divine stuff, substances, states of being, but gives himself for us and our salvation. This is supremely represented in the self-giving nature of love taught and exhibited in person by Jesus: "This is my commandment, that you love one another as I have loved you. Greater love has no one than this: to lay down one's life for one's friends" (Jn. 15:12, 13).

---

[33]Torrance delivers the same critique of limited atonement and double-predestination which are acts generated from the sheer will of God imposed upon creation. Being causal they are deterministic. The sovereign will of God is not grasped in the personal and particular terms of Christ. See Thomas F. Torrance, "Universalism or Election?" *Scottish Journal of Theology* 2, no. 3 (1949): 310–18.

[34]See Tit. 2:14; 1 Tim. 2:6; Gal. 1:4; 2.20; and Eph. 5:2, 25 for the phrase "gave himself."

THE PERSONAL QUALIFICATIONS OF ONTO-RELATIONS BY JESUS CHRIST

There are many other ways that Torrance brings out how the personal qualifies the kind of onto-relations involved between God and humans in Jesus Christ. We can touch on only a few and very briefly.

Only persons can relate to one another by means of promise-making and keeping. Covenant making and keeping is the prominent biblical form of this kind of interaction. Relationships involving this dynamic involve freely choosing, deciding, and giving in particular by one person to another. It involves personal trust and hope in the fulfillment and the exercise of faithfulness. An impersonal, generic, and mechanical interaction cannot generate such a covenant relationship. But the God of covenant love does just that, at a level that involves our very being. The God of grace is true to his Word, true to his promises, true to his covenant—because of his faithfulness. This is a faithfulness enacted first and foremost in Jesus culminating in his resurrection from the dead.

Only persons can engage in personal *self*-disclosure and *self*-giving that contribute to personal relationship forming, growing, sustained, and renewed—this is what we find enacted in Jesus, first in relationship to the Father and then in relationship to us. An impersonal tool, instrument, law, method or technique, concept or ideal cannot accomplish this.[35] The personal nature of such an exchange requires freedom to truly give and receive in a way that contributes to relationships of love.

Such personal relationships of promise, self-disclosure, self-giving all in freedom involve deliberating, deciding, intending, choosing, and purposing. These are other dimensions of the personal that qualify the kind of onto-relations that lie at the root of Torrance's theological synthesis.

And finally, such personal relationships require personal communication in truth and faithfulness. Personal interaction, when most personal, includes words deliberately spoken to disclose to one's own particular inner thoughts, concerns, intentions, motivations, purposes, and responses to another person who can receive them. And such personal disclosures are often meant to facilitate ongoing interaction and the harmonization or repair of relationship so that the free interchange of the gifts of self-disclosure and self-giving might increase. Communication of this personal sort engenders response, true interaction. The relationship engendered by such communication is not simply one way but reciprocal. It is open-ended, responsive, not controlled, or predetermined. The result, when realizing its purpose, is a rich *history* of relationship with a memory and a hope for fulfillment.

JESUS, THE PERSONALIZING PERSON

Such personal relationships are not static, fixed, mechanical, and causal. In fact, the dynamics of such interactive personal relationship contributes to what Torrance calls "personalizing." Through them we become more personal, able to be and relate on a more and more personal basis. The source of personalization is God through Jesus Christ,

---

[35] See Karl Barth on the basic form of humanity being mutual speaking and hearing, seeing eye to eye, serving one another freely and gladly. Barth, *CD* III/2, 250–4. Both Barth and Torrance refer to Buber's work, *I and Thou*. See also Gary W. Deddo, *Karl Barth's Theology of Relations: Trinitarian, Christological and Human*, 2 vols. (Eugene, OR: Wipf & Stock, 2015).

for he is the personalizing Person and we, in personal onto-relationship with him, are personalized persons.[36] Such relationships are personally creative, transforming, renewing, sanctifying, and ultimately glorifying. In such relationships there is a real becoming what we could never be (ontically) without the personal gift exchange characteristic of God's relationship with us in Christ and by the Spirit. Such relationships, as Torrance so often repeats, are person-constituting relations.[37] They are, in a word, particular expressions of God-like love (*agape*), full of grace and truth, mirroring and participating in Jesus's onto-relational relationship to the Father and Spirit and the intra-triune relationships themselves.

CONCLUSION: THE PERSONAL DISCLOSED IN JESUS QUALIFIES EVERY DOCTRINE

For Torrance the personal as disclosed in Jesus qualifies every doctrine of the Christian faith: Trinity, Jesus Christ, the Holy Spirit, creation, providence, covenant, atonement, reconciliation, election, salvation, the Kingdom of God, providence, glory, evil, and final judgment. The personal qualifies every aspect of the Christian life: birth, rebirth, repentance, forgiveness, justification, sanctification, glorification, reconciliation, faith, hope, love, being the church under the Word of God, the worship and mission of the church. Without the personal infusing each doctrine at its root, each will inevitably be shaped by relatively impersonal, static, fixed, mechanical, deterministic, or deistic assumptions. As a result, Christian worship, faith and obedience, and mission will fail to bear as faithful a witness as it might to the truth and reality of the triune God revealed in Jesus Christ in words and deeds, in the academy, in our communities and world.

---

[36] "We must remember that in all his healing and saving relations with us Jesus Christ is engaged in personalising and humanising (never depersonalising or dehumanising) activity, so that in all our relations with him we are made more truly and fully human in our personal response of faith than ever before. This takes place in us through the creative activity of the Holy Spirit as he unites us to the perfect humanity of the Lord Jesus conceived by the Holy Spirit, born of the Virgin Mary and raised again from the dead," Thomas F. Torrance, *The Mediation of Christ: Evangelical Theology and Scientific Culture*, 2nd edition (Colorado Springs, CO: Helmers and Howard, 1992), xii.

[37] "God interacts personally and intelligibly with us and communicates himself to us in such a personalising way or person-constituting way that he establishes relations of intimate reciprocity between us and himself within which our knowing of God becomes interlocked with God's knowing of himself," Torrance, *The Christian Doctrine of God*, 88.

CHAPTER ELEVEN

Thomas F. Torrance and the Trinity

CHRISTOPHER R. J. HOLMES

Torrance says many helpful things about divine things. His corpus provides a rich platform for exploring theology proper, that is, the doctrine of God. In this chapter, I take up his well-known text, published in 1996, *The Christian Doctrine of God, One Being Three Persons*.[1] This book presents the fullest vision of Torrance's theology proper. We see in it three important themes that I shall address. First, Torrance unites theology and economy. Second, he reworks venerable terms like "being" and "person" in light of "the transformed meaning they are given within the doctrine of the Trinity itself."[2] Third and last, he explicitly anchors trinitarian doctrine in Christology. In what follows, I unfold these themes, offering along the way a few judgments as to what is and is not profitable in them.

Torrance begins his subtle account of the doctrine of God by reminding the reader that the "truth of Holy Trinity is more to be adored than expressed."[3] This is important. There is nowhere in Torrance's presentation where one gets the sense that he stands above the subject matter. Instead, there is a doxological spirit at work in his writings. We must be alert to the deep spiritual dimension of the doctrine of the Trinity. The very Being of God speaks to us and acts "upon us in an intensely personal way."[4] Torrance calls this *theopoiesis* or *theosis*, meaning "we humans are admitted to an intimate sharing of what is divine."[5] This is not to say, however, that our nature as humans "is deified through what might be called *theotic actuality*."[6] We do not become God but are rendered transparent to God. Accordingly, Torrance recognizes the self-involving character of trinitarian reflection, again its spiritual character. Our faculties are to be mortified and vivified by the Being and Act about which we write. We are personally addressed by the object at hand.

This point helps us to understand the tone of Torrance's work. It is edifying theological scholarship. For Torrance, theology proper is not about inhabiting Scripture and the best of the tradition for their own sake. Rather, trinitarian theology is about attending to them so as to describe the One whose self-revelation saves and renews all humankind.

---

[1] Thomas F. Torrance, *The Christian Doctrine of God, One Being Three Persons* (Edinburgh: T&T Clark, 1996).
[2] Ibid., xi.
[3] Ibid., ix.
[4] Ibid., 42.
[5] Ibid., 96.
[6] Ibid., 95 n. 52.

THEOLOGY AND ECONOMY

We move, now, on to our first theme: the relation of theology and economy, who God is in himself, antecedently and eternally, and who God is in relation to us, who are not God. We pursue this first because it reflects Torrance's commitment to a robustly *Christian* doctrine of God, one that has the doctrine of the Trinity at its center. Torrance argues that who God is in himself is what he is toward us in Jesus Christ. The Gospel is not only grounded in God's inner life but is demonstrative of God himself. In a programmatic statement, Torrance writes, "The economic Trinity and the ontological Trinity overlap with one another and belong to one another, and can no more be separated than the Act of God can be separated from his Being or his Being from his Act."[7] Note, first, how Torrance identifies the economic Trinity with the ontological Trinity; and second, how Torrance does not make space for the doctrine of the one God over and against, say, a Thomas Aquinas, for whom the one essence of God is treated in advance of the Trinity of persons. Note, last, how God's divine nature is expounded by his evangelical activity. The good news is disclosive of God's very self. Revelation has the character of *self*-revelation by Jesus Christ and in the Holy Spirit. The burden of Torrance's trinitarian theology is to show how in Jesus, the incarnate Word and the Spirit God's very self is communicated: again, revelation as self-communication.

Having said that, are we to think that Torrance does not in any way *distinguish* the economic from the ontological Trinity? By no means: there is oneness and also distinction between economy and theology. If so, how do we speak responsibly of that oneness and distinction? Here Torrance introduces a key concept, the *homoousion*. "The *homoousion* expresses at once the distinction and the oneness between the incarnate Son and the Father, so it enables us to speak both of the distinction and of the oneness between the economic and ontological Trinity."[8] What is he saying? In terms of the distinction between the immanent and economic, we know the Trinity through encountering, in faith, the incarnate Son. The truth to which Torrance is gesturing is that the Trinity (the threeness of the three) is known via the revealed oneness of the three. The distinction between the incarnate Son and his Father is not only economic but also ontological. Once again, however, we are talking about distinction and not separation. In coming to us, the incarnate Son does not cease to be who he has always been, God. God acts as man in his beloved Son by the power of the Spirit.

Stated differently, the two main concerns of the doctrine of the Trinity are distinction and oneness. This is an ontological matter, and such matters must be rightly handled, epistemologically speaking. Ontology concerns the *homoousion*. Without the *homoousion* in play, the distinction and oneness of the three, as well as the relationship between the economic and immanent, will remain opaque. The *homoousion* is the hermeneutical key. Without it, the doctrine of God will at best remain sub-Christian. The *homoousion* is the key to understanding the inseparability of God's Word and Act, toward the inside and the outside. Word and act are, to use some technical language, intrinsic "to the self-subsistence of his Person."[9]

Given Torrance's antipathy toward Greek—read dualist—forms of thinking, his embrace of the *homoousion* may at first seem quite surprising, perhaps even unsettling,

---

[7] Ibid., 8.
[8] Ibid., 30.
[9] Ibid., 40.

given its provenance in Greek metaphysics. What is important to note is that it is not for Torrance the term itself that is significant. Rather, what is significant is the adaptability of the *homoousion* to the truths presented to us in Scripture. Torrance calls this "thinking realities through statements."[10] We are able to apprehend via the *homoousion* something of the reality of the three in their hypostatic interrelations. These interrelations are not at any remove from God's personal being. Put differently, when it comes to Jesus and the Father and their Spirit, there exists an essential and substantial relation. The three are equal in being; one being is common to them, and so there is an "unbroken relation in Being and Act between Jesus Christ and God the Father."[11] The gift of the *homoousion*, writes Torrance, is such that it encourages articulation of this "unbroken relation ... upon which the whole substance of the Gospel finally depends."[12]

Crucial to note so far is the conditioned character of theology proper. Theology remains theological only insofar as the life, death, and resurrection of Jesus Christ, in fulfillment of the promise made to Israel, determines our thinking. Torrance does not think that what happens to Jesus determines his being. Instead, Jesus's being is revealed to us via his life, death, and resurrection. Indeed, Torrance is after an ontology that is transparent to the Gospel—hence his formulation of *homoousion*. But again, the expression *homoousion* does not stand on its own. It is serviceable to the Gospel only in so far as it enables the church to affirm that God is in himself what he does among us. If the *homoousion* is not amenable to wonder, prayer, and praise of the God we meet in Scripture, then it is not sound doctrine.

Torrance uses the turn of phrase "stratified structure" to unpack the relationship of the doctrine of the Trinity to "evangelical experience."[13] Trinitarian doctrine builds upon—it does not impose upon—the events of the Gospel. Its function is pedagogical, helping us map the relation between who God is for us in Jesus Christ and who God is in his inner life. Indeed, we see that there is no gap between the two. The doctrine of the Trinity does not refer us to itself but rather to events, to the fulfillment of covenant promises that are demonstrative of God as God is in himself. In Torrance's words, we "advance from the evangelical and doxological level of intuitive knowing to the explicitly theological level."[14] We use a word like *homoousion* not so as to betray "evangelical experience" but rather to clarify what that experience communicates regarding *theo*logy. The *homoousion* encourages recognition of three "objective self-identifying Subsistences" as true of "God's Being and Activity."[15]

Another technical term that helps us elucidate this "stratified structure" is that of *perichoresis*. The doctrine of the Trinity uses this term so as not to obviate "evangelical experience" but to show that such experience rests upon and assumes "the identity of the divine Being and the intrinsic unity of the three divine Persons."[16] Furthermore, *perichoresis* does not simply work at the ontological level but at the economic as well. What is true of God in relation to us is true of God as one who transcends us: each dimension is inseparable from the other. There is profound *homoousial* relation with

---

[10] Ibid., 44.
[11] Ibid., 72.
[12] Ibid.
[13] Ibid., 83.
[14] Ibid., 94.
[15] Ibid., 92.
[16] Ibid., 102.

respect to theology and economy, and the content of that intimacy is the Word made flesh. That said, Torrance is at pains to remind us that "we cannot think of the ontological Trinity as if it were constituted by or dependent on the economic Trinity."[17] The economy reveals and thus does not impact in any way, shape, or form the ontological Trinity.

The doctrinal heresies Torrance thereby avoids are tritheism and modalism. Tritheism exaggerates their personal differences while modalism ignores them. Following Greek Fathers such as Athanasius and Gregory Nazianzen, Torrance insists that "God really is indivisibly and eternally in himself the *one indivisible Being, three coequal Persons* which he is toward us."[18] Torrance's language of "*personal being*" is in the service of showing us this indivisibility. When it comes to the Trinity, ontology and revelation are one and the same, though, as we have seen, they unfold each other. To talk about Yahweh's Being, as we must, is to talk about how "Being and his revealed being are one and the same."[19] What he becomes in relation to us is demonstrative of, as Torrance says in *The Doctrine of Jesus Christ*, the fact that "he *is* first and eternal Father, Son and Holy Spirit in himself alone."[20]

The epistemological consequences of this are many. Chief among them, as we are noticing, is that key Greek terms like *homoousios* and *perichoresis*, come to mean different things than their Platonic, Aristotelian, and Stoic predecessors intended. They become, in Torrance's charged words, "radically 'un-Greek.'"[21] Torrance is not against forms of thought that sound Greek. What he is against, however, is any sense in which we can know God apart from God's self-determination as disclosed in the Gospel. It is the Gospel that teaches us to speak of *ousia* as denoting personal being. Here we see the Gospel reworking terms in ways that are original, surprising, and subversive. The Gospel demands that we say that God in his very being is an "intensely personal Communion."[22] To be sure, Torrance's concern is, ultimately, pastoral. He is sensitive to the moral and ecclesiological consequences of God's "*personal being*," namely, that "in worshipping and praying to each Person we worship and pray to the whole undivided Godhead, *one Being, three Persons*."[23]

One of the motifs present in Torrance's theology proper is Communion. Though each divine person is wholly and truly God—God the Father, God the Son, and God the Spirit—there exists perfect Communion among the three. The three "are in themselves" Communion.[24] Communion is not something they create; it is, rather, what they are. Not surprisingly, the soteriological consequences of the Communion motif are prominent. We are through the power of the Holy Spirit united to Christ in whom we participate in the Communion of the three: Father, Son, and Holy Spirit. The mediator, Jesus Christ, unites in his one Person divinity and humanity. His union of the two in his one Person is, as Torrance notes, an "atoning union."[25] The Lord Jesus assumes our fallenness in order to restore it from within his personal being and act for us and for our salvation. It is through that union that we share in the Communion of the three. That sharing is our salvation.

---

[17] Ibid., 108–9.
[18] Ibid., 115.
[19] Ibid., 116.
[20] Thomas F. Torrance, *The Doctrine of Jesus Christ* (Eugene, OR: Wipf & Stock, 2002), 107.
[21] Torrance, *The Christian Doctrine of God*, 128.
[22] Ibid., 133.
[23] Ibid., 134.
[24] Ibid., 148.
[25] Ibid., 144.

Torrance's strong doctrine of the Holy Spirit comes to the forefront in his unfolding of the Communion motif. He describes the Spirit as, for example, "the freedom of God to actualise his relation with us." The Lord God is free in the person of the Spirit to be our God. Furthermore, the Spirit is "the freedom of God to actualise our relation with himself."[26] We are not free in and of ourselves, but only in the Lord, who is the Spirit. Again, Torrance thinks that we cannot render ourselves continuous with God. It is the Spirit—and not we ourselves—who actualizes the reconciliation that Christ effects for us. The Lord relates us to himself in the Spirit. The Spirit, in other words, acts among us as he acts in God, binding us to the Father through the Son. This is what the Spirit does as the love of the Father for the Son and the Son for the Father.

The Godhead is completely present in the Spirit, as is the case in the Father and Son. Though the Spirit proceeds from the *being* of the Father, the Spirit is no less God because the Spirit is from another, and the Father is not more divine because the Father is from no one. Rather, their relations one to another belong to them as persons. The Spirit's procession is not extrinsic to who the Spirit is. The Godhead is completely in the Spirit as one who proceeds. Once again, the *homoousion* comes into play. The *homoousion* reminds us that the relations between the Spirit and the other two persons are real, essential, true of God's personal Being *in se*. The three radically indwell one another constituting thereby "the Communion of Love or the movement of reciprocal Loving which is identical with the One Being of God."[27] The Spirit, following Augustine, is, not surprisingly, as the heart of this Communion as the Love of the first person for the second person and the second person for the first person. As such, the Spirit coexists with and in-exists in the Father and Son and the Son and the Father. Their relations are *homoousial*. Their oneness is displayed in their communion for the three are, inseparably, one.

Although my interest in this chapter is Torrance's theology proper, it is worth noting how Torrance draws upon the tradition in constructing his theology proper. Torrance is indeed a theologian of the church catholic. He quotes Augustine and Hilary when it comes to the Latin west and liberally cites Athanasius and the Cappadocians when it comes to the Greek east. Interestingly, when it comes to unfolding the implications of the *homoousion*, it is Cyril of Alexandria who wins the day. Of Cyril, Torrance notes "he brought together the emphasis of Athanasius upon the one Being of the homoousial Trinity with Gregory Nazianzen's conception of an indivisible but internally differentiated Trinity of real hypostatic relations continuously and actively subsisting in the Godhead."[28] Cyril recognizes, following Athanasius, that one Being is common to the three; God's Being is personal Being. What Cyril also recognizes, following Gregory Nazianzen, is that God's Being is "internally differentiated." The three are really three; their relations are real, indeed internal to the one divine essence itself. The relations of the three one to another are not extrinsic to them but "real hypostatic relations." Their relations, moreover, as Cyril realizes, do not minimize what is unique to each but rather become the basis for their unity. The perichoresis of the three is not a speculative matter but rather has deeply soteriological implications. The one God shows us to be who he eternally is in his saving self-revelation in the Son and Spirit. To use a quite technical term, their interrelations, on display as it were in the economy of salvation, are "onto-relations."[29] There are not

---

[26]Ibid., 152.
[27]Ibid., 165.
[28]Ibid., 171–2.
[29]Ibid., 173.

any persons behind their relations. Likewise, their relations just are the Godhead. So for Torrance: "Each Person is in himself whole God of whole God."[30]

The Cyrilian imprint of Torrance's theology proper is not also without its Athanasian and Cappadocian imprint. As is well known, Torrance is a fan of Athanasius (especially) and of Gregory Nazianzen. What they help us recognize is that God is an undivided whole. Each "Person is a 'whole of a whole.'"[31] This is again not to take away or detract from the strongly personal distinctions within the life of the triune God. Noteworthy, and in keeping with Torrance's doxological approach, is his appreciation of the Cappadocians sensitivity toward the doctrine's impact upon "spiritual life and worship."[32] There is no sense in which these quite precise concepts negate the impetus to worship and give thanks. Rather, these precise concepts interpret the economy of salvation, unfolding thereby the soteriological consequences of the *homoousion* as applied to God's action in the economy.

One of the very great strengths of Torrance's doctrine of God begins to emerge at this point. As with Barth, Torrance is set against reading back elements of the divine economy into the divine life. A strict asymmetry must be maintained between them: theology and then economy. The divine life is the wellspring of the economy and is not impacted by it. When it comes to Christ's suffering, Torrance notes that it "cannot be read back into the eternal hypostatic relations and distinctions subsisting in the Holy Trinity."[33] Torrance honors the independence of God in relation to all that is not God. At the same time, Torrance insists that Christ's incarnate life "falls within the life of God and that his passion belongs to the very Being of God."[34] He is not suggesting that the being of God is passible, that God is impacted by his passion. His passion, rather, is revelatory of his being.

This is a salutary move, but Torrance (as with Barth) does not always practice it as consistently as he might. This is seen, for example, in his warm comments on Jürgen Moltmann's book *The Crucified God*, which first appeared in German in 1968.[35] Torrance praises Moltmann for articulating the "identity between the almightiness of God and the weakness of the Man on the Cross."[36] Torrance writes, furthermore, "What even could be more astonishing, and utterly new even for God, than *God crucified and risen again*?"[37] Torrance applauds Moltmann's articulation of the trinitarian dimension of the cross. Moltmann's "insistence upon this is one of the merits of … *The Crucified God*" though Torrance also insists that Moltmann's "somewhat tritheistic understanding of the unity, rather than the oneness, of the Father, the Son and the Holy Spirit … damages this insight."[38]

---

[30] Ibid., 174.

[31] Ibid., 179.

[32] Ibid.

[33] Ibid., 180.

[34] Ibid., 246.

[35] Jürgen Moltmann, *Der gekreuzigte Gott*, ET. *The Crucified God: The Cross of Christ as the Foundation and Criticism of Christian Theology*, trans. R. A. Wilson and John Bowden (Minneapolis, MN: Fortress Press, 1983).

[36] Torrance, *The Christian Doctrine of God*, 215.

[37] Ibid., 238.

[38] Ibid., 247. We could add to this his warm endorsement of the equally problematic work by Alan E. Lewis, *Between Cross and Resurrection: A Theology of Holy Saturday* (Grand Rapids, MI: Eerdmans, 2001). Torrance describes it on the back dust jacket as "the most remarkable and moving book I have ever read." This endorsement is strange given the fact that Lewis directly buys into some of Moltmann's most problematic ideas. I think Torrance was expressing his appreciation for someone dying of cancer to be able to write a book like that. But that endorsement is indeed puzzling. I sincerely doubt that Torrance would agree with Lewis that God is on his way toward becoming who he will be by relating with us. In fact, he explicitly rejects that idea by insisting that God's becoming refers only to the fact that God is a living God.

Frankly, I do not know how to hold together Torrance's insistence that we "cannot read back" onto the divine life Christ's suffering and his enthusiastic embrace of Moltmann. Moltmann's influence upon Torrance is felt when Torrance writes that "we cannot but think of the saving passion of Christ as internal to the Person of God the Son become man."[39] We must be careful here. When Torrance says "internal," he means that the Son takes our sin into his own personal being thereby overcoming it. As Torrance writes in *The Trinitarian Faith*, "Thus we may say of God in Christ that he both suffered and did not suffer, for through the eternal tranquility of his divine impassibility he took upon himself our passibility and redeemed it."[40] Indeed, Torrance does not confuse the processions of the persons—that whereby each is—with their missions—what each is in relation to us. Rather, Torrance, unlike Moltmann, resists the notion that the economic Trinity has a retroactive effect upon the immanent. Torrance recognizes that the Son, as very God, "has stooped to take upon himself our passion, our hurt and suffering, and to exhaust it in his divine impassibility."[41]

Furthermore, Torrance holds on the one hand that "God is impassible in the sense that he remains eternally and changelessly the same." Yes and amen. On the other hand, he argues "we cannot but hold that God is passible in that what he is not by nature he in fact became in taking upon himself 'the form of a servant.'"[42] This may seem to indicate Moltmann's triumph. Quite the opposite, thankfully: Torrance insists that the God who exists impassibly in perfect love and freedom becomes passible for us as our Savior. The Son of God who became flesh for us, taking the form of a servant, does not cease to be the Son of God and therefore impassible. His taking the form of a servant does not diminish his impassibility. In his one person, he unites humanity and divinity, without confusion and change. His great condescension shows us the depths of his impassible being. Even under the opposite—the cross—he remains himself, the eternally begotten Son of the Father. His mission does not impinge upon his eternal person. As Torrance notes, the Lord "brought his *serenity* ... to bear redemptively upon our passion."[43]

BEING AND PERSON

Another point that is somewhat mystifying in what is, overall, a profitable unfolding of theology proper, is Torrance's chastisement of the Cappadocians for championing "the uncaused Person" rather than "Being" of the Father as the source of divinity.[44] While this is not the place to contest the rigor of Torrance's reading of the Cappadocians, I wonder whether he is being too critical of them in arguing that they rob "*ousia* of its profound *personal* sense," a sense "that was so prominent at Nicaea," by emphasizing the Person rather than the Being of the Father as the source of the Godhead.[45] Athanasius and Epiphanius save the day as it were by laying the foundation for "the great work of Cyril

---

[39]Ibid., 251.

[40]Thomas F. Torrance, *The Trinitarian Faith: The Evangelical Theology of the Ancient Catholic Church* (Edinburgh: T&T Clark, 1988), 185.

[41]Ibid., 186.

[42]Torrance, *The Christian Doctrine of God*, 250.

[43]Torrance, *The Trinitarian Faith*, 185.

[44]Torrance, *The Christian Doctrine of God*, 181.

[45]Ibid., 182.

of Alexandria."⁴⁶ It was Cyril who, building upon Athanasius and Epiphanius, argued that talk of procession is anchored "from the one Being of God the Father which is common to the Son and the Spirit."⁴⁷ In short, my sense is that Gregory may not be as far off the mark as Torrance thinks because for Gregory Nazianzen the Father's relation to the Son is internal to the divine essence itself. Regardless, the point remains: the Son's deity is not "derived."⁴⁸

Torrance praises the Cappadocians (especially Gregory Nazianzen) for "an indivisible but internally differentiated Trinity of real hypostatic relations continuously and actively subsisting in the Godhead" and yet criticizes them (really, Gregory) for averring that it is the uncaused Person rather than Being of the Father that is the source of divinity. I do not think this is as problematic as I once thought. The point is, really, quite simple: there is an "internally differentiated Trinity," an order to the persons but no subordination of being. As Torrance helpfully notes in relation to the *Filioque* controversy, "The whole Godhead belongs to each divine Person as it belongs to all of them, and it belongs to all of them as it belongs to each of them."⁴⁹

These points of reservation aside, Torrance makes a point that resonates deeply with the classical tradition and the Scriptures upon which it rests, namely, that each of the three is fully God, and "all three have and are one and the same Godhead."⁵⁰ Where Torrance seems to at least also mildly diverge from the tradition is in his sense that there exists "a dynamic three-way reciprocity."⁵¹ Does the Father receive anything, ontologically speaking, from the Son and Spirit? Is not the Father simply the one who begets, who is from no one, and the Son and Spirit begottenness (the Son) and procession (the Spirit)? There is of course reciprocity in the economy. The Gospel narratives attest this. The three cohere and in-exist. "Perichoretic relations characterise both the hypostatic subsistences and the hypostatic activities of the three divine Persons, so that they are not only Triune in Being but are Triune in Activity."⁵² Put again, *perichoresis* is a matter of describing the relations of the Trinitarian persons. And yet, you can say that without inferring that the Father receives his Being in a reciprocal sense from the Son. The Father is the Being who begets and is as such from no one, the Son the Being who is begotten and as such *from* the Father. There is not any distinction in terms of their deity.

Another way to raise this point, without hopefully trying to offer an account of the *how* of the relations, is to draw attention, with Torrance, to the deep truth that "the incommunicable properties distinguishing them do not divide them from one another but on the contrary integrate them in their subsistent reciprocal relations."⁵³ There is something right about what Torrance is arguing, namely, that what distinguishes them—their differing origins—also integrates them. I wonder, however, whether integration language necessarily encourages us to take the further step toward that of reciprocity. Does not the Father's monarchy prevent us from saying that he is in some sense caused in relation to the Son? Does not reciprocity imply, at least subtly, a degree of causality,

---

⁴⁶Ibid., 185.
⁴⁷Ibid., 186.
⁴⁸Ibid., 185.
⁴⁹Ibid., 190.
⁵⁰Ibid., 184.
⁵¹Ibid., 197.
⁵²Ibid.
⁵³Ibid., 202.

that is, that the Son somehow causes the Father? The answer may at first sight appear to be yes. However, Torrance, as always, is subtle. He is thoroughly opposed to introducing the language of causality into the Trinitarian relations. There is not a kind of consecutive structure in terms of the Father's deity in relation to that of the Son and Spirit. Each person is again, as Torrance notes of Athanasius in *The Trinitarian Faith*, "whole of the whole."[54]

TRINITY AND CHRISTOLOGY

Moving on from this point, Torrance's theology proper provides us with significant clues as to the shape of other doctrines. The Christological concentration of his doctrine of God allows him to say, for example, that "we may really understand something of the wonderful nature and work of the Creator himself, as it would be quite impossible otherwise," when Christology is in play.[55] Christ is the key to the doctrine of creation, epistemologically and ontologically. We know through Christ that creation's beginning, center, and end is in Christ. The Creator's attributes obliquely manifest in creation are profoundly clear and on display in Christ. So for Torrance we "define omnipotence by the Nature and Being of God as he has revealed himself to us in his creative and redemptive activity."[56] Not only do we recognize God as Creator through his redemptive activity, we understand God's attributes in that way too. There is for Torrance no sharp distinction between what is communicable and what in incommunicable in God. All of God is communicated to us in his creative and redemptive activity, which is not to say that God is thereby exhausted. God remains sovereign and free. There is, following Barth's lead, "a total otherness in being and a complete disparity in nature between the Creator and the creature."[57] This "total otherness" does not, however, preclude God from revealing himself as he is for us and for our salvation.

The doctrine of creation, then, is clearly derivative of the doctrine of the Trinity. Only insofar as we are able to think of "this one God in his intrinsically homoousial and perichoretic relations as Father, Son and Holy Spirit" are we "to think of him as Sovereign Creator."[58] Regardless of which doctrine we are considering, we are not allowed to steer clear of the "homoousial and perichoretic" relations of the three. There is identity between God the Creator and Redeemer, just as there is "identity between the almightiness of God and the weakness of the Man on the Cross."[59] The God who is always Father is free to create, the God who is always Son is free to save, to make himself nothing, doing thereby something that is new even for himself, and all that for us and for our salvation. There is oneness with respect to God's inner being and God's acts toward the outside. God is utterly consistent in all that he accomplishes in his self-disclosure. Though the living Lord does new things, things new even for himself, he is not thereby changed. I think it is fair to say that Torrance thinks that God's being is impacted, but unfair to say that his being is changed by anything that he does. We must always recognize

---

[54]Ibid., 238.
[55]Ibid., 204.
[56]Ibid.
[57]Ibid., 207.
[58]Ibid., 212.
[59]Ibid., 215.

the "intrinsic simplicity and homogeneity of his divine Being."[60] And yet, this recognition does not detract from the utter dynamism of the divine being itself. God's "intrinsic simplicity and homogeneity" gloss his "living reality and self-consistency." Simplicity and homogeneity, insofar as Torrance understand them, do not in the least imply that God is static. Rather, because of the oneness in being, essence and agency between the Father and the incarnate Son, "any thought of God as impassible in the Greek or Stoic sense" is forbidden.[61]

This leads Torrance to audacious places, doctrinally speaking. As we noted earlier, in terms of his dependence on Moltmann, the passion is not limited to the Son. The *homoousial* principle demands that we say that the Son's passion "in his union with us in history" is one with "the transcendent passion of God the Father."[62] The oneness in being and agency between the three leads further to Torrance's affirmation that "the whole undivided Trinity was involved in the atoning passion of Christ."[63] It is this oneness between God in himself and for us, between theology and economy, that illumines everything Torrance writes. All of God is involved in all that God does. God, for Torrance, is as God does.

CRITICAL ASSESSMENT

Having laid out the basic features of Torrance's theology proper, it is time to step back for a moment to assess its merits, and in a way that is sensitive to Torrance's own terms. Though my own thinking has taken something of a more "Thomistic" turn since I first discovered Torrance's writings as a newly minted ThD and Seminary Professor, I remain grateful for Torrance's presentation of the *homoousial* and perichoretic relations of Father, Son, and Spirit. Though Torrance tilts toward Barth at many points (and at times, rather surprisingly in my view, toward Moltmann), he tilts as much if not more toward the Greek Fathers. Though I do not want to contest the rigor of his readings—I have no reason to doubt their accuracy—I find it fascinating that Torrance, like Calvin himself, found so much to work with in the Greek and, to a lesser extent, Latin Fathers, for example Hilary. The Hellenization thesis that von Harnack so popularized does not have much of a hold on Torrance.[64]

Though Torrance is critical of the Cappadocians at points, he nonetheless remains extremely sympathetic. Athanasius and Epiphanius, too, as well as Cyril, emerge as Torrance's (and our) teachers. Appreciative words are also said about Augustine's *On the Trinity*. Torrance reads Barth as working with and advancing insights arrived at in the Patristic era, even if Barth himself does not always realize that. Torrance's influences are eclectic you might say. Like Thomas, he will take up different voices in the tradition

---

[60]Ibid., 236.

[61]Ibid., 251.

[62]Ibid., 253.

[63]Ibid., 255.

[64]See, for example, Torrance's fine article "Scientific Hermeneutics, According to St. Thomas Aquinas," *Journal of Theological Studies* 2 (1962): 259–89. Rather than writing off Thomas as metaphysical and therefore abstract, Torrance commends Thomas, though not without articulating a few reservations, concluding that "we must acknowledge unhesitatingly the immense contribution of St. Thomas, not least in the judicious and rationale handling of the material, and his application of careful scientific method to biblical and theological interpretation," ibid., 289.

insofar as they help him inhabit the deep things of God. Voices like Gregory Nazianzen help Torrance to articulate *ousia* as *"being in its internal relations."*[65] Even a contemporary figure like Moltmann is praised for bringing forward the trinitarian character of "God crucified."

Torrance wants the Trinity to bear as much relation to salvation history through Jesus Christ as is possible. Accordingly, the doctrine of the Trinity is downstream from Christology. Torrance wants to restore in his most mature and last significant systematic work on the doctrine of God "the classical Greek patristic understanding of the Holy Trinity within the framework of the Church's confession of the Gospel of the incarnation and the mystery of divine salvation."[66] Trinity illuminates the doctrine of the incarnation and salvation; indeed, any doctrine is harmed when unfolded apart from the Trinity.

What is strikingly absent in Torrance's doctrine of God is a doctrine of God's attributes. Barth, as is well known, treats us to a remarkable account of the perfections of God's love and freedom. I find it fascinating that a tract of the doctrine of God to which Barth gives so much attention (as did Thomas) is one that Torrance does not take up. For example, we are not treated in *The Christian Doctrine of God* to an account of those perfections of the one and triune God that the economy, as Torrance understands it, elicits.

What is also worth pointing out is that Torrance, though sensitive to the doxological import of trinitarian doctrine, adopts a form and method that, although originating in the vocation to praise and adore the glorious and blessed Trinity, is not always so overt in championing that vocation. "Listening obedience" matters, as Torrance notes in *The Trinitarian Faith*, but Torrance, though assuming the need to love the one to whom we listen, does not make love for him explicit to his method.[67] I say this because not too long ago I read another extremely significant contribution to the Christian Doctrine of God, namely, Katherine Sonderegger's *Systematic Theology: vol. 1: The Attributes of God*.[68] In Sonderegger's offering, theology's object—the unicity of God—overtly determines the form that her text takes. The voice and method of her work are overtly doxological, though not less scientific because of that. In other words, the devotional frame is, in Sonderegger's work, more prominent. Torrance's text is more straightforwardly scientific in its orientation, whereas a text like Sonderegger's, though equally scientific, pursues the objective reality lying at the heart of theology in a more explicitly personal way. Sonderegger is more attuned to "the personal dimension" of the doctrine of God. The doctrine of God involves not only what we say but also how we say it.[69]

Torrance is certainly Barth's pupil. Many of the basic moves in his theology proper are derived from Barth. Though notable differences remain, most especially in terms of the scant attention Torrance gives to the divine attributes, and of Torrance's worries regarding Barth's reading of the Son's obedience back into the inner life of God, the affinities are, nonetheless, far greater. That said, an apparent difference between the two is found in their respective uses of Scripture. Barth's doctrine of God is replete

---

[65]Torrance, *The Christian Doctrine of God*, 182.

[66]Ibid., 10.

[67]Torrance, *The Trinitarian Faith*, 21. See further Torrance's chapter on "Faith and Godliness" in *The Trinitarian Faith*, 13–46.

[68]Katherine Sonderegger, *Systematic Theology*: vol. 1: *The Attributes of God* (Minneapolis, MN: Fortress Press, 2015).

[69]See further A. N. Williams, *Architecture of Theology: Structure, System, and Ratio* (Oxford: Oxford University Press, 2011), 27, 135.

(in the fine print) with exegesis of Scripture. Torrance assumes Scripture but does not actually exegete it in the way that Barth does in the small-print sections of the *Church Dogmatics*. Though Torrance does offer a wonderful chapter on "The Biblical Frame" in *The Christian Doctrine of God*,[70] his theology does not read as scriptural commentary in the same way as much of the *Church Dogmatics* does. For example, I would have liked to have seen Torrance use Scripture to justify his sense of Moltmann's "somewhat tritheistic understanding of the divinity unity."[71] What dimension of the biblical testimony does Moltmann help him to hear? Engagement with Scripture would also provide another benefit, that is a kind of greater existential immediacy. Torrance's presentation of theology proper is nuanced yes, but the modes of expression are at times cumbersome, as with his propensity to write overlong sentences. Would a more direct engagement with Scripture have helped to tighten things up along the way?

That said, Torrance has done so very many things so very well. He helps us appreciate the lasting import of the classical conciliar tradition. It took great doctrinal courage for Torrance to depend upon a tract of the tradition that many in our von Harnack-influenced day—as was the case with Torrance's day—find irrelevant. Do, for example, Athanasius, Gregory Nazianzen, and Epiphanius really speak to us today? Yes, because they are instruments used by God's Spirit to keep Christ's church one, holy, catholic, and apostolic. Their teaching helps us to hear the Scriptures afresh, and to discern their overtly trinitarian character. That Torrance, a Reformed theologian, would lean so heavily on the Greek east shows a kind of receptive ecumenism that serves as a model for us all. Indeed, though I do not agree with everyone of Torrance's moves, the way that he gets to where he does is edifying. He demonstrates genuine confidence in the promise of the Gospel. God will never leave his church without teachers and shepherds who by the grace of the Spirit lead the people of God throughout the ages into all truth.

Torrance also teaches us the importance of disregarding disciplinary boundaries. That Torrance, a dogmatic theologian in the Reformed tradition, happily exegetes Greek and Latin theologians with a view to their trinitarian promise belies a kind of confidence in the truth's perspicacity. The dogmatic theologian is free to draw upon all and everywhere, though with the priority of course given to the Scriptures, so as to hear the trinitarian Word contained therein. This means that Torrance sits fairly lightly upon the specialist scholarship available to him. He simply reads these figures, shows their biblical import, and tries to demonstrate how theology's object—the triune God—determines theology's form. Torrance opens up tracts of the tradition not as an archaeologist but as a preacher of sorts, one who wants to hear the scriptural Word and its ontological import. Torrance knows enough to know that he needs help in hearing that Word, and so we are edified by his efforts in his theology proper to hear the scriptural Word together with other gifted Greek and Latin hearers of the same.

In sum, Torrance's theology proper leaves much for the church to digest. The *homoousial* principle instructs us in terms of the indivisibility of theology and economy, of God in himself and of God in relation to us. Honoring the aseity of God, Torrance points to the saving economy of Jesus Christ in fulfillment of the promises made to Israel as the place wherein we encounter God's *self*-disclosure for us and for our salvation. There is much that he teaches the contemporary Christian church, and the church is bettered for listening.

---

[70]Torrance, "The Biblical Frame" in *The Christian Doctrine of God*, 32–72.
[71]Ibid., 247.

CHAPTER TWELVE

Incarnation and Atonement

THOMAS A. NOBLE

Throughout his years as Professor of Christian Dogmatics at New College, Edinburgh, from 1952 to 1979, Thomas F. Torrance set his students in the second-year Dogmatics class an essay on the topic, "The Relationship between the Incarnation and the Atonement." There were six departments in the college, which was then the Divinity Faculty of the University of Edinburgh.[1] Each was headed by a professor assisted by three lecturers.[2] The Department of Divinity addressed issues of philosophical and contemporary theology. It was headed at first by John Baillie, and then for most of Torrance's years, by his contemporary, John McIntyre, and the division of labor meant that it was the professor of Divinity who lectured on the doctrine of the Trinity. As professor of Christian Dogmatics, Torrance lectured on Christology and Soteriology. His major works on the Trinity were not published till after his "retirement" in 1979.

In fact, Torrance concentrated in his major writing during the 1960s on theological methodology, and particularly his development of the comparison of the method of theology with the method of the natural sciences. His first *magnum opus* was *Theological Science*, published in 1969.[3] He did not publish a book on Christology and Soteriology till his Didsbury Lectures, *The Mediation of Christ*, first published in 1983.[4] All during these years, however, he was developing and delivering the lectures which were published posthumously as *Incarnation: The Person and Life of Christ* and *Atonement: The Person and Work of Christ*.[5]

The essay Torrance set for his students in the Christian Dogmatics II class therefore took them right to the heart of his approach to theology, for his Trinitarian doctrine arose from the confession of faith in Jesus Christ as Lord and Savior. It was the encounter with Christ at the "evangelical and doxological level" which led through the confession of his deity (expressed in the *homoousion* of the Nicene Creed) to the awareness of what he called "the evangelical Trinity," the Father, the Son, and the Holy Spirit revealed in the

---

[1] Now known as "The School of Divinity."

[2] In American terminology, these would be "associate professors."

[3] Thomas F. Torrance, *Theological Science* (London: Oxford University Press, 1969; 2nd edition, Edinburgh: T&T Clark, 1996).

[4] Thomas F. Torrance, *The Mediation of Christ* (Exeter: The Paternoster Press, 1983). It was my privilege to invite him to give these Didsbury Lectures, and I had suggested a series on Athanasius. This first edition only contained the four lectures. The second edition, published by T&T Clark in 1992, added the fifth chapter, "The Atonement and the Holy Trinity."

[5] Thomas F. Torrance, *Incarnation: The Person and Life of Christ*, ed. Robert T. Walker (Downers Grove, IL: IVP Academic/Milton Keynes: Paternoster, 2008); and *Atonement: The Person and Work of Christ*, ed. Robert T. Walker (Downers Grove, IL: IVP Academic/ Milton Keynes: Paternoster, 2009).

economy of salvation. This led upwards to the confession of God as Triune not only in his saving action in the world (the economic Trinity or Trinity ad extra), but the confession of God as eternally triune in his own eternal being (the ontological or immanent Trinity).[6] Although McIntyre, not Torrance, lectured on the Trinity to the second-year Divinity class, those who took Christian Dogmatics III in the third year of their BD course did study Pneumatology and Trinity.[7]

After the introductory "General Theology" class, taught jointly by the two theology departments in the first year of the BD degree course, the starting point for those who chose further studies in Dogmatics in the second year of study was Christology and Soteriology, considered not as isolated loci, but in integration. The question which the student had to face therefore was how to construct this essay: Should one begin with the Incarnation and move toward the Atonement? Or should one begin with the Atonement and move toward the Incarnation? Was Soteriology to be understood from Christology, or Christology from Atonement? Should one follow the *ordo essendi* (the order of being), the ontological order beginning with who Christ is eternally? Or should one begin with the *ordo cognoscendi* (the order of knowing), beginning with his atoning death proclaimed in the Gospel? The two doctrines had to be considered together as mutually informing each other, but the practical business of organizing the structure of the essay seemed to leave little choice but to begin with one or the other!

The arguments for beginning with the doctrine of the Incarnation were strong. In the organization of the lecture course in the Christian Dogmatics II class, Christology was considered in the autumn term before Soteriology was considered in the spring term. When James Torrance lectured to the class, he laid great stress that we must begin (as Bonhoeffer had written) with the "Who?" question: "Who is Jesus Christ?"[8] The same order of Christology before Soteriology can now be seen too in the published version of Torrance's earliest lectures, given at Auburn Seminary in Upper New York State in the academic year 1938–39.[9] After five preparatory chapters, the doctrine of the Incarnation is expounded in chapter 6. That is followed by chapters on the preexistence of Christ (chapter 7), and on "The Humiliation of Christ" (chapter 8). Although Torrance refers to these lectures as "my Lectures on Christology and Soteriology,"[10] in fact there is not a full doctrine of the Atonement such as he later developed. Chapter 8 examines "Jesus the Incarnate Servant," the doctrine of the Virgin Birth, the vicarious humanity of Christ, and his sinlessness. Chapter 9, "The Significance of the Humanity of Christ," does have one brief section on its significance for redemption. In it, Torrance quotes his mentor, H. R. Mackintosh, on the necessity of the humanity of Christ for the atonement,[11] and adds this comment: "How could Christ have died *for us*, how could he have borne *our*

---

[6]See chapter 4, "The Trinitarian Mind," in *The Christian Doctrine of God, One Being Three Persons* (Edinburgh: T&T Clark, 1996), 73–111; and the summary of the three "levels" in Dick O. Eugenio, *Communion with the Triune God: The Trinitarian Soteriology of T.F. Torrance* (Eugene, OR: Pickwick, 2014), 11–23.

[7]In the traditional structure of university education, now largely abandoned, each "class" lasted the whole of the academic year through the autumn, spring, and summer terms with final examinations in June.

[8]Dietrich Bonhoeffer, *Christology* (London: Collins, 1960), 27–40. This was one of the set seminar texts for the Christian Dogmatics II class.

[9]Thomas F. Torrance, *The Doctrine of Jesus Christ* (Eugene, OR: Wipf & Stock, 2002).

[10]Ibid., "Preface," ii.

[11]The quotation is from H. R. Mackintosh, *The Doctrine of the Person of Christ* (Edinburgh: T&T Clark, 1912), 405.

guilt and *our* sin and carried it away had he not *really and actually been Man?*"[12] But this is not developed. An integration of Christology and Soteriology is clearly advocated: "We cannot therefore properly think of the Incarnation apart from the Atonement, or of the Atonement apart from the Incarnation."[13] But the Soteriological aspects are not developed and expounded until his Edinburgh lectures.

The Edinburgh students did not have those Auburn lectures available, but the order of approach in the Dogmatics II class might suggest that it was better to begin the essay with the Incarnation and work toward its implications for the doctrine of the Atonement. Despite that, it will be more enlightening for us here in this chapter to begin with Torrance's doctrine of the Atonement. That will help us to see more clearly where Torrance accepted and agreed with the doctrine of the Atonement which was so central to the evangelical tradition from which he came, and also see more clearly where his focus on the Incarnation refined, deepened, and corrected the traditional focus on "Christ crucified."[14] Robert T. Walker considers this as the better way to approach Torrance's theology. He writes: "Torrance can often be read as beginning with the incarnation, and often misread, particularly by students and non-theologians, as emphasizing its importance at the expense of the atonement and the cross." Walker argues that "the starting point of his theology is the crucified and risen Jesus Christ, and that it is from this viewpoint that he sees the link with incarnation and its importance."[15]

THE SCOTTISH EVANGELICAL TRADITION

David Bebbington defined the evangelical tradition as having four characteristics: conversionism, activism, biblicism, and crucicentrism.[16] The last of these, crucicentrism, was particularly evident in the dominant Scottish theologians at the turn of the twentieth century. James Denney, Professor of New Testament and Principal of the United Free Church College in Glasgow, published his classic work, *The Death of Christ,* in 1902. Denney even went so far as to criticize the fathers and the Nicene Creed for focusing too much on the incarnation instead of the atoning death of Christ.[17] P. T. Forsyth, the Scottish Congregationalist, published guest lectures as *The Cruciality of the Cross* in 1909[18] and a fuller set of extempory addresses, *The Work of Christ,* in 1910.[19] Both of these major figures belonged to the Scottish evangelical tradition which had rejected Ritschlian Liberalism but which had also fought to defend the validity of biblical criticism advanced by William Robertson Smith, George Adam Smith, and others, against the beginnings of the fundamentalism which was later to flourish in the 1920s. Torrance's professor

---

[12]Torrance, *The Doctrine of Jesus Christ,* 135.

[13]Ibid., 85.

[14]This was the order which I adopted in writing the essay when in the Dogmatics II class in 1974–75, and the professor's evaluation of the essay (in his almost illegible red scribble!) seems to offer an endorsement of this strategy.

[15]Robert T. Walker, "Incarnation and Atonement: Their Relation and Inter-Relation in the Theology of T.F. Torrance," *Participatio* 3 (2012): 1–63. Cf., 16–17.

[16]David W. Bebbington, *Evangelicalism in Modern Britain: A History from the 1730s to the 1980s* (London and New York: Routledge, 1989), 2–17. While those are useful markers for the historian, the theologian cannot see these as a sufficient characterization of evangelical theology and must insist that it begins not with the eighteenth-century "revival" but with the Reformation.

[17]James Denney, *The Death of Christ* (London: Hodder and Stoughton, 1902), 324. See page 179 in the later version, edited by R. V. G. Tasker (London: Tyndale Press, 1951).

[18]P. T. Forsyth, *The Cruciality of the Cross* (London: Hodder and Stoughton, 1909).

[19]P. T. Forsyth, *The Work of Christ* (London: Hodder and Stoughton, 1910).

and mentor, H. R. Mackintosh, belonged like Denney to the evangelical tradition of the United Free Church of Scotland.[20]

Mackintosh's major publications included *The Person of Jesus Christ* and *The Christian Experience of Forgiveness*.[21] In the latter, Mackintosh has a chapter on the Atonement in which he declares: "The history of theology proves to the hilt that the great ideas of Atonement and Incarnation lost the life-blood of meaning when they drift apart from each other."[22] He proceeds to quote his late colleague, James Denney, with approval:

> It is a common idea that Socinianism (or Unitarianism) is specially connected with the denial of the Incarnation. It began historically with the denial of the Atonement. It is with the denial of the Atonement that it always begins anew, and it cannot be too clearly pointed out that to begin here is to end, sooner or later, with putting Christ out of the Christian religion altogether.[23]

To some extent this was a reaction against a contemporary movement, particularly among Anglicans, to center theology in the incarnation and life of Jesus, rather than in the cross.[24]

These were the leading theologians of the Scottish evangelical tradition to which the Torrance family belonged, and consequently, it is important to see that T. F. Torrance in no way denied the crucicentric emphasis of that tradition. But what he did achieve was to deepen that focus on the cross and the resurrection by demonstrating how a more profound understanding of the atonement emerges when it is informed by a deeper Patristic understanding of the Incarnation. For him, the theology of the Fathers and the theology of the Reformers were complementary. The former emphasized "the-*being*-of-God-in-his-acts" and the latter "the-*acts*-of-God-in-his-being."[25] To clarify the way in which Torrance deepened the Reformation perspective with the Patristic perspective, we shall therefore begin with his doctrine of the Atonement.

ATONEMENT: THE PERSON AND WORK OF CHRIST

Torrance's exposition of the doctrine of the Atonement is given in the second volume of his Edinburgh lectures, *Atonement: The Person and Work of Christ*.[26] He begins two chapters of biblical theology with the caveat that the atonement is a mystery and cannot

---

[20]The Free Church of Scotland, which began with the Disruption in 1843 when the evangelical wing of the Church of Scotland left their churches and manses, united with the United Presbyterian Church to form the United Free Church in 1900. The resulting U.F. Church was larger than the remaining established Church of Scotland when the two united in 1929.

[21]H. R. Mackintosh, *The Person of Jesus Christ* (Edinburgh: T&T Clark, 1912), and *The Christian Experience of Forgiveness* (London: Nisbet, 1927); republished in the Fontana Books series (London and Glasgow: Collins) in 1961. See the illuminating discussion of Mackintosh in Andrew Purves, *Exploring Christology and Atonement: Conversations with John McLeod Campbell, H. R. Mackintosh and T. F. Torrance* (Downers Grove, IL: IVP Academic, 2015).

[22]Mackintosh, *Forgiveness* (1961 Fontana edition), 181.

[23]Denney, *The Death of Christ*, 320.

[24]Notably in Charles Gore, *The Incarnation of the Son of God* (London: John Murray, 1891), the 1891 Bampton Lectures. Cf. Denney, *The Death of Christ*, 320–7.

[25]Torrance, *Incarnation*, 85.

[26]The editor's synopsis in pages ix–xxxiv of Torrance, *Atonement*, should be read along with the following paragraphs helping us to see the structure of the lectures and therefore to grasp Torrance's doctrine as a whole. There is a later exposition of the Patristic doctrine of the Atonement in Thomas F. Torrance, *The Trinitarian Faith: The Evangelical Theology of the Ancient Catholic Church* (Edinburgh: T&T Clark, 1988), 145–90.

be explained by a "theory." As the high priest entered behind the veil on the Day of Atonement, so Christ completed the atonement within the mystery of his relationship with the Father. Torrance then takes his starting point from the two definitive sayings of Jesus himself. "This is my body given for you ... This is my blood of the [new] covenant," (Mk. 14:22-24) is expounded in the first chapter by examining the Old Testament doctrine of the covenant and the New Testament doctrine of Christ as the Mediator of the New Covenant.[27] The other saying, "The Son of Man came not to be served but to serve and to give his life a ransom for many," (Mk. 10:45 and Mt. 20:28) is expounded in the second chapter with a particular focus on the word "ransom."[28]

The saying about the blood of the covenant prompts Torrance to highlight the key significance of the sacrificial worship inaugurated under the Mosaic covenant and therefore the priesthood of Christ the Mediator "who fulfils the covenant in that he is the embodied communion between God and man," and who is "himself the cult, both the high priest and the victim in one person." The saying about Christ's life given as a "ransom" leads to an examination of what this meant by exploring the Old Testament background behind the word.[29] Torrance highlights three key Hebrew words, but he was not simply engaging in the fashion of word study so severely criticized by his younger Scottish contemporary, James Barr.[30] This was an examination of what we would now call three overlapping "models" which it was convenient to identify by using three Hebrew terms, *padah*, *kipper*, and *go'el*.[31] The *padah* model was the deliverance of Israel out of Egypt and the "house of bondage" which indicated "redemption out of divine judgment and alien oppression into the liberty of the kingdom of God."[32] The *kipper* model was that of the priestly sacrifices in which sin was "covered," that is to say, "blotted out." That *expiation* brought about *propitiation*: both meanings were needed. But this was not humanity propitiating God: this was God's action through the priestly sacrifices. "God is primarily the subject for it is ultimately God himself who atones, who blots out sin, pardons it, casts it behind his back, invalidates it or annuls it."[33] The *go'el* model is that of the kinsman-redeemer bringing "redemption out of slavery or forfeited rights through a kinship in blood and property."[34]

Three historic emphases in the church's doctrine of the atonement are then seen to correlate with these: *padah* redemption with the dramatic or *Christus Victor* aspect; the *kipper* model with the cultic-forensic aspect; and the *go'el* model with the moral influence

---

[27]Torrance, *Atonement*, 1–24.

[28]Ibid., 25–60. Behind Torrance's discussion of these texts we may detect the influence of James Denney, *The Death of Christ*, 39–56.

[29]It may be necessary to disabuse some readers of the misunderstanding propagated by some superficial textbooks that the concept of ransom implies the notion of paying the ransom to Satan. That Origenist speculation reappeared in Gregory of Nyssa's "Catechetical Oration," but was denounced by Gregory Nazianzen and never dominant. Torrance's investigation of the Old Testament background provides a more solid interpretation of Mark 10:45.

[30]See the criticisms of Torrance in James Barr, *The Semantics of Biblical Language* (Oxford: Oxford University Press, 1961).

[31]The use of the notion of models as definitive metaphors was first advanced by Ian T. Ramsey, Bishop of Durham from 1966 till his death in 1972, and has since been taken up by such theologians as Janet Soskice, Sallie McFague, and Colin Gunton. Gunton particularly employed this in his approach to the atonement. See *The Actuality of the Atonement: A Study of Metaphor, Rationality and the Christian Tradition* (Edinburgh T&T Clark, 1988).

[32]Torrance, *Atonement*, 29.

[33]Ibid., 34.

[34]Ibid., 44.

aspect, but importantly also with the ontological aspect of atonement in the Greek Fathers. Torrance also correlates with those the historic *triplex munus* (threefold office) of king, priest, and prophet. We may speculate that had these lectures ever been rewritten as the intended dogmatics, this structure may have given shape to the whole doctrine.

As it is, only the priestly office is given full treatment, but the Old Testament "tension" between priest and prophet, or word and liturgy, is part of that exploration in chapter 3, along with the priestly mediation of the incarnate and ascended Son in the epistle to the Hebrews. Chapter 4 considers atonement as justification with particular reference to the apostle Paul. The question how God can be just and the justifier of the ungodly leads into consideration of the role of the law. The death of Christ was an expiatory sacrifice, the judgment of the judge, the atoning death of "the one for the many." This brings Torrance to "the problem of substitution," which would be "utterly impossible" and "immoral" if construed *only* in forensic terms. Only the Creator Word could be such a substitute, providing an "essentially corporate" justification for humanity.[35] Justification has a backward reference in the undoing of the past and guilt and a forward reference as a completed reality awaiting disclosure.

Torrance's lectures then turn to "Atonement as Reconciliation":[36] our justification is not an end in itself for in it the legal relation is transcended. It is not merely a matter of guilt canceled but of a new relation to God in which we are reconciled as his dear children. A study of *katallage*, originally translated as "atonement" but today as "reconciliation," brings out its close connection to *antallage*, "exchange." Reconciliation is "through substitutionary exchange and expiation." But notably, Torrance insists that reconciliation was completed not just by the action of, but in the *person* of, the incarnate Son, worked out in the hypostatic union from birth to death. It is (as Calvin called it) "the wondrous exchange" in which Christ took our place that we might take his. "God takes on himself his own rejection of humanity and directs to them only the positive act of acceptance." Torrance adds this comment:

> Because of the blood of Christ there is no positive decision of God to reject anyone, but only the gracious decision to accept them, and that decision has once and for all been enacted in the cross and resurrection so that nothing in heaven and earth can change it or undo it or reverse it. To reverse it would be to bring Christ back to the cross again, and to deny the reality of what he has already done. *That decision is not altered if man refuses it, but if someone goes to hell, they go because they dash themselves in judgement against an unalterable positive act of divine reconciliation that offers to them only the divine love.*[37]

What is clear here is that Torrance stood in the mainstream of the Scottish evangelicalism of James Orr, James Denney, P. T. Forsyth, and H. R. Mackintosh in rejecting the "high" Calvinism of double predestination and limited atonement still maintained by the Princeton theologians, the Hodges and Warfield. With all of them he maintained that this is an objective atonement, but, there is a subjective sequel: "It must be worked through

---

[35]Ibid., 125–8.
[36]Ibid., chapter 5, 137–70.
[37]Ibid., 157–8, italics original.

the heart and mind of men and women, until they are brought to acquiesce in the divine judgement on sin and are restored in heart and mind to communion with God."[38]

Atonement also has to be understood as redemption.[39] Torrance returns to the term *lytron* (ransom) and the cognates terms, *lyo* (release) and *apolytrosis* (redemption), and relates this cluster of concepts to *kipper, go'el,* and *padah*. He considers the "mighty act" of redemption, giving a full place to the role of the Holy Spirit. He considers the "range" of redemption, and, given the inseparability of atonement and incarnation, he rejects any notion of "limited atonement" as impossible. "God's election cannot be separated from Christ and is essentially corporate."[40] In eschatological perspective, redemption is cosmic.

But the end is not yet. While attention has so far been concentrated on the death of Christ, Torrance does not consider that a full doctrine of the atonement can ignore the resurrection and ascension. He explains in chapter 7 that the resurrection is inseparable from the person of the incarnate Son and part of the very being of Christ as Mediator.[41] It is both passive (Jesus was raised) and active (Jesus rose). He triumphed over the grave because of his sinlessness so that his resurrection is the holding firm of the hypostatic union (God and humanity in one Person) through death and hell. The resurrection reveals that the virgin birth was the human birth of the almighty Creator-Word. The resurrection is the fulfillment of justification, meaning that it is not just forensic, but "an active sharing in Christ's righteousness." As a fully bodily resurrection, it was the redemption of the whole human being.

A further chapter is added on "The Nature of the Resurrection Event," exploring its relationship to space and time and the theological factors essential to interpreting this more-than-historical event.[42] Similarly, in a chapter on the ascension and the *parousia*, Torrance considers the nature of the event of the ascension, its relation to space and time, and its significance for the threefold office of king, priest, and prophet. The ascension creates "an eschatological pause" in the midst of the one event of the *parousia*.[43] Further chapters follow on the biblical witness to Jesus Christ, the one church of God in Jesus Christ, and the eschatological perspective of the gospel.

So far, it is clear that in writing about the atonement, Torrance strove to develop his doctrine from Holy Scripture, and that consequently he affirmed the comprehensive approach including all three "offices" which marked out the evangelical tradition rooted in the Reformation. The *padah* note of kingly victory is there (as in Patristic doctrine), but the focus is more on the priesthood of Christ and his self-offering as a "ransom" (*lytron* or *kopher*). But while the forensic model is affirmed as a necessary part of that (as in Reformation doctrine), it is not sufficient in itself. God in Christ not only acted to provide propitiation, but also expiation; not only justification, but sanctification. The prospective aspect (advocated by McLeod Campbell) was essential to the doctrine: we were not only pardoned but raised in Christ to a new life in which Christ gave us to share in his filial relationship with the Father. That is the heart of atonement. Third, the prophetic office was fulfilled not just in the revelation of God's love in the cross, but in the *go'el* model of

---

[38]Ibid.
[39]Ibid., chapter 6, 171–200.
[40]Ibid., 183.
[41]Ibid., 201–42.
[42]Ibid., chapter 9, 243–64.
[43]Torrance, *Atonement*, chapter 10, 265–314.

the kinsman-redeemer who took our poverty in the "wondrous exchange" that we might share in his riches.

What becomes clear however is that these aspects of the atonement cannot be plumbed in any depth without a deeper understanding of the doctrine of the incarnation. This is where Torrance goes deeper than the evangelical tradition which he inherited.

INCARNATION: THE PERSON AND LIFE OF CHRIST

It is an interesting question how original Torrance was in relating the atonement to the Incarnation. His own tendency was to claim that the doctrine he was presenting was the historic doctrine of the church as expounded by the Greek Fathers, particularly Irenaeus, Athanasius, Gregory Nazianzen, and Cyril of Alexandria.[44] His claim was that their doctrine of the *vicarious humanity* of Christ was largely lost in the Western, Latin church after the fifth century,[45] but recovered in the theology of Calvin, Knox, and the Scottish tradition which he traced through Robert Bruce, Hugh Binning, and John McLeod Campbell. It was championed in the twentieth century by Karl Barth.[46] Historians of doctrine have been critical of these claims, and it is best to admit that, while Torrance was immensely erudite, he did not think like an historian. He did not employ the methods of what we may call "theological history," but of true and genuine historical *theology*. He was not reading these predecessors to establish what was peculiar to them in their specific historical context: rather, he was interested in their common witness to the objective revelation in the Word-made-flesh. He treated them as contemporary conversation partners, and he accentuated their common agreement on the doctrine which he championed and expounded more explicitly and comprehensively than any other. But while he may have brought out the saving significance of the Incarnation more fully, he was surely right in seeing the common thread in their thinking. And since theology does not stand still but has developed through the Christian centuries, he was surely right that his conclusions were the ones for which they prepared the way and to which, therefore, they pointed.

The deeper understanding of the atonement which came through integrating the doctrine with that of the Incarnation may be most clearly outlined under three headings: the Hypostatic Union, the *homoousion*, and the vicarious humanity.

---

[44]See Jason Robert Radcliff, *Thomas F. Torrance and the Church Fathers: A Reformed, Evangelical, and Ecumenical Reconstruction of the Patristic Tradition* (Eugene, OR: Pickwick, 2014). Radcliff argues that Torrance "imaginatively reconstructs the Greek Fathers in the light of the evangelical tenets of the Reformation," 183.

[45]See Thomas F. Torrance, "Karl Barth and the Latin Heresy," *Scottish Journal of Theology* 39, no. 4 (1986): 461–82.

[46]See Peter Cass, *Christ Condemned in the Flesh: Thomas F. Torrance's Doctrine of Soteriology and Its Ecumenical Significance* (Saarbrücken: VDM Verlag Dr Müller, 2009) for an examination of Torrance's account of Knox and this Scottish tradition. Torrance clearly differentiates this tradition of "Evangelical Calvinism" from the "Federal Calvinism" of Samuel Rutherford and the Westminster Confession of Faith in Thomas F. Torrance, *Scottish Theology from John Knox to John McLeod Campbell* (Edinburgh: T&T Clark, 1996). Cass concludes that the roots of Torrance's doctrine are to be found in Bruce but that he was most influenced by McLeod Campbell.

The Hypostatic Union

This phrase, the "Hypostatic Union," is taken from the language of the Chalcedonian Definition as understood in the light of the Christology of Cyril of Alexandria.[47] It refers to the union of two *physeis* or "natures"—deity and humanity—in the one *hypostasis* or "Person" of the Son of God. But the Greek Patristic language or conceptuality is not the root of the doctrine. As Torrance makes clear in the opening chapters of *Incarnation: The Person and Life of Christ*, this is the doctrine of the Incarnation firmly rooted in the New Testament and foreshadowed in the Old. The task of Christology is not to prove or establish the doctrine of the Incarnation, but "to yield the obedience of our mind to what is given, which is God's self-revelation in its objective reality, Jesus Christ."[48] This is the fundamental *mystery* of the Person of Christ which we cannot understand or explain out of our own knowledge: "He is God and very God, and yet man and very man: God and man become one person. We know Christ in the mystery of that duality in unity."[49]

It must be emphasized that the Hypostatic Union is what Torrance calls "the starting point." Christology does not begin "from below" with the human Jesus (as Pannenberg argued). But neither does it begin "from above," that is, from the deity, which Pannenberg wrongly argued was the method of orthodox Christology from the Fathers to Barth. Rather the doctrine of Christ begins from the confession of the "two-in-one," from the recognition that this is the Word become flesh. It is that confession, that the risen, human Jesus is "My Lord and my God" (Jn. 20:28), which is the beginning of Christology and of all Christian faith. The first point in Torrance's "outline" of the doctrine of the Person of Christ at the end of Chapter Two of *Incarnation* is therefore "the mystery of true God and man in one person."[50] That is the starting point.

Torrance begins with the biblical basis for this in the New Testament *kerygma*, bringing knowledge of Christ as he truly is by the Spirit.[51] Through the *kerygma*, the preaching of the gospel, we "encounter" Jesus Christ himself as he "steps out of the pages of the New Testament and confronts us face to face and reveals himself personally to us."[52] (Despite the common misunderstanding of Melanchthon's dictum, we only know Christ's "benefits" as we know Christ.)[53] But the New Testament gospel can only be understood in the light of the Old Testament covenant with Israel.[54] Torrance expanded considerably on this point in his Didsbury Lectures, explaining the methodological aspects. Whereas much modern thinking was dominated by "dichotomous," "analytical," and "abstractive" modes of thought, modern science since the field theory of James Clerk Maxwell and the "relativity" theory of Albert Einstein had developed "dynamic, relational and holistic ways of thinking."[55] So in biblical studies and theology, we needed to get beyond the dominance of the analytical thinking which divided the human Jesus from God the Father

---

[47] See the introduction to Torrance's emphasis on the Hypostatic Union in Elmer M. Colyer, *How to Read T.F. Torrance: Understanding His Trinitarian and Scientific Theology* (Downers Grove, IL: IVP Academic, 2001), 81–4.

[48] Torrance, *Incarnation*, 1.

[49] Ibid., 3.

[50] Ibid., 83.

[51] Ibid., chapter 1, esp. 10–32.

[52] Ibid., 33.

[53] Melanchthon's dictum, *Christum cognoscere eius beneficia cognoscere*, has been misinterpreted to mean that only knowing the *benefits* and not Christ himself is what matters.

[54] Torrance, *Incarnation*, 37–44.

[55] Torrance, *The Mediation of Christ* (Exeter: Paternoster, 1983), 2.

and divided Jesus from his historical context in the history and culture of Israel. Jesus could not be understood if he were seen as a mere man abstracted from his relationship with the Father or abstracted from his human "matrix" in Israel. His relationship to God and his relationship to Israel are part of who he was and is.

It follows then that we must "go to school with Israel." "God's revelation of himself through the medium of Israel has provided mankind with permanent structures of thought and speech about him," and chief among those is God's election of Israel in the covenant to form a "community of reciprocity." This covenant relationship, however, was with a sinful people, so that it involved a running conflict between divine revelation and what St Paul called "the carnal mind."[56] The Old Covenant is therefore the necessary background to understanding the Incarnation and the *new* Israel. It provides us with the necessary "conceptual tools."[57] Torrance goes on to explain in chapter 2 of *Incarnation*, that the Incarnation was the event in which the Word became flesh, the Son became the Servant, but the classic passage in Philippians 2:6-11 puts this in the context of the whole story, speaking of "the descent and ascent of the Son."

Having shown in these first two chapters how the story is biblical, Torrance proceeds in the next stage of his lectures to expound the *effecting* of the union in the event of "his birth into our humanity" (chapter 3) and the "*continuous* union in the historical life and obedience" (chapter 4). Christology can only be grasped by following this narrative. The doctrine of the virgin birth is not a biological explanation, but is part of the mystery, teaching us "the reality of the humanity of Jesus" but also "the disqualification of human capabilities." It signifies the new creation coming out of the old and sets the pattern of the initiative of grace incorporating the response of faith.[58] Torrance traces the "continuous union" through the obedient life of Jesus. He has been elected "the one for the many" and so is our "substitute," the judge who takes our judgment. His life reveals his faithfulness toward the Father in a life of utter dependence and obedience, and also his faithfulness toward humankind as the shepherd of the sheep and king of the kingdom. And it is that ministry as our shepherd and king which led straight to the cross, which was the moment of final judgment, resulting in the reconstitution of his messianic community as the church after his resurrection.

The tracing in these two chapters of the biblical narrative of Christ, understood as the fulfillment of the Old Testament, brings Torrance to a deeper consideration of the *mystery* of Christ (chapter 5), and thus to a full chapter on "The Hypostatic Union" (chapter 6). In the light of the incarnation and incarnate life, it is now possible to see the full ontological significance of the Union. But Torrance is very aware of the danger of Chalcedonian Christology that we reduce "the movement of love and grace into a static relationship," or "state the doctrine of Christ purely in substantive or ontological terms, without adequate attention to his action and saving mission in history." In other words, "Hypostatic union and atoning reconciliation cannot be properly expounded apart from each other."[59] On the one hand, reconciliation was achieved not only by what Christ *did* in his life and death, but by what he *became* in his incarnation and therefore who he *is* as

---

[56]These sentences employ the sub-headings in chapter 1 of *The Mediation*. See further Thomas F. Torrance, "The Divine Vocation and Destiny of Israel in World History," in *The Witness of the Jews to God*, ed. David W. Torrance (Edinburgh: Handsel Press, 1982), 85–104.

[57]Torrance, *Mediation* (1992), 18.

[58]Torrance's doctrine of the virgin birth reflects that of Barth in *CD* I, 2, §15. Students in the Dogmatics II class had to produce a précis of that section of Barth's *Dogmatics*.

[59]Torrance, *Incarnation*, 182–3.

the God-man. This union of God and humanity is "at-one-ment." But on the other hand, that union had to be tested in his death: and in his resurrection and exaltation we see that the union and communion between God and humankind is irreversibly completed in his risen and exalted Person. He *is* the revelation and he *is* the reconciliation. God is revealed to humanity and humanity is reconciled to God *in him*—in his very Person.

Human *being*, that is to say, our common human nature, is united to the *being* of God *in Christ*: this is the ontological reality of the irreversible Hypostatic Union. Yet this is best understood not in static terms as if one inert entity has been united to another inert entity, but as the "bidirectional" movement in which Christ as God actively represents God to humanity, and Christ as man actively represents humanity to God.[60] This is (as Calvin called it) "the wondrous exchange."[61]

The homoousion

Second, as part of this doctrine of the Hypostatic Union, it is necessary to insist on the *homoousion*, that is to say, on the true and full *deity* of Christ.[62] It had to be truly God who became one of us in the Incarnation: the true deity of Christ is essential to atonement. Torrance makes this clear in his Christology lectures in commenting on John 1: "*The Word is God the Creator*—Word by whom all things are made."[63] He underlines the importance of this. The deity of Christ is "the guarantee that salvation is the work of God." He explains: "If Christ is not God, if God is not fully and wholly present in Christ, and identical with Christ, then God does not reconcile the world to himself, and the work of Jesus is not eternally valid, but is only temporal and contingent and relative."[64] The deity of Christ is essential for *revelation*, for only God can reveal God:

> This identity of Christ's revelation with God's self-revelation is the ground of our assurance and certainty that what we know and he whom we know in and through Jesus Christ, is none other than the Lord God himself, and that there is nothing in God essential to our knowledge of him which is hid from us.[65]

The deity of Christ is thus essential for *salvation*:

> The whole of our salvation depends on the fact that it is God in Christ who suffers and bears the sins of the world, and reconciles the world to himself ... It is important to see that if the deity of Christ is denied, then the cross becomes a terrible monstrosity. If Jesus Christ is man only and not also God, then we lose faith in God and man. We lose faith in God because how could we believe in a God who allows the best man that ever lived to be hounded to death on the cross ... ? ... Put Jesus Christ a man on the cross, and put God in heaven, like some distant and imprisoned God in his own lonely, abstract deity, and you cannot believe in him, in a god such that he is monstrously unconcerned with our life, and who does not lift a finger to help Jesus ... Put God in heaven, and Jesus on

---

[60]For this useful word "bidirectional" see Purves, *Exploring Christology and Atonement*, especially chapter 6, 199–240.

[61]Torrance, *Atonement*, 151.

[62]See Colyer, *How to Read T.F. Torrance*, 70–81.

[63]Torrance, *Incarnation*, 60.

[64]Ibid., 188.

[65]Ibid., 188–9.

the cross only as a man, and you destroy all hope and trust, and preach a doctrine of the blackest and most dismal despair. Denial of the deity of Christ destroys faith in God and in man, and turns the cross into the bottomless pit of darkness.[66]

Curiously however, although those passages are eloquent on the necessity of the deity of Christ to the atonement, Torrance did not use the Greek word *homoousios* in the original Didsbury Lectures, *The Mediation of Christ*.[67] This is the technical term from the Nicene Creed which insists on the full deity of Christ, coined at the Council of Nicaea in AD 325, and defended by Torrance's greatest theological hero, Athanasius of Alexandria. The word does appear in his Edinburgh lectures, published as *Incarnation*, but only in reference to Chalcedon in the section where Torrance discusses the Patristic terminology.[68] It appears too in other more technical articles, or in his later works on the Trinity, *The Trinitarian Faith* and *The Christian Doctrine of God*.

In *The Trinitarian Faith*, Torrance explains the "hermeneutical significance" of the *homoousion*, namely, that by clarifying "the inner structure" of the gospel through obedience to the teaching of Holy Scripture, it established the primacy of Scripture in the mind of the church.[69] He also explains its "evangelical significance,"[70] namely, that the oneness in being of the Father and the Son means that we truly know God since the revelation of the Son was the self-revelation of the Father. This is the cognitive aspect of atonement: that in knowing Christ we truly know God. If however, the actions of Christ are not the action of God, "then the bottom falls out of the Gospel."[71] The *homoousion* or "oneness in being" of the Father and the Son is thus the point of access to the Christian doctrine of God since it means that "what God is in Jesus Christ he is inherently in himself."[72] Its full implication is drawn in the doctrine of the Trinity which declares Father, Son, and Holy Spirit to be "one Being."[73]

The vicarious humanity

If the emphasis on the *homoousion* accentuates the deity of Christ, this is complemented within the doctrine of the Hypostatic Union with the emphasis on the full humanity of Christ, and this is the third aspect we need to note. At Chalcedon this was affirmed by a second use of the word *homoousion,* that Christ was of "one being" with us in his human nature. Torrance brings out the soteriological significance by referring to this as the *vicarious humanity* of Christ. The Western Christian tradition, particularly from Anselm onward, has spoken of the *vicarious atonement*. By derivation, the word means substantially the same as

---

[66] Ibid., 189–90.

[67] The word does appear in chapter 5, which was added to the book in the second edition.

[68] Ibid., 203.

[69] Torrance, *The Trinitarian Faith*, 125–32.

[70] Ibid., 132–45.

[71] Ibid., 138.

[72] Torrance often articulates this maxim, but it may be found for example in his paper, "The Atonement: The Singularity of Christ and the Finality of the Cross: The Atonement and the Moral Order," in *Universalism and the Doctrine of Hell*, ed. Nigel M. de S. Cameron (Carlisle: Paternoster/Grand Rapids, MI: Baker, 1992), 223–56.

[73] See Torrance, *Incarnation*, 17–484. See also the more advanced and technical exposition and defense of the concept of *ousia* in *The Christian Doctrine of God, One Being Three Persons* (Edinburgh: T&T Clark, 1996), 112–35.

"substitutionary" although some have tried to find a subtle differentiation between them. It means that Christ died *in our place*. But Torrance wanted to expand that understanding. For him, we must say not only that his death was vicarious or substitutionary, but, like Irenaeus, that his whole life was—his birth, life, death, resurrection, and exaltation. He is also concerned that the notion of substitution should not be confined to a *forensic* understanding of the cross. There *is* a forensic dimension to the atonement, but that must not be understood in a crude and simplistic way, turning God into a monster. Rather it has to be seen as in the context of the whole vicarious movement of incarnation, incarnate life, death, resurrection, and ascension—the whole descent and ascent, the "bidirectional" movement in the hymn of Philippians 2:6-11. The cross must not be isolated as the sole point of atonement, understood *only* as penal; but has to be seen in the context of the incarnation and incarnate life in which Christ took and lived out a truly human life in our human flesh. The cross was the culmination and center, the turning point of the whole movement, but the whole of his humanity and human life was "vicarious."

That began in his birth, when he, God the Word, assumed our human flesh. And for Torrance, it is vital to see that, since it was our fallen human flesh which needed to be rectified, reconciled, and resurrected as the new humanity, then it *had to be* that same fallen human flesh which he assumed. We have to say with Paul that "he was made in the likeness of sinful flesh, and was even made a curse for us."[74] To say that he was a sinless man who suffered in place of sinful humanity in order to bring pardon and justification is true: he *was* sinless and he *did* procure our justification. But that is not enough: that is only one aspect. To stop there is to make the incarnation merely a preliminary to atonement and to isolate the cross as not the final moment, but the *only* moment of atonement. We also have to affirm that the immortal Son of God assumed our decaying, mortal humanity in order that we might become immortal through his resurrection. That is the ontological aspect: he brought not only pardon but eternal life. Further, only if the sinless Son of God assumed our fallen, sinful humanity could he purify and sanctify it through his own holiness, culminating in his own self-sacrificing death, so that we might be holy and sinless *in him* at the last day. Only in that way could he truly be the Lamb of God who bears away the sins of the world.[75]

There can no longer be any doubt that Torrance was in line here with the Patristic consensus, accurately reflected in the well-known aphorism of Gregory Nazianzen, "The unassumed is the unhealed."[76] He marshals the evidence in his exhaustive footnotes in *The Trinitarian Faith*.[77] Jerome Van Kuiken has gathered the evidence to show that the assumption of our fallen, sinful humanity in order to sanctify it in his own Person and through his life and death is not only the doctrine of the Greek Fathers: Irenaeus, Athanasius, Nazianzen, Nyssen, and Cyril, but also, in the Latin west: Tertullian, Hilary,

---

[74]Torrance, *Incarnation*, 61, referring to Rom. 8:3 and Gal. 3:13.

[75]The assumption of our fallen humanity is found again and again in Torrance's writings, but for examples, see *Incarnation*, 61–5, *Mediation* (1992), 39–42, 61, 70–2.

[76]Gregory Nazianzen, "Letter 101" (To Cledonius), most accessible in *Nicene and Post-Nicene Fathers*, second series, vol. 7:440. Peter Cass is correct that while this first of all stressed against Apollinaris that this was a full humanity, including a human mind, Apollinaris wanted to exclude the mind since it was sinful. For Nazianzen, that was precisely why the Son assumed a human mind—to sanctify it! See Cass, *Christ Condemned Sin in the Flesh*, 160–1.

[77]Torrance, *The Trinitarian Faith*, chapter 5, "The Incarnate Saviour," and especially the section on "The Atonement," 154–90.

Ambrose, Augustine, and Leo the Great.[78] But Torrance drew the lines of connection more explicitly and comprehensively than any of them.

At this point, however, Torrance found himself engaged in controversy, primarily because of the conviction of some that this doctrine compromised the sinlessness of Christ. If that were true, it would be a serious, indeed a fatal charge. The Christian mind could never tolerate anything which compromised the sinlessness of Christ. But the charge is a false one arising from an historic misunderstanding particularly rooted in the history of Scottish theology and especially in the theology of the brilliant early-nineteenth-century preacher, Edward Irving. Irving deserves credit and even sympathy for the way in which he wrestled with the Christological issues in order to portray Christ as "touched with the feeling of our infirmities" in such a way that his victory in the power of the Holy Spirit could also be ours. However, while denying that Christ shared in the guilt of original sin, and asserting that he was free of actual sin, Irving taught that in his human birth the Son took our "constitutional sin," the law of sin and death at work in the flesh.[79] It is quite understandable therefore that the mainstream of Reformed Scottish thought saw this as compromising the sinlessness of Christ and rejected Irving as heretical.[80] But what is clear is that Torrance did not agree with Irving here.

Perhaps Torrance did not always make himself sufficiently clear at this point, but in his early Auburn lectures (which remained unpublished till the end of his life), he clearly differentiated his position from that of Irving. While Christ assumed our common "sinful flesh" from his mother, and while it was still "fallen" in him during his earthly life in the sense that it suffered from infirmities, temptation, and mortality, yet it was sanctified and so sinless from the moment of conception. Torrance specifically rejects Irving.[81] And although he did not always highlight this clearly in later years,[82] yet in response to criticism from Donald Macleod, he left no doubt that his position had not changed.[83] Rejecting Macleod's static conception of Christ, he insisted that "in the very act of taking our fallen Adamic nature the Son of God redeemed, renewed and sanctified it AT THE SAME TIME ... The only human nature which our Lord HAD, therefore, was utterly pure and sinless."[84] He could not be clearer.

What must also be said, however, is that while the humanity of Christ was sinless, his sanctification of humanity was not finished at the point of his human birth. That, as Paul Molnar points out, would be the so-called physicalist view that redemption was complete when the holy divine nature of Christ communicated its holiness to the human nature so that nothing further was needed.[85] Rather, for Torrance, the

---

[78]E. Jerome Van Kuiken, *Christ's Humanity in Current and Ancient Controversy: Fallen or Not?* (London: Bloomsbury T&T Clark, 2017).

[79]For a clear and succinct summary of Irving's doctrine, see Van Kuiken, *Christ's Humanity*, 12–21.

[80]Van Kuiken traces this through Marcus Dods the elder, A. B. Bruce, even (interestingly) H. R. Mackintosh, down to Donald Macleod.

[81]Torrance, *The Doctrine of Jesus Christ*, 122–3. See Van Kuiken, *Christ's Humanity*, 32–4.

[82]It is clearly stated, however. See, for example, *The Mediation* (1992), 40: "But St Paul taught that in the very act of God's incarnational assumption of our fallen nature he cleansed and sanctified it in Jesus Christ."

[83]See Van Kuiken, *Christ's Humanity*, 37.

[84]Thomas F. Torrance, "Christ's Human Nature," *The Monthly Record of the Free Church of Scotland* (May 1984): 114. Upper case lettering original. Italics were obviously not enough to emphasize the point!

[85]Paul D. Molnar, *Thomas F. Torrance: Theologian of the Trinity* (Farnham and Burlington, VT: Ashgate, 2009), 142–3.

sanctification of our human nature in his Person was carried through continuously to "perfection" (Heb 2:10; 5:9) in his life of consecrated faith and obedience,[86] and finally secured only through his death and resurrection. This was not some kind of quasi-chemical reaction, but fully *personal* action in which Christ restores us to true personhood.[87]

Here Torrance's use of the Patristic terminology of *anhypostasis* and *enhypostasis* is helpful.[88] In opposition to Nestorius, Cyril of Alexandria insisted that the Word assumed *anhypostatic* humanity, that is to say, our *common* fallen human nature, but not an already existent human person (or *hypostasis*). Yet the later coining of the term *enhypostasis* made it clear that the still fallen, mortal (but sinless) human nature of Christ had its center in the Person (*hypostasis*) of the Son of God. Therefore, this is not merely God *in* man (i.e., in common human nature), but God *as a man*, a distinct human being with a fully human mind, soul, will, and body. It was not sufficient therefore that the Word became human: the becoming incarnate by human birth did not complete the work of salvation. It was also necessary that *as a distinct human being*, the Incarnate One should sanctify human life through his free human obedience, and that this human consecration to the will of God throughout his life and ministry was carried right through to the ultimate self-sacrifice on the cross.[89] Both the incarnation and the incarnate life-unto-death are essential to atonement. And yet it was only through his atoning death and triumphant resurrection that our humanity was raised immortal and perfected by the Spirit in his Person, opening the way for us to be with him in the new creation.

The contemporary importance of Torrance's interrelating of incarnation and atonement and his focus on the vicarious humanity of Christ is (as Christian D. Kettler has argued) that he speaks to the reality of human salvation without falling into the anthropocentrism of so much recent theology.[90]

CONCLUSION

The ecumenical significance of Torrance is to be seen in the way in which his witness to the truth of the atonement and the gospel revealed in Holy Scripture brings together the soteriological concerns of Eastern and Western churches. He does not deny the forensic concerns of his own Western tradition but deepens their often narrow expression by

---

[86]Torrance proposed that *pistis Iesou Christou* in Rom. 3:21, Gal. 3:22, and elsewhere should be translated not as "faith in Christ" but as the "faith of Christ;" a view later championed by Richard B, Hays, *The Faith of Jesus Christ* (Atlanta, GA: SBL press, 1983/ Grand Rapids, MI: Eerdmans, 2002).

[87]See Torrance, *Mediation* (1992), 67–72 on "The Personalizing and Humanizing Activity of Christ."

[88]Torrance, *Incarnation*, 84, 228–32.

[89]According to Torrance, this also illumines the "logic of grace" by which we may each freely respond in faith in the light of the perfect response Christ has already perfected for us, thus ruling out both monergism and synergism. See Colyer, *How to Read T.F. Torrance*, 118–23.

[90]See Christian D. Kettler, *The Vicarious Humanity of Christ and the Reality of Salvation* (Lanham, MD: University Press of America, 1991), especially 121–54. See also Kettler, *The God Who Believes: Faith, Doubt, and the Vicarious Humanity of Christ* (Eugene, OR: Cascade Books, 2005); *The God Who Rejoices: Joy, Despair, and the Vicarious Humanity of Christ* (Eugene, OR: Cascade Books, 2010); and *The Breadth and Depth of the Atonement: The Vicarious Humanity of Christ in the Church, the World, and the Self: Essays, 1990–2015* (Eugene, OR: Pickwick Publications, 2017).

placing them within the wider ontological framework of the Eastern fathers, "grounding his teaching on the atonement in the Father-Son relationship, the incarnation, the hypostatic union of the two natures in one Person and in the triune being of God."[91] Right at the heart of this profound understanding of the gospel is the way in which Torrance articulates the church's faith in the integration of the doctrines of Incarnation and atonement.

---

[91]Cass, *Christ Condemned in the Flesh*, 152.

CHAPTER THIRTEEN

The Innovative Fruitfulness of *an/en-hypostasis* in Thomas F. Torrance

ROBERT T. WALKER

At first sight *an-* and *en-hypostasis* are abstract terms, far removed from anything of real importance for ordinary understanding of the gospel. Torrance would have agreed, for he warned that in themselves they are abstruse, technical terms which only make sense when translated back into the language of the gospels and ordinary experience. Important as they are, they can only point to the reality of Jesus as known through the New Testament. Only when that is done, can one begin to see the significance of the *an/en-hypostasis* couplet. Just as Einstein's famous special-relativity equation ($E = mc^2$) means nothing without a knowledge of physics, so the *an/en-hypostasis* formula means nothing without a living faith in Christ as God and man. The *an/en-hypostasis* couplet not only succinctly summarizes the nature of Christ's person, but pinpoints how this *is* and is *not* to be understood. While Torrance uses *an/en-hypostasis* primarily Christologically for understanding key aspects of Christ's person and ministry, he uses it also very innovatively to give a Christological understanding of the relation between Christ and the church, and Christ and human faith. As such, *an/en-hypostasis* could hardly be more important for grasping all these aspects of Torrance's Christology but also for avoiding misunderstanding of his theology at crucial points.

As a New College student (1934–37), Torrance was struck by the use of the couplet in Calvinist theology and then "gripped" when in Auburn (1938–39) by the way Barth used it.[1] Thereafter, he makes significant references to it throughout his career, particularly in major works, but given its importance for him, it may be thought remarkable he did not make more of it. The reason, however, is that he regarded it as "theological algebra," not as the "flesh and blood"[2] substance of the faith. It was a precise technical formula, necessary and extremely useful for giving us in a nutshell an understanding we could not have without it, but which was not the living substance of the Gospel; as already noted, it

---

[1] Thomas F. Torrance, *Karl Barth, Biblical and Evangelical Theologian* (Edinburgh: T&T Clark 1990), 124–5. See Karl Barth, *Church Dogmatics* (Edinburgh: T&T Clark, 1954) I/2. 163–5. A reading of the Barth text here, page 165 in particular, makes it clear why Torrance was so struck by Barth's comments on the couplet and his high approval of making it a dogma and affording it the same careful consideration it received in early Christology.

[2] Thomas F. Torrance, *Incarnation: The Person and Life of Christ*, ed. Robert T. Walker (Downers Grove, IL: IVP Academic/Milton Keynes: Paternoster, 2008), 233.

had to be translated back into the ordinary language of faith for its meaning and supreme significance to be appreciated.

This chapter therefore moves from an account of the doctrine of Christ in normal theological and biblical language to the use of *an-* and *en-hypostasis* in its explication. There are three main foci of Torrance's theology: the Trinity, Christology, and the relation between Christ, the church, and faith. These can be regarded as concentric circles of theological understanding, narrowing down from the Trinity as the widest to the *an-* and *en-hypostasis* couplet as the narrowest and as the innermost and most technical circle in Christology. Several key characteristics of Torrance's theology can be seen as lying behind *an-* and *en-hypostasis* and exemplified in it,[3] but the chapter begins with the second main focus of his theology, the centrality of the hypostatic union for the doctrine of Christ, before detailing the ways in which the couplet crystallizes the Christological nerve center of Torrance's theology in what we might call his "theological shorthand."

THE CENTRALITY OF THE HYPOSTATIC UNION FOR CHRISTOLOGY AND SOTERIOLOGY

The pivotal centrality of the hypostatic union for Torrance is not only that Christ is true God and true man in one person but that this "*one person acts both from the side of God and from the side of man,* both in his divine acts and in his human acts, and that these acts are really and truly identical in the person of the mediator."[4] What is essential is that the action of God and the action of man are indivisibly one and unbreakable in the person of the mediator. With revelation and reconciliation for example, it is not just that they mutually involve each other (for there can be no revelation without reconciliation through the cleansing of sin, and no reconciliation without revelation, for it is only the true revelation of God which can reconcile the human mind by the converting revelation of divine truth and light) but that they can only happen together, at the same time, in the one person of the mediator. Torrance proceeds therefore to spell out how essential the hypostatic union is, as the action of God and man in one person, to the whole action and logic of revelation and atoning reconciliation. Only God can save humanity, but he can only do so if he is also human, God acting *as man*, in *one person*.

> There are not two actions in the life and death of Jesus Christ, but one action by the God-man, one action which is at once manward and Godward. It was act in our place, and yet act of God for us. It is the doctrine of the union of two natures in one person which is thus the mainstay of a doctrine of atoning reconciliation.[5]

The holding firm of the hypostatic union through death and judgment means the union established in incarnation is carried through into resurrection. With atoning reconciliation completed, the way was open for Christ's royal ascension into heaven where he received

---

[3]The following factors are all pivotal: Trinitarian Christocentrism; the intensely personal nature of God; dogmatics as the systematic ordering of doctrine around, and held together in, Christ; independence and originality, particularly in seeing new connections of ideas. Also, key and often under-appreciated in him are: familiarity with Scripture and faithfulness to its logic; the endeavor to work out a theology in dynamic not static terms; the influence of the Scottish philosophical tradition.

[4]Torrance, *Incarnation*, 183, italics original.

[5]Ibid., 195, 196.

the Spirit for us (Acts 2:33). Having received the Spirit for us, Christ could then send him to complete in us what he had already completed in himself.[6] As Torrance puts it:

> Once the breach between humanity and God had been healed on the cross ... then the way was open for God to pour his Spirit upon man, and for man through the same Spirit to draw near to God in Christ. With the enmity of the human mind done away and the veil of darkness it entailed torn aside, the way was open for humanity to enter into that intimate communion with God within which alone real revelation could be fulfilled, not only from the side of the giving God, but from the side of receiving humanity, not only from the side of grace but *from the side of faith*.[7]

The role of the Spirit is to unite us to Christ (that through indwelling union with him we may live from his fullness) and to take Christ's prayer, "Abba, Father," and his faith, and put them on our lips and in our hearts. The role of the Spirit, in other words, is to work in us what he has already worked in Christ. Only then in the "subjectification [in us] of the perfected reality of atonement"[8] is the act of atonement and redemption regarded as completed and actualized in us through our being incorporated into Christ and his redemption,[9] as we await its full unveiling at his *parousia*.[10] Thus the faith that we have is genuinely ours, but it is *Christ's faith in us*, and both are realities, Christ's faith for us *and* our faith, the latter inseparable from the former and in it.[11] For Torrance, this is the mystery of grace, the mystery of Christ, and the mystery of Christ in us, that by grace the reality of what Christ has worked for us in our human nature, has through the Spirit become genuinely ours, *our* willing act. The whole meaning of grace is that the reality of Christ's own human faith-for-us-and-in our-place and the reality of our human faith are held together, and far from being a contradiction actually comprise the whole meaning of the logic of grace. As Torrance said so often, "All of God means all of man."[12] The logic of grace is "all of God and all of man," not "some of God and some of man." For Torrance, this is true of *all* the relations of God and his creatures, not least of God and man, and this is precisely where his use of the *an-/en-hypostasis* couplet is so significant and innovative.

The final main focus of Torrance theology is on the relation between Christ and human faith, the corporate relation of Christ to the church and within that of Christ and all members individually. Both the church and her members live by the faith of Christ himself, but as already mentioned, the atonement does not reach its end until Christ through the Spirit completes in us, corporately and individually, what he has won for us in himself. Torrance therefore lays great stress on Christ coming to all *personally* to ask of us *personal* relations in love and trust. This stress is very clear in Torrance's dogmatics lectures but his fullest treatment of it is in *The Mediation of Christ* where

---

[6]See Thomas F. Torrance, *Atonement: The Person and Work of Christ*, ed. Robert T. Walker (Downers Grove, IL: IVP Academic/Milton Keynes: Paternoster, 2009), 320–1, where Torrance speaks of both Christ and the Father as sending the Spirit. In the unity of the Trinity both are true. Likewise, it is true to say that what *Christ* had completed in himself, he had completed *through* the Spirit and equally true to speak of what the *Spirit* had completed in Christ.

[7]Ibid., 328.

[8]Ibid., 178–9.

[9]Ibid.

[10]Ibid., 309.

[11]The biblical verse which best encapsulates this for Torrance is Galatians 2:20; See Torrance, *Incarnation* 28; and *The Mediation of Christ* (Exeter: Paternoster, 1983), 98.

[12]Torrance, *The Mediation of Christ*, xii–xiii.

the whole chapter "The Mediation of Christ in Our Human Response" is of great significance.[13] Torrance here makes the relation between the faith of Christ and our faith unambiguously clear and it is a matter of regret that he can still be accused of belittling the need for faith, even by those with a very good understanding of him otherwise. To the extent they do so, they have failed at this point to grasp and interpret Torrance in terms of the categories and biblical logic he is arguing for.[14] It is to be hoped that careful consideration of his use of *an-* and *en-hypostasis* and the logic of grace at this point may enable a reconsideration of Torrance and an interpretation of him in terms of the biblical, theological, and philosophical lens he is working with.

ANHYPOSTASIS AND *ENHYPOSTASIS* IN GENERAL

The hypostatic union states that the divine and human natures (each in their full integrity) are united in one person. *Anhypostasis* and *enhypostasis* put it differently, narrowing it down even more precisely by specifying more exactly the nature of the relation between the reality of the divine nature and that of the human nature. Where the hypostatic union says, "reality of God and reality of man, united in one person," the *an-/en-hypostasis* couplet simply makes two statements about the nature of the reality of the humanity of Christ: (i) *the humanity of Christ has no independent existence* by itself: it depends totally on the action of God becoming man without any action from the human side and (ii) *the humanity of Christ is fully personal* in *the person of the Son* of God, that is, fully human, real, personal, and individual *in* the Son. But crucially the *an-/en-hypostasis* couplet adds a critical rider: (iii) *an- and en-hypostasis cannot be separated and are only valid together*.

In insisting that all three statements being taken together, the *an-/en-hypostasis* couplet reinforces and strengthens all three of the basic tenets on the hypostatic union, the reality of the divine nature, the reality of the human nature, and their unity in one person. In doing so the couplet clarifies and strengthens the "logic of grace" and does all this by (i) strengthening the action of God by marking the incarnation as *wholly* the action and work of God, (ii) strengthening the reality of Jesus's humanity by making clear its *individuality and personal being,* (iii) strengthening and at the same time personalizing the union and "logic of grace," strengthening it by making the humanity *totally dependent* on the divinity for its very existence (without belittling in any way its *complete human reality*), and personalizing it by narrowing down the union from being simply one in the one hypostasis of the Son, to being one *in* a Jesus who is fully personal *in* the one hypostasis of the Son. Personal knowledge of the Son comes only through personal knowledge of the human Jesus. In line with Torrance's emphasis on the fact that God in his triune being is inherently personal and therefore known only personally, this means that the personal element is further reinforced when knowledge of God comes only through personal knowledge of his only Son and image become personal human in Jesus of Nazareth.

By insisting on the inseparability of *an- and en-hypostasis,* and therefore on the inseparability of the divine person of the Son from the individual human personhood or personalness of Jesus, Torrance not only strengthens each tenet of the hypostatic

---

[13]Ibid., xii, 73–98. See especially 81–6, 92–98, but also the sections on Worship and Sacraments.

[14]See Michael Bauman, *Roundtable: Conversations with European Theologians* (Grand Rapids, MI: Baker Book House, 1990), 112, for Torrance's comment on this as the reason theologians could continue to misunderstand him.

union but also emphasizes that the salvation in Jesus Christ is inescapably personal and inescapably known only personally.

THE OCCURRENCE AND DEVELOPMENT OF *AN-* AND *EN-HYPOSTASIS* IN TORRANCE

While his most extensive and important statements on them occur in *Incarnation*, *Theological Science* and *Conflict and Agreement in the Church*, the importance of *an-* and *en-hypostasis* for Torrance's theology as a whole is to be found not in the number of times he refers to them in his published writings generally but in how and when he uses them.[15] It is also significant that the references span his whole career from his time at New College.

The early writings (1938–42): The Christological analogy

In three works published in 1941–42,[16] as well as in his Auburn Lectures in 1938–39,[17] it is significant that Torrance uses the Christological analogy as the key and the norm for understanding not just the place and nature of reason, but the relations of God and man in general and indeed all Christian doctrine. He takes the "hypostatic union," the way in which the deity and humanity of Christ are united in his one person "without change, confusion, division or separation," as the key to understanding *all* the relations of God and man and therefore as the norm for *all* Christian doctrine and theological understanding, a position which remained fundamental to him.

The following quotation from *The Modern Theological Debate* sets out one of Torrance's first statements of how the hypostatic union of God and man in Christ is to be seen not simply as *the unique and central union* found in his person, but as a wider generic category describing *the same type of relatedness* in *all* the relations between God and humanity. Torrance argues that as the incarnation is the ground of all knowledge of God, the way he acted there must be taken as the basic pattern of all knowledge of God. The union of God and man in the person of Christ is then the pattern for every doctrine in Christian dogmatics, in soteriology and epistemology, as well as in Christology itself.

---

[15]Apart from his dogmatics lectures, *Incarnation*, 84–5, 228–32 (and *Atonement*), there are significant references to *an-* and *en-hypostasis* in his three major works, *Theological Science* (London: Oxford University Press, 1969; 2nd edition, Edinburgh: T&T Clark, 1996), 217–18, 269; *The Trinitarian Faith: The Evangelical Theology of the Ancient Catholic Church* (Edinburgh: T&T Clark, 1988), 230, cf. 226; and *The Christian Doctrine of God, One Being Three Persons* (Edinburgh: T&T Clark, 1996), 160. See also *Conflict and Agreement in the Church*, vol. 1 (London: Lutterworth Press, 1959), 242–9; *Theology in Reconstruction* (London: SCM Press, 1965), 131; *Theology in Reconciliation* (London: Geoffrey Chapman, 1975), 166; *Space, Time and Resurrection* (Edinburgh: Handsel Press, 1976), 51, 55; *Karl Barth, Biblical and Evangelical Theologian* (Edinburgh: T&T Clark, 1990), 124–5; *Scottish Theology* (Edinburgh; T&T Clark, 1996), 71; Thomas F. Torrance, "The Atonement: The Singularity of Christ and the Finality of the Cross: The Atonement and the Moral Order," *Universalism and the Doctrine of Hell*, ed. Nigel M. De S. Cameron (Carlisle: Paternoster Press/Grand Rapids, MI: Baker Book House: 1992), 230.

[16]Thomas F. Torrance, The Modern Theological Debate: Notes of three addresses delivered at the T.S.P.U. Conference, Bewdley, December 30–January 2, 1941 (Issued for Private Circulation by the Theological Students' Prayer Union of the Inter-Varsity Fellowship of Evangelical Unions, 39 Bedford Square, London, W.C.1.); Thomas F. Torrance "Predestination in Christ," *Evangelical Quarterly* 13 (1941): 108–41; Thomas F. Torrance, "The Place and Function of Reason in Christian Theology," *Evangelical Quarterly* 14 (1942): 22–41, originally Torrance's Presidential Address to the New College Theological Society.

[17]Thomas F. Torrance, *The Doctrine of Jesus Christ* (Eugene, OR: Wipf & Stock, 2002), 115.

The hypostatic union here describes both the central union of God and man in Christ *and* the same "kind of union" or "relatedness" "found throughout the whole body of theology and not elsewhere," a type of union which is "parallel to" but "secondary" to the primary union in Christ.[18]

> Any human thought of God is dependent upon the Incarnation, the coming of God to man out of a sheer act of grace, and His becoming one with man in personal union with Jesus of Nazareth; therefore we must turn thither, for what happened there and then must once and for all be the basic norm of theological knowledge. The fundamental material form which underlies all other forms, material and formal, is the central paradox of the Person of Christ, where we have God and Man together; here is the basic pattern and ground of all knowledge of God (even that proleptic to the Incarnation) and of every doctrine in dogmatics which deals with the relations between God and man, whether in the realm of salvation or of epistemology. The basic form here may be called the "hypostatic union", by which is meant not simply the personal (consubstantial) union between God and man in Jesus Christ, but just *that kind of union* which of all unions is unique. In other words, the expression "hypostatic union" becomes a kind of category which describes a certain relatedness, found throughout the whole body of theology and not elsewhere; a relatedness secondary and parallel to the central relatedness of God and Man in Christ, or a secondary kind of hypostatic union.[19]

The same thoughts, adapted and expanded for their context, are expressed in virtually identical language in "The Place and Function of Reason."[20] It is highly illuminating to find Torrance realizing and stressing, in all three of these earliest publications, the pivotal significance of the hypostatic union and Chalcedonian formula for the whole of theology.

Between his first extended use of the couplet in his *Scottish Journal of Theology* Article of 1954, his use of it in *Theological Science* in 1969, and his Christology dogmatics lectures of 1952–76 (published as *Incarnation*), it is impossible to say when and how much his theology of the couplet developed. What we can say is that the basic concepts which are brought together and summed up by *an-* and *en-hypostasis* were already there as least as early as 1941–42.

Torrance does not in any of the three writings from this period (or in his Auburn lectures) refer to *anhypostasis* and *enhypostasis*, but as already mentioned, he does argue that *the hypostatic union is the pattern for all relations between God and man*. Elaborating on this in "Predestination in Christ," Torrance stresses that the humanity of Christ had no independent existence apart from the incarnation. It was wholly the work of God and if the eternal Word had not become incarnate there would have been no Jesus. Nevertheless, he was a real man, fully human in every way, a particular individual, Jesus of Nazareth, in whom God meets us personally and individually, calling us to real human decision.

Five elements here may be singled out as being of fundamental importance: (i) the humanity of Jesus has no existence apart from incarnation—it is wholly the work of

---

[18]Torrance would not in later writings speak of a "secondary kind" of "hypostatic union," preferring to limit the term to Christ and preferring to speak of other unions as analogous to it, but he would certainly continue to see the union in Christ as a pattern for all God's relations with the church and humanity in general. Cf. Torrance *The Doctrine of Jesus Christ,* 115, where all God does in Grace "reflects" "the altogether unique hypostatic union of the two natures in the one Person of Christ." Cf. also *Atonement,* 336–40, esp. 336–9.

[19]Torrance, "The Modern Theological Debate," 17.

[20]Torrance, "The Place and Function of Reason," 39; cf., "The Modern Theological Debate," 17–18.

grace;[21] (ii) the humanity of Jesus is fully real, personal, and particular;[22] (iii) in Christ God meets us personally and individually, calling us to decision in his work of grace;[23] (iv) our human decision of faith is genuinely ours and is fully human, but (like the humanity of Christ) has no independent existence apart from the divine decision on our behalf;[24] (v) the pattern of the hypostatic union in Christ, and of the virgin birth, is the analogy and pattern for the relation between the divine decision of grace and the human decision of faith.[25] Torrance sees here that the hypostatic union is the analogy for the relation between election and faith:[26] just as the humanity of Jesus had no existence apart from the incarnation but was nevertheless real humanity, so human decision has no existence apart from the divine decision but is nevertheless real human decision.[27] Although Torrance does not in the early writings cited use the terms *anhypostasis* and *enhypostasis*, he has, by the time of the dogmatics lectures, clearly thought through into much greater precision and articulated the concepts involved with the help of the terms *an-* and *en-hypostasis*, thereby providing a significant deepening and precision to the earlier writings.

Torrance's fully developed understanding of an- and en-hypostasis

Anhypostasis means that "the human nature of Jesus never existed apart from the incarnation of God the Son," "that his human nature had *no independent subsistence* or *hypostasis*, no independent centre of personal being."[28] In other words, if the eternal Son had not become man there would have been no Jesus of Nazareth. *Enhypostasis* means that the humanity of Jesus was fully human, real, individual, and personal *in* the person of the eternal Son. "That is, the human nature from the first moment of its existence had its *hypostasis* or personal subsistence *in* the personal subsistence of God the Son. That is the meaning of *en-hypostasis*."[29] Taken together, as they must always be for Torrance, *anhypostasis* and *enhypostasis* help to safeguard the dynamic nature of the hypostatic union.

> This doctrine of the *anhypostasia* and *enhypostasia* is a very careful way of stating that we cannot think of the hypostatic union statically, but must think of it on the one hand in terms of the great divine act of grace in the incarnation and on the other hand in terms of the dynamic personal union carried through the whole life of Jesus Christ.[30]

Torrance stresses that the hypostatic union "cannot be understood apart from the reconciling and atoning work of God the Son" and "has to be stated in essentially soteriological terms" and therefore in dynamic terms.[31]

---

[21] Torrance, "Predestination in Christ," 128–9.

[22] Ibid., 128.

[23] Ibid., 112–13.

[24] Ibid., 130; *The Doctrine of Jesus Christ*, 20.

[25] Torrance, "Predestination in Christ," 129.

[26] Ibid., 130–1.

[27] Ibid.

[28] Torrance, *Incarnation*, 229; cf. 84.

[29] Ibid.

[30] Ibid., 84.

[31] Ibid., 85; "It is in this way that we seek to deliver the Chalcedonian doctrine of Christ from the tendency involved in the Greek terms to state the doctrine of Christ statically and metaphysically," ibid.

The complementary emphases of anhypostasis and enhypostasis

In *anhypostasis* the emphasis falls on (i) God's *sheer act of grace* in Christ, (ii) the *once for all* nature of the hypostatic union and on (iii) Jesus Christ as *man* in the incarnation, while in *enhypostasis* the emphasis is on (i) the *obedient life* of the Son, (ii) the *continuous* nature of the personal union in him and on (iii) Jesus Christ as *a* man in the incarnation. It is striking that in publications (or lectures) Torrance will often explain a theological doctrine and then comment that one aspect of it represents the *anhypostatic* element in it and the other the *enhypostatic*. The quotations below illustrate Torrance's careful reflection and ordering of the theological significance of *an-* and *en-hypostasis* in their essential inseparability.

> (i) The union of the two natures in the person of Jesus Christ as thus expressed is stated in the light of the transcendent act of grace in the incarnation of the one eternal Son on the one hand, and in the light of the obedient life of the incarnate Son on earth, on the other hand. This is the doctrine of the *anyhpostasia* and *enhypostasia* regarded in their complementarity.[32]

> (ii) The incarnation involves a union of God and man in Christ accomplished once and for all, but it also involves a living union continuous throughout the life of the historical Jesus Christ moving from his birth to his resurrection. To this once and for all union corresponds the *anhypostasia*, and to the continuous personal union throughout the life of Christ corresponds the *enhypostasia*.[33]

> (iii) The *anhypostasia* stresses the *general* humanity of Jesus, the human nature assumed by the Son with its *hypostasis* in the Son, but *enhypostasia* stresses the *particular* humanity of the one man Jesus, whose person is not other than the person of the divine Son.[34]

The incarnation was the union of the Word of God with mankind in solidarity with all men and women; yet it was union with one man, or rather such a union with all humanity that it was achieved and wrought out in and through this one man, Jesus of Bethlehem and Nazareth for all men and women … It was the incarnation of the creator Word, by whom the whole of mankind is made and in whom all cohere. Here we have the union of the universal Word and one human creature created by that Word which makes Jesus *at once man, and a man*.[35]

The fact that Jesus Christ is *man* means for Torrance that *as man* he has assumed the human nature of all humanity and in that human nature has worked out the salvation of all. The fact that he is *a man* means that the salvation he has achieved has been worked in his one human person, remains identical with his particular person and is therefore only to be known in personal encounter and union with him individually. As *man* he has worked out the salvation of all (*anhypostasis*) but as *a man* he has done so in his own particular humanity and unique person (*enhypostasis*).

Torrance's use of *an-* and *en-hypostasis* is a striking illustration of his originality in taking terms from classical theology, seeing their potential and putting them together to

---

[32]Ibid., 84; cf. 232.
[33]Ibid., 85.
[34]Ibid., 230.
[35]Ibid., 230–1.

create a specialized, theological, instrument of considerable explanatory fruitfulness. He has thought out the meaning of *anhypostasis,* of *enhypostasis,* and of both together, and been able to see several implications.

Torrance argues that by itself *anhypostasis* would mean that salvation was automatic, for "apart from the doctrine of *enhypostasia* in addition to it, *anhypostasia* could only mean a solidarity between Christ and all mankind which was, so to speak, only ontological and therefore physical and mechanical—a causal and necessitarian solidarity."[36] Torrance goes on to spell out here in a way he does nowhere else in his writings the explicit Christological basis for one of his most fundamental concepts, that *salvation is not automatic but personal*. He commonly states elsewhere, for example in the chapter on reconciliation in *Atonement,* that the reconciliation and truth of Jesus Christ is identical with his living personal presence and therefore always personal, never automatic, in its dealings with us.[37] In *Incarnation,* Torrance connects the personal nature of Christian truth to the *enhypostatic* aspect in the person of Christ, grounding it on the fact that Jesus is not just *man* in general (the *anhypostatic* element) but *a* man who therefore meets us individually. Salvation for all (*anhypostasis*) exists only in the shape of a particular man Jesus Christ (*enhypostasis*) and is therefore not automatic but only known personally in individual encounter with him. Speaking of Christ's seeking a solidarity with us in all the various modes of personal interaction within society, Torrance outlines some of the details of that interaction and describes it as his "solidarity with our human life by acutely personal modes of existence, and encounter, and communion."[38] Torrance also suggests at this point, then likewise spells out in a way he does nowhere else in his writings, the Christological basis for one of his most fundamental and characteristic concepts, that in his very assumption of fallen flesh Christ sanctified it and converted it back to God.

In these passages in *Incarnation,* Torrance suggests that the linkage of *an-* and *en-hypostasis* can show how together they help us understand how Christ assumed fallen flesh but without sin.

> The doctrine of *anhypostasia and enhypostasia* (put together as one concept) helps us also to understand or express how God the Son was made in the likeness of our flesh of sin, and yet was not himself a sinner; how he became one with us in the continuity of our adamic and fallen existence in such a way as to make contact with us in the very roots of our sinning being, and yet did not himself repeat our "original sin" but vanquished it, and broke its continuity within our human nature. He assumed our corrupt and estranged humanity, but in such a way as at the same time to heal and sanctify in himself what he assumed.[39]

Torrance then proceeds to elaborate, in the two following paragraphs,[40] how *anhypostasia* can be used to show how Christ assumed our fallen nature and original sin, and

---

[36] Ibid., 231.

[37] "This reconciliation encounters us personally ... asking of us personal relations with it. This reconciliation is truth in the form of personal being and therefore we can only know it and relate ourselves to it personally, so that we cannot in any sense think of reconciliation as automatically effective in its continued operation, but quite the reverse," Torrance, *Atonement,* 167.

[38] Torrance, *Incarnation,* 231.

[39] Ibid., 231–2.

[40] Ibid., 232.

enhypostasia to show how by his obedience and sinlessness he expiated sin and restored us to the Father in purity and truth. Thus, *Anhypostasis*: God as *anhypostatic* man assumes our fallen nature, the original sin of all humanity; *Enhypostasis*: God as *enhypostatic* man enters "our personal human structure of existence," enters "into personal relations with sinners," in order to "assume personally" our sin and guilt, expiate it and restore us to the Father. Torrance also sees a further implication in the Son of God's not uniting himself to a pre-existent person:

> In the doctrine of *anhypostasia*, we state that the Son did not join himself to an independent personality existing on its own as an individual. That is, he so took possession of human nature, as to set aside that which divides us human beings from one another, our independent centers of personality, and to assume that which unites us with one another, the possession of the same or common human nature.[41]

For Torrance, therefore, the teaching of *anhypostasia*, that the humanity of Jesus had no existence independent of the incarnation, carries with it *ipso facto* the further implication that it had no independent center of personality. It means also that since the Son did not unite himself to such an independent center, he thereby set aside what divides us as separate human personalities and assumed only what we all share in common. Torrance's argument here highlights the *anhypostatic* element in the person of Jesus that his humanity is purely the act of the eternal Son and reinforces his linking of *anhypostasia* to the Son's assumption of the human nature of all and his acting in it as "*man*" for their salvation. At the same time, the inseparability of *an-* and *en-hypostasia* signifies that this does not mean that Jesus does not act personally or individually as "a man" and Torrance immediately goes on in the same passage to speak about the *enhypostatic* ministry of Jesus in personal encounter.

Torrance's Lund article of 1954,[42] in his application of *an-* and *en-hypostasis* to the relation of Christ to the church, marks an intermediate stage between his first explicit application of it to Christ and his clear application of it to faith in *Theological Science* in 1969. In the 1954 article, Torrance first explains the application and meaning of the terms as applied to Christ and stresses their inseparability. He then applies them secondly to the atonement, a matter he describes as being one of "supreme importance" as it highlights and focuses attention on the fact that the atonement is not just act of God, but act of man, and yet not two actions but one, of God *as man*, as man *in our place*, in an act of radical substitution for us in incarnation, crucifixion, and resurrection. Torrance argues that for the church this means crucifixion with Christ and incorporation into his resurrection, the way of baptism and communion, the way of the cross, the only way to ecumenical reunion and the resurrection of the one body. Torrance then discusses the analogy of Christ and suggests the application of the *an/en-hypostatic* relation in him cautiously[43] to the church:

---

[41]Ibid., 231.

[42]For Torrance's whole argument here see *Conflict and Agreement in the Church*, vol. 1, "The Atonement and the Oneness of the Church" (London: Lutterworth Press, 1959), 238–62, esp. 242–9 (reprinted from *Scottish Journal of Theology* 7, no. 3, "The Atonement and the Oneness of the Church" [1954]: 245–69, esp. 249–56).

[43]Torrance's caution may spring from this being his first explicit application of *an-* and *en-hypostasia* outwith Christology, but given his early realization of the normative significance of the Christological analogy, it may simply be that in the ecumenical context of Lund he wishes to introduce the novelty of the application with care.

Within the orbit of this whole relation between Christ and His Church and within the analogical form which it demands, we may seek cautiously to apply the conceptions of *anhypostasia* and *enhypostasia* to the Church. *Anhypostasia* would then mean that the Church as Body of Christ has no *per se* existence, no independent *hypostasis*, apart from atonement and communion through the Holy Spirit. *Enhypostasia*, however, would mean that the Church is given in Christ real *hypostasis* through incorporation, and therefore concrete function in union with Him. That is why to speak of the Church as the Body of Christ is no mere figure of speech but describes an ontological reality, *enhypostatic*[44] in Christ and wholly dependent on Him.[45]

Just as the humanity of Jesus is *anhypostatic* with no reality of its own independent of the incarnation, so the church has no reality or life in itself apart from Christ and communion with him in the Spirit. But equally, just as the humanity of Jesus is *enhypostatic* and fully real in the person of the Son, so the description of the church as the body of Christ is not just figurative but indicates the reality of its human existence and ministry in inseparable union with him. Just as Jesus Christ is fully real, individual, and personal in the person of the Son, so the church is affirmed as an "ontological reality" in him. In other words, and in a nutshell, *as the divinity of Christ is to his humanity, so is the whole Christ, the risen God-man to the church*. The church owes its very being and life entirely to the *anhypostatic* act of God in Christ, but in Christ the church is *enhypostatically* real *in Christ*, real in being, life, and very humanity in him.

Although Torrance nowhere applies *an-* and *en-hypostasis* explicitly to human faith in so many words, he does, in *Theological Science*, make it unambiguously clear that they apply to all human decision, response, and thinking.[46] That being so, it must be clear that this applies just as much to faith also. Everything therefore that Torrance has said about *an-* and *en-hypostasia* in the Church[47] must apply also to human faith in general, not least to the faith of its own members. In other words, and in a nutshell, *as the divinity of Christ is to his humanity, so is the risen faith of Christ himself to our human faith*. As the human birth of Christ was entirely dependent on the anhypostatic act of God, so the birth of human faith in us is entirely the *anhypostatic* act of God in Christ through the Spirit, but just as the humanity of Jesus was entirely *enhypostatically* real in the person of the Son, so our human faith is our genuine human act, *enhypostatically* real *in* the risen Christ, where it is not swallowed up but remains our genuine human faith, real *in* his faith.

Although Torrance never used the language of *an-* and *en-hypostasis* for the nature of human faith, his emphasis on the reality of faith as the gift of grace (human act yet divine act in the relation of grace, *our* faith yet *Christ's* in us) is a constituent element of his New Testament understanding from the very beginning and characteristically comes out most strongly when discussing the meaning of the virgin birth, the sacraments of baptism and the Lord's supper, and worship, and prayer.[48]

---

[44]Italics added here.
[45]*Conflict and Agreement*, 1, 247–8. Cf., "The Atonement and the Oneness of the Church," 254–5.
[46]Torrance, *Theological Science*, 218.
[47]*Conflict and Agreement*, 1, 242–9. Cf., "The Atonement and the Oneness of the Church," 249–56.
[48]Torrance, *Incarnation*, 100–4; and *Mediation of Christ*, 80–98.

THE INNOVATIVE FRUITFULNESS OF THE CONCEPTS OF *AN-* AND *EN-HYPOSTASIS*

With the aid of all the determinant factors behind his theology outlined above, Torrance has been able to see and understand seemingly abstract concepts such as *an-* and *en-hypostasis* and see their great fruitfulness in (a) focusing on pivotally central aspects of Christology and encapsulating them so concisely, essentially and neatly, as to enable a rigor of understanding and insight we would not have without them and would not be able to express, let alone think so purely and elegantly; (b) enabling us to hold together the mystery of Christ, the mystery of Christ and the church, and the mystery of Christ in us, in a way that remains true both to the reality of God, the reality of man, and the nature of the relation between them without subjugating them together in a false logical system that negates the mystery itself and the mystery of how the bible can hold together things which we deem contradictory.

SUMMARY

As innovatively understood by Torrance, *an-* and *en-hypostasis* can help us to better understand, express, and hold together: (i) the *dynamic* aspect of Christ's ministry as man with his being and act as God, holding together the continuing union alongside the once for all union, the saving significance of Christ's human life and ministry alongside his incarnational assumption of our humanity; (ii) the nature of Christ as both *man* and *a man*, that the salvation completed in Christ for all humanity is *not automatic* but *always personal* and comes to us individually in Christ; (iii) how Christ assumed *fallen nature* and original sin, yet remained *sinless*, and in the deepest personal interaction with sinners undid guilt and restored them to God in purity and love; (iv) that as *anhypostatic*, Christ assumes what unites us, our common human nature, but sets aside what divides us, our independent centers of personality, while as *enhypostatic* and personal himself Christ encounters us "by acutely personal modes of existence, and encounter, and communion."[49]

A NOTE ON THE PLACE AND FUNCTION OF TECHNICAL TERMS IN THEOLOGY

Important as *anhypostasis* and *enhypostasis* are for Torrance, he was careful not to use them more than he felt necessary and in *Incarnation* has a half-page statement in the form of a "note" on their use in theology.[50] In *Theological Science,* the first of his two statements on the place of concepts such as hypostatic union and *anhypostasia* and *enhypostasia* is somewhat fuller if less technical, designed perhaps for the non-theologian as well as the theologian. The various statements complement each other nicely. He begins his first statement in *Theological Science* with a *caveat* on the doctrine of the hypostatic union and a warning that it is not to be used as a fundamental truth, or as the foundational idea of a theological system, as though it had truth in itself. In itself it is nothing and its only function is to point to the reality of Jesus Christ.[51]

---

[49]Torrance, *Incarnation,* 231.

[50]Ibid., 233.

[51]"A word of warning is now in place: we cannot turn the doctrine of the hypostatic union into ideological truth, and use it as the masterful idea of a system of thought. The notion of the hypostatic union is nothing in itself, for it does not have its truth in itself. Its function is to point us to the reality, Jesus Christ," *Theological Science,* 217.

Torrance continues his statement by saying that the hypostatic union needs to be understood as "the logic of Grace" establishing "the logic of Christ," with the two logics being held together in the irreversible relation of grace of God to man, of *anhypostasia* to *enhypostasia*. The "logic of Grace" is the unconditional love of God, from which creation and all else derives, establishing the "logic of Christ," the divine–human reality of Jesus Christ for our salvation, with the two logics being related to one another as *anhypostasia* to *enhypostasia*. *Anhypostasia* asserts that the humanity of Christ and all human reality and knowledge of God owe their existence to the logic of Grace, entirely to the act of God. *Enhypostasia* asserts that God always acts as grace, that is, in such a way as in his action to establish the genuine reality of humanity and human knowledge, not override them.

> To use severely technical terms, we may say that the logic of Grace and the logic of Christ are to be related to one another as the doctrines of *anhypostasia* and *enhypostasia*. In this way we can say two very important things with theological accuracy. *Anhypostasia* asserts the unconditional priority of Grace, that everything in theological knowledge derives from God's Grace, while all truths and their relations within our thinking must reflect the movement of Grace. But *enhypostasia* asserts that God's Grace acts only as Grace. God does not override but makes us free.[52]

Torrance concludes his statement here with the assertion that just as *enhypostasia* affirms that in his person as Son of God the humanity of Jesus is unambiguously full, authentic, and complete humanity, so in our knowledge of God it affirms equally its full and unimpaired reality as genuine *human* knowledge of God.

> Just as the doctrine of *enhypostasia* asserts the full unimpaired reality of the humanity of the historical Jesus as the humanity of the Son of God, so it affirms in our theological knowledge full and unimpaired place for human decision, human response and human thinking in relation to the Truth of God's Grace.
>
> That two-fold truth of the doctrine of *anhypostasia* and *enhypostasia* is what we have to keep clearly in mind in thinking out the interior logic of theological thought.[53]

Here unambiguously, Torrance states the place of *anhypostasia* and *enhypostasia* in "the interior logic of theological thought."[54] The twofold truth of *anhypostasia* and *enhypostasia* enables us to state with "theological accuracy" the fundamental pattern or "interior logic" not just of the person of Jesus Christ himself in his humanity but of "all the other doctrines of the faith in Christ." Torrance makes clear here that he regards *anhypostasia* and *enhypostasia* as terms to be applied to *all* our human thinking and response to grace. If this is so, it may be asked why Torrance does not make the point more often, other than here where, by speaking of *enhypostasia* affirming

---

[52]Torrance, *Theological Science*, 217. The passage in Torrance continues, "In merciful and loving condescension He gathers us into union with Himself, constituting us as His dear children who share His life and love. In this way He sets us on our feet as persons in personal relation with Him, affirming and recreating our humanity in communion with Him; He bestows His love freely upon us and asks of us the free love of our hearts; He takes our cause upon Himself and makes provision for true response on our part as we are allowed to share in the human life and response of Jesus to the Father," ibid., 217–18.

[53]Ibid., 218. This quotation continues and concludes that in the previous footnote.

[54]For all the references in *Theological Science* to interior logic, inner logic, inner rationality, see the index under "logic": "inner logic."

"in our theological knowledge full and unimpaired place for human decision, human response and human thinking in relation to the Truth of God's Grace," he makes it clear that the orbit of *anhypostasia* and *enhypostasia* includes the human response of faith?

Why does Torrance not apply *anhypostasia* and *enhypostasia* more generally to faith? The answer is twofold: (i) he does not need to since he has already made it clear in his writings that the analogy of Christ extends to all Christian doctrine and has in addition spelled out the way in which the virgin birth of Jesus as man is the pattern for our human response of faith.[55] Without using the technical terms of *an-* and *en-hypostas-is/ia* as such, he has applied the same logic in other language. (ii) For Torrance, *anhypostasia* and *enhypostasia* are technical terms to be used sparingly in theology, since while they are of great importance in enabling us to understand the truth of Christ more precisely they are in themselves abstract statements and not the reality of Jesus Christ himself. For the most part, therefore, Torrance uses the "flesh and blood"[56] language of Christian belief, biblical language, and more accessible theological concepts, reserving the more specialized concepts and highly technical terms of theology for occasions when the extra precision of terms like *anhypostasia* and *enhypostasia* can be of real benefit.

In a passage in *Theological Science* and in one in *Incarnation*, in the chapter on the hypostatic union where he has a "note" on the use of theological terms, Torrance explains the place of technical terms such as *an-* and *en-hypostasia* and their function as a kind of "theological algebra."[57]

Torrance regards technical terms like *an-* and *en-hypostasia* as specialized lenses or "disclosure models" through which we may look to see the revelation of Christ in greater clarity. He also thinks of them as a kind of "theological algebra" enabling us to see the inner connections of Christology more precisely. The constant temptation, however, is to dwell too much in these formalized concepts and to lose hold of reality. The theologian therefore must continually transpose technical theological concepts back into the "flesh and blood" of living faith. Although *an-* and *en-hypostasia* can never in themselves encapsulate the reality of Christology, they may, used appropriately, allow its inner structures and logic to be grasped more truly. The following quotation is Torrance's succinct and precise summary of his views in *Incarnation*:

A note on the use of theological terms such as "anhypostasia" and "enhypostasia"

All technical theological terms such as these are to be used like "disclosure models", as cognitive instruments, helping us to allow the reality of Christ to show through to us more clearly. As in natural science we must often cast our thought about certain connections into mathematical or algebraical form in order to see how those connections work out in the most consistent and rigorous way, so here we may well think of "*anhypostasia* and *enhypostasia*" as a sort of "theological algebra" to help us work out the "inner logic" in christology more consistently and purely. But once we see the connections more clearly in this way, they have to be translated back into "the

---

[55]Torrance, *Incarnation*, 100–2; "Predestination in Christ," 129.

[56]Torrance, *Incarnation*, 233.

[57]Torrance, *Theological Science*, 269; and *Incarnation*, 233.

flesh and blood" of reality, translated back into terms of the person and work of Christ himself. Just as in a natural science, we may have to resort to algebra to work out the connections using algebra like a computer as it were, to compute for us what our brains are incapable of doing by themselves, but must then translate the algebra back into "physical statements" in order to discern the real relations in empirical reality, so we must do much the same here. *Anhypostasia* and *enhypostasia* together do not themselves contain the "stuff" of christology, but they may be, rightly used, theological instruments or lenses through which we may discern more deeply and clearly the ontological structures of the incarnation.[58]

In his second statement in *Theological Science*, Torrance makes very much the same points but more fully, bringing out both the necessity and fruitfulness of such theological concepts but also their danger. The danger behind such technical concepts, the temptation to dwell in them, springs from their very necessity. The theologian "must" says Torrance, construct a careful "theological notation" which will "lay bare the essential structure of theological knowledge" and enable its implications to be worked out beyond what is possible simply from immediate experience. Having done that, the theologian must eschew the temptation to dwell in such "theological algebra" since it is only when it is translated back into normal language and existence that there can be real growth in knowledge and understanding of its living implications.[59]

Torrance goes on to emphasize the "remarkable" usefulness and fertility of concepts such as *an-* and *en-hypostasia* before restating the dangers in their becoming detached from reality and the need to maintain the connection between them and the living reality of personal being. The passage contains Torrance's fullest statement on the range and power of *an-* and *en-hypostasia* to illuminate understanding not only of Christ himself, and other doctrines in their Christological coherence around him, but the true form in which many theological difficulties are to be conceived and from which they can be fruitfully understood.

> A striking example of this "theological algebra" is the compound conception of *anhypostasia* and *enhypostasia* which, taken together with the doctrine of the hypostatic union, serves to bring out the essential logic of Grace and logic of Christ, not only in our understanding of Christ Himself but in the other doctrines that are organized round the Incarnation as their centre of reference. Used in this way the conception of *anhypostasia* and *enhypostasia* is remarkably fertile in its power to throw light on many difficulties and to reveal the true form in which many relations are to be conceived.[60]

---

[58] Torrance, *Incarnation*, 233.

[59] The theologian "must engage in logical, as well as metaphysical, thinking to unfold the *inner logic* of his subject-matter and to construct the kind of 'calculus' he needs for this end, that is, a rigorous theological notation which will enable him not only to lay bare the essential structure of theological knowledge in its dogmatic integration but which will enable him to work out its implications beyond the range of his immediate experience ... The pure theologian cannot do without this formal notation any more than the physicist can do without his algebra, but the theologian is constantly tempted to dwell too much in his 'theological algebra' and to let it do all his thinking for him, when it is only by translating it back into the actual forms and conditions of existence that he can grow in his knowledge and understand its material implications," *Theological Science*, 269.

[60] Ibid.; Torrance continues, "But like all formalizations it can become dangerous for it inevitably detaches theological statement from its hold on reality if it is turned into a basic statement rather than a cognitive tool. Regarded in itself the conception is merely a sort of 'algebraic formula' and therefore must be transposed back into the living and actual forms of personal being if we are to think theologically and not just 'theologistically', so to speak."

In the innovative and fruitful use to which he puts the *an-* and *en-hypostasia* concepts, but also in his own sparing employment of them, Torrance's theology itself illustrates everything he says in this passage.

UNDERSTANDING *AN-* AND *EN-HYPOSTASIS*

This section will consider the question of how best to understand the logic of *an-* and *en-hypostasis* in the various sets of relations in which it can be applied. It will be argued that the basic problem is *attempting to understand the logic of Grace*, which, simply because it is grace, the sovereign, free, unmerited, uncompelled act of God establishing creation and humanity alongside him (then re-establishing them in Christ), cannot be understood in terms of logical connection, because there is none (other than the miracle of God's love and grace). It is the problem of attempting to understand logically the relation of different realities connected only by grace. *An-* and *en- hypostasis* do not attempt to solve the problem of the connection, they simply bring it into acute focus and state it as it is, God and man together (or God and creation), in the mystery of grace.

It will therefore be shown that in all the different sets of relations between God and creation the problem is one of understanding the very nature of the connection as being one of grace. The three sets in chronological order are (i) God and creation, (ii) God and man in the person of Christ, and (iii) Christ (as God-man) and human faith. Common to all three is the basic problem of understanding the relation of two realities, completely different in nature yet inescapably related to each other, even when there is no discernible or apprehensible mode of connection. It is the mystery of realities discernibly and essentially related but separated by the mystery of their connection across an unfathomable gap. It will be argued that in the nature of the case, this gap is logically unfathomable and must therefore remain mystery to creaturely eyes. It will be further suggested that we can come to understand precisely why this gap is unfathomable and that when this happens, the mystery is understood to be the mystery and miracle of grace, of creation, incarnation, and Pentecost. It will be stressed that the three sets are essentially related and that seeing each in the light of the others helps make the logic of their common mystery all the more compelling.

While based on, and made possible by, the logic of creation, the logic of incarnation ("the logic of Grace" and "the logic of Christ") must be the primary logic and only in its light can the logic of creation and Pentecost be most fully appreciated, while it is only in the light of these two that the logic of incarnation itself can in turn be appreciated even more deeply.

The *logic of creation* is that God has brought into being out of nothing an entirely new reality to exist alongside him with its own very different nature, reality, and intelligibility. The relation between God and the universe is that of creation, but creation out of nothing, and the "nothing" is the impenetrable gap or void which exists between the two realities and which we cannot possibly understand, just as we cannot possibly grasp how God can create out of nothing. Yet we know he is real (through revelation) and we are real, and that by grace we are wholly dependent on him for being, yet coexist alongside him with our own reality and nature and measure of freedom.

The *logic of incarnation* is somewhat similar to that of creation in being the relation, across a void of nothingness, of the same two realities each with their own different being, but with the difference that this time the Creator has himself crossed the gap to become one of the creatures he had made. Not only so, he has become a genuine creature while remaining what he was before, Creator.

The *logic of Pentecost* is that through the Spirit everything won for us in Christ becomes ours, and is ours, with a relation of identity between them. How can there be a relation of identity between them? Christ does not become us, and we do not become Christ, yet he has so identified himself with us that he has taken on himself our human nature, and in our humanity stood in for us in such a way as to make the response of faith for every one of us. When through the Spirit our eyes and hearts are opened to see that the response he has made for us is ours, then through the Spirit, that response and faith of Christ is made ours, on our lips and in our hearts. Our faith is then Christ's faith, Christ's faith now in us, yet it is genuinely ours, genuine human faith and genuinely our act. How can it be both at once? Yet it is. That is the mystery of the virgin birth, the mystery of faith, of Christ in us.[61]

There are two further "logics" which are somewhat analogous and can help in understanding the essential relation between very different realities, the logic of statements and the logic of pictures.

Statements point beyond themselves to the reality they refer to (and if true statements, point faithfully to it). The *logic of statements* is that what they say in words points to a reality true beyond them in real being. The relation between them (once the statement is understood and the reality perceived) is obvious and thought can move naturally from the statement to the reality, then back to the statement for a comprehension of the reality. *But*, the important point for Torrance is that there is a logical gap between the statement and the reality: one has to move beyond the statement to the reality to understand it and ascertain its validity. The logic of statements as Torrance understands it and states it is "*a statement cannot state, how it is a statement, of that which it states.*"[62] Although Torrance does not use the term "logic of statements" he did in lectures commonly use the statement just quoted to refer to the fact that theological statements do not hold the truth of God in themselves and that one must pass beyond its statements to the reality and truth of God himself.[63]

The *logic of pictures* is parallel to and essentially the same as the logic of statements and it was similarly commonly used by Torrance in lectures. It runs, "*A picture cannot picture, how it is a picture, of that which it pictures.*" Once again, one must see both the picture *and* the object or scene painted to understand the nature of the relation between the two, the type of picture it is, and the faithfulness of the representation. If one simply sees the picture, and not the reality, then it is still possible to pass to the object but only in imagination and only because one is already well acquainted with the referential function of pictures.

In all these cases, there is a gap or void which cannot be put into words or logicalized. Our thoughts can focus on one side of the gap or the other, terminating on each in turn, moving from one to the other, understanding the connection but unable to specify it in words. In the case of statements and pictures it is much easier to see or understand the relation across the gap, while in the first three (creation, incarnation, and Pentecost) the gap cannot be bridged from the human side, only crossed from the divine side. Nevertheless, there is, to some extent at least, an analogical relation between the two

---

[61]Ephesians 5:32, the "mystery" of "Christ and the church"; Colossians 1:27, "this mystery which is Christ in [us] you." Cf. Galatians 2.20, the mystery of I yet not I "but Christ who lives in me."

[62]Cf. Torrance, *Theological Science*, 348–9.

[63]Torrance, *Reality and Evangelical Theology* (Philadelphia, PA: Westminster Press, 1982), 145–9.

types of gap and this can help in understanding *how it is possible to know the realities on different sides of a gap as real realities,* yet find it difficult to logically comprehend the real coexistence of *both* realities across an unspecifiable gap when we cannot comprehend the "how" of the gap. We can therefore find ourselves bridging the gap by logicalizing and dismissing it through sitting loose to the full integrity of one or other of the realities thereby enabling them to be falsely united in a logical system.

The basic challenge of *an-* and *en-hypostasis* is the challenge of comprehending how *anhypostasis and enhypostasis* can really go together, that the humanity of Christ can be wholly the act of God and yet fully and genuinely human. Christ through the Spirit establishes his faith in our hearts. It is his act, yet by grace our act. Our faith now exists alongside his, two realities, and in faith we perceive the identity between them, between Christ's faith and what has become ours and we know our faith as a sharing in his. While we can understand this as the miracle, nature, and fact of grace, we cannot understand the "how" of it. The challenge therefore becomes the one of seeing how the reality of Christ's human faith for us can and does coexist alongside the reality of our faith without belittling it. It is therefore ultimately the difficulty of comprehending also our own existence as creatures totally dependent on God, and yet really existent and with our own genuine if limited freedom. It is the difficulty of seeing how we can really coexist personally alongside God as his creatures. Ultimately, it is the challenge we have in accepting the incomprehensibility yet reality of the grace of God, *that it establishes human reality alongside divine reality*. Just as the humanity of Jesus was *enhypostatically* real in the person of the Son, so analogously is our faith *enhypostatically* real in Christ's risen faith. The relation of Jesus's humanity to his divinity becomes the pattern for the relation of our faith to his risen faith. Just as both his humanity and divinity were real in his person, so both our faith and Christ's faith are real in union with him (and he with us) through the Spirit. Human and divine reality coexist in the miracle of grace. We can only endeavor to look at the reality of Christ himself to see that what we cannot comprehend (his reality as God, as man, one person) is the new, irrefutable, personalizing fact, the reality of what-God-is-and-has-done-and-ever-will-be-in-Christ, and endeavor to let it reshape all our thinking around the "new gate,"[64] "the logic of grace," establishing "the logic of Christ," establishing "the logic of the church" and "the logic of faith," thereby setting the logic of creation right back on its proper basis and revealing its true nature as creaturely reality.

In the way it pinpoints the logic of grace in the person of Christ, *an-* and *en-hypostasis* highlight the mystery of Christ in its starkest simplicity and enable the same logic of grace to be seen analogously as the guide and pattern for understanding all action of the triune God in creation and redemption. "All of God means all of man."

---

[64]A reference to Luther's dictum that someone comprehending the gospel for the first time is like "a cow staring at a new gate."

CHAPTER FOURTEEN

"Jesus Christ Is Our Human Response to God"

Divine and Human Agency in the Theology of Thomas F. Torrance

CHRISTIAN D. KETTLER

"Jesus Christ *is* our human response to God."[1] With this statement, Thomas F. Torrance, in a nutshell, audaciously contributes to the perennial debate concerning the relationship between God's action and human action. Is it God alone in the end *(monergism)* or humanity cooperating with God *(synergism)*? Does Torrance present himself as the most obvious monergist of all, if our human responses are supposedly "overridden" by Christ's, or is he on to something somewhat subtle, which may be his greatest theological heritage, perhaps even rivaling his work on the dialogue between theology and science? For Torrance is claiming that the classic Nicene-Chalcedonian tradition of Christology has not taken its own doctrine of *vere homo* seriously enough, and especially extending that into the atonement.[2] This thesis will be explored in terms of, first, knowledge of the triune God and creation. Knowledge of God involves the "two-fold movement" of reciprocity found both in the incarnation and that of Israel, the "you will be my people" in which God is deeply involved, not just the "I will be your God." Second, the centrality of the vicarious humanity of Christ to the human response to the Word of God features Christ as not just God in the flesh, but also "the hearing man," for us and in our place. The feebleness of our faith cries out for his faith (Gal 2:20). Third, so justification by faith is not just centered on our faith but God's grace. We know through Christ's faith through the Spirit in the church. Our believing is not obliterated, however, but grounded in the faith of Jesus, who continues to pray for us as our High Priest (Heb 7:25), so that we might participate in his life and ministry even now, in that taste of the kingdom of God.

---

[1] Thomas F. Torrance, *The Mediation of Christ*, 2nd edition (Colorado Springs, CO: Helmers and Howard, 1992), 80.
[2] See the additional connection with the hypostatic union, *theosis,* and union with Christ in Thomas F. Torrance, *Conflict and Agreement in the Church*, vol. 2 (1959, Eugene, OR: Wipf & Stock, 1996), 90–1.

KNOWLEDGE OF THE TRIUNE GOD AND CREATION

The one being, three persons of the Trinity revealed by the incarnate Word demonstrates a relationality in God that Torrance calls "onto-relations."[3] We have genuine knowledge of God in Jesus Christ because the being of God is known in his act, a favorite theme in Torrance's and Karl Barth's thought, which Torrance sees as Athanasian and Nicene.[4] This action is deeply personal so that "we cannot truly know God without being reconciled and renewed in Jesus Christ."[5] Theological knowledge cannot be separated from soteriology.

The emphasis upon Christ's response on our behalf and in our place is integral for Torrance even at the epistemological beginnings of theology. Genuine knowledge will only occur when there is a faithful response to the Word.[6] An acute problem occurs when one seeks to know divine agency and human agency logically in the sense that "all of grace" would mean "none of man."[7] This coincides with Torrance's massive work on the relationship between classical Christian theology and modern science, particularly physics. What most of modern theology and philosophy have not embraced, that modern science has, is that the art of the scientific question lets itself be questioned, to be embraced by reality beyond our own logic.[8] This is similar to the patristic teaching on knowing God *kata phusin* (κατὰ φύσιν) according to God's nature, knowing God in a "godly way."[9] For Torrance, this reflects the reality of modern scientific thinking: there is "one way of knowing," allowing nature to speak to us, but different "modes of rationality" that need to be respected.[10] In both theological and natural science it is necessary to "renounce ourselves," to forget old ways of thinking. Discipleship means we have no rational option but to follow Jesus, though to the world that may seem irrational. To deny yourself and follow the carpenter seems that way but there is a deeper logic at work.[11]

Creation is to be understood as a *contingent*, non-necessary creation, given as a gift of the grace of God.[12] However, it is also a contingence given with its own rationality, paving the way for the rise of modern science. Unfortunately, the "deistically detached" determinism of Newton and others advocated "a closed continuum of cause and effect"

---

[3] Thomas F. Torrance, *The Christian Doctrine of God, One Being Three Persons* (Edinburgh: T&T Clark, 1996), 157; *The Mediation of Christ*, 47.

[4] Torrance, *The Christian Doctrine of God*, 164.

[5] Thomas F. Torrance, *Theological Science* (New York: Oxford University Press, 1969), 41; *The Trinitarian Faith: The Evangelical Faith of the Ancient Catholic Church* (Edinburgh: T&T Clark, 1988), 54–6. See also the place of Michael Polanyi's "personal knowledge" in Torrance's thought: "The Place of Michael Polanyi in the Modern Philosophy of Science," in *Transformation and Convergence in the Frame of Knowledge* (Grand Rapids, MI: Eerdmans, 1984), 107–73; *Belief in Science and in Christian Life*, ed. Thomas F. Torrance (Edinburgh: The Handsel Press, 1980); and "Michael Polanyi and the Christian Faith: A Personal Report," in *Theological and Natural Science* (Eugene, OR: Wipf & Stock, 2002), 127–34.

[6] Torrance, *The Mediation of Christ*, 24–5; See also Elmer M. Colyer, *How to Read T.F. Torrance* (Downers Grove, IL: InterVarsity Press, 2008), 109.

[7] Colyer, *How to Read T.F. Torrance*, 120.

[8] Thomas F. Torrance, *God and Rationality* (Oxford: Oxford University Press, 1971), 54.

[9] Torrance, *The Trinitarian Faith*, 37–8.

[10] Thomas F. Torrance, *The Ground and Grammar of Theology* (Charlottesville: University Press of Virginia, 1980), 9; *God and Rationality*, 92.

[11] Thomas F. Torrance, "The Place of Christology in Biblical and Dogmatic Theology," in *Theology in Reconstruction* (Grand Rapids, MI: Eerdmans, 1965), 133.

[12] Thomas F. Torrance, *Divine and Contingent Order* (New York: Oxford University Press, 1981), vii–viii, 34–6, 110.

and a "rigid mechanical determinism."[13] Following the unfortunate heritage of dualistic thinking in the West—from Plato through Kant—the relationship between divine and human agency greatly suffered. A "yawning gap," Torrance argues, was created "between the otherworldly and this-worldly, the divine and the human," typical of much of modern theology that can now speak of Christ only in terms of "mythology," divorcing the empirical from the historical.[14] This "logico-causal" epistemology should be substituted by a *participatory* paradigm that does not put the burden on the Christian but on Christ and his accomplishment.[15] Gary Deddo suggests that here we can see the replacement of the Holy Spirit as agent for causal and impersonal habits of mind.[16]

The triune God revealed by Jesus Christ, exists eternally in *perichoresis,* in mutual love and reciprocity, one God in three persons, who never exists apart from the other two.[17] Therefore, in seeing Jesus, we see the Father and the Spirit as well, a reciprocal relationship, a reciprocity, which all relationships of love demand.[18] The "two-fold movement" or bidirectional reality of the incarnation is a reflection of whom God is from all eternity: one who loves and is loved. The incarnation may be a new event for God; love is not.[19]

Torrance is quick to cite Athanasius's concern that salvation be about "the whole man."[20] This includes the mind, as it did for Paul in Romans 12:2 ("be transformed by the renewal of your minds"). The incarnation and the atonement did not leave the mind untouched ("unbaptised reason"), as seems to be the case often in the history of theology, Protestant and Catholic, conservative and liberal.[21] At the essence of this is Torrance's belief that God took up our fallen human nature in the incarnation, in order to come to us and convert us as we are.

For Torrance the question of divine and human relationships is not a "zero-sum game" in which the more God is given the glory, the less place there is for the human.[22] As some end up saying, the more a response is fully human, the less can God be said to have acted.[23] However, Torrance teaches that the Son has provided the "faithful answer" to God's self-revelation before we have a chance to do otherwise.[24] Christ does ask a personal response of us, but "the response in word is put into our mouth by the Truth

---

[13] Thomas F. Torrance, *Christian Theology and Scientific Culture* (Belfast: Christian Journals Ltd., 1980), 133.

[14] Ibid., 134.

[15] Alexandra Radcliff, *The Claim of the Humanity of Christ: Salvation and Sanctification in the Theology of T. F. and J. B. Torrance* (Eugene, OR: Pickwick Publications, 2016), 146.

[16] Gary Deddo, "The Holy Spirit in T. F. Torrance's Theology," in *The Promise of Trinitarian Theology*, ed. Elmer M. Colyer (Lanham, MD: Rowman & Littlefield, 2001), 106.

[17] Torrance, *The Christian Doctrine of God,* 174.

[18] Ibid., 133; *The Trinitarian Faith,* 149.

[19] Torrance, *The Christian Doctrine of God,* 144. See Christian D. Kettler, *The God Who Loves and Is Loved: The Vicarious Humanity of Christ and the Response of Love* (Eugene, OR: Cascade, forthcoming).

[20] Thomas F. Torrance, "Athanasius: A Study in the Foundations of Classical Theology," in *Theology in Reconciliation: Essays towards Evangelical and Catholic Unity in West and East* (Grand Rapids, MI: Eerdmans, 1975), 230.

[21] Thomas F. Torrance, *Atonement: The Person and Work of Christ*, ed. Robert T. Walker (Downers Grove, IL: IVP Academic/Milton Keynes: Paternoster, 2009), 437, 440–7.

[22] Todd Speidell, *Fully Human in Christ: The Incarnation as the End of Christian Ethics* (Eugene, OR: Wipf & Stock, 2016), 9.

[23] Colyer, *How to Read T.F. Torrance,* 119.

[24] Torrance, *The Christian Doctrine of God,* 1.

Himself."[25] This is because of the incarnation. "'All of grace' does not mean 'nothing of man,'" Torrance is fond of saying, but, moreover, *"all of grace means all of man."*[26] Part of the problem, Torrance sees, is the wrong use of logic in the relationship of grace and the human will.[27] Thinking of these matters in logical or causal categories, however, does not mean to think illogically when one comes to such a complex and ineffable object, as Torrance's studies in theological and natural science teach him, but to think beyond appearances.[28] Torrance's mentor Karl Barth was often criticized for his insistence that salvation is all of grace. That could only mean that human beings were nothing, said his critics.[29] "The Latin heresy," which Torrance accuses western theology of propagating, is seen here, in contrast to the East and its doctrine of "the unassumed is the unhealed," including the assumption of our alienated minds.

Logically, God and human beings can only be juxtaposed, the Creator and the creature. We are not to be caught in this logical conundrum. Todd Speidell argues that, in contrast to John Webster's criticism that the vicarious humanity of Christ does not leave room for our response, rather, it creates room for our humanity that did not exist there before.[30] Cyril of Alexandria used to point to Moses's burning bush that was not consumed, so also Christ's humanity is not consumed by his deity as an act of pure grace.[31] Just as there was space for Jesus to act as a human being and still be God, so there is also a place for our genuine human responses and for God still genuinely to act. *All of grace means all of man.*[32] Torrance is able to say this because of his Nicene-Chalcedonian Christology which holds that Jesus is "fully God, fully human."

THE VICARIOUS HUMANITY OF CHRIST AND THE HUMAN RESPONSE OF THE WORD OF GOD

The Nicene-Chalcedonian Christology makes this even more so, because of Torrance's creative theology of what he calls not just the "vicarious death" of Christ but more fully the "vicarious *humanity*" of Christ, a major theme throughout his work. In fact, in an interview during his year as Moderator of the Church of Scotland, Torrance spoke of his theology, while being "deeply Nicene and doxological":

> "The cutting edge" of "my theology" would be, I suppose, what I call "the vicarious humanity of Christ"—the fact that Jesus Christ even in His humanity takes our place

---

[25] Thomas F. Torrance, "Introduction," in *The School of Faith: The Catechisms of the Reformed Faith*, trans. and ed. Thomas F. Torrance (New York: Harper and Row, 1959), xxxiii.

[26] Torrance, *The Mediation of Christ*, xii.

[27] Colyer, *How to Read T.F. Torrance*, 120.

[28] See Torrance, *Christian Theology and Scientific Culture*, 130–7, on the problem of applying logic to predestination.

[29] Thomas F. Torrance, "Karl Barth and the Latin Heresy," in *Divine Interpretation: Studies in Medieval and Modern Hermeneutics*, ed. Adam Nigh and Todd Speidell (Eugene, OR: Pickwick Publications, 2017), 63.

[30] Speidell, *Fully Human in Christ*, 9. Cf. John Webster, *Barth's Ethics of Reconciliation* (Cambridge: Cambridge University Press, 1995), 171; "The Christian in Revolt: Some Reflections on *The Christian Life*," in *Reckoning with Barth: Essays in Commemoration of the Centenary of Karl Barth's Birth*, ed. Nigel Biggar (London: Mowbray, 1988), 126.

[31] Thomas F. Torrance, *Incarnation: The Person and Life of Christ*, ed. Robert T. Walker (Downers Grove, IL: IVP Academic/Milton Keynes: Paternoster, 2008), 9.

[32] Torrance, *The Mediation of Christ*, xii.

in faith, prayer, worship, mediating all we are and do in His name toward the Father—but really believing, praying and worshipping Him in our place in such a way that He is our worship, and our faith is a sharing in His faith and our prayer a sharing in His prayer.[33]

Grace demands that God is free to descend and submit himself to the limitations of humanity, creating a "correlation and correspondence," which includes not just revelation but the response as well, "a true and faithful response."[34] The doctrine of election means that grace acts without prior human action.[35] So also justification by grace is not a denial of natural goodness but "that man is set upon a whole new basis in Grace."[36] This "hearing of man" is a part of revelation itself, "the all-significant middle term" of "the vicarious humanity of Christ," as substitute and representative in a radical way, "including every aspect of human response to Him: such as trusting and obeying, understanding and knowing, loving and worshipping."[37] He is the Word of God who has already heard the word.[38] However, where does a genuine response from believing human being come in? Jesus's humanity "invalidates all other ways of response."[39] Created humanity's responses are only "derived from, grounded in, and shaped by the very humanity of the Word" which we then proceed to read about in the narrative of the Gospels.[40] Torrance uses an endearing illustration of how the faith of Jesus is the basis for our faith, by telling of his young daughter learning to walk as she nonetheless grasped upon his strong hand.[41] The incarnation as "truth in the flesh" means that faith is not something far off but within and in union with humanity—the faith of the Son—not simply an external command or invitation.[42]

Torrance grounds such a reality on Galatians 2:19-20, combining union with Christ with the vicarious humanity of Christ: "I have been crucified *with Christ;* and it is no longer I who live, but Christ who lives *in me.* And the life I live I live by *the faith of the Son of God,* who loved me and gave himself for me." Note that Torrance translates "the faith *of* the Son of God," a translation scholars are increasingly preferring, stressing

---

[33]Thomas F. Torrance cited in R. D. Kernohan, "Tom Torrance: The Man and the Reputation," *Life and Work* 32, no. 5 (1976): 14. The most important writings on the vicarious humanity of Christ are found in Thomas F. Torrance, "The Mediation of Christ in our Human Response," in *The Mediation of Christ*, 73–98; "The Word of God and the Response of Man," in *God and Rationality*, 133–64; James B. Torrance, "The Vicarious Humanity of Christ," in *The Incarnation: Ecumenical Studies in the Nicene-Constantinopolitan Creed*, ed. T. F. Torrance (Edinburgh: Handsel Press, 1981), 127–47. The present writer has contributed several books exploring the implications of the doctrine of the vicarious humanity of Christ for contemporary theology, the church, and Christian life, beginning with *The Vicarious Humanity of Christ and the Reality of Salvation* (Lanham, MD: University Press of America, 1992); then *The God Who Believes: Faith, Doubt, and the Vicarious Humanity of Christ* (Eugene, OR: Cascade Books, 2005); *The God Who Rejoices: Joy, Despair, and the Vicarious Humanity of Christ* (Eugene, OR: Cascade Books, 2010); and most recently, *The Breadth and Depth of the Atonement: The Vicarious Humanity of Christ in the Church, the World, and the Self: Essays, 1990–2015* (Eugene, OR: Pickwick Publications, 2017).

[34]Torrance, "The Word of God and the Response of Man," 144–5.

[35]Thomas F. Torrance, *Theological Science* (Oxford: Oxford University Press, 1969), 86, 96–7.

[36]Ibid., 103.

[37]Ibid., "The Word of God and the Response of Man," 145.

[38]Torrance, *Theology in Reconstruction*, 157.

[39]. Torrance, "The Word of God and the Response of Man," 145.

[40]Ibid., 146.

[41]Torrance, *The Mediation of Christ*, 83.

[42]Torrance, *Incarnation*, 64.

the vicarious faith of Christ.[43] His faith is that which picks up our faltering, imperfect faith and believes in our place.[44] This does not denigrate our faith, because it is only through his faith that we can believe.[45] This includes all of our human responses to God, which even though they are Christ's, are still our responses. This is one aspect of Torrance's thought that his critics frequently fail to see, who criticize him for not allowing a place for a human response.[46] Our faith "is laid hold of, enveloped, and upheld by his unswerving faithfulness."[47] The question is, has Torrance obliterated any *distinction* between our responses and Christ's response? However, that is clearly the same objection one would have of Paul over Galatians 2:19-20, "I have been crucified with Christ ..." Again, is there in this objection more of the "logico-causal" mechanistic Aristotelian or Newtonian categories that are at work? Here, Torrance contends, one finds that the goal of faith is in the real text of the New Testament Scriptures, the humanity of Christ.[48]

Union with Christ is key to Torrance's understanding of divine and human agency. It is novel in some respects to traditional understandings, which find the union caused by justification, as an element of the *ordo salutis* (order of salvation). Torrance is clear to explain that there is one union between God and humanity, and that is the incarnation of the Word of God in Jesus Christ in his life, death, and resurrection.[49] The assumption of our human nature includes the sanctifying of our humanity, so there is a genuine atonement in the incarnation, ontologically grounded, beginning with the day of his birth: "Thus incarnation in the narrower sense of the term is itself redeeming event."[50] His holiness contrasts with our unholiness; his purity our impurity. Therefore, this "sanctifying union" does away with unholiness, impurity, and original sin.

Crucial to the union is its connection to the vicarious humanity of Christ as not only dealing with a "negative righteousness" but also presenting Christ's "positive righteousness" to us in the Son's faithful obedience to the Father. Otherwise, Christ's righteousness is only forensic and external to us. Therefore, union with Christ is not just a consequence of justification but also an essential component of the atonement, of who Christ is in relation to who we are, of the integration of the incarnation and atonement, and of the working together of divine and human agencies. The result is that we can now share in a filial relation with the Father through the Son.

Union with Christ is founded on the priesthood of Christ. Torrance is fond of quoting the words of Athanasius concerning Christ as priest: "He became Mediator between God and man in order that he might minister the things of God to us and the things of ours to God."[51] It is as our priest that Christ takes upon himself our prayers and worship, to appear before the holiness of the Father, something we are not able to do.[52] Human

---

[43]See *The Faith of Jesus Christ: Exegetical, Biblical, and Theological Studies*, ed. Michael F. Bird and Preston M. Sprinkle (Peabody, MA: Hendrickson, 2009).

[44]Torrance, *The Mediation of Christ*, 98.

[45]Thomas F. Torrance, "Preaching Jesus Christ," in Thomas F. Torrance, James B. Torrance, and David W. Torrance, *A Passion for Christ* (Edinburgh: The Handsel Press and Lenoir: PLC Publications, 1999), 24–5.

[46]*Contra* John Webster, "T. F. Torrance, 1915–2007," *International Journal of Systematic Theology* 10, no. 4 (2008): 371. See also his *Barth's Ethics of Reconciliation* (Cambridge: Cambridge University Press, 1995), 171.

[47]Torrance, "Preaching Jesus Christ," 25.

[48]Thomas F. Torrance, *Reality and Evangelical Theology* (Philadelphia, PA: Westminster Press, 1982), 93.

[49]Torrance, *Incarnation*, 81–2.

[50]Ibid., 82.

[51]Athanasius, *Against the Arians*, 4.6, cited by Torrance, *Theology in Reconciliation*, 110.

[52]Ibid., 114.

agency is enabled by the priesthood of Christ. This is only true, however, if Christ is truly our substitute, not just our representative, only an exemplary. The latter is what has happened in church history, Torrance contends.[53] Worship tends to be only that which we offer, not Christ's. This is so much so, that God is able to provide both the divine initiative "from the side of God toward humanity and from the side of humanity toward God … he propitiates himself."[54] We do not need to do anything to complete it but only to receive it gratefully.[55]

God deals with our sins in the active and passive obedience of the incarnate Son (see Phil. 2:5-11), beginning with "His incarnational union of our human nature with His divine nature."[56] The union of divine and human natures in Christ, the hypostatic union, therefore, has chief importance when it comes to understanding the relationship between divine agency and human agency. This "saving and sanctifying union, in which we are given to share … belongs to the very substance of our faith."[57] This is a paradox, to be sure. So also, both freedom and necessity govern human agency. We enter a room freely but bound by the unconditional knowledge of the room we have entered.[58]

In a discussion of Craig's catechism (1581), Torrance notices the danger of creating a second union with Christ (a "spiritual" union) in addition to the one union with Christ in the incarnation (the "carnal" union, "carnal" in the sense of the Word made *flesh*, or *carnis*).[59] As common thinking as this may be, does this not create something else to be added to the finished work of Christ "before it is real for us"? Does this not simply repeat the error of Roman Catholics and their *ex opere operato* view of the sacraments, as well as Protestants whose doctrine of union with Christ is effected by faith or by conversion? Torrance's concern is simply for the centrality of Christ in salvation, not the church or our faith. When the latter two take control, one is slipping into a doctrine either of human cooperation or of conditional grace, both manifestations of synergism. "There is only one union with Christ, that which He has wrought out with us in His birth and life and death and resurrection and in which He gives us to share through the gift of the Holy Spirit."[60] This is why Torrance can answer the question, "When were you born again?" by saying, "when Jesus Christ was born of the Virgin Mary and rose again from the virgin tomb, the first-born from the dead."[61] The center is on the incarnation, but there is still a place for sharing in that as the gift of the Holy Spirit, the time of personal faith. Torrance's point, however, is that "we are not saved by the act of our believing."[62] "Justifying faith" should never be seen as a "condition" for salvation. No, it is in relying on "the vicarious faith of Christ" that "we are really free to believe," without using faith for some "ulterior motive."

Who is the Christ with whom we are in union? He is one person, two natures, the *hypostatic union* of the creeds, which has great relevance for Torrance in establishing

---

[53] Ibid., 115–6, 133–4.

[54] Torrance, *Atonement*, 68.

[55] Paul D. Molnar, *Thomas F. Torrance: Theologian of the Trinity* (Farnham and Burlington, VT: Ashgate, 2009), 293.

[56] Torrance, "Introduction," in *The School of Faith*, lxxxvi.

[57] Ibid.

[58] Torrance, *Theological Science*, 36.

[59] Ibid., cvii.

[60] Ibid.

[61] Torrance, *The Mediation of Christ*, 85–6.

[62] Torrance, "Introduction," in *The School of Faith*, cix.

a basis for human agency in light of divine action. Christ himself demonstrates that we are no longer to separate the supernatural acts of God from the natural acts of humanity (Torrance's critique of dualistic thinking is appropriate here), just as one is not to separate the eschatology of the "already" from the "not yet." One does not "replace" the other.[63] So Torrance frequently uses the Patristic nomenclatures *anhypostasia* and *enhypostasia* to establish the integrity of both divine and human natures within the one person of Christ. Christ has no other existence apart from union with God (*anhypostasia* = "no person"). So also, God's existence comes in this one man, Jesus of Nazareth (*enhypostasia* = "in person").[64] Thus Torrance seeks to avoid much of the criticism of the two natures as flat "substances," by emphasizing the "living" union between the divine and human natures of Christ, his being known in the acts of salvation.

The *enhypostasia* establishes the uniqueness of God's reconciling action in the person of the historical Jesus of Nazareth, where he is chosen (elect) for all. Here the doctrines of election and substitution come together in Christ.[65] Judgment is not separated from the one in whom God and humanity have become one in the hypostatic union, fully God, fully human, as Chalcedon puts it.[66] Jesus not only utters "the word of truth" but also "the answer of man," the genuine agency of human beings.[67] Divine and human agency have no other place to be than in this genuine "word and answer" of the hypostatic union.

The hypostatic union, of course, cannot be known apart from God's reconciling acts in Jesus Christ, just as the being of God cannot be known known apart from his act.[68] Jesus Christ is one person, so the divine cannot be set asunder from the human in him ("not to be separated" in Chalcedon). There is no place for war between divine agency and human agency. Therefore, the act of the incarnation does not split the Father–Son relationship, even with the bearing of divine judgment on the cross.[69]

How then, for Torrance, does the human agency of Christ connect with our human agency? The role of the Holy Spirit, within Torrance's Christocentric theology, has prominent place, particularly as the place where the vicarious humanity of Christ "corresponds" with our humanity. "The Spirit echoes the intercession of Christ," connecting us with his priestly intercession (Rom. 8:26-27).[70] This is the very Spirit of Jesus, the Spirit in which he was born, baptized, and offered himself to the Father. He comes because of our weakness, Paul says in Romans, we do not know how to pray, so the Spirit intercedes for us in prayer (Rom. 8:34). Human agency does not have to depend on the sophistication or correctness of its prayers. The Spirit connects us with the vicarious prayer of Christ, our ascended High Priest who continues to pray for us at the right hand of the Father (Heb 7:25).[71] Pentecost signifies for us the giving of the Holy Spirit, not as a new event apart from the incarnation, but as the actualization of the incarnation and

---

[63] Ray S. Anderson, *The Seasons of Hope: Empowering Faith through the Practice of Hope* (Eugene, OR: Wipf & Stock, 2008), 95.
[64] Torrance, *Incarnation*, 84; *Theology in Reconstruction*, 131; Colyer, *How to Read T.F. Torrance*, 118–19.
[65] Torrance, *Incarnation*, 109.
[66] Ibid., 111.
[67] Ibid., 114.
[68] Ibid., 184.
[69] Ibid., 149.
[70] Ibid., 136.
[71] Ibid., 137.

atonement "subjectively within the personal lives of men and women with their decisions and living actions and upholding them creatively in their real relation with God."[72]

Since Jesus is not only the Word of God but also "Believer," his humanity can be vicarious, for us and in our place.[73] He has already believed "apart from your ever believing in him."[74] Torrance continues with dramatic words: "He has bound you to himself by his love in a way that he will never let you go, for even if you refuse him and damn yourself in hell his love will never cease. Therefore, repent and believe in Jesus Christ as your Lord and Savior."[75] Christ is our human response to God:

> He has acted in your place in the whole range of your human life and activity, including your personal decisions, and your responses to God's love, and even your acts of faith. He has believed for you, fulfilled your human response to God, and even made your personal decision for you, so that he acknowledges you before God as one who has already responded to God in him, who has already believed in God through him, and whose personal decision is already implicated in Christ's self-offering to the Father, so that in Jesus Christ you are already accepted in him. Therefore, renounce yourself, take up your cross and follow Jesus as your Lord and Saviour.[76]

This is the actualization, not just the possibility, of salvation in Christ. Salvation is in Christ's hands (and not just the sovereign God of most forms of monergism), not in our hands. Nonetheless, this is true discipleship. This is part of what it means to "renounce yourself," according to Torrance.[77] Torrance will not allow another source to enable Christ's work to "take effect" in us.[78]

Often viewed as irrelevant to "practical" Christianity, Torrance sees the ascension as the result of the incarnation; from God taking humanity's place, now humanity goes to "God's place," heaven, being exalted with Christ, who sits at the right hand of the Father.[79] Our humanity goes with the ascended Christ, so that our humanity, our human response, is part of his time in heaven. Human agency is now no longer to be thought of apart from divine agency. We see our eschatological hope from the resurrection to the ascension, in the One who waits for us.[80] His waiting, of course, is not without action, for he has poured for his Spirit upon us, for the sake of the continuing ministry of Jesus Christ through the church in the world (Acts 2:33), where even worship is led by the ascended Christ, our High Priest.[81] This is all as Christ continues to intercede for us by prayer (Heb. 7:25).[82]

---

[72]Torrance, *Atonement,* 189, 368.

[73]Torrance, *Theology in Reconstruction,* 131. However, Jesus is "not a Christian, saved by God," 136.

[74]Torrance, *The Mediation of Christ,* 94.

[75]Ibid.

[76]Ibid.

[77]Ibid.

[78]Thomas Smail, *The Giving Gift: The Holy Spirit in Person* (London: Hodder and Stoughton, 1988), 109–12.

[79]Torrance, *Atonement,* 287.

[80]Thomas F. Torrance, *Royal Priesthood: A Theology of Ordained Ministry*. 2nd edn (Edinburgh: T&T Clark, 1993), 43–5.

[81]Thomas F. Torrance, *Space, Time and Resurrection* (Grand Rapids, MI: Eerdmans, 1976), 117, *Atonement,* 270, 278.

[82]Torrance, *Atonement,* 274.

JUSTIFICATION BY GRACE AND PARTICIPATION BY FAITH THROUGH THE SPIRIT IN THE CHURCH

More fundamental to Torrance than the various themes of a typical *ordo salutis*, Elmer Colyer observes, is Torrance's striking claim that Jesus *is* our human response to God in the vicarious humanity of Christ.[83] This has great implications for justification by faith, or as Torrance prefers, justification *by grace*. Torrance observes that one of John Calvin's contributions was to reverse the *ordo salutis* of the medieval church and put union with Christ before justification and sanctification.[84] Justification by *grace*, by God's initiative (Rom. 3:24; Eph. 2:8), is emphasized by Torrance, to head off any idea that it is our acts of believing that save us.[85] It is "the faithful and obedient life of Jesus Christ," "the vicarious faith of Christ" that we can rely on. "It is only on this basis that we are really free to believe and have faith in Christ without the ulterior motive of using faith to secure our salvation."[86] Our response can only be that of "thanksgiving" for this movement "from the side of man."

Such a view of justification leaves no room for merit, as is true for any Reformation view. Torrance tells the story of his day as a young pastor in which an agitated elder had heard Torrance's sermon on justification by grace and approached him after the sermon: "Do you mean to say that being an elder for forty years does not count for my salvation?" he asked. Torrance's response was equally as blunt: "It is not what we are or do, but what Christ alone has done and continues to do for us as our Lord and Saviour, that counts. It is by his grace alone that we are put in the right by God, and by his grace alone that we are saved, and live day by day as Christians."[87] Therefore, the young Torrance in his doctoral dissertation on grace in the Apostolic Fathers did not find a robust freedom from merit in them but still on "the debit side of an account with God," so that "they did not live from God so much as toward God."[88]

As Torrance further puts it, since there is no divorce between Christ's Word and Act in his Person, he "is *himself* our *justification, redemption, mediation and propitiation; he is himself the resurrection and the life*," citing 1 Corinthians 1:30 and John 11:25, what he calls "the absolute singularity of Christ," our great High Priest.[89] These actions are more than the "results and consequences" of Christ's actions which would satisfy Smail's critique of Torrance.[90] As the righteousness of God, Christ is both the creator and answer of righteousness in his "obedience of faith," the one true "satisfaction" to the Father.[91]

---

[83] Colyer, *How to Read T.F. Torrance*, 112.

[84] Thomas F. Torrance, "The Distinctive Character of the Reformed Tradition," in *Incarnational Ministry: Essays in Honor of Ray S. Anderson*, ed. Christian D. Kettler and Todd H. Speidell (Colorado Springs, CO: Helmers and Howard, 1990), 6.

[85] Torrance, *The School of Faith*, cix.

[86] Ibid.

[87] Thomas F. Torrance, "My Parish Ministry: Alyth, 1940–43," in *Gospel, Church, and Ministry: Thomas F. Torrance Collected Studies* I, ed. Jock Stein (Eugene, OR: Pickwick Publications, 2012), 40.

[88] Thomas F. Torrance, *The Doctrine of Grace in the Apostolic Fathers* (1948, Eugene, OR: Wipf & Stock, 1996), 94–5.

[89] Thomas F. Torrance, "The Atonement, the Singularity of Christ and the Finality of the Cross: The Atonement and the Moral Order," in *Universalism and the Doctrine of Hell*, ed. Nigel M. de S. Cameron (Grand Rapids, MI: Baker, 1993), 232–3; "Karl Barth and the Latin Heresy," 59. See also Colyer, *How to Read T.F. Torrance*, 111–12.

[90] Smail, *The Giving Gift*, 109–12; Kettler, *The Breadth and Depth of the Atonement*, 99.

[91] Torrance, *Atonement*, 103.

Justification, for Torrance, is not just a forensic, non-imputation of our sins through the pardon of Christ, but a "positive sharing in His human righteousness."[92] An "atoning exchange" (2 Cor. 8:9) takes place, which is a part of our union with Christ, in which Christ deals with the "actual sins" of our fallen human nature as well as original sin. This is the "wonderful exchange" of Calvin's *Institutes*.[93] But this is can be found as well in the Fathers, such as the Epistle to Diognetes as "the sweet exchange."[94] The importance of this is great, Torrance contends, for we need the union of our human nature with his divine nature in order to benefit from his righteousness, his "perfect filial relation" on earth with the Father.

Union with Christ is the predecessor of justification by grace, in contrast with scholastic Calvinism and its *ordo salutis*. The life, death, and resurrection of the Son who took upon himself our fallen human nature, brings about this "holy union," establishing genuine contact with who we are now, in order to "sanctify" it.[95] Therefore, justification by grace includes the incarnation itself in a narrower sense as a redeeming event, not just the cross, or even personal faith. This act "entirely displaces" the autonomous human will and its "self-justification," since a real man, Jesus Christ, has responded to the act of God for us and in our place.[96] We are able to see the saving significance of the humanity of Jesus in terms of the atonement in light of the union of the human and divine natures.[97] What place, then, can Torrance claim for a genuine human response? his critics ask. How does Torrance respond to this?

Justification as part of union with Christ means that justification is essentially "corporate," that those who are justified include the entirety of humanity.[98] So then Torrance can naturally speak of our "participation" in justification, in the righteousness of Christ.[99] Participation brings a genuine place for our human agency that is, nonetheless, based on the human agency of Jesus Christ. We can now participate in that which has already been accomplished, justification.[100] Eucharistic participation becomes especially meaningful as the means by which the "accomplished" act of the Lord continues to be meaningful, as a "continual participation in Christ's new humanity."[101]

Participation is where our human agency becomes intertwined with the work of the Holy Spirit, "the two-way activity" (God toward humanity and humanity toward God) of the Spirit that corresponds and coordinates with the "two-way movement" of the incarnation, the descent and the ascent in Jesus with us today.[102] This is the Holy Spirit's participation in the continuing vicarious humanity of Christ, working within and among us, ruling out synergism.[103]

---

[92] Torrance, *The School of Faith*, lxxxvi.

[93] John Calvin, *Institutes of the Christian Religion*, ed. John T. McNeill, trans. Ford L. Battles, Library of Christian Classics 20 and 21 (Philadelphia, PA: Westminster Press), 4.17.2; Torrance, *The Trinitarian Faith*, 179.

[94] *The Epistle to Diognetus* 9.2; Torrance, *The Trinitarian Faith*, 179.

[95] Torrance, *Incarnation*, 82.

[96] Ibid., 123.

[97] Torrance, *The School of Faith*, lxxxvi.

[98] Torrance, *Atonement*, 128.

[99] Ibid., 133–4.

[100] Ibid., 134.

[101] Ibid., 136.

[102] Torrance, *The Christian Doctrine of God*, 153; George Hunsinger, "The Dimension of Depth: Thomas F. Torrance on the Sacraments," in *The Promise of Trinitarian Theology*, 153.

[103] Torrance, *Theology in Reconciliation*, 136.

Participation is based on the very triune being of God as relational. In fact, the Father, the Son, and the Holy Spirit only know each other as such in their persons, their "onto-relations."[104] The early church knew this by the term *perichoresis* or "a circle of reciprocal relations."[105] "Reciprocity" can mean that a free will exists because it is made free by God ("If the Son makes you free, you will be free indeed," Jn. 8:36), but only as it exists in reciprocity with God.

"Reciprocity" is important for Torrance, for he sees the biblical creation of a "community of reciprocity" created by God in Israel, taking seriously language that comes in the context of community.[106] What is most difficult, however, for us to accept, is that the response is created *for us, vicariously,* "bending" back our wills.[107] The vicarious humanity of Christ takes away our place, for our sake. We may find it difficult to see the genuine freedom in that, until we see the freedom of Jesus, freedom in obedience.

The foundational "community of reciprocity" is Israel, where history in "its innermost being and life" actualizes the covenant.[108] The life of Israel creates a reciprocity from the side of humanity in acts of atonement, especially in terms of the Hebrew *gaal* (kinsman-redeemer), and *kipper* (expiation and propitiation).[109] The fact that God himself is one being, three persons, Father, Son, and Holy Spirit, a "communion in love" in himself, means that he desires to create a "community of personal reciprocity in love."[110]

Israel provides the "matrix" or "womb" to understand the worship of the Son to the Father, the basis for the worship in the church.[111] Therefore, Jesus Christ as our great High Priest prays because we are unable and worships because we are unable. However, we can participate through that worship by the Spirit in the church. "In a very real sense Christ Jesus is himself our worship."[112] We may worship "for Christ's sake," motivated by him, but that is different from worshipping "with him and in him," for that is when we have access "through him into the immediate presence of God."[113] Jesus as the true worshipper ("the Offerer and the Offering" in Chrysostom's Liturgy)[114] cannot possess "authentic human agency" and represent us vicariously in worship unless he has a truly human mind, which the Apollinarians denied.[115] As such, he becomes the judgment against all false "priesthoods" created by human beings throughout time.[116] This can include *sacramental sacerdotalism*, but also a Protestant *psychological sacerdotalism*. Both take the form of

---

[104]Ibid., 157; *The Mediation of Christ,* 47.

[105]Torrance, *The Christian Doctrine of God,* 174.

[106]Torrance, *God and Rationality,* 146–53; *The Mediation of Christ,* chapters 1 and 2.

[107]Thomas F. Torrance, *When Christ Comes and Comes Again* (1957, Eugene, OR: Wipf & Stock, 1996), 42–3; *Theology in Reconstruction,* 126, 132, 157; *The Mediation of Christ,* 79–80; *Incarnation,* 212; and *Atonement,* 70.

[108]Torrance, *Atonement,* 43.

[109]Ibid., 33–65.

[110]Thomas F. Torrance, *Trinitarian Perspectives: Toward Doctrinal Agreement* (Edinburgh: T&T Clark, 1994), 3.

[111]Torrance, *The Mediation of Christ,* 5–46.

[112]Torrance, *Royal Priesthood,* xvi.

[113]Thomas F. Torrance, "The Paschal Mystery of Christ and the Eucharist," in *Theology in Reconciliation,* 134.

[114]"The Prayer of the Cherubic Hymn," in *Service Book of the Holy Eastern Orthodox Catholic and Apostolic Church* (Antiochian Orthodox Christian Archdiocese of North America, 1997), 105.

[115]Thomas F. Torrance, "The Mind of Christ in Worship: The Problem of Apollinarianism in the Liturgy," in *Theology in Reconciliation,* 150, 118, 176. See also *The Mediation of Christ,* 86–92.

[116]Torrance, "The Mind of Christ in Worship," 206.

"worship as man's self-expression." The baptism of Christ is the "one baptism" for the church, the one response of obedience that begins his ministry, in which our baptisms participate, not simply as acts of obedience.[117] This is a reciprocity that God creates, that is not dependent upon us, not remaining detached from and untouched by us, but as created by the Holy Spirit.[118] Ultimately, this is a sacrament of God's faithfulness and the ground of our faith.[119] We also bring nothing to the eucharistic sacrifice. Such "communities of reciprocity" have Christ as their worshipper in terms of not only representation but also substitution.[120] This again is a place to see the one act of Christ once and for all not only in terms of his sacrifice, but also as we participate eucharistically daily and eternally with the ascended and eternal Christ.[121] Eucharistic worship means to "echo" the eternal intercession of Christ.[122] The "echo," Robert Stamps observes, reflects the importance of the Word, the auditive, in Torrance's theology.[123]

Such life under the resurrection and ascension of Jesus is life delivered from what Torrance calls "nomistic" (*nomos* = "law") existence, that is a law of a life of "necessity," of determinism and fatalism, of fallen human nature under the judgment of the law, rather than that of freedom.[124] Justification, the resurrection, and the ascension of Jesus deliver us from the bondage of time not by its annihilation but by its recreation. Here is the place of the Holy Spirit who intercedes for us and actualizes Christ for us, "in believing response and brings us into union himself."[125]

Participation through union with Christ, even to the point of the cross, for Torrance, then leads us to the process of *theosis*, or "deification" or "godliness."[126] The source of this is from such Eastern Fathers as Athanasius, who said that the Son "became man that we might be made divine," or "godly."[127] However, in Torrance's words, "we are not made divine but are preserved in our humanity."[128] This is part of the twofold movement from God to humanity and humanity to God, so that "he might minister the things of God to us and of us to God (Athanasius)" is the goal of the Christian life.[129] The things "of us to God" connecting with the vicarious humanity of Christ are not done in an impersonal way, such as in an absorption by a divine force.[130] This view of *theosis* "lifts

---

[117]Thomas F. Torrance, "The One Baptism Common to Christ and the Church," in *Theology in Reconciliation*, 87–8.

[118]Ibid., 100.

[119]Ibid., 103–4.

[120]Torrance, *Space, Time and Resurrection*, 116.

[121]George Hunsinger, *The Eucharist and Ecumenism* (Cambridge: Cambridge University Press, 2008), 156.

[122]Torrance, *Conflict and Agreement in the Church*, vol. 2, 176.

[123]Robert J. Stamps, *The Sacrament of the Word Made Flesh: The Eucharistic Theology of Thomas F. Torrance* (Eugene, OR: Wipf & Stock, 2007), 220–1.

[124]Torrance, *Atonement*, 253–5; *Space, Time and Resurrection*, 96–8, Molnar, *Thomas F. Torrance: Theologian of the Trinity*, 243–4.

[125]Torrance, *The Mediation of Christ*, 110, 117.

[126]See Myk Habets, *Theosis in the Theology of Thomas Torrance*. Ashgate New Critical Thinking in Religion, Theology and Biblical Studies (Farnham: Ashgate, 2009).

[127]Athanasius, *De inc.*, 54.3, cited by Torrance, *The Trinitarian Faith*, 156.

[128]Torrance, *The Mediation of Christ*, 64.

[129]Athanasius, *De inc.*, 4.6, cited by Torrance, *The Trinitarian Faith*, 154; and "Athanasius: A Study in the Foundations of Classical Theology," in *Theology and Reconciliation*, 228.

[130]Jason Radcliff, *Thomas F. Torrance and the Church Fathers: A Reformed, Evangelical, and Ecumenical Reconstruction of the Patristic Tradition* (Eugene, OR: Pickwick Publications, 2014), 97–8.

us up in Christ to enjoy a new fullness of human life in a blessed communion with divine life."[131] Christ is the one who "personalizes" and "humanizes" through our participation in his humanity, the reality of *theosis,* sharing in life with the triune God.[132]

Some do not see Torrance as permitting genuine human freedom. John Webster sees the vicarious humanity of Christ as threatening to "absorb" the humanity of others, versus Barth's approach in which he "graciously evokes corresponding patterns of being."[133] Emphasizing "a unique, vicarious work" of Christ can immobilize the Christian life, according to Webster, failing to give direction for responsibilities and obligations.[134] However, this surely misses the significance of the *ontological* depth of the vicarious humanity, particularly in its connection with union with Christ, which provides a power far beyond that of the moral exhortation that Webster seems to promote. What "evokes" more than the closeness of our union with Christ as his sons and daughters? An *imitatio* by itself still keeps Jesus the teacher at a distance, however we may revere him.

We can rest in such "realized eschatology" that "our adoption, sanctification and regeneration have already taken place in Christ."[135] Does such an objectification of salvation inevitably lead to universalism? Many have thought so, but Torrance does not agree. Again, the problem of "logico-causal" thinking arises. Atonement may be objectified, but that does not rule out human agency.[136] There is something inexplicable and baffling, Torrance contends, when someone rejects the gospel. "That is to say, if people are damned, they are damned by the gospel."[137] The sin of humanity never nullifies the unconditional grace of God. The love of God never ends: "for even if you refuse him and damn yourself in hell his love will never cease."[138]

CONCLUSION

Both monergists and synergists will find much to criticize in Torrance's view on divine and human agency, but they will also find much that will challenge their traditional positions. In an age of "analytical theology" which promotes "precision," Torrance's emphasis on a paradox between the divine and the human may seem incoherent to some. Torrance himself warns of a certain "vertigo" in dealing with realities such as the ascension, the Spirit, and the Trinity.[139] Torrance, with the Fathers, would add that the Trinity, for example, is more to be adored than expressed.[140] He quickly reminds us that

---

[131]Torrance, *The Trinitarian Faith,* 189. See also page 155 on salvation as taking place within the being and life of God; "The Relevance of Orthodoxy," in *T. F. Torrance and Eastern Orthodoxy,* ed. Matthew Baker and Todd Speidell (Eugene, OR: Wipf & Stock, 2015), 336.

[132]Thomas F. Torrance, "The Goodness and Dignity of Man in the Christian Tradition," *Modern Theology* 4, no. 4 (1988): 320; *The Mediation of Christ,* 67–72.

[133]Webster, *Barth's Ethics of Reconciliation,* 171.

[134]John Webster, "Christology, Imitability, and Ethics," *Scottish Journal of Theology* 39, no. 3 (1986): 310–11, 317, 322–3.

[135]Torrance, *Theology in Reconciliation,* 89. See also Hunsinger, "The Dimension of Depth," 161.

[136]Andrew Purves, *Exploring Christology and Atonement: Conversations with John McLeod Campbell, H. R. Mackintosh and T. F. Torrance* (Downers Grove, IL: InterVarsity Press, 2015), 223.

[137]Torrance, "Preaching Jesus Christ," 31; *Atonement,* 156–8.

[138]Torrance, *The Mediation of Christ,* 94.

[139]Torrance, *Space, Time, and Resurrection,* 136.

[140]Torrance, *The Christian Doctrine of God,* ix; *The Trinitarian Faith,* 46.

the hypostatic union of the divine and human natures in Christ both communicate the deity of Christ and preserve our true humanity. Based on the Pauline doctrine of being "in Christ" (2 Cor. 5:17), this becomes a key for Torrance in enabling him to speak of our participation by faith through the Spirit in the Son's obedient response to the Father, the vicarious humanity of Christ, as the essence of the atonement. As Torrance adds, citing Cyril of Alexandria, not only do we pray *with* Christ, but we also pray *through* and, most importantly, *in* Christ.[141] Nevertheless, the "inner citadel" of human freedom that has been built up in humanity especially since the Enlightenment is a perennial foe for the church. On the basis of the hypostatic union and the vicarious humanity of Christ the church will be able to provide a new vision of what it means to be human; a new vision of being human in terms of both freedom and obedience to God. The gospel truth of the hypostatic union and our union with Christ stands strong against the force of "logico-causal" thinking.

Torrance achieves, despite his critics, a merging of the Reformation doctrine of justification by grace through faith with the Patristic doctrine of *theosis* ("deification"), in order to provide a divinely centered, relational paradigm for divine and human agency, based on the grace of union with the vicarious humanity of Christ and participation in the life of God. The Pauline declaration of "Not I, but Christ" (Gal. 2:20) sings of sharing in God's life and still maintains a Reformed distinction between the Creator and the creature. Such teaching brings great implications for practical theology, particularly in spiritual formation and pastoral care, where legalism or license burdens many Christians. The personal nature of Torrance's "onto-relational" soteriology has great promise where one seeks to find the meeting of divine and human agency in the mediation of Jesus Christ.

---

[141]Torrance, *Theology in Reconciliation*, 176.

CHAPTER FIFTEEN

Thomas F. Torrance and Ecclesiology

KATE TYLER

INTRODUCTION

Unlike the *magnum opus* of Karl Barth, whose *Church Dogmatics* directly evokes the idea that theology is done by and for the Church, Thomas Torrance's theology is often considered abstractive, overly technical, and not easily accessible to the uninitiated reader. This is an unfortunate association, for Torrance has much to say to the Church in an era where continued focus on missional praxis sometimes leaves the deeper theological foundations of ecclesiology and missiology lying backstage while the "latest and greatest" ideas for revitalizing the Church are played out before the audience.

As a dogmatic theologian, Torrance's theological structure is centered on the incarnation of Jesus Christ, one of the three persons of the triune God.[1] Consequently, Torrance's ecclesiology constantly dialogues with Christology and the doctrine of the Trinity. This brief précis will begin with a survey of Torrance's service to the Church and its mission. The key relationships between ecclesiology and Christology and the Trinity will be highlighted before the continuity and discontinuity of the Church throughout history is addressed. This will open up the way for more detailed ecclesiological reflection, where we will focus on the nature of order, the attributes of the church, and the word, sacraments, and ministry. This will all contribute to our observations on Torrance's contributions to missiology, and the ecumenical movement.

A MISSIONARY BIOGRAPHY

Service to the Church and its mission was a central tenet of Torrance's sense of vocation. His missional impulse was formed by twelve years spent on the mission field in China, before returning to Scotland with his mother and siblings while his father remained in China for a further seven years. Torrance entered divinity studies at New College intending to work as a missionary in Tibet, but throughout his time studying in Edinburgh he came to reenvision his vocation as that of an academic theologian whose call was to

---

[1] Torrance preferred "dogmatic" over "systematic," for while a systematic theologian might focus on the logic and rationality of a particular system, dogmatic theology was theology done in response to the self-revelation of God in Jesus Christ. Torrance thus considers "proper theology" to be "dogmatic theology." Thomas F. Torrance, *The Ground and Grammar of Theology* (Charlottesville: University Press of Virginia, 1980), 48–51.

serve the Church and its mission. One particularly influential voice in his life during this time was his lecturer Hugh Ross Mackintosh who issued the challenge that "a theology which failed to sustain and encourage a missionary or evangelistic attitude was not a theology worthy of the name" and also encouraged his students to test each doctrine by asking how it would be received on the mission field.[2] Mackintosh was an example for Torrance of how a theologian could serve the Church and its mission from within the university world.[3]

After a scholarship year of postgraduate study with Karl Barth in Germany, Torrance's first appointment was a year teaching at Auburn Theological Seminary in New York. Although he was offered a professorship at Princeton University, he returned to Scotland before the start of the Second World War to serve in army chaplaincy. Chaplains were required to complete two years of ordained ministry before being accepted for military service, so after a further brief postgraduate stint at Oxford, Torrance became a Presbyterian minister in the rural parish of Alyth in order to meet these requirements and "to bring a serious and solid dose of reality to his academic reflection."[4] He then served as a chaplain in the Middle East, after which he returned to Alyth and then moved to the larger parish of Beechgrove, completing ten years of pastoral ministry. Torrance attributes his time in parish ministry with giving his theology a practical grounding, later observing that visitation to people's homes had taught him much about how to best communicate the gospel message,[5] as well as the "relevance and healing power of the Word of God."[6]

Having remained an active participant in the academic world during his time as a minister, including launching the *Scottish Journal of Theology*, Torrance commenced lecturing at New College in 1952. He first held the Chair of Ecclesiastical History, and then the Chair of Christian Dogmatics, the latter having responsibility for teaching Christology, soteriology, and ecclesiology. It was during the first portion of his time at New College that Torrance was most involved in ecumenical dialogue. He served on the Faith and Order Commission from 1948 until 1962, contributing an essay entitled "Eschatology and Eucharist" to the *Intercommunion* report circulated for discussion at the Faith and Order conference in 1952 at Lund, where he was in attendance.[7] Torrance published a number of other essays and articles on the Church during this period, many of which are collated in the two volumes of *Conflict and Agreement in the Church*, alongside *Theology in Reconciliation* and *Theology in Reconstruction*.[8] Torrance held the Chair of Christian Dogmatics until his retirement from New College in 1979, after which he went on to be involved with other ecumenical efforts which developed out of his personal friendships and theological relationships. The most significant of these was the Orthodox–Reformed dialogue on the doctrine of the Holy Trinity, an example of the sort

---

[2] Alister E. McGrath, *T. F. Torrance: An Intellectual Biography* (Edinburgh: T&T Clark, 1999), 29–31.

[3] Ibid., 31. Part of Mackintosh's appeal for Torrance was his appreciation for the work of Karl Barth, since the first volume of *Church Dogmatics* had just been translated into English. Torrance would also go on to follow in Mackintosh's professional footsteps; Mackintosh was also a minister in the Beechgrove Parish, as well as Professor at New College.

[4] Ibid., 60.

[5] Thomas F. Torrance, *Gospel, Church and Ministry*, ed. Jock Stein, *Thomas F. Torrance Collected Studies*, vol. 1 (Eugene, OR: Pickwick Publications, 2012), 51.

[6] Ibid., 35.

[7] Stanley S. MacLean, *Resurrection, Apocalypse, and the Kingdom of Christ*, Princeton Theological Monograph Series (Eugene, OR: Pickwick Publications, 2012), 126.

[8] Ibid., 103.

of robust theological dialogue that Torrance felt was necessary for true ecumenism.[9] It was also in his retirement that Torrance was twice able to visit the Xiang people among whom his father had labored faithfully in China.[10]

A CHRISTOCENTRIC AND TRINITARIAN ECCLESIOLOGY

Colyer aptly observes that "Torrance thinks out every aspect of his ecclesiology in an essentially christocentric, pneumatological and trinitarian manner."[11] This Christological and trinitarian approach is paradigmatic for Torrance, for he holds that the doctrine of the Trinity belongs "to the essential structure of faith in God and to the intrinsic grammar of Christian thought,"[12] while the incarnation and the pattern of the hypostatic union exercise a regulative influence on theological methodology. Just as Christology takes into account both Christ's divinity, "in the light of what he is in himself in his internal relations with God," and his humanity, drawing on the "actual matrix of interrelations from which he sprang as Son of David and Son of Mary,"[13] so too the Christological pattern involves holding two dimensions in relation, offering a model for dealing with theological paradox. However, because the hypostatic union is "grounded in, derived from, and is continually upheld" by the relations of the three triune persons,[14] Christology cannot be separated from the doctrine of the Trinity. Consequently, "to speak of Jesus as Son of God means, in the same breath, speech about the Father and the Holy Spirit. No doctrine of the person of Christ in his divine and human being is possible, except in that eternal mystery and in that Trinitarian context."[15]

This paradigm plays out in Torrance's preference for the language of the "body of Christ" over the many other New Testament images that describe the people of God. Torrance argues that the body of Christ is the fullest and the most Christological image for the Church, directing our attention to Christ as the head of the Church since it is only in him that Christians are formed into one body.[16] Because humans are incorporated into Christ through the Spirit, "body of Christ" is "no mere figure of speech but describes an ontological reality."[17] It is a somatic and pneumatic reality.[18] This is where the work of the Holy Spirit comes into clear focus, for "the Communion of the Spirit has to be understood as correlative to the union of God and man wrought out in the Life and

---

[9]Thomas F. Torrance, *Conflict and Agreement in the Church: Order and Disorder*, vol. 1 (Eugene, OR: Wipf & Stock, 1996), 228. Torrance observes that the issue with the early Faith and Order conferences after the formation of the WCC in 1948 was a reluctance to "get down to bed-rock, to a proper theological basis and dogmatic procedure."

[10]Alister E. McGrath, *Thomas F. Torrance: An Intellectual Biography* (Edinburgh: T&T Clark, 1999), 238–40.

[11]Elmer M. Colyer, *How to Read T.F. Torrance: Understanding His Trinitarian & Scientific Theology* (Downers Grove, IL: InterVarsity Press, 2001), 262.

[12]Torrance, *The Ground and Grammar of Theology*, 40.

[13]Thomas F. Torrance, *The Mediation of Christ* (Edinburgh: T&T Clark, 1992), 3.

[14]Ibid., 65.

[15]Thomas F. Torrance, *Incarnation: The Person and Life of Christ*, ed. Robert T. Walker (Downers Grove, IL: IVP Academic/Milton Keynes: Paternoster, 2008), 164.

[16]Thomas F. Torrance, "What Is the Church," *Ecumenical Review* 11, no. 1 (October 1958): 6.

[17]Torrance, *Conflict and Agreement: Order and Disorder*, 248. See also Thomas F. Torrance, *Royal Priesthood* (Edinburgh: Oliver and Boyd Ltd, 1955), 29–35.

[18]Torrance, *The Trinitarian Faith: The Evangelical Theology of the Ancient Catholic Church* (Edinburgh: T&T Clark, 1993), 290.

Work of Jesus Christ."[19] Torrance derives this realist understanding of union with Christ through the Spirit from Irenaeus,[20] emphasizing that the Spirit outworks subjectively what has been accomplished objectively in Christ.[21]

It is worth commenting on Torrance's use of analogy in relation to his frequent taking up of the analogy of the body of Christ. Analogical language describes ontological reality. Neinhardt observes that Torrance uses analogy as a disclosure model to show "similarity within dissimilarity … a partial likeness or reflection which is true but not exhaustive."[22] Just as scientific research uses analogical language to cross-reference, using images on one level to refer to an imageless reality on a higher level,[23] Torrance argues that there is an analogical correspondence between Christ and the Church. This is a true, ontological relation between the head and the members, which Torrance describes as an "analogy of relations," or "an analogical correspondence of opposites," since to use the language of an "analogy of being" would be to wrongly suggest an equal ontological identity between the Creator and the creature.[24] God creates the world in divine freedom, and while the world remains dependent on God, God is not dependent on the world. This leads to the "asymmetrical relation between God and the world."[25] In the same way, it is only through God's gracious acts that the Church is enabled to participate in the trinitarian life through union with Christ in the Spirit. Torrance notes that Barth refers to this as the "analogy of grace," wherein humans do not have any inherent capacity to know God beyond that which God gifts to us in the incarnation and through the work of the Spirit.[26] It is thus that the Church exists in a framework of contingent relationality. It remains part of creation, but is graced by God in being set apart through the work of the Spirit and the "particularity of the Incarnation."[27]

In order to avoid speaking of the Church as having "divine" and "human" elements, because to suggest that divine and human elements are united in the Church as a parallel to the divine and human natures of Christ would be a misuse of theological analogy,[28] Torrance instead identifies its "vertical" and "horizontal" dimensions. Christ is still the One from whom this language is derived, since it is in Christ alone that the vertical dimension of divinity, and the horizontal dimension of humanity uniquely meet. However, while Christ's two natures are united in his one person, and cannot be confused, changed, divided, or separated, the vertical and horizontal dimensions of the Church are not united in the same way. Thus, the vertical dimension of the Church is the reality that humanity is genuinely invited to participate in the *koinonia* of the Holy Trinity through union with Christ, but only in a way appropriate to our creatureliness. The horizontal dimension is the concrete and historical existence of the Church in space and time as a visible entity

---

[19] Thomas F. Torrance, ed., *The School of Faith: The Catechisms of the Reformed Church* (Eugene, OR: Wipf & Stock Publishers, 1996), cvi.

[20] Torrance, *The Trinitarian Faith*, 254.

[21] Torrance, *The School of Faith*, cvi.

[22] W. Jim Neidhardt, "Introduction," in Thomas F. Torrance, *The Christian Frame of Mind: Reason, Order, and Openness in Theology and Natural Science* (Eugene, OR: Wipf & Stock, 2015), xxvii.

[23] Torrance, *The Ground and Grammar of Theology*, 115–17.

[24] Thomas F. Torrance, *The Christian Doctrine of God, One Being Three Persons* (Edinburgh: T&T Clark Ltd., 1996), 219–20.

[25] Thomas F. Torrance, *Divine and Contingent Order* (Edinburgh: T&T Clark, 1998), 34.

[26] Torrance, *Theology in Reconstruction* (Grand Rapids, MI: Eerdmans, 1965), 113–16.

[27] Torrance, *Conflict and Agreement: Order and Disorder*, 17.

[28] Torrance, *Theology in Reconstruction*, 185.

within human society. The Church's vertical dimension shapes its horizontal dimension only as Christ himself is actively at work within the Church; participation in the life of the Trinity is what makes the Church the body of Christ, in distinction to every other organization or institution.[29]

Koinonia, or communion, is the central motif which Torrance uses to describe both the triune God and the community of the Church. Because "the three divine Persons mutually dwell in one another and coinhere or inexist in one another while nevertheless remaining other than one another and distinct from one another,"[30] Father, Son, and Spirit are not separate individuals.[31] It is this "ever-living ever-loving Being, the *Being for Others* which the three divine Persons have in common,"[32] which is the basis of God's freedom to seek and create fellowship with humanity. "In loving us in the gift of his dear Son and the mission of his Spirit he loves us with the very Love which he is."[33] This is why Torrance argues that the Church does not merely mirror the triune love by attempting to love each other as the triune persons love each other. Instead, through the influence of the vertical dimension on the horizontal dimension, the Church's life is formed into "a community of reciprocity among [humankind], which through the Spirit is rooted in and reflects the trinitarian relations in God himself."[34] The Church has a creaturely *koinonia* which correlates to the triune *koinonia*. Thus, it is the community that results from the intersection of the vertical and horizontal dimensions, so that

> the community of reciprocity which we have with God is actualised within the reciprocities we have with one another in human society, but in such a creative way that our reciprocities with one another are organised and informed by the intelligible presence of God through his Word and Spirit indwelling the Church, and are at the same time deployed in the service of God's love and will for all mankind.[35]

A CHURCH LIVING BETWEEN THE TIMES

Although the incarnation and Pentecost open up a new understanding for the life of God's people, Torrance does not limit the existence of the Church to the messianic community shaped by the pouring out of the Holy Spirit. He holds that "there is only one people and Church of God throughout all ages from the beginning of creation to the end."[36] This one church has three distinct phases, and it is Christ's physical, incarnate presence in space and time that marks the transitions between phases.

The first phase is Israel's history, beginning with creation and intensified in the establishment of the Abrahamic covenant.[37] The Church comes into existence from the moment when God

---

[29]Thomas F. Torrance, *Atonement: The Person and Work of Christ*, ed. Robert T. Walker (Downers Grove, IL: IVP Academic/Milton Keynes: Paternoster, 2009), 295.
[30]Torrance, *Christian Doctrine of God*, 102.
[31]Ibid., 125.
[32]Ibid., 133.
[33]Ibid., 5.
[34]Torrance, *The Trinitarian Faith*, 250.
[35]Thomas F. Torrance, *Reality and Scientific Theology* (Eugene, OR: Wipf & Stock Publishers, 2001), 119.
[36]Torrance, *Theology in Reconstruction*, 193.
[37]Torrance, *The School of Faith*, cxx.

calls Abraham and his descendants, and promises to make them "the instrument through which all peoples were to be blessed."[38] Israel is the Church in a preparatory form. God shaped its historical existence in such a way that it became a "womb for the incarnation."[39] This involved establishing the concepts necessary for Christ's salvific work to be understood, whether Israel's formation as a covenantal community in order to demonstrate God's unswerving faithfulness,[40] human understanding being adapted to articulate divine revelation as God spoke to Israel and called them to be his people,[41] the various Old Testament images for redemption,[42] or any other concepts which are taken up by the New Testament to illuminate the work of Christ, from the need for sacrifice and atonement right through to the anticipation of the servant-messiah.[43] Although God did not reveal the rich inner communion of his triune life to Israel before Christ's incarnation, there is no contradiction between the Jewish monotheism of the Old Testament, and the triune revelation of the New Testament. God was at work preparing the way for Jesus to fulfill the prophetic anticipation of a Savior, and so without being ingrafted into Israel, Torrance argues, "the Church on earth and in history does not have the promise of the fulness of Spirit."[44]

The second phase of the Church's life is inaugurated through Christ's obedient life, death, resurrection, and ascension, and the sending of the Spirit. Jesus became a human, living and ministering among the people of Israel, culminating in his vicarious death as humankind's substitute and representative, and his victorious resurrection. Christ has already completed the work of reconciliation but has held back its full unveiling in order to allow time for the Church to proclaim the gospel through witness and service, and for the world to freely respond with repentance and belief. In the time between the "penultimate and the ultimate acts of the *Heilgeschichte*,"[45] the Church is subject to the ambiguities of fallen time and the consequences of sin.[46] Yet it already proleptically lives "in the midst of the advent-presence of Christ,"[47] accessing the promises of God by faith. Living by faith and not by sight, in the overlap of an age marked by sin and the hope of the new creation, this is "the time of the patience of Jesus between His ascension and His *parousia*."[48] This is the phase of the Church's life which Torrance writes the most about; the Church is already the body of Christ, and is still to become one body.[49]

The third phase of the people of God lies in the future, and yet overlaps with the current phase of the Church's existence. The Church will receive its "final and eternal

---

[38]Torrance, *Theology in Reconstruction*, 193.

[39]Ibid., 145.

[40]Torrance, *Conflict and Agreement: Order and Disorder*, 289.

[41]Torrance, *The Mediation of Christ*, 7–9.

[42]Torrance groups the redemptive threads of the Old Testament into three strands; the cost of redemption, the covering-over of sin, and the relational basis for redemption, and argues that all three converge most closely in identification with the servant of the Lord and the new exodus. See Torrance, "Redemption in the Light of the Old Testament," in *Atonement,* ed. Robert Walker, 25–60.

[43]Torrance, *The Mediation of Christ*, 18.

[44]Torrance, *The School of Faith*, cxx.

[45]Torrance, *Conflict and Agreement: Order and Disorder*, 17. Heilgeschichte may be translated as salvation history.

[46]Torrance, *Atonement*, 342.

[47]Torrance, *The Trinitarian Faith*, 300.

[48]Torrance, *Royal Priesthood*, 63.

[49]Ibid., 44–6.

form when Christ comes again to judge and renew his creation."[50] Thus, the significance of the *eschaton* is not so much the historical event which will end the current age of human history, but rather the person of Jesus Christ whose return will ultimately and absolutely transform human existence and time.[51] Torrance takes his cue from Calvin to argue that "eschatology properly speaking is the application of Christology to the Kingdom of Christ and to the work of the Church in history,"[52] focusing on the import of the kingdom of God for the Church's life now. As MacLean notes of Torrance's eschatology, if the Church "ignores the eschatological element" of its historical existence, it not only loses its vision of the future, but "loses sight of its union with Christ."[53] Eschatology involves a time-gap between the objective accomplishment of the salvation of all things in Christ, and the full consummation of the kingdom. The Church thus lives "under the pressure of the imminent Advent of our Lord and Saviour."[54] This will not be the termination of time, but rather God bringing history to its *telos*, for, "the eschatological acts of God run throughout time to their end at the consummation of time; they are teleological as well as eschatological, for they are not just abrupt acts abrogating or terminating time, but rather acts that gather up time in the fulfilling of the divine purpose."[55]

Held together, these three stages of the one Church demonstrate the continuity of Torrance's view of salvation history. The Old and New Testaments are a complementary account of what God has done, is doing, and will do in calling a people to himself to journey toward the redemption of all things in Christ.

A CHURCH RIGHTLY ORDERED

In what follows, we will consider the second phase of the Church within Torrance's theological vision. It is in the time between Christ's ascension and return that the Church has its vocation, and it is also during this time where diversity in ecclesiological issues arises. This includes questions about the shape of the Church's historical life, such as institutional organization, the ministry of word and sacrament, forms of worship, and the proclamation of the good news. Torrance weights his consideration of these elements from a theological perspective rather than focusing on the visible ordering of the Church. In this Torrance follows the Fathers, who sought to develop right belief about the Trinity instead of focusing on developing rules for the Church. The Fathers focused on faithfulness to apostolic teaching rather than seeking to develop a "definite ecclesiology,"[56] and by extension, the ecumenical Councils produced "the kind of theology of God and Christ that is forced upon us by the actual interaction of God with the universe he has made … [and in response] we find ourselves committed to saying fundamental things about God and the world, Christ and the Spirit, and the Church."[57] Situating himself within this

---

[50] Torrance, *Theology in Reconstruction*, 193.

[51] Torrance, *Royal Priesthood*, 49.

[52] Ibid., 43; See also Thomas F. Torrance, *Kingdom and Church: A Study in the Theology of the Reformation* (Eugene, OR: Wipf & Stock Publishers, 1996), 101.

[53] MacLean, *Resurrection, Apocalypse and the Kingdom of Christ*, 193.

[54] Thomas Torrance, "Answer to God," *Biblical Theology* 2, no. 1 (1951): 15.

[55] Thomas F. Torrance, *Space, Time and Resurrection* (Edinburgh: The Handsel Press, 1976), 151.

[56] Torrance, *The Trinitarian Faith*, 255.

[57] Torrance, *The Ground and Grammar of Theology*, 50.

tradition, Torrance argues that humankind's participation in the Trinity is the "primary truth" that should be given "precedence over all questions of external form, organisation and structure" of the Church.[58]

But what of the tension between the way things are, and the way things are intended to be? In its most theological sense, order is the way that God intends for things to be. In contrast, disorder emerges as the consequence of sin. "It belongs to the very nature of sin to divide, to disrupt, to be anarchic—sin is lawlessness, *anomia*. The opposite of all that is order, harmony, communion."[59] However, this description of order as harmony and communion does not mean that the primary task of the Church is to be peaceful and gentle, for "when the Christian Church bears faithful witness to God, there is no department in human life that does not feel its penetrating challenge, no region of human experience that is not disturbed and does not suffer upheaval."[60] This is why Torrance is fond of the biblical image of bread yeast to describe the role of the Church in relation to society; it has an "aggressive function … the army of God created for offensive action."[61] Just as a little yeast causes a large loaf of bread to rise, so too the Church's role is to challenge the whole of human society.

Central to the sin-caused disorder of the time between, and the divine reordering of all things, is the relationship between the two dimensions of the Church's existence. Although the Church is already a new creation, justified and holy as it shares in Christ's self-sanctification through its vertical dimension,[62] it also has a horizontal dimension for it is composed of sinful men and women, subject to the limitations and frustrations of fallen time.[63] It is this ongoing dynamic which dictates the ordering of the Church's life in the time between the ascension and the *parousia*. While all things in heaven and earth will be reordered according to the will of God, there is a redemptive reordering that takes place in a limited and anticipatory way in the time between the ages. This corresponds with Flett's observation that for Torrance, order is a relational concept—the reordering of all creation is inherent to God's redemptive activity, leading toward the *telos* of creation of reconciliation between God and his creation.[64]

Because of the Church's eschatological orientation, involving a "sort of a hypostatic union between the eternal and the temporal in the form of new time,"[65] its existence within the tensions of the present age creates the need for structure that serves rather than controls the Church. Torrance illustrates this using the metaphor of scaffolding; this limited reordering is like a temporary scaffolding built to support the presently hidden but eternal reality of the Church. The scaffolding will be taken down once when the building is complete—that is, at the return of Christ.[66] Helpful here is the delineation that Torrance makes between the Nicene attributes of the Church, and the visible elements

---

[58]Torrance, *The Trinitarian Faith*, 275.

[59]Torrance, *Gospel, Church, and Ministry*, 93.

[60]Thomas Torrance, *The Apocalypse Today* (London: James Clarke, 1960), 86.

[61]Torrance, *Gospel, Church and Culture*, 77. Torrance's chapter "The Place of the Church in the World," 74–84, demonstrates Torrance's frustration with the Church's assimilation into society and lack of radical witness.

[62]Torrance, "What Is the Church," 12.

[63]Ibid.

[64]Eric G. Flett, *Persons, Powers, and Pluralities: Towards a Trinitarian Theology of Culture* (Eugene, OR: Pickwick Publications, 2011), 90–115.

[65]Torrance, *Atonement*, 410.

[66]Torrance, *Gospel, Church and Ministry*, 98.

of the Church's life. Whereas oneness, holiness, catholicity, and apostolicity describe the essential being of the Church as derived from relationship with the triune God, the "word of God purely preached, the sacraments of the gospel rightly administered, and godly discipline," are considered part of the temporary scaffolding given to the Church in the time between the ages. The Nicene attributes are not "independent qualities inhering in the church, but are affirmations of the nature of the church,"[67] while visible elements of the Church's life such as word and sacrament only "indicate where the true church is to be found; they do not define it or describe it but point to it."[68] These temporal elements will not necessarily endure into the age to come.

ATTRIBUTES: ONE, HOLY, CATHOLIC, AND APOSTOLIC

The Church is one, holy, catholic, and apostolic because its head is Jesus Christ and it is in him. Although the realization of these attributes within the Church's life is imperfect in the current age, Torrance's description of the two dimensions of the Church helps us to contextualize the Nicene marks as attributes which will be fully realized eschatologically. Oneness, holiness, catholicity, and apostolicity derive from the vertical dimension, and are imperfectly lived out in the horizontal dimension.

Oneness

For Torrance, the oneness of the Church is inseparable from the uniqueness of Jesus Christ. Oneness is derived from the Church's ontological relation to Christ, rather than the idea of the Church as a singular, monolithic entity.[69] Although the full manifestation of this oneness is a mystery hidden in Christ awaiting eschatological fullness, the one church spans all space and time, and "comprises a diversity as wide as the creation itself."[70] Within this oneness, both Jew and Gentile are included; Torrance argues that although the greatest schism in the Church is the separation of Jew and Gentile, in Christ, Jew and Gentile will one day cohere in unity.[71] It is on the basis of the Church's oneness that Torrance rejects a division between the church triumphant and militant, and invisible and visible, arguing that "there is only one body"[72] encompassing all dimensions of the gathered and scattered people of God.

Holiness

The Church's holiness is not to do with the individual or corporate morality of its members, but because it is a people "in holy relation to holy God through the Holy Spirit."[73] In its

---

[67]Torrance, *Atonement*, 380.

[68]Ibid., 381.

[69]Torrance, *Conflict and Agreement: Order and Disorder*, 264–5.

[70]Torrance, *Atonement*, 381.

[71]Thomas F. Torrance, *Theology in Reconciliation: Essays towards Evangelical and Catholic Unity in East and West* (Eugene, OR: Wipf & Stock Publishers, 1996), 24–7. Torrance argues, "That does not simply mean that Jews will eventually become Christians and members of the One Holy Catholic Church, but that within the one Church of Christ, the Israel of God, there will be a special place for Israel as a people." See "Israel and the Incarnation of God," in *Conflict and Agreement: Order and Disorder*, 298.

[72]Torrance, *Atonement*, 384.

[73]Ibid., 386.

vertical dimension the Church is a people set apart through union with Christ, while in its horizontal dimension the Church wrestles with its call to holiness, just as Israel wrestled with the tension of being a covenant people that wanted the freedom to be like the nations that surrounded them.[74] Although the Church participates in the fallen world, by continually submitting itself to the judgment and cleansing of Christ and remembering that it is justified by grace alone, the Church is daily renewed in the holiness of the Son,[75] "justified in Christ and made holy with his holiness."[76] Holiness is also related to oneness and catholicity, for "ecumenicity and catholicity imply, involve and interpenetrate each other in the sanctification of the Church through Christ and in the Spirit."[77]

Catholicity

Torrance parallels catholicity and ecumenicity as cognate terms,[78] both referring to the "inner wholeness or essential universality" of the Church's relation to Christ.[79] He has a distinct preference for the language of ecumenicity, suggesting that catholicity is more juridical and institutional in sense, while ecumenicity is more evangelical and theological.[80] Catholicity refers to "the fullness of the church in all its height and depth and length and breadth, in the height of holiness and depth of truth, in the length of its history and the breadth of its expansion in the world."[81] It is a dynamic concept, rather than being static and unchanging; Torrance speaks of both a catholicity of extension when referring to the mission of the Church to reach out to the very ends of the earth, and a catholicity of depth, the church's grounding in the "fullness and comprehensiveness of Jesus Christ and the holy Trinity."[82] The Church is whole in Christ in its vertical dimension, even though it is presently fragmented in its horizontal dimension.

Apostolicity

Apostolicity "is the actual norm (*ecclesia apostolica*) for our true understanding of the other 'marks.'"[83] Oneness, holiness, and catholicity are measured in relation to apostolicity. To be apostolic is to be faithful to the revelation of Christ uniquely passed on through the apostles by the Spirit,[84] and so the apostolic Church remains "identical with itself in its apostolic foundation in Christ."[85] Because Christ has withdrawn himself from time, the Church must constantly return to the time of Christ's historical life as the basis for its own existence in space and time.[86] In the footsteps of the apostles, the

---

[74] Ibid., 385.
[75] Ibid., 388.
[76] Torrance, *The Trinitarian Faith*, 282.
[77] Torrance, *Theology in Reconciliation*, 17.
[78] Ibid.
[79] Ibid.
[80] Ibid., 18–19.
[81] Torrance, *Atonement*, 389.
[82] Ibid., 391.
[83] Torrance, *Theology in Reconciliation*, 17.
[84] Torrance, *Theology in Reconstruction*, 134–40.
[85] Torrance, *Conflict and Agreement: Order and Disorder*, 166.
[86] Torrance, *Gospel, Church and Ministry*, 102–3.

Church "moves out into history shaped and moulded by the apostolic tradition in both doctrine and in ordinances, and so continues to proclaim the apostolic *kērygma* and to be ordered in its life by the apostolic commands."[87] On this basis Torrance argues that ministerial succession, as in the succession of bishops, is nothing more than a sign that points to the true apostolicity of the Church in Christ; apostolic succession is measured by fidelity to apostolic teaching rather than by the laying on of hands from one generation to another.[88] Thus, in its vertical dimension the Church is always rightly ordered because the apostolic tradition is the ongoing revelation of Christ. However, even though in its horizontal dimension the Church is often distracted from faithfulness to ancient truths, as God's people choose each day to live oriented to the "new time" of the risen Christ, the Church is made able by the Spirit to point to the eschatological reality of Jesus's reign over all creation. While the Church is related *supernaturally* to Christ in the Spirit, it has its *historical* relation to Christ through the apostolic witness.[89]

WORD, SACRAMENTS, AND MINISTRY

In the same way that the Nicene attributes of the Church will be fully manifest eschatologically, the proclamation of the word, the sacraments, and the ministry also anticipate eschatological fullness. As forms of "temporary scaffolding," they will pass away when Christ returns. Torrance's approach to these elements of the Church's life is to view them stereoscopically, drawing this idea from Michael Polanyi. Two images are taken separately, slightly apart, but when held together, the two-dimensional images combine to provide one three-dimensional image.[90] The two images are the historical rite, and the reality that lies behind it. It is only when we look at the rite and the reality together that we gain the true sense of what is taking place. This approach is aptly termed "the dimension of depth" by Hunsinger[91] and is described by Torrance utilizing the metaphor of looking through a window. When we look through a window, it is what lies beyond the window that is the center of our attention. We do not usually stop to inspect the glass unless it somehow mars our vision.[92] In the same way, it is the reality of what God is doing that is really at stake, rather than the rites themselves. While this language is used of the sacraments by Torrance, he also applies it to biblical interpretation,[93] the knowledge of God through worship,[94] and baptism.[95] The word, the ministry, and the

---

[87] Torrance, *Atonement*, 396.

[88] Torrance, *Royal Priesthood*, 68–70.

[89] Torrance, *Atonement*, 394.

[90] Thomas F. Torrance, "The Place of Michael Polanyi in the Modern Philosophy of Science," in *Transformation and Convergence in the Frame of Knowledge* (Eugene, OR: Wipf & Stock, 1998), 107–74, especially 125.

[91] George Hunsinger, "The Dimension of Depth: Thomas F. Torrance on the Sacraments of Baptism and the Lord's Supper," *Scottish Journal of Theology* 54, no. 2 (2001): 155–76. Torrance uses the term in relation to baptism (*Theology in Reconciliation*, 83, 88–90), and in relation to the Eucharist (*Theology in Reconciliation*, 108, 119).

[92] Thomas F. Torrance, *Conflict and Agreement: The Ministry and Sacraments of the Gospel* (Eugene, OR: Wipf & Stock Publishers, 1996), 110–11.

[93] Torrance, *Christian Doctrine of God*, 47; Torrance, *Reality and Evangelical Theology*, 106.

[94] Torrance, *Christian Doctrine of God*, 90.

[95] Torrance, *Theology in Reconciliation*, 88.

sacraments are tools of revelation and signs of participation, but are far more than mere historical rituals because of their dimension of depth, leading to the triune God.

The Word

In Christ, "the Word of God has taken historical form and is now never without that historical form."[96] God's word is inseparable from the historical self-proclamation of Christ—in both word and deed he bore witness to himself, for God's word is never mere speech but always filled with power.[97] Jesus remains in control of the Church's proclamation, its *kērygma* about him.[98] It is the kerygmatic self-revelation of God in Christ that is the real content of Scripture; the human, written words of the apostles repose upon Christ's own *kērygma*. In this way, "the Word of the Kingdom is identical with Christ Himself."[99]

It follows that it is the living God's self-revelation in Scripture that occupies Torrance's attention, which means he often bypasses the textual detail which occupies exegetical scholars. He is not particularly interested in grammatical or linguistic exegesis except for in a few rare places where such work illuminates a theological point.[100] Webster helpfully observes that the engine of Torrance's "semantically oriented interpretation"[101] of Scripture "was a theology of biblical language as a sign of revelation, possessed of a depth by virtue of its relation to the realities to which it testifies and not simply terminating in its syntactic surface."[102] This form of interpretation involves penetrating, indwelling, and listening to the word of God through Scripture.[103] This has both theological and historical elements; using the idea of stereoscopic vision, in biblical interpretation, theological truth and historical reality are held together.

The word of God must be communicated and received afresh in each generation.[104] This is one of the tasks of the Church in the time between the ages,[105] so that the role of any man or woman who preaches is that of an ambassador who declares a word that is not their own. A preacher's task is limited to explaining Scripture in a way that is accessible to its contemporary hearers and doing so in a way that meets the standard of the word of God.[106] Preaching is both evangelical and theological, *kerygmatic* and didactic, an act of proclamation and yet only ever a response to divine revelation. Torrance's key observations about preaching are that it must refuse to separate the "historical Christ" from the "theological" Christ, emphasize the staggering reality of God becoming human,

---

[96] Torrance, *Incarnation*, 13.

[97] Torrance, *Conflict and Agreement: Ministry and Sacraments*, 67.

[98] Torrance, *Incarnation*, 14.

[99] Torrance, *Conflict and Agreement: Ministry and Sacraments*, 61–2.

[100] For example, see Torrance, *Conflict and Agreement: Order and Disorder*, 285–7.

[101] John Webster, *The Domain of the Word: Scripture and Theological Reason* (London, New York: T&T Clark, 2012), 104.

[102] Ibid., 102–3.

[103] Ibid., 104–6. Webster has a critically appreciative view of Torrance's use of Scripture, noting that for a theologian who is so insistent on the concreteness of revelation within space and time, more attention needed to be paid to the process of revelation being received and recorded and the "creaturely coefficient of revelation" (110).

[104] Torrance, *The School of Faith*, lxvi–xlvii.

[105] Torrance, *Gospel, Church and Ministry*, 102.

[106] Thomas F. Torrance, *When Christ Comes and Comes Again* (Eugene, OR: Wipf & Stock, 1996), 6–10.

and keep the Cross central.[107] However it is ultimately the work of the Spirit to take up the preached word and to so fill it with Christ's own presence that human words are enabled beyond their own capacity to carry divine revelation. Through the Church, Christ "lets his Word be heard, so that as the Church bears witness to him and proclaims the Gospel of salvation in his Name, he himself through the Spirit is immediately present validating that Word as his own, and communicating himself to men through it."[108]

The Sacraments

Linking *sacramentum* with its Greek origin, *mystērion,* Torrance returns to the idea of an analogical relationship again; the relationship between the sacraments, and the reality which they signify, is one of "analogy involving something of identity and something of difference."[109] Thus, Torrance emphasizes that it is the union of God and humanity in Christ that is the glorious mystery of the gospel, rather than the sacraments themselves. As he explains, "The primary *mysterium* or *sacramentum* is Jesus Christ himself, the incarnate reality of the Son of God who has incorporated himself into our humanity and assimilated the people of God into himself as his own body."[110] Baptism and the Lord's Supper are derivative or secondary mysteries in the sense that they refer us to the ultimate mystery of the gospel, but the analogical relationship here is entirely governed by Christ.[111] More than simple acts of memorial, there is a strong relation between the sign and the reality which the sign signifies, for the reality which the sign signifies is not reduced to being encompassed by the sign.[112] Torrance draws on Calvin's language of signification to suggest that we should think of baptism and the eucharist as pointing beyond themselves to what Christ has done for us,[113] and enabling our participation in that work. According to Christ's promise and command, the outward sign and inward reality are indivisible.[114] This way of describing the sacraments is different to the Augustinian description of "outward and visible signs of inward and invisible grace"[115] and is why Torrance maintains that the elements—whether water, bread, or wine—are instrumental, and not just symbolic.[116] The sacraments are "divinely provided, dominically appointed ways of response and obedience of a radically vicarious kind,"[117] through which we are "raised up to share in the life of God."[118]

Torrance reflects that the sacraments in particular "are ordinances of Christ belonging to the eschatological reserve between the moment of the First Advent and the moment of Final Advent."[119] At Christ's *parousia,* the need for the sacraments will cease. Since the

---

[107]Torrance, "Preaching Christ Today," in *Gospel, Church and Ministry,* 220–57.
[108]Torrance, *Space, Time and Resurrection,* 120.
[109]Torrance, *Conflict and Agreement: Ministry and Sacraments,* 141.
[110]Torrance, *Theology in Reconciliation,* 82.
[111]Torrance, *Conflict and Agreement: Ministry and Sacraments,* 141–2.
[112]Ibid., 145.
[113]Ibid., 140–1.
[114]Ibid., 141.
[115]Torrance, *Theology in Reconciliation,* 122.
[116]Hunsinger, "The Dimension of Depth," 169.
[117]Torrance, *The Mediation of Christ,* 89.
[118]Torrance, *Conflict and Agreement: Ministry and Sacraments,* 145.
[119]Torrance, *Royal Priesthood,* 48.

fullness of the gospel is not yet manifest, the sacraments are signs which anticipate the mystery of the gospel. Gifted to the pilgrim church for the sustenance and renewal of its life between the times, the sacraments are signs of the new creation within fallen space and time, they accompany the word of God as it is communicated through Scripture, and are the way in which humanity is miraculously enabled to participate in union with Christ while awaiting his second coming.[120]

The relationship between the two sacraments points to the tension between the ambiguities of fallen time, and the fact that reconciliation is already accomplished in Christ. Baptism reminds us that we are in Christ once and for all, while the Eucharist is a gift given for the renewal of our faith and as a sign of the unity of the Church.[121] Baptism is the "sacrament of substitution"[122] and the "sacrament of justification."[123] The Eucharist is the "sacrament of sanctification."[124] This is to do with the fact that "in Baptism we have particularly to do with the objective and perfected event, and in the Eucharist we have to do particularly with participation in that completed reality in the conditions of time."[125] Baptism and the Eucharist direct us away from ourselves to Christ, and are actions to which we can add nothing; although we are commanded to participate in them, it is Christ's action in our place that is important.[126]

The Ministry of the Church

The Church's ministry is undertaken in the name of Christ and in reliance on the Spirit. In sending the twelve apostles out to minister in his name, Jesus commissioned them to continue his mission, rather than giving them their own mission. As for the apostles, so for the Church; *kērygma*, or proclamation, is in this sense "such proclamation that by the Holy Spirit it becomes the actualization of that event among men."[127] Unless the Spirit is actively at work as the redeemer, the Church's proclamation remains empty. The Church is called to engage in the ministry of Christ—which is always His ministry, not ours—through witness, stewardship, and service.[128] Describing the ministry of the Church, Torrance uses the helpful description of the movement from *soma* (body) to *pleroma* (fullness). The Church is the body of Christ, and its mission is to proclaim the gospel to all people in all places in all times, moving from its current particularity to a future universality.[129] Although Torrance is cautious about the phrase "the priesthood of all believers" because of the danger of a "ruinous individualism,"[130] he argues that ministry is "primarily corporate."[131] Just as every believer is baptized into Christ, so too every believer is called to the corporate priesthood; the difference is that the Church's

---

[120]Torrance, *Atonement*, 305–7.
[121]Torrance, *Royal Priesthood*, 64, 84.
[122]Ibid., 33.
[123]Torrance, *Atonement*, 307.
[124]Ibid.
[125]Torrance, *Conflict and Agreement: Order and Disorder*, 258.
[126]Torrance, *The Mediation of Christ*, 90.
[127]Torrance, *Conflict and Agreement: Ministry and Sacraments*, 158.
[128]Torrance, *Royal Priesthood*, 37–8.
[129]Ibid., 26.
[130]Ibid., 35 n. 1.
[131]Ibid., 35.

ministry is "a ministry of redeemed sinners, whereas [Christ's] ministry is that of the redeemer."[132] While there are diverse gifts within the body, every Christian shares in the same ministry, which is the ministry of Christ.

However, some are set apart for leadership within the Church. Torrance derives his understanding of ordained ministry from the Old Testament tradition of the priesthood but reinterprets this in accordance with the life and ministry of Christ. Jesus fulfills all the requirements of the covenant as the superior mediator between God and human. In discontinuity with the Old Testament priesthood, ordained ministers do not represent humanity to God, for as Molnar observes, "that would impinge on the living Christ."[133] It is Christ alone who is our substitute and our representative before the Father. As with word and sacrament, the efficacy of a minister is not found in their actions but rather through the empowerment of the Spirit. As those ordained to the ministry of word and sacrament proclaim the gospel, the Spirit is present, making real what is declared.[134] The ordained priesthood is therefore not a calling to elevated status but of humility and service. Those ordained are called to follow Christ's model of servant ministry; deacons, priests, and bishops are "nothing more than servants of Christ, and, at the same time, servants of the people in Christ."[135] Torrance suggests we should think of deacons as those who lead the congregation in worship, priests as shepherds who feed the flock through word and sacrament, and bishops as watchmen whose task is to minister to the priests.[136] Although Torrance was ordained in the Church of Scotland, he notes that while there is no biblical ground for the office of elder, the kind of ministry exercised by Presbyterian elders is in fact that of the deacon, and calls for the Presbyterian Church to associate the office of elder with the ministry of the deacon, thus creating elder-deacons.[137]

Finally, Torrance strongly supported the ordination of women. While he makes use of many standard theological arguments for gender equality, his primary reasoning is Christological. Emphasizing that Christ assumed humanity and thus included all humanity within himself, rather than specifically assuming masculinity, Torrance insists:

> In Jesus Christ the order of redemption has intersected the order of creation and set it upon a new basis altogether. Henceforth the full equality of man and woman is a divine ordinance that applies to all the behaviour and activity of the "new man" in Christ, and so to the entire life and mission of the Church as the Body of Christ in the world.[138]

A CHURCH CALLED TO PROCLAMATION

Given Torrance's formative experiences on the mission field, and his own initial sense of being called to missions, which gained clarity as a calling to serve the mission of the Church as a theologian, it is unsurprising that he wrote a significant amount of material on the

---

[132]Torrance, *Atonement*, 357.

[133]Paul D. Molnar, *Thomas F. Torrance: Theologian of the Trinity* (Farnham: Ashgate, 2009), 291.

[134]Torrance, *Atonement*, 280–1.

[135]Torrance, *Royal Priesthood*, 91, quoting Calvin, *Institutes*, 4.8.1.

[136]Ibid., 102–3.

[137]Torrance, "The Eldership in the Reformed Church," *Scottish Journal of Theology* 37, no. 4 (1984): 503–12.

[138]Torrance, *Gospel, Church, and Ministry*, 207–8.

mission and ministry of the Church. His missiological ecclesiology is closely linked with his ecumenical theology. Torrance insists that if the Church is truly to be a community that proclaims Christ's reconciliation to the world, it must first experience internal reconciliation. The church's ecumenical task goes hand in hand with its evangelical task—it must proclaim the reconciliation of God to all humankind, but this proclamation must first be heard and responded to by the divided Church.[139]

Standing apart from every other human organization, the Church is "the community in which God has put his name, as the Body with which Christ identifies himself in the world, and as the unique place where God is immediately present to us through the Holy Spirit in his very own being as God."[140] It is the presence of God with his people that sets the Church apart and gives it a unique purpose. The church is a community set apart for witness, to be the "trysting place" where humankind is made able to meet with God.[141] Just as Jesus was sent, so too he sent the apostles out in his name, to continue his mission.[142] This returns us to the idea of apostolicity, for the apostolic church is one that continues in the apostolic tradition by participating in the mission of Christ.[143]

Because the Church is apostolic, it is also already one, holy and catholic. It is incumbent that the Church works toward living out these attributes as best it can while it awaits the *parousia*. What is at stake is not the Church itself, but rather the reality which it bears witness to, for the Church is an earthen vessel bearing heavenly treasure—it is not the container that is valuable, but that which it holds.[144] As Torrance comments:

> [This] is why it is more and more imperative that the doctrines of the person and of the work of Christ should engage our full attention, even when pressing problems of ecclesiology bear down upon us. Nothing must be allowed to decentralize the Gospel—the Church is but a poor earthen vessel bearing the heavenly treasure, and it is the heavenly treasure that counts, not the earthen vessel.[145]

The metaphor of an earthen vessel bearing heavenly treasure demonstrates well the Church's role of witness within Torrance's thought. Witness and mission are only able to be properly undertaken in dependence on Christ's presence through the Spirit; as Molnar succinctly explains, "it is always Christ who is the enabling condition of the church's witness."[146] This applies also to the Church's witness through service, for as Ziegler notes, "the pattern for her life and work finds its significance only in directing the world's attention towards her risen and ascended Lord."[147] Because Jesus has established "the people of God within the processes and structured patterns of history as a coherent body,"[148] the Church has been given structures for the current phase of its life. Nevertheless, this structure serves the mission of the Church as "a communion

---

[139]Torrance, *Theology in Reconciliation*, 23.

[140]Torrance, *The Trinitarian Faith*, 282.

[141]Torrance, *Gospel, Church and Ministry*, 108.

[142]Torrance, *The Trinitarian Faith*, 286.

[143]Ibid., 287.

[144]Torrance, *Conflict and Agreement: Order and Disorder*, 18.

[145]Ibid., 18.

[146]Molnar, *Thomas F. Torrance*, 292.

[147]Geordie Ziegler, *Trinitarian Grace and Participation: An Entry into the Theology of T. F. Torrance* (Minneapolis, MN: Fortress Press, 2017), 203.

[148]Torrance, *Atonement*, 295.

of love through which the life of God flows out in love towards every human being."[149] This is not to say that the task of witness will be an easy one; indeed, Torrance draws on the image of two witnesses from the Book of Revelation to observe "it is impossible for a person who has really eaten the book in the hand of the angel to have sweetness and comfort only without facing the consequences of bearing witness."[150] Nevertheless:

> It is therefore the mission of the church to bring to all nations and races the message of hope and by the witness of its word and life to summon them to the obedience of the gospel, that the love of God in Jesus Christ may be poured out upon them by the Spirit, breaking down all barriers, healing all divisions, and gathering them together as one universal flock to meet the coming of the great shepherd, the one Lord and saviour of all.[151]

A Missional and Ecumenical Theology of Reconciliation

Torrance posits that the Church's "ontological unity" is the basis for its "dynamic unity" with Christ—a unity not only in being, but also in action.[152] As those who have been reconciled to Christ, the Church is called to proclaim reconciliation to the world. This theme of reconciliation is central to Torrance's theology of mission, and demonstrates his appreciation for the method of biblical theology, holding the Old and New Testaments together as one cohesive narrative.[153] Genesis 1–2 indicate God's intention for humanity to live in unhindered relationship with God, and on this basis, to live in open relationship with each other. However, sin causes a separation between God and humanity. The Old Testament is the story both of humankind's failed efforts to bind themselves together and of God's kindness in establishing a covenant with Israel as part of his redemptive plan to bring reconciliation to all things. Noting the division at Babel in Genesis 11, and its reversal in Acts 2 when the Spirit is poured out as the antithesis to the separation of the nations, Torrance observes that where sin divides, the Spirit reconciles and reunites.[154] Through Christ descending to assume humanity, gathering us to himself and atoning for us, and then ascending to return to the Father, we are restored to communion with God.[155]

That God has reconciled the world to himself in Christ is the basis for the Church's mission, because "in being sent by Christ into the world to proclaim what God has done in him, the Church is constituted a reconciling as well as a reconciled community."[156] This returns to the model we explored earlier where the vertical dimension of the Church's life shapes its horizontal dimension. The Church is not the mediator of reconciliation, but it is to live out the reality of the reconciliation which Christ has already accomplished on

---

[149] Ibid., 375.

[150] Torrance, *The Apocalypse Today*, 85.

[151] Torrance, *Atonement*, 343.

[152] Torrance, *Theology in Reconciliation*, 21–3.

[153] MacLean, *Resurrection, Apocalypse, and the Kingdom of Christ*, 117. MacLean observes that a hallmark of Torrance's eschatology is his emphasis on the unity of the whole Bible and particularly the integration of the present and the future.

[154] Torrance, *Atonement*, 383.

[155] Torrance, *Incarnation*, 77.

[156] Torrance, *Theology in Reconciliation*, 7.

the Cross. Unity is an eschatological reality for the Church as it exists in the midst of the disorder of the creation but constantly reaches toward the fullness of the new creation.[157] It breaks into the present although it is not fully manifest; in Christ, the Church is already one body formed by the Spirit yet in another sense, it still awaits the full realization of its unity.[158]

> The oneness of the Church is derived solely from Christ Himself ... is grounded upon His unique action for the Church ... and is maintained and secured by the fact that He alone is the Head of the Church ... Because He gathers up the whole Church in Himself (Eph. 1:10, 22), because He is the One and the Many, He alone constitutes and forms the *many* of the Church into *one*.[159]

However, because this unity is not yet fully manifest, there is a need for ecumenical theology. While the driving force for the initial ecumenical impulse of Edinburgh 1910 was the need for cooperation on the mission field since the divisions of the sending Churches limited the efficacy of their missionaries' proclamation,[160] Torrance saw the ecumenical movement as an "upsurge of the original spirit of the Reformation in seeking the renewal of the Church as the one Body of Christ."[161] He suggested that the "inner intention" of the Reformation was the recentralization of Christ and the Trinity, and that this was now being carried through to fullness by the ecumenical movement. Torrance saw his own work as standing in this tradition with its Christocentric and trinitarian foundations.[162] He served the World Council of Churches in various capacities from the late 1940s until the early 1960s, but became frustrated by its leaning toward social action rather than a concern for theological orthodoxy. Shepherd notes that Torrance's participation in the World Council of Churches waned in proportion to his growing sense that the WCC had lost its way theologically,[163] while MacLean notes that Torrance's message to the ecumenical movement in the 1950s was "Repent!"[164]

By contrast, it was a theological dialogue between the Reformed Church and the Orthodox Church in the 1970s and 1980s which best represents the style of Torrance's theological engagement with the ecumenical movement. This dialogue emerged from Torrance's involvement in the Faith and Order Commission, particularly his service to the "Special Commission on Christ and his Church," where he had served with a number of Orthodox theologians. These theological contacts continued through the years, and led to Torrance proposing a formal dialogue between the Reformed Church and the Orthodox Church. His vision was a dialogue on the Trinity which followed Athanasius and Cyril rather than the Cappadocians in order to "cut behind" some of the differences between East and West and would lend itself to "fuller accord" in

---

[157] Torrance, *Conflict and Agreement: Order and Disorder*, 196–7.
[158] Torrance, *Royal Priesthood*, 46.
[159] Torrance, *Conflict and Agreement: Order and Disorder*, 265.
[160] Torrance, *Theology in Reconciliation*, 47.
[161] Ibid., 41.
[162] Ibid., 44.
[163] Albert L. Shepherd, "The Body of Christ Analogy in T. F. Torrance's Ecclesiology," *Participatio* 6 (2016): 70–1.
[164] MacLean, *Resurrection, Apocalypse, and the Kingdom of Christ*, 91.

further doctrinal conversations.[165] A series of consultations took place over a decade and a half, cochaired by Thomas Torrance and George Dragas, and concluding with the release of the Orthodox–Reformed "Agreed Statement on the Holy Trinity." Although the singular voice of the Statement has been described as an "extraordinary theological and ecumenical achievement,"[166] for the way that it spoke with one voice rather than setting two positions side by side as do the majority of bilateral ecumenical statements, further dialogues between the Reformed and Orthodox "have not fulfilled the promise of the Agreed Statement on the Holy Trinity."[167] Nevertheless, the "Agreed Statement" and accompanying documents stand as an example of Torrance's vision of ecumenical partnership undergirded by genuine theological agreement resulting in the reconciliation of the Churches.

CONCLUSION

Torrance's ecclesiology remains fruitful ground for further investigation, not least in his commitment to faithful witness.[168] We began by acknowledging that Torrance's vocation to serve the church has shaped his theological career. Although Torrance was rarely engaged in what might be considered "traditional" missionary activity, his immense theological output has certainly left a missional legacy. The significance of his career is measured by the foundations laid in the lives of many pastors, theologians, and missionaries; those who heard Torrance during his life, and those who benefit from his written work. However, McGrath rightly observes that for all the magnitude of his intellectual achievements, Torrance may have preferred "to be remembered as one who both knew and proclaimed the faithfulness of God in the midst of the uncertainties and anxieties of this world."[169]

Torrance's vision of God's faithfulness shaped his hope for the Church in the current age. The eschatological *telos* of the Church is that of a redeemed and reconciled body, which is one, holy, catholic, and apostolic, united with Jesus Christ through the Holy Spirit. The Church is already that which God intends it to be. However, between the ascension and *parousia* the Church is still a pilgrim people, on the way, wrestling with the ambiguities of order and the influence of sin. It is in this space that Torrance's theological vision invokes the faithfulness of God to the Church, for it exists in the eschatological pause between the first and second coming of Christ and heralds the glorious reality of Christ's body which will one day be fully manifest.

---

[165]Thomas F. Torrance, ed., *Theological Dialogue between Orthodox and Reformed Churches*, 2 vols., vol. 1 (Edinburgh: Scottish Academic Press, 1985), xi.

[166]Joseph D. Small, "Orthodox and Reformed in Dialogue: The Agreed Statement on the Holy Trinity," in *The Witness of Bartholomew I, Ecumenical Patriarch*, ed. William G. Rusch (Grand Rapids, MI: Eerdmans, 2013), 122.

[167]Ibid., 125.

[168]Myk Habets, *Theology in Transposition: A Constructive Appraisal of T.F. Torrance* (Minneapolis: Fortress Press, 2013), 198.

[169]McGrath, *Thomas F. Torrance*, 241.

CHAPTER SIXTEEN

"Not I, but Christ"

Thomas F. Torrance on the Christian Life

E. JEROME VAN KUIKEN

In the year of his eightieth birthday, Thomas F. Torrance recalled, "Galatians 2:20 has long been for me a passage of primary importance."[1] Concentrated within this single verse is Torrance's doctrine of the Christian life.[2] It is a life in which Christ and his virtues—his life, his faith, his love—radically displace one's own "I" so as to annihilate all self-reliance. Yet the self itself is not annihilated but established. Christ's life makes us live. His constant faith and love enable and enfold our own fluctuating faith and love. Thus, the Christian life includes both an objective "primary pole" (Christ's ongoing initiative on our behalf) and a subjective "secondary pole" (our Christ-empowered response to his activity).[3] Torrance's home tradition of Reformed theology typically speaks of the doctrine of the Christian life using the language of sanctification. This chapter will follow suit by studying Torrance's view in terms of objective and subjective sanctification (along with overlapping terms of his like "participation" and "personalization") before ending with an overview of present and proposed developments of his material on the Christian life.

OBJECTIVE SANCTIFICATION: OUR HOLINESS IN CHRIST

Torrance's conviction that the "primary pole" of the Christian life lies outside of ourselves prompted his robust account of sanctification's objective grounding in the great truths of Christian orthodoxy: Trinity, Incarnation, and Atonement. Since his views on these dogmas receive in-depth treatment elsewhere in this volume, what follows is simply a survey of how they fund Torrance's teaching on objective sanctification.[4] We shall explore six loci: (1) the Ontological and Economic Trinity, (2) the hypostatic union and

---

[1] Thomas F. Torrance, "Preaching Christ Today," in *Preaching Christ Today: The Gospel and Scientific Thinking* (Grand Rapids, MI: Eerdmans, 1994), 31. Torrance delivered this address in 1993 (ibid., viii). For further comments on and bibliography of Torrance's use of Gal. 2:20, see Thomas F. Torrance, *Incarnation: The Person and Life of Christ*, ed. Robert T. Walker (Downers Grove, IL: IVP Academic/Milton Keynes: Paternoster, 2008), 28 n. 40.

[2] See the comments of Andrew Purves, "'I yet Not I but Christ': Galatians 2:20 and the Christian Life in the Theology of T. F. Torrance," *Participatio* Supplemental, vol. 2 (2013): 25.

[3] Torrance, *Preaching*, 31–2.

[4] Consequently, footnoted citations from Torrance's works are meant to be suggestive, not exhaustive.

an/en-hypostasis couplet, (3) the Chalcedonian safeguards against Christological heresies, (4) the *non-assumptus* and fallenness of Christ's vicarious humanity, (5) Christ's atoning total substitution, and (6) the Atonement as the "end" of ethics.

The Ontological and Economic Trinity

The ultimate foundation of Christian life and holiness lies in the life and holiness of the triune God.[5] Within the Ontological Trinity, that life and holiness take the form of an eternal communion of Persons (*hypostases*) who are who they are by virtue of their relationships to one another. The most fundamental reality, then, is both personal and personalizing. Each divine Person is distinct: the Father is not the Son, who is not the Holy Spirit. Yet their distinction is without division, for each Person indwells the others in the mysterious coinherence called *perichoresis*, each one upholding each other's uniqueness within the unity of the Divine Being.

While the Trinity is self-sufficient, it is not self-absorbed. Neither by necessity nor by caprice but in gracious freedom, God wills to share life and love with that which is not God. This will of God results in creation and—due to the absurd irruption of evil into God's good world—redemption. God's relationship with the world in creation and redemption follows a single pattern, that of the Economic Trinity: all things come from the Father, through the Son, in the Holy Spirit, and are called to return their life, love, and worship in the Spirit, through the Son, to the Father. The aim of the Trinity's activity is creaturely participation in God's objective life.

The an/en-hypostatic union

This aim reaches full realization in the Incarnation. By the will of the Father and in the power of the Spirit, God the Son bonds with the created order so as to become a man. Because it is through the Son that all things exist, his becoming a particular human being affects the whole of humanity and the cosmos.[6] The Son joins himself to humanity in such a way that the divine nature and human nature are united in one Person (*hypostasis*), the Son. The human nature taken up by the Son has two aspects. Considered in itself, apart from him as Son or Word, it is *anhypostatic*, having no personhood of its own. In the Incarnation, the Son assumes a human nature, not a human person. But considered in its union with the Son, his human nature is *enhypostatic*: it participates in his Personhood, being personalized in him even as the Person of the Son is humanized in it (though without diluting his deity). He does not merely impersonate a human person.[7] Torrance sees the

---

[5]Torrance states his mature doctrine of the Trinity in Thomas F. Torrance, *The Christian Doctrine of God, One Being Three Persons*, Cornerstones edition (London: Bloomsbury T&T Clark, 2016). Torrance's entire theology is rooted in the Trinity, as two authoritative introductions to his thought rightly recognize: Elmer M. Colyer, *How to Read T.F. Torrance: Understanding His Trinitarian & Scientific Theology* (Downers Grove, IL: InterVarsity, 2001), and Paul D. Molnar, *Thomas F. Torrance: Theologian of the Trinity* (Farnham, UK: Ashgate, 2009; repr. London: Routledge, 2016). Two recent expositions of his trinitarian soteriology are Dick O. Eugenio, *Communion with the Triune God: The Trinitarian Soteriology of T. F. Torrance* (Eugene, OR: Pickwick, 2014) and Geordie W. Ziegler, *Trinitarian Grace and Participation: An Entry into the Theology of T. F. Torrance* (Minneapolis, MN: Fortress, 2017).

[6]Thomas F. Torrance, "The Atonement. The Singularity of Christ and the Finality of the Cross: The Atonement and the Moral Order," in *Universalism and the Doctrine of Hell*, ed. Nigel S. de S. Cameron (Grand Rapids, MI: Baker, 1992), 230–2, 244–5, 249, 254–6.

[7]Torrance, *Incarnation*, 207, 211–12, 228–33.

hypostatic union, with its dual aspects of *anhypostasis* and *enhypostasis* (abbreviated as the "*an/en-hypostasis* couplet"), as the objective paradigm for all divine–human relations.[8]

Chalcedon's Countermoves to Christological Heresies

Every paradigm must be properly understood. To interpret the hypostatic union aright, Torrance looks to the Definition of Chalcedon (AD 451). This ecumenical statement affirms that in the one Person of Christ are two natures, divine and human, "without confusion, without conversion, without division, and without separation."[9] The first two adverbial phrases exclude a pair of heresies that undermine Christ's humanity: Docetism, in which the celestial Christ only seems human, and Eutychianism, in which Christ's humanity so blends with his deity as to dilute his human properties. Chalcedon's second two phrases deny heresies that divorce the divine from Christ's creaturely nature: adoptionism (or Ebionism), which reduces Christ to a mere God-approved man; Arianism, which ranks him as the highest created being but leaves him infinitely less than God Most High; and Nestorianism, which posits two persons in Christ—one divine, one human—who partner together to produce salvation.[10] Chalcedon's four safeguards ensure that a truly participatory relationship exists between Christ's deity and humanity. The sanctification of his human nature (addressed below) does not require its erasure in whole or in part by his deity. Nor does it demand autonomous creaturely effort, with or without divine assistance. Christ's divinity sanctifies his humanity, enabling instead of disabling it to fulfill his Father's will.[11]

The Assumption of a Full, Fallen Human Nature

From Chalcedon's doctrine of the Incarnation, it follows that the divine Son took on (or "assumed") a complete human nature, including a body, mind, and will. No one has expressed the importance of this point more pithily than the Church Father Gregory Nazianzen, in an epigram known as the *non-assumptus*: "the unassumed is the unhealed."[12] Christ must have a full human nature in order to heal our humanity fully. But Torrance took Nazianzen to mean not only that the Son assumed an ontologically whole human nature but also that he assumed it in its postlapsarian condition.[13] This claim has occasioned much controversy and misunderstanding, and so we must examine it carefully.[14]

For Torrance, this claim is biblical: the Son came "in the likeness of sinful flesh" (Rom. 8:3) and was "made sin" (2 Cor. 5:21) not in the weak sense of looking like a sinner

---

[8]Thomas F. Torrance, *Theological Science* (London: Oxford University Press, 1969), 216–19; cf., Thomas F. Torrance, "Predestination in Christ," *Evangelical Quarterly* 13 (1941): 129–30.

[9]Quoted in Torrance, *Incarnation*, 200. Cf., his full discussion on pages 198–212.

[10]Torrance, "Predestination in Christ," 129–30.

[11]Torrance, *Incarnation*, 207–12.

[12]*Epistle* 101.5; Torrance quotes this slogan frequently, for example, in his *Karl Barth, Biblical and Evangelical Theologian* (Edinburgh: T&T Clark, 1990), 103, 202, 231.

[13]For example, Torrance, *Incarnation*, 61–5; Thomas F. Torrance, *The Mediation of Christ*, rev. edition (Colorado Springs, CO: Helmers & Howard, 1992), 39–42.

[14]E. Jerome Van Kuiken, *Christ's Humanity in Current and Ancient Controversy: Fallen or Not?* (London: Bloomsbury T&T Clark, 2017) offers extensive analysis of the controversy. The following paragraphs draw from pages 31–43.

or being counted as one but in a stronger, ontological sense. The claim is also simply rational: From where else would Christ derive his human nature but from humanity, all of whom are fallen? For him to have become incarnate in a nature created *de novo* would render him alien to us and defeat God's purpose of reestablishing fellowship with Adam's rebel race. Moreover, to interpret the *non-assumptus* in terms of a prelapsarian human nature calls into question how salvation is achieved: Does a neutral-natured Christ simply set sinners a moral example? Is his perfect obedience in a perfect human nature merely credited to our account to cancel our debt of iniquity? How then may we be saved from the original sin that festers in the depths of our being? Is Jesus but half a savior, pardoning our wrongdoings but leaving our wrongbeing to the Holy Spirit to cure?

Torrance insists that what Christ assumed, he healed first *in himself*: sanctification is wrought out within the Incarnate One before we are given to share in it through the Holy Spirit. The act of assumption was itself a healing, hallowing act that began in Christ's virginal conception and continued until his resurrection. This is not to say that Christ's self-sanctification was ever partial, leaving room for any vestige of depravity within him. On the contrary, at every moment, his consecration and purity were complete in that moment. But that consecration and purity were constantly under pressure from the limitations, temptations, and persecutions of existence in a fallen world. Christ's holiness was a victory to be maintained at every step until he finished his mission. Not only, though, did he bear the external hostility of sinners and the devil, as well as the internal frailty of his own flesh; he also bore the wrath of God against the sinful humanity whose nature he sinlessly wore. Thus, by his spotless obedience in our nature and his acceptance of its condemnation, he "condemned sin in the flesh" (Rom. 8:3) and continuously converted it into conformity to God's will.[15]

Torrance's discussions of the *non-assumptus* can leave readers with the mistaken impression that he has compromised Christ's perfect sinlessness or has lapsed into incoherence.[16] Here the *an/en-hypostasis* couplet clarifies his meaning. Whenever Torrance speaks of the human nature assumed by Christ as sinful, depraved, and the like, he is viewing it anhypostatically—that is, apart from its sanctifying union with the Person of Christ. Whenever Torrance speaks of Christ's humanity as sinless, pure, and holy, that humanity is being considered enhypostatically.[17]

Total Substitution

Christ's lifelong healing and conversion of human nature in himself forbids us from limiting his atoning substitution for us to his death alone. Rather, his whole life from

---

[15]Torrance, *Incarnation*, and Thomas F. Torrance, *Atonement: The Person and Work of Christ*, ed. Robert T. Walker (Downers Grove, IL: IVP Academic/Milton Keynes: Paternoster, 2009), expound at length on this paragraph's material.

[16]For example, Donald Macleod, *Jesus Is Lord: Christology Yesterday and Today* (Fearn, UK: Mentor, 2000), 126–32; Oliver Crisp, "Did Christ Have a *Fallen* Human Nature?," *International Journal of Systematic Theology* 6, no. 3 (2004): 270–88; repr. in Crisp, *Divinity and Humanity: The Incarnation Reconsidered* (Cambridge: Cambridge University Press, 2007), 90–117; Peter Cass, *Christ Condemned Sin in the Flesh: Thomas F. Torrance's Doctrine of Soteriology and Its Ecumenical Significance* (Saarbrücken, Germany: Dr. Müller, 2009); Kevin Chiarot, *The Unassumed Is the Unhealed: The Humanity of Christ in the Theology of T. F. Torrance* (Eugene, OR: Pickwick, 2013). For rebuttals, see Van Kuiken, *Christ's Humanity*, 40, 42, 85–7, 161–2, 170–1.

[17]Myk Habets, *Theology in Transposition: A Constructive Appraisal of T. F. Torrance* (Minneapolis: Fortress, 2013), 190 n. 118; cf., Kye Won Lee, *Living in Union with Christ: The Practical Theology of Thomas F. Torrance* (New York: Peter Lang, 2003), 129 n. 108, 301, 308.

conception and birth to resurrection and ascension stands in for us and reconciles us to God. This is Torrance's doctrine of *total substitution*. There is nothing we do to contribute to our salvation or Christian life that Christ has not already done on our behalf. His is a "vicarious humanity," representing us in our flesh and in our stead from beginning to end. He has perfectly been born from above for us, repented and believed for us, prayed and obeyed for us, suffered judgment and godforsakenness for us, and been raised from the tomb to the right hand of God for us. To deny the totality of Christ's substitution at any point is to create an Achilles's heel in the body of salvation, a vulnerable spot at which we must rely on our own repentance, faith, obedience, and such. But given our weakness and depravity, we cannot repent enough, believe adequately, or obey perfectly on our own, and so our salvation would fall under jeopardy. Even if we deluded ourselves into thinking our efforts were sufficient, we would only lapse into Pharisaical pride and the Pelagian heresy that one may save oneself. But because of Christ's total substitution in his vicarious humanity, we may and must depend wholly on him at every moment of the Christian life.[18] Herein lies our assurance of salvation: not in turning inward to regard ourselves and our spiritual condition, for that is to take up the very posture of self-centeredness from which Christ came to deliver us! Rather, we discover a sense of security in salvation by looking away from ourselves to Christ, who is our election, sanctification, and redemption.[19]

Christ the "End" of Ethics

The atoning work of Christ transforms not only human nature but also the moral order itself. Torrance adapts Kierkegaard's phrase to speak of the "soteriological suspension of ethics."[20] Torrance expositor Todd Speidell refers to Christ as the "end" of ethics, playing on the *double entendre* of "end": on the one hand, the Atonement brings about the cessation ("end") of legalism, for all human attempts to achieve righteousness by the Law only strengthen sin's grip; on the other hand, our reconciliation in Christ fulfills the purpose ("end") for which we were created, a purpose that the Law could only promise and prefigure but never achieve—an intimate childlike relationship with a loving heavenly Father.[21] Through the mediation of Christ, who has obeyed the Father perfectly on our behalf, we are freed from the mediation of the Law in our relationship to God.[22] The personal objectivity of Christ as the one who for us has "fulfill[ed] all righteousness" (Mt. 3:15) replaces the impersonal objectivity of the Law and the subjectivity of our self-effort to keep it. In Christ we are recipients of unconditional grace, and even in our faithlessness he remains faithful for our sake.[23]

---

[18]Torrance, *Preaching*, 30–8; *Mediation*, 79–98.

[19]Thomas F. Torrance, *When Christ Comes and Comes Again* (Grand Rapids, MI: Eerdmans, 1957), 74–5; Alexandra S. Radcliff, *The Claim of Humanity in Christ: Salvation and Sanctification in the Theology of T. F. and J. B. Torrance* (Eugene, OR: Pickwick, 2016), 187.

[20]Torrance, "The Atonement," 252. For background and reflections on Torrance's phrase, see Christopher Holmes, "'Renewal through Union': Thomas F. Torrance on the New Basis of Ethics," *Participatio* 5 (2015): 45–55.

[21]Todd Speidell, *Fully Human in Christ: The Incarnation as the End of Christian Ethics* (Eugene, OR: Wipf & Stock, 2016), ix.

[22]Torrance, "The Atonement," 249–54.

[23]Ibid., *Preaching*, 35–8.

The Problem of Abstraction

Torrance's doctrine of objective sanctification in Christ as surveyed above has come in for criticism due to its level of abstraction. Echoing Colin Gunton, Myk Habets finds inexcusable "Torrance's minimal treatment of the details of Jesus' human life on earth."[24] Geordie Ziegler questions whether "a formulaic mode is the most effective approach for the kind of personal dynamism Torrance seeks" rather than a more narratival mode.[25] Ironically, these critiques echo Torrance's early mentor, Hugh Ross Mackintosh, who complained of the ancient Church Fathers' development of orthodox formulae, "and thus by degrees the Church's memories of the human life of Jesus faded into oblivion."[26] Torrance's rigorous attention to and extension of these ancient formulae appears to have landed him in the same neglect of the biblical accounts.

A Solution: Torrance on the Life of Christ

Appearances, though, can mislead. In fact, Torrance did attend to the details of the biblical narratives in two of the genres in which he wrote: his sermons and his Christology lectures at New College, University of Edinburgh. Torrance's unpublished sermon manuscripts range across the breadth of Scripture, including all four Gospels' accounts of Jesus's birth, temptations, and ministry, as well as the events of Holy Week.[27] A published collection of sermons entitled *When Christ Comes and Comes Again* likewise covers a number of passages from the Gospels.[28]

As for the New College lectures, their editor notes that they "provide what is effectively an extended theological commentary on the bible."[29] As such, their significance is crucial:

> These lectures ... represent the starting point and centre of all his thinking. If the focus of his later work appeared to be on [other] issues ..., that was only because the doctrine of Christ and the biblical understanding behind it remained the foundation from which he was thinking out other issues. It is the lectures which more than anything else unfold the biblical and theological roots of his thought.[30]

In these lectures we read that Christ regenerated our humanity in his virginal conception and birth; overcame our ignorance in his boyhood growth in wisdom; repented in our stead at his baptism; defeated temptation for us in the desert; bore our sorrows and afflictions in his healings; wrestled against the powers of evil in his exorcisms; revealed God's Kingdom in his teachings; prayed against our self-will in Gethsemane; fully satisfied

---

[24]Habets, *Theology in Transposition*, 167. He has leveled the same critique in his earlier work, *Theosis in the Theology of Thomas Torrance* (Farnham, UK: Ashgate, 2009), 82 n. 154, 196. Cf. Colin E. Gunton, "Being and Person: T.F. Torrance's Doctrine of God," in *The Promise of Trinitarian Theology: Theologians in Dialogue with T. F. Torrance*, ed. Elmer M. Colyer (Lanham, MD: Rowman & Littlefield, 2001), 132.

[25]Ziegler, *Trinitarian Grace*, 297.

[26]H. R. Mackintosh, *The Doctrine of the Person of Jesus Christ* (Edinburgh: T&T Clark, 1912; repr. 1920), 222. On Mackintosh's influence on Torrance, see Alister E. McGrath, *Thomas F. Torrance: An Intellectual Biography* (London: T&T Clark, 1999), 29–33, 163–4.

[27]Torrance's unpublished sermons may be found in The Thomas F. Torrance Manuscript Collection, Special Collections, Princeton Theological Seminary Library, Boxes 38–47. For detailed lists, see http://manuscripts.ptsem.edu/collection/223 or Eugenio, *Communion*, 219–28.

[28]Torrance, *When Christ Comes*.

[29]Robert T. Walker, "Introduction," in Torrance, *Incarnation*, xi. This volume and its sequel, *Atonement*, comprise Torrance's New College Christology lectures.

[30]Ibid., x–xi. Cf., Molnar, *Torrance*, 342–3, on Torrance's handling of Christ's earthly life.

God's judgment and triumphed over evil on our behalf in his crucifixion and resurrection; and ever intercedes for us and governs us by his Spirit as the ascended Lord. By all these means, our conversion, reconciliation, and sanctification are forever secured in the objectivity of Christ's vicarious humanity.

SUBJECTIVE SANCTIFICATION: CHRIST'S HOLINESS IN US

Although Torrance strongly and thoroughly articulated the objectivity of our sanctification in the Trinity, Incarnation, and Atonement, he also insisted that God's agency does not eliminate our own. Our sanctification is "all of grace," yes, but the corollary is not therefore "nothing of man" but rather "all of man." This is what Torrance terms "the logic of grace."[31] God's activity noncompetitively enables instead of canceling out our own activity while denying all our efforts at autonomy and self-justification. Consequently, the half-dozen loci of objective sanctification considered above correspond to six aspects of subjective sanctification: (1) the Church as the earthly locus of the Trinity, (2) the "hypostatic" relationship between grace and faith, (3) the anthropological correlates of Chalcedon's Christological heresies, (4) Torrance's Reformed rehabilitation of *theosis*, (5) the Holy Spirit's purveyance to us of Christ's total substitution, and (6) evangelical (not legal) ethics. We move now to study each aspect in turn.

From the One Holy Trinity to the One Holy Church

The objective activity of the Economic Trinity in history brings forth the Church, the people of God. Each Person of the indivisible Godhead plays a distinct role in the formation of the Church. The Father elects to have a body of people who are the recipients of his love and the representatives of his glory; hence election in relation to the Church is primarily corporate, not individual. The Son hypostatically unites with human nature so as to reconcile the world to God, gathers around himself a band of disciples, and commissions them to proclaim by word and sacrament his atoning grace. The Spirit poured out from the Father through the Son at Pentecost actualizes union between individuals and Christ, as well as communion with the whole Trinity and with one's fellow believers. The Church, then, is the earthly temple and analogue of the heavenly Godhead. As such, her distinctive marks share in and reflect those of the triune God. As the Trinity is one, so the Church is to be one and undivided amid the diversity of persons within her. As the Lord is holy, so the Church is sanctified through participation in the self-sanctification of Christ, a participation enabled by means of the hallowing Spirit. As God has loved the world in its entirety, so the Church is called to catholicity, to flesh out the universal scope of the reconciliation wrought by Christ. And as God's love led to the sending of the Son and Spirit to give the world salvation, so is the Church apostolic, sent to all nations with the gospel. Thus the Church forms the matrix in which individuals come to faith and join in worship of God, thereby participating at a creaturely level in the eternal life and love of the Ontological Trinity.[32] This participation in God

---

[31]Torrance, "The Atonement," 230; *Mediation*, xii; *Theological Science*, 214–6. Here and throughout his corpus, Torrance uses "man" as inclusive of both sexes.
[32]Thomas F. Torrance, *The Trinitarian Faith: The Evangelical Theology of the Ancient Catholic Church,* 2nd edition (London: Bloomsbury T&T Clark, 2016), 252–82; *Atonement*, 342–3, 349–400.

takes particular form in the sacraments. Torrance strongly affirms paedobaptism and sees Christian baptism as an incorporation into Christ's own Jordan baptism. Both of these moves tend to accent the priority of divine initiative and the objectivity of baptism even amid our subjective baptismal experience. Likewise, in the Eucharist Christ is really though mysteriously present to nourish us in our union with him and communion with the Trinity and fellow Christians.[33]

From Christ's Hypostatic Union to Christians' Union with Christ

As stated earlier, Torrance sees Christ's hypostatic union as paradigmatic for divine–human relations, particularly in conversion and the Christian life. According to Torrance, "There is a kind of hypostatic union between Grace [sic] and faith, through the Holy Spirit." The human nature assumed by the Son is anhypostatic, devoid of any independent personhood, but becomes *enhypostatic* upon its assumption by the Son, such that his human mind and volition think and will in concurrence with his divine mind and will. By analogy with the *anhypostasis*, there is no independently existing faith within us when the Holy Spirit graciously initiates our encounter with Christ. That personal encounter is personalizing, though, as in the *enhypostasis*: we find ourselves thinking and willing in repentant faith. The Annunciation serves as a further analogy: God's decision of grace that Mary shall bear the Messiah comes before and enables her decision of faith to submit to God's will. As in the physical birth of Christ, so in the spiritual rebirth of Christians, God's gracious initiative evokes our believing response.[34]

Yet here the mystery of evil rears its head. Not everyone responds believingly to the divine initiative. Torrance flatly rejects any explanation that narrows the range of the Father's election, the Son's atonement, and the Spirit's drawing so that a portion of humankind is left untouched by salvific grace. He likewise denies the syllogism that since salvation is solely by grace and grace has come to all persons, therefore all definitively will be saved in the end. Why some spurn God's cruciform love and end in damnation is inexplicable, just as is the very presence of evil in God's good creation. Evil is essentially irrational, an absurdity irreconcilable with logic. The grim irony remains that the very grace that enables our communion with God becomes the basis of our greater condemnation if we refuse it.[35]

From Christological to Anthropological Heresies

If Christ's hypostatic union is the paradigm for the relation of God's grace to our response, then the Chalcedonian safeguards should prove heuristic for preventing heretical views of grace. On the one hand, just as there must be no blending of Christ's divine and human natures, so must there be none in the relation of the divine and human elements in salvation. A Docetic Christology corresponds to theological determinism, in which humans' seeming choices are merely shadows cast by God's choices. Similarly,

---

[33]Thomas F. Torrance, *Theology in Reconciliation: Essays towards Evangelical and Catholic Unity in East and West* (London: Geoffrey Chapman, 1975), 82–138; *Trinitarian Faith*, 282–98; Ziegler, *Trinitarian Grace*, 205–38.

[34]Torrance, "Predestination," 127–31; quotation from page 130. On Christ as the "personalising Person," see *Mediation*, 67–9. For critique of Torrance's application of the *an/en-hypostasis* couplet and the term "hypostatic union" beyond Christology, see Ziegler, *Trinitarian Grace*, 294–8.

[35]Torrance, "Predestination," 121–6, 139 nn. 65, 67; "The Atonement," 244–8.

Eutychianism finds its anthropological echo in "a doctrine of mystic infused grace" that blurs the boundaries between Creator and creature. On the other hand, no separation may be countenanced between Christ's divinity and humanity or between the divine and human decisions in salvation. An Ebionite Christology parallels a Pelagian soteriology: both rely on minimally graced human efforts to accomplish salvation. Nestorianism's dual-partner Christ exemplifies synergism, in which God contributes only part of what is necessary for redemption and humans themselves are obliged to make good the rest. The Arian Christ is neither truly God nor truly human but stands in the metaphysical gap between the two as a mediating creature. The Roman Catholic notion of created grace functions in the same fashion as an intermediary *tertium quid*.[36] A proper doctrine of grace will dodge all these errors.

From Non-assumptus *to* Theosis

The Church Fathers paired the divine Word's condescension to human flesh (Jn. 1:14) with a corresponding exaltation of redeemed humanity to become partakers in the divine nature (2 Pet. 1:4). According to the famous epigram of Athanasius, "He was made man that we might be made divine."[37] Gregory Nazianzen, who taught that "the unassumed is the unhealed," also coined the term *theosis* for this "be[ing] made divine."[38] Torrance's early handling of the doctrine of *theosis* reflected a Protestant prejudice against it as a case of Hellenistic metaphysical mysticism, a view he later abandoned.[39] In August of 1964, he gave an address to the World Alliance of Reformed Churches in which he sought to rehabilitate *theosis* for Reformed theology. To translate this term as "*deification*" or "*divinization*" is inaccurate, Torrance insisted. Just as God does not cease to be God in the Incarnation, so humans remain human in *theosis*. What the term really refers to is our sharing in the very life of God by the grace of the all-holy Spirit, who stoops to our weakness and raises us up into communion with the Most High.[40] After 1964, Torrance continued to exposit *theosis* and the related term *theopoiesis* along the same lines, albeit infrequently.[41] Myk Habets has noted that Torrance preferred to communicate the same concept via terms like "union, communion, participation ... humanising, personalising and atoning exchange."[42] Far from metamorphozing into gods, then, *theosis* for Torrance

---

[36]Torrance, "Predestination," 129–31, 140 n. 75. Torrance's sprawling, tangled sentence structure obscures his correlations. See also Torrance, "The Roman Doctrine of Grace from the Point of View of Reformed Theology," *Theology in Reconstruction* (London: SCM Press, 1965), 169–91.

[37]*De incarnatione* 54, quoted in Torrance, *Trinitarian Faith*, 188.

[38]Christopher A. Beeley, *Gregory of Nazianzus on the Trinity and the Knowledge of God: In Your Light We Shall See Light* (Oxford: Oxford University Press, 2008), 117.

[39]Thomas F. Torrance, *The Doctrine of Grace in the Apostolic Fathers* (Edinburgh: Oliver & Boyd, 1948), 140 n. 3, cited in Ziegler, *Trinitarian Grace*, 252 n. 43, who credits Torrance's shift to his correspondence with Orthodox theologian Georges Florovsky in the 1950s. However, in *Christian Doctrine of God* he still rejected the "Platonising translation of theosis as 'Deification,'" 95–6.

[40]Thomas F. Torrance, "Come, Creator Spirit, for the Renewal of Worship and Witness," in *Theology in Reconstruction* (Grand Rapids, MI: Eerdmans, 1966), repr. in *Theological Foundations for Ministry*, ed. Ray S. Anderson (Edinburgh: T&T Clark, 1979), 373.

[41]Torrance, *Trinitarian Faith*, 138–42, 183–4, 188–90, 231 n. 193, 264–6, 305; ibid., *The Christian Doctrine of God*, 95–7, 151.

[42]Habets, *Theosis*, 15. See the whole of Habets's book for the biblical and historical background of the doctrine of *theosis* and its outworking in Torrance's theology; cf., concurring and corrective comments in Eugenio, *Communion*, 71–2.

meant becoming conformed to the true humanity found in the Person of Christ and so finding our own true humanness and personhood.[43]

From Total Substitution to Total Participation

By means of their theotic communion with the Holy Spirit, Christians' union with Christ becomes actualized in their individual lives and they participate in his total substitution. At every point, Christ's perfect obedience on our behalf does not exclude but includes our own feeble, faltering obedience. Torrance opposes any evangelism that places the burden of adequately repenting and believing, deciding for and converting to Christ upon the hearer. Our response to the gospel will always be inadequate when measured by God's holy standard. Proper evangelism calls us to cast ourselves upon Christ, who has supplied perfectly the penitence, faith, conversion, and decision that enable our own. As baptizands we share in the one baptism of Christ himself. At worship and prayer, we join in the perpetual adoration and intercession offered by our ascended great high priest in heaven. In the Eucharist we continually partake of his once-for-all sacrifice. Through Christian service we act as co-laborers with Christ, who came to serve the needy and save the lost. Nor do we serve only when it is convenient or out of an expectation of reward or fear of punishment. No, Christ's total substitution summons our total submission to his call to service, even as it frees us from mercenary motives unworthy of his pure self-giving love. This paradox of liberty from anxious self-interest and liberty for wholehearted obedience lies at the root of the relation between Christ's total substitution and our total participation.[44]

While Torrance affirms that the Spirit subjectively actualizes our objective union with Christ and his benefits, he is keen to ward off any identification of the Holy Spirit with the human spirit or of Christ's benefits (such as election, regeneration, and sanctification) with any psychological experience. Monasticism, pietism, revivalism, nineteenth-century liberalism, and twentieth-century existentialism and personalism all have succumbed to these reductionisms, but the essential objectivity of the Spirit and of Christ's benefits must remain uncompromised.[45] Torrance offers a similar qualification when he celebrates the fresh emphasis on the Holy Spirit generated by the Pentecostal and Charismatic Movements. These movements' adherents rightly expect Christ to act miraculously today through his Spirit, just as he did during his earthly ministry. But they wrongly tend to focus on the miracles themselves instead of on the Son whom the Spirit has been sent to glorify.[46] Neither Pentecostals nor liberals nor anyone else may be permitted to twist our total participation in Christ into a total assimilation of Christ to ourselves.

From the "End" of Ethics to Evangelical Ethics

Since our total participation in Christ's total substitution frees us for unselfish obedience, there is a place for Christian ethics, rightly understood. We no longer relate to God at a distance by means of the mediation of the Law, with its commandments externally

---

[43]Cf., Torrance, *Mediation*, 67–72, on Christ as "personalising Person" and "humanising man."

[44]Thomas F. Torrance, "The Word of God and the Response of Man," in *God and Rationality* (Oxford: Oxford University Press, 1971), repr. in Anderson, *Theological Foundations*, 125–32; Torrance, *Mediation*, 81–98.

[45]Torrance, "Come, Creator Spirit," 372–5; *When Christ Comes*, 67–9, 73–5.

[46]Thomas F. Torrance, "The Church in the New Era of Scientific and Cosmological Change," in *Theology in Reconciliation*, repr. in Anderson, *Theological Foundations*, 773–6.

imposed upon us because the "is" of our sinful nature stands at odds with the "ought" of God's holy will. Now we share through the Spirit in the Son's relationship with his Father, and God's love within us inwardly compels us to please him.[47] This ethic of love is a properly evangelical (i.e., gospel-grounded) ethic as opposed to the old legal ethic. Its stimulus is gratitude for unconditional grace, not anxiety to impress God or others. Its shape is Christian service in union with the servant Christ.

What does such service look like? Torrance sketches two answers. Negatively, service with Christ will rebuff the devil's desert temptation to embrace sociopolitical, coercive power, and worldly prestige. Nor will the Church forfeit her ministries of mercy to state-run programs. Positively, Christian service involves intercession, evangelism, and the reconciliation of churchly divisions. In relation to scientific endeavor (a key interest of Torrance's), Christian service means pursuing pure science to the praise of the Creator and applied science to the resolution of humankind's crises of poverty and starvation, all the while respecting rather than exploiting nature.[48]

The Problem of Abstraction, Again

Despite his descriptions of the Christian life, numerous sympathetic commentators have faulted Torrance for inadequate attention to the particulars of Christian experience and ethics.[49] His tendency toward abstraction in relation to Christ's own life corresponds to abstraction in relation to the Christian life. As we have seen, however, in the former case we have in the New College lectures a sustained systematic treatment of Christ's life, which Torrance's more abstract writings presuppose. We have no such resource from his pen on the subject of the Christian life.[50] Instead, Torrance seems content to outline the broad contours of subjective sanctification and service, leaving most of the specifics to his readers' Spirit-led imagination.

A Solution: Torrance's Occasional Pieces and Overall Project

Although Torrance never penned a thorough treatment of the practicalities of Christian experience or ethics, we may look to his occasional writings on these subjects for partial coverage. As we found with the life of Christ, so also here Torrance's sermons give specifics that his more scholarly works often omit. Notably, in his preaching Torrance strongly insisted that his hearers must decide for Christ, exercise a lively faith, and work

---

[47]Torrance, "The Atonement," 249–54.

[48]Torrance, "The Word of God," 132–4; "Service in Jesus Christ," in *Service in Christ*, ed. James I. McCord and T. H. L. Parker (London: Epworth Press, 1966), repr. in Anderson, *Theological Foundations*, 726–33; Torrance, "The Church in the New Era," 762–3.

[49]For example, Ray S. Anderson, "Reading T. F. Torrance as a Practical Theologian," in Colyer, *Promise*, 177; Lee, *Living*, 310–5; David Fergusson, "The Ascension of Christ: Its Significance in the Theology of T. F. Torrance," *Participatio* 3 (2012): 106–7; Habets, *Theosis*, 152, 162, 186, 189, 196; Eugenio, *Communion*, 75, 208–11, 213; Andrew Purves, *Exploring Christology and Atonement: Conversations with John McLeod Campbell, H. R. Mackintosh and T. F. Torrance* (Downers Grove, IL: InterVarsity, 2015), 101–2, 239–40; Radcliff, *Claim*, 109–12, 117, 126, 128, 159–60, 189; Ziegler, *Trinitarian Grace*, 298–300; John Webster, foreword to Ziegler, *Trinitarian Grace*, xi, as well as in other of Webster's writings, as documented in Todd H. Speidell, "The Soteriological Suspension of the Ethical in the Theology of T. F. Torrance," *Participatio* 5 (2015): 57–60. Speidell's article is reprinted in *Fully Human*, 1–37.

[50]One good reason for this omission is that at New College Torrance was assigned to teach Christian dogmatics, not ethics (which fell under the purview of a different university department), as pointed out in Speidell, "Soteriological Suspension," 60.

out their salvation if they were to be Christians indeed, all the while recognizing the grounding of their actions in Christ's acting on their behalf.[51] Dick Eugenio accounts for the difference between Torrance's scholarship and sermons in terms of their differing intended audiences: in the former, he almost exclusively stressed Christ's objective accomplishment of redemption over against evangelicals' (and, one might add, liberal Christians') preoccupation with religious experience. In the latter, he addressed parishioners whose federal Calvinism predisposed them to such a strong emphasis on the objectivity of salvation that they were in danger of downplaying its subjective side.[52]

In the arena of Christian ethics, Todd Speidell similarly rebuts Torrance's critics by pointing to occasional pieces in which Torrance directly addressed five specific ethical questions.[53] Rearranging Speidell's sequence to match the order of one standard summary of biblical ethics—the Decalogue—illumines the breadth of Torrance's coverage:

- *I am the Lord your God who brought you out of Egypt; no other gods; no idols; no misuse of the Lord's name*: Torrance defended traditional (masculine) language for God, claiming that to alter or abandon it is to exchange divine revelation (albeit accommodated to our creaturely condition) for mythologizing, idolatrous projectionism.
- *Honor your father and mother (respect human authorities)*: Perhaps unexpectedly in view of his stance on God-talk, Torrance advocated that ordained ministry should be open not only to men (spiritual "fathers" or "padres")[54] but equally to women. As both sexes receive holy baptism, so may both receive holy orders.
- *No murder*: Torrance argued that the unborn are persons and therefore that abortion is immoral.
- *No false witness*: One must both tell and do the truth, Torrance urged.
- *The Ten Words taken as a whole*: Torrance wrote a defense of legal realism, the understanding that law has its basis in nature, against legal positivism, the theory that law is purely the creation of human caprice.

Viewed through the grid of the Decalogue, the lacunae in Speidell's case studies are sexual (*No adultery; no coveting your neighbor's wife*) and economic (*Work six days, rest the seventh; no theft; no coveting your neighbor's goods*). Yet concerning the latter, Speidell recounts how Torrance's parish ministry included a monthly study of the Sermon on the Mount, which prompted a parishioner to raise his workers' salaries.[55] Concerning

---

[51] Torrance, *When Christ Comes*; Eugenio, *Communion*, 73–7; Radcliff, *Claim*, 177 (both Eugenio and Radcliff use unpublished sermons from The Thomas F. Torrance Manuscript Collection). Cf., McGrath, *Torrance*, 62–5, on Torrance's parish ministry.

[52] Eugenio, *Communion*, 75, 208–9. Cf. McGrath, *Torrance*, 65.

[53] Speidell, "Soteriological Suspension," 83–90. The occasional pieces upon which Speidell draws are (in the order of his usage) Thomas F. Torrance: *The Ministry of Women* (Edinburgh: Handsel, 1992); "The Christian Apprehension of God the Father," in *Speaking the Christian God: The Holy Trinity and the Challenge of Feminism*, ed. Alvin Kimel (Grand Rapids, MI: Eerdmans, 1992), pp. 120–43; *The Soul and Person of the Unborn Child* (Edinburgh: Handsel, 1999); *The Christian Doctrine of Marriage* (Edinburgh: Handsel, 1992); *The Being and Nature of the Unborn Child* (Lenior, NC: Glen Lorien Books, 2000); "The Ethical Implications of Anselm's *De Veritate*," *Theologische Zeitschrift* 24 (1968): 309–11, 314–19; *Juridical Law and Physical Law: Toward a Realist Foundation for Human Law* (Eugene, OR: Wipf & Stock, 1997).

[54] Torrance himself had served as a "padre" (military chaplain) in the Second World War (McGrath, *Torrance*, 69–76).

[55] Speidell, "Soteriological Suspension," 78.

the former, Torrance did write a booklet on *The Christian Doctrine of Marriage*, in which he affirmed male–female union rather than individuality as foundational to human existence.[56] He also published a response to a query regarding homosexuality. Appealing to Scripture and science, he opined that churches should welcome persons experiencing same-sex attraction just like anyone else on the expectation of repentant faith. Homosexual practice, though, should not be condoned.[57] We conclude that Torrance covered the main loci of biblical ethics, however minimally or controversially.

Beyond Torrance's handful of discussions of particular ethical issues, Speidell discerns the ethical implication of Torrance's whole project of uprooting dualistic thinking. While "Torrance does resist a programmatic ethic of moral deeds and misdeeds, virtues and vices," still "*one can read the entirety of Torrance's body of work as a theology of reconciliation on all levels of life: personal, social, historical, political, and cosmic.*"[58] Seen from this angle, a profound ethical vision lies behind Torrance's special scholarly concerns with reconciling Christianity and science,[59] overcoming the churches' divisions through ecumenical dialogue,[60] and healing the rift between Christians and Jews.[61] Nor is this ethical vision divorced from an evangelistic intention. As the son of missionaries, Torrance saw himself as a missionary to academia, engaged in the evangelization of the dualistic Western mind and culture.[62] The whole of Torrance's prodigious oeuvre is a massive missional enterprise.

Another Solution: Christ in the Life of Torrance

Besides focusing on particular writings of Torrance's or eyeing the intent and implications of his work as a whole, there is another way to meet the charge that he neglected the details of the Christian life. A former student, Ray Anderson, once lamented that it was hard to read Torrance as a practical theologian because he was so prolix on doctrine and terse on ethics.[63] Torrance's reply was telling: he referred to his practice of praying before and after his university lectures; to the experiential lessons of pastoral ministry that were greater than anything learned through reading, especially his visits in parishioners' homes to read Scripture and pray; and to the encouragement in ministry that he always gained when thinking of Christ's vicarious humanity.[64] Based on Torrance's own response, we may look to his Christian living, not just his writings, for practical direction.

Throughout his childhood, Torrance's home observed daily family worship consisting of Scripture reading, kneeling prayer, and hymn singing. His parents also encouraged their children by word and example to pray privately, read through the bible once or twice per year, memorize Scripture, and evangelize.[65] Torrance carried these spiritual disciplines

---

[56] Ibid., 85–6, uses this booklet in his discussion of abortion.
[57] Thomas F. Torrance, "Thomas Torrance Responds," in Colyer, *Promise*, 323–4.
[58] Speidell, "Soteriological Suspension," 65, 64 (italics his).
[59] McGrath, *Torrance*, 195–236; Colyer, *How*, 45–6.
[60] McGrath, *Torrance*, 94–102; Colyer, *How*, 46–7.
[61] Torrance, *Mediation*, xi.
[62] McGrath, *Torrance*, 29–31, 42, 75–6; Colyer, *How*, 35–6, 51; Torrance, *Atonement*, 437–47.
[63] Anderson, "Reading T. F. Torrance," 177.
[64] Torrance, "Thomas Torrance Responds," 322.
[65] McGrath, *Torrance*, 13; David W. Torrance, "Thomas Forsyth Torrance: Minister of the Gospel, Pastor, and Evangelical Theologian," in Colyer, *Promise*, 3–5. (Note: All references simply to "Torrance" refer to T. F.)

into adulthood. He continued to read through the Bible once or twice annually.[66] As his reply to Anderson indicates, he read Scripture to parishioners and prayed with them and students.[67] He was active in the Scottish Church Society, which promoted sacramental and liturgical revitalization.[68] His evangelistic efforts during his student days, wartime chaplaincy service, parish ministry, and teaching career bore fruit (sometimes strikingly).[69] So conditioned was he by the spiritual formation of his upbringing that he maintained a lifelong unshakeable conviction of God's reality and his own spiritual need.[70] He credited his parents with bequeathing to him a "theological instinct," a reflexive sharing in the "mind of Christ," that governed his judgments in ministry and theology—including his evaluations of students and colleagues![71]

DEVELOPING TORRANCE'S VISION OF THE CHRISTIAN LIFE

Due to his unshakeable convictions and confidence of access to the mind of Christ, as well as his vigorous intellect and personality, Torrance was often an overpowering presence. His historical reconstructions drowned out the distinctions of past theologians' views from his own.[72] His students (and other interlocutors) found it daunting to attempt to reason with him or express dissent.[73] If in his theologizing the figure of Christ seems so to predominate that the rest of us risk eclipse, perhaps the same may be said of the figure of Torrance! Yet as we have seen, like Christ he was also a personalizing person who nurtured as well as challenged his students. They and their own students, along with others sympathetic to Torrance's theology, have further developed his vision of the Christian life.

All too briefly, we may sketch some of these developments. In the 1970s Ray Anderson pioneered the use of Torrance's perspective in pastoral theology.[74] Andrew Purves and,

---

[66]Torrance, *Preaching*, 12; cf., ibid., *Karl Barth*, 83.

[67]For reminiscences on Torrance's prayers before lecturing, see the editor's comments in Torrance, *Incarnation*, x, and *Atonement*, 451. On Torrance's traveling to Athens to pray with a dying former student, as well as going to pray with his New College rival John McIntyre when McIntyre was ill, see George Dion Dragas, "T. F. Torrance as a Theologian for Our Times: An Eastern Orthodox Assessment" (lecture presented at the annual meeting of the Thomas F. Torrance Theological Society, Chicago, November 16, 2012. Cited October 26, 2018. Online: http://www.youtube.com/watch?v=Frhvk-MY3dg), 00:31:10–00:34:10.

[68]Ziegler, *Trinitarian Grace*, 205.

[69]David Torrance, "Thomas Forsyth Torrance," 6, 16; McGrath, *T. F. Torrance*, 54–8; Torrance, *When Christ Comes*, 108; cf., Ray S. Anderson, "The Practical Theology of Thomas F. Torrance," *Participatio* 1 (2009): 65.

[70]McGrath, *Torrance*, 13; Torrance, *Theological Science*, v.

[71]Torrance, *Karl Barth*, 83; *Atonement*, 445; in personal conversation, Thomas Noble has recalled how, while he was a student at New College, Torrance reflected on some of his colleagues who did not appear to be truly regenerate.

[72]Lee, *Living in Union with Christ*, 6–7; David Fergusson, "Torrance as a Scottish Theologian," *Participatio* 2 (2010): 86–7; Jason Robert Radcliff, *Thomas F. Torrance and the Church Fathers: A Reformed, Evangelical, and Ecumenical Reconstruction of the Patristic Tradition* (Eugene, OR: Pickwick, 2014), 116 n. 9, 147–55, 193. (Note: All references simply to "Radcliff" refer to Alexandra.) Thomas A. Noble, "T. F. Torrance on the Centenary of His Birth: A Biographical and Theological Synopsis with Some Personal Reminiscences," *Participatio* 4 (2013): 10–11, 23, 26–8, acknowledges this tendency and offers a partial defense. Cf. Molnar, *Torrance*, 325–6, 338–9.

[73]Anderson, "Practical Theology," 64–5; Fergusson, "Torrance," 87; Colyer, *How*, 51; Dragas, "T. F. Torrance," 00:49:17–00:54:15.

[74]See the chapter on Anderson in this volume.

most recently, Geordie Ziegler have added their own contributions.[75] For a quarter century, Christian Kettler has explored the implications of Christ's vicarious humanity for a range of existential and ethical issues, such as our experiences of faith, doubt, joy, and despair; globalization; aesthetics; genetic engineering; and self-perception.[76] Christopher Holmes and Todd Speidell have released their own Torrance-themed constructive studies of ethics, while Eric Flett has explored the implications of Torrance's thought for a theology of culture.[77] With Torrance's encouragement, Nazarene theologian Thomas Noble has sought to ground the Wesleyan doctrine of "Christian perfection" (or as Noble prefers, "Christian perfecting") in Christ's vicarious humanity.[78] Alexandra Radcliff similarly places Torrance's theology in conversation with Pentecostal–Charismatic Christianity.[79] Both Noble and Radcliff supplement Torrance's reserved account of subjective sanctification with an optimism about the degree to which Christ may actualize his victory over sin in the lives of those in communion with him. But both also spurn any notion of Christians' absolute sinlessness and heed Torrance's warnings against self-effort and mechanistic models of an *ordo salutis*.

Further development of Torrance's vision requires revisiting its roots. This chapter has pointed to his unpublished sermons and personal life as resources for subjective sanctification. Scholars, ministers, and laypeople alike would benefit from the publication of these sermons and the writing of a more comprehensive biography than presently is available.[80] By these means, weary souls may find rest and self-satisfied souls, conviction through one who lived by the apostolic testimony, "Not I, but Christ."

---

[75]Andrew Purves, *Reconstructing Pastoral Theology: A Christological Foundation* (Louisville, KY: Westminster John Knox, 2004); ibid., *Exploring*; Ziegler, *Trinitarian Grace*; ibid., "Is It Time for a Reformation of Spiritual Formation? Recovering Ontology," *Journal of Spiritual Formation and Soul Care* 2, no. 1 (2018): 74–92.

[76]Christian D. Kettler, *The God Who Believes: Faith, Doubt, and the Vicarious Humanity of Christ* (Eugene, OR: Cascade, 2005); ibid., *The God Who Rejoices: Joy, Despair, and the Vicarious Humanity of Christ* (Eugene, OR: Cascade, 2010); and ibid., *The Breadth and Depth of the Atonement: The Vicarious Humanity of Christ in the Church, the World, and the Self: Essays, 1990–2015* (Eugene, OR: Pickwick, 2017).

[77]Christopher R. J. Holmes, *Ethics in the Presence of Christ* (London: T&T Clark, 2012); Speidell, *Fully Human*; Eric Flett, *Persons, Powers, and Pluralities: Toward a Trinitarian Theology of Culture* (Cambridge: James Clarke, 2012).

[78]Thomas A. Noble, *Holy Trinity: Holy People: The Theology of Christian Perfecting* (Eugene, OR: Cascade, 2013); on Torrance's encouragement, see page xii.

[79]Radcliff, *Claim*.

[80]The only book-length biography is McGrath, *Torrance*, which is specifically an intellectual biography (as the subtitle states) and so rather selective.

CHAPTER SEVENTEEN

Theologia Is *Eusebia*

Thomas F. Torrance's Church Homiletics

MYK HABETS

The Very Reverend Thomas Forsyth Torrance (1913–2007) is known and renowned throughout the world of academic theology as a "theologian's theologian." By that it is meant that many, but by no means all, of his academic works are dense and meticulous pieces of historical and constructive theology which canvass the fields of Christian dogmatics, science, philosophy, art, and culture. His sermons by contrast are immensely and attractively readable and accessible. His American exegete, Professor Elmer Colyer, has depicted Torrance as "a theological heavyweight whose writing style can be dense to the point of obscurity," his works contain an "enigmatic prose and overly compressed composition," and "this problem of obscurity is exacerbated by the somewhat unorganized character of [his] publications."[1] While true, that is not the last word Colyer has to say of Torrance's written work as he goes on to add that "the difficulty of Torrance's theology was frustrating, yet I repeatedly found myself coming to understand what I had always tacitly believed as a Christian in a way that deepened my faith and clarified my grasp of the theological structure of the Gospel."[2] This sense of indebtedness to the theology of Thomas Torrance is shared by many contemporary theologians around the world.

While theologically rigorous in content, idiosyncratic in style, and voluminous in output, Torrance's theology is also deeply pastoral, engaging, and evangelical. While latent in his more academic books and articles, these elements of his theology are nonetheless present, lurking beneath the surface of the syntax, informing the theology. So true is this that the real goal and point of Torrance's work is not simply to communicate information but to place the living Christ, clothed with his Gospel at the center, as the one who, through the power of the Holy Spirit transforms us through our union with him. His was a work of evangelism as much as it was a contribution to human knowledge. Reflecting on his missionary sensibilities Torrance wrote, "This orientation to mission was built into the fabric of my mind, and has never faded—by its essential nature Christian theology has always had for me an evangelistic thrust."[3]

---

[1] Elmer M. Colyer, *How to Read T.F. Torrance: Understanding His Trinitarian and Scientific Theology* (Downers Grove, IL: InterVarsity Press, 2001), 15–16.

[2] Ibid., 18.

[3] The Thomas F. Torrance Manuscript Collection, Special Collections, Princeton Theological Seminary Library, Box 10, T. F. Torrance, "Itinerarium Mentis in Deum: My Theological Development," 1. Henceforth title of the work, SC (Special Collections), followed by the box number and page if relevant. So here it would be: "Itinerarium Mentis in Deum: My Theological Development," SC, 10:1.

Upon Torrance's retirement from New College, the University of Edinburgh, John McIntyre rightly commented:

> But his aim is not solely to enlighten intellectually: it is rather to impart such a lively sense of the claim of the Word of God upon us all, that our obedience manifests itself not only in integrity of thought, but also in faithfulness in proclamation and care in counselling. Theology ordered to the ministry has always been the sequence of his intention.[4]

McIntyre's words are absolutely correct and this call to training men and women for the ministry was a large part of Torrance's decision to stay in Edinburgh, a University which trains ordinands for the Kirk, rather than succeed Barth upon his retirement in his chair in Basel. Torrance was fond to point out from his favorite theologian, Athanasius of Alexandria, that true knowledge of God—*theologia*—actually equals or is equivalent to godliness and worship—*eusebia*—such that godly faith in and worship of the Holy Trinity belong wholly to a proper understanding or knowledge of God.[5]

Given the propensity for misunderstanding Torrance's evangelistic and doxological theology, this chapter presents the key elements of Torrance's theology in a way that is easily understood and clearly presented. While Torrance always wanted to write a popular exposition of the Christian faith, time and circumstances never permitted. However, we do have a rather full collection of his early sermons to reflect upon, sermons which explicitly show the evangelical, pastoral, and experiential aspects of his faith and thought. My goal in providing an overview of these sermons is that those familiar with Torrance's work may appreciate the underlying assumptions and biblical commitments which drove his more academic program, while for those unfamiliar with Torrance, this material may be edifying and encouraging in its clear portrayal of crucial elements of the Gospel of Jesus Christ.

THE GENERAL CONTEXT AND STYLE OF THE SERMONS

For a decade Torrance was minister at two Scottish Kirk parishes: Alyth Barony Parish Church and Beechgrove Church. Torrance's time in Alyth and Aberdeen have been recorded in his memoirs and discussed several times in recent works, most especially in Alister McGrath's biography. What follows introduces both parishes and the general tenor of the sermons he gave there.

The Barony Parish in Alyth 1940–43, 1945–47

Torrance's first parish was in the Scottish town of Alyth, a small town of around three thousand people and Torrance quickly came to respect and love the congregants.[6] Torrance was particularly impressed with the elders of the Kirk, men he calls "godly farmers, very friendly and intelligent people."[7] Torrance's ordination to the ministry

---

[4] John McIntyre, "Thomas Forsyth Torrance," *New College Bulletin* 10 (August 1979), SC, 197:1.

[5] See Thomas F. Torrance, *The Christian Doctrine of God, One Being Three Persons* (Edinburgh: T&T Clark, 1996), 73–82. Reissued as Thomas F. Torrance, *The Christian Doctrine of God, One Being Three Persons*. T&T Clark Cornerstones (Edinburgh: Bloomsbury T&T Clark, 2016), 73–82.

[6] See "My Parish Ministry: Alyth. 1940-1943," SC, 10. Torrance's memoir of his time in Alyth has been anthologized in *Gospel, Church, and Ministry. Thomas F. Torrance Collected Studies 1*, ed. Jock Stein (Eugene, OR: Pickwick Publications, 2012), 25–73. All further references will be taken from this more easily accessible published version.

[7] "My Parish Ministry: Alyth, 1940–43," 27.

of Word and Sacrament and his induction as minister of the Alyth Barony Parish Kirk in the Presbytery of Meigle, Perthshire, Scotland was on Wednesday, March 20, 1940. Torrance would be minister of the Alyth Church until 1947, with a brief break in ministry when he saw war service as a chaplain under the Church of Scotland Huts and Canteens.

Early in his time at Alyth Robert Hastie, the minister of St Andrew's Church, Blairgowie, learned of Torrance's interest in John Calvin and so gave him his complete set of Calvin's *Commentaries, Institutes*, and *Treatises*. Torrance notes these "proved a godsend to me in my preparation for the two sermons I had to preach each Sunday, morning and evening, and for my continued theological study and writing."[8] In addition to Calvin's works Torrance also drew heavily in his sermon preparation from Alexander MacLaren's *Biblical Expositions* and Joseph Parker's sermons.

As McGrath notes in his intellectual biography of Torrance, "His preaching over his period at Alyth shows him to be a man who is passionately concerned to turn nominal Christians into believers, and believers into disciples."[9] This seems an accurate assessment of Torrance's time at Alyth. Indeed, one of the sermons he preached when being "interviewed" for the position was from John 3:7 on the theme "you must be born again," so that, as Torrance says, "the people from Alyth would know that I was concerned to preach the gospel."[10] This concern for the gospel and for his congregants led Torrance to maintain a rigorous schedule of home visitation which, when he reflected on his time in Alyth, he considered one of "the most rewarding and fruitful aspects of my ministry."[11] But Torrance did not see his ministry as a series of atomized pieces; rather, each part was related to the whole so that the visitation "served to complement my rather theological sermons,"[12] and the visitation helped clarify what Torrance believed needed to be preached on Sundays, so that "I could not separate my preaching in Alyth from my house to house visitation of the congregation."[13]

Ministering in a local parish in the 1940s meant serving a people who were at war. This had a profound impact upon Torrance and his ministry. The congregation in Alyth was not immune to the casualties of war and was often deeply impacted by the deaths of servicemen, sons, brothers, uncles, and fathers of those in the congregation. One member alone lost three sons in the war. Against the backdrop of the war Torrance sought to address the concerns of his people in his sermons. "The subjects for my sermons week by week reflected very much my regular pastoral concern, and seemed to select themselves in answer to the congregation, and the country's engagement in the war, when the needs of the sons, and sometimes the daughters, of Alyth people, called for special response in congregational worship and prayer."[14]

In his memoirs Torrance makes mention of one particular way in which his sermons had to address war concerns of several of these "daughters." The war department established a camp in the parish for many hundreds of Poles who had been recruited and were trained for war service. This caused problems, specifically the relations of the Polish soldiers to the women in Alyth with whom many struck up sexual relationships.

---

[8] Ibid., 38–9.
[9] Alister E. McGrath, *Thomas F. Torrance: An Intellectual Biography* (Edinburgh: T&T Clark, 1999), 62.
[10] "My Parish Ministry: Alyth, 1940–43," 29.
[11] Ibid., 35.
[12] Ibid.
[13] Ibid.
[14] Ibid., 39.

Reflecting on the situation Torrance was horrified that this sort of thing went on, "It was particularly disturbing when some of these women were married and had husbands who were away at war."[15] Torrance felt he had to address this situation "if only in a back-handed or oblique way" and so he incorporated into his sermons words to the effect that husbands were being stabbed in the back by the behavior of their wives at home. "My mother thought one of these sermons was rather 'stingy and heart-searching' ... but I did not feel I could be easy on them or turn a blind eye to what seemed to be happening."[16]

Torrance singles out several sermon series of this time for specific mention. He preached a series through the book of Revelation "designed to strengthen the faith of the congregation by spelling out the implications of St. John's apocalyptic visions for people's outlook upon the war, and the struggle in which the country was engaged with the evil forces of tyranny and oppression."[17] The sermons apparently met with a fine reception and helped people in their faith. Torrance began to repeat this series in his subsequent parish in Beechgrove, but found they met with little interest and so he abandoned them.[18] They would eventually be published upon the request of some friends.[19]

A second series Torrance mentions is on the Epistle to the Romans, which he decided to preach on at the request of a congregant. Torrance had been reluctant to preach on Romans given the theological nature of the book but his congregant, John Welch, believed that the congregation, a certain man in particular, needed to hear the teaching on justification by grace. Torrance writes, "I could not but agree to that."[20] Nineteen sermons on Romans preached by Torrance remain in the Special Collections archive at Princeton Theological Seminary, the bulk of which were preached between September 1942 and May 1943. Torrance typically took an entire chapter of Romans as his text and sought to expound the central theme of the chapter to his congregation. The emphasis throughout these sermons is on justification by grace alone, the place of the law after grace, and the centrality of the work of Jesus Christ for our salvation.

In a sermon on Romans 1, Torrance clarifies the need for Christ's forgiveness of our good as well as our evil.

> My friend, when Jesus Christ forgives you, He forgives your good as well as your evil. Yes, He forgives your good. You know that at the communion table: you feel shame for your whole being, for your good just as much as for your wrong, because you feel ashamed of yourself. Therefore no Christian who really receives forgiveness from Christ, no believer who receives the righteousness of God as a gift, can also make protestations about his own goodness, his own worthiness, his own service, his own dutifulness and righteousness.[21]

From Romans 2 he seeks to situate the law in its rightful place.

> What is the Law? It is the impress of God's revelation left behind in history, in the lives of men. It is the tremendous impression made upon men by the impact of a mighty act

---

[15] Ibid., 57.
[16] Ibid.
[17] Ibid., 39.
[18] "Aberdeen. 1947–1950," SC, 10:9.
[19] Thomas F. Torrance, *The Apocalypse Today* (London: James Clarke, 1959).
[20] "My Parish Ministry: Alyth, 1940–43," 39.
[21] "Sermon on Romans 1.16-18" (Alyth: December 13, 1942), SC, 45:6.

long ago—but now what is it? It is a heap of clinkers marking a fiery miracle—and little more. It is a burnt-out crater disclosing the place where God has once spoken; the Law is simply a desert Wadi, or a dry canal which in a past generation and under different conditions had been filled with the living water of faith and clear understanding of the truth, but now it is empty, and the banks of the canal are formed out of the hard and fast commandments rules and regulations, the residue of a live moment somewhere in past history. The men who have the law are the men who live in this empty canal. Yes, it may well be, that they are stamped with the imprint of the true God, because they possess the form of traditional religion, but the canal is empty—that is the tragic fact—the living water is gone! The Jews are the people who live on the banks of this empty canal—and still are living there. But that applies to the Christian Church as well. "Thou hast a name that thou livest and art dead" said an angel in the book of Revelation. This picture about the Law applies to us as well therefore.[22]

Torrance notes that his preaching on justification met with some resistance from his congregation, yet he continued to preach the doctrine of grace alone.

The evening services at Alyth were less formal than the morning services. Torrance singles out a series on 1 John which he preached in order to show its evangelical and practical application to daily life. In these evening services Torrance modeled a form of service popular in some churches today where the sermon is brief, and the congregation is invited to verbally respond with questions and discussion. The Special Collections archive contains fourteen sermons from 1 John, dating from April 1940 to May 5, 1946, but it is unclear when the particular series Torrance mentions was given. This is not surprising given the fact that Torrance began the habit of preaching from handwritten notes. He tells us, "I found it hard work to prepare two sermons each week—it took most of each morning and afternoon. I wrote out all my sermons (as Mackintosh told us), but sometimes in the evening service I preached only from notes, which my mother preferred!"[23] Many of these handwritten sermons remain in the archive but many others are absent. It also appears that Torrance's sermons became more extemporaneous over time.

A significant feature I wish to make mention of from his preaching at Alyth are his quarterly Communion sermons. The quarterly seasons of Holy Communion stand out in Torrance's mind as "very wonderful and rewarding."[24] He notes that in the Scottish tradition what became known as "action sermons" preached at Holy Communion on the thankful celebration of the Eucharist (or *actio gratiarum*) had often initiated seasons of evangelical revival. "I came to understand why that was so, for it is at Holy Communion above all that we see Christ face to face and handle things unseen and feed upon his body and blood by faith."[25] It is there that Torrance experienced the reality of the vicarious humanity of Christ, of his redeeming sacrifice, and of how Christ's faith not ours is the all-important part of the Gospel that redeemed sinners have to grasp hold of. "Thus it was at Holy Communion that I found it easiest to proclaim and make clear to people what the unconditional grace of God's saving love really is."[26] It is my own view that these

---

[22] "Sermon on Romans 2" (Alyth: December 27, 1942), SC, 45:9.
[23] "My Parish Ministry: Alyth, 1940–43," 46.
[24] Ibid.
[25] Ibid., 47.
[26] Ibid.

Communion sermons reveal the heart of Torrance's theology, and indeed, the heart of Torrance himself.

One final aspect of Torrance's preaching during his time in Alyth deserves mention. Curiously, the archive contains a number of sermons Torrance gave in German. His memoir mentions that in 1945–46 the War Department established a camp in Alyth for prisoners of war, waiting for repatriation. As Torrance knew German from his time studying with Barth in Basel in 1937–38, he was asked to take services for German Internees, some of whom were prisoners of war. During these services Torrance was concerned to preach the gospel "in which I made use of and adapted some of the published sermons of Emil Brunner. They were more helpful to me in that ministry than Karl Barth's sermons."[27]

After his war service Torrance returned to Alyth and took up his ministerial position. Pastoral visitation took up much of his time as well as the usual sermon preparation. Although the socialization and secularization of life and thought, as Torrance terms it, had not gripped the people of Alyth as much as the rest of Britain and Europe, and he was still committed to the preaching of the Gospel, he:

> had a deeper concern to overcome the tendency to damage the relation between belief in Christ and belief in God which had resulted from a resort to natural theology fostered by liberal theologians and ministers. I was haunted by the question of a mortally wounded young soldier ... about whether God was *really* like Jesus. I was all the more concerned to encourage theological change throughout the Kirk, and to help restore in it the centrality of the crucified and risen Lord Jesus Christ.

In addition, "This also had the effect of deepening my concern for more liturgical worship, and for more attention to the celebration of Holy Communion."[28] These aspects of Torrance's preaching are borne out in the sermons he preached throughout the 1940s.

Beechgrove Parish 1947–50

In July 1947 Torrance was visited by a deputation of elders from Beechgrove Church in Aberdeen asking him to consider being their minister. After due consideration Torrance was inducted into Beechgrove Church, Aberdeen on Wednesday November 12, 1947.[29] Torrance would remain at Beechgrove until 1950 when he took up the "Church Chair" of ecclesiastical history at the University of Edinburgh. Several factors went into the decision to move to Aberdeen. First, with a growing family the stipend at Beechgrove was almost double that of Alyth. Second, the proximity to the Faculty of Divinity at Aberdeen, especially Donald McKinnon, a close friend of Torrance's, was hugely attractive. Finally, the history of Beechgrove and its ministers was a tradition that Torrance identified with.

Beechgrove was a very different church from Alyth. It was a congregation of 1,300 people, and was an urban, university church.

> I was soon to find out that it was a very different congregation from that of the Barony Church in Alyth, for to it belonged many teachers, lecturers, doctors, solicitors ... insurance agents, and business people, but only a few working class people. And there

---

[27] Ibid., 56. As an interesting aside, Barth thought Torrance's German was terrible and Torrance returned the compliment thinking Barth's Latin was terrible.
[28] Ibid., 60.
[29] Ibid., 73.

were also in the congregation quite a few students from elsewhere as well as from Aberdeen itself.[30]

Its first minister was Hugh Ross Mackintosh (1901–04) who left to become Professor of Christian Dogmatics at New College in Edinburgh. He was followed by F. J. Rae for fifteen years, then by A. J. Gossip for seven years, then the much-loved James S. Stewart before he moved to North Morningside Church in Edinburgh and then became Professor of New Testament Theology at New College, then Roderick Bethune, Torrance's immediate successor who was there for twelve years. "It was a great ministerial tradition into which I had been ingrafted, but it gave me a great heart to have had among them H R Mackintosh and J S Stewart from whom I had learned so much."[31]

The long heritage of good theology and good preaching at Beechgrove was somewhat intimidating to Torrance, however:

> I was later to write to Beechgrove to say that I came to them in great fear and trembling, sensible of my weakness and yet of the high calling to minister to them the Word of God, but I soon learned that they were a people who minister to the minister out of their wealth of spiritual life and tradition. Few ministers could have been so encouraged and strengthened in their ministry as I was by the Kirk Session, men who had themselves been ordained as elders to share with the minister the pastoral care of the flock. My own indebtedness to them was unbounded, not least for their understanding and sympathy and prayer, and wise guidance in public affairs.[32]

Both the building and the people came to be fondly appreciated by Torrance. Of the building he wrote:

> Beechgrove Church was a very imposing and beautiful granite edifice with a magnificent Spire which could be seen several miles away. The interior of the Church was no less inspiring …. While I was much impressed with the beauty of the building, I was to be no less impressed by the atmosphere of worship when its members were assembled at a service.[33]

But it was the people who held his heart.

> Shortly before I went to Beechgrove a friend wrote to tell me that of all the churches he knew Beechgrove was the easiest in which to preach. I proved that to be true, but I also found that Beechgrove was the easiest in which to pray. Public prayer, as Mackintosh used to tell us in New College, is the most arduous part of the ministry; but in Beechgrove I found a spirit of devotion and prayerfulness which encouraged and stimulated praise and intercession, and was an unending source of strength to minister and congregation alike.[34]

The emphasis on the liturgy and on Holy Communion impressed upon Torrance in Alyth continued to have an impact upon Torrance's ministry after the war at

---

[30] "Aberdeen. 1947–1950," SC, 10:2.
[31] Ibid., 3.
[32] Ibid.
[33] Ibid., 1.
[34] Ibid., 3. The archive at PTS contains a number of Torrance's public prayers from throughout his career, many of which show some of the ways in which his theology worked itself out in prayer and devotion.

Beechgrove. "The celebrations of the Lord's Supper at Beechgrove, made me think much more profoundly about the atoning sacrifice and passion of the Lamb of God, and its bearing upon our celebration of Holy Communion."[35] Reflecting on the seasons of Holy Communion we read:

> It was at the Communion Seasons that the relations between minister and congregation were especially deepened. I conducted the Communion Services in the full liturgy of our *Book of Common Order* under the guidance of the 1940 edition for which professor William Manson of New College had been largely responsible, but with which apparently many in the congregation were not too familiar, but which I found to be Eucharistically very profound and right.[36]

By this stage Torrance's mature theology of union and communion was already clearly evident, as seen in his Eucharistic theology and practice.

> I cannot but link the celebration of Holy Communion or the Eucharist, with the ascension of the crucified and risen Lord Jesus as the great High Priest who ever lives before the face of the Father to make intercession for us, and yet is really personally present with us in the Eucharistic celebration of his redeeming love at the breaking of the bread. The celebration of the vicarious passion of the Lord Jesus at Holy Communion is surely appointed to echo on earth his heavenly intercession above.[37]

The centrality of Christ, a hallmark of Torrance's theology, was clearly evident in his Beechgrove sermons. For instance, in the Beechgrove Church newsletter for April 1949, the minister's editorial by Torrance is a sermon on Mathew 18:20, "where two or three are gathered together in my name, there am I in the midst of them." In that sermon Torrance emphasizes the centrality of Christ.

> What is it that makes a Christian Church? When Christians gather together for worship, sing their hymns, have their devotions, and make their offerings, all that is deeply significant. But after all that only constitutes the roof under which the Church meets. What constitutes the essence of the Church? That question is answered by our text: "Where two or three are gathered together there *am I* in the midst of them." The essence of the Church is the living Lord Jesus Christ. Where He is present and worshipped, there you have the Christian Church. Where He is not present, you have a sham Church.[38]

Such a Christ-centered church is one gathered around the Word written:

> That is why we gather here around the Word of God. It is here we hear the voice of Christ speaking to us, revealing Himself to us, and as we answer Him with our devotion and bear witness to Him as Saviour and Lord, the Church is founded upon a rock. That is what it means to meet *in the name of Christ*: to meet in such a way as to listen to His Gospel and to surrender ourselves to His love. When we do that Jesus Christ is alive in our midst. There is a living presence amongst us which fills us with life and power.[39]

---

[35] "Aberdeen. 1947–1950," SC, 10:6.
[36] Ibid., 5.
[37] Ibid., 6.
[38] "Beechgrove Church Publications" (April 1949), SC, 20:2, col. 1.
[39] Ibid., 2, col. 2.

During his time in Aberdeen Torrance was heavily involved in theological activity: he regularly attended the Creed Association in Edinburgh and the sessions of the Scottish Church Theological Society. He launched the *Scottish Journal of Theology* in 1948 with J. K. S. Reid, his published PhD, *The Doctrine of Grace in the Apostolic Fathers* was issued by Oliver and Boyd at this time, and he reviewed a large number of books for the *Scottish Journal of Theology* which he was editing. In 1949 his work *Calvin's Doctrine of Man* was published by Lutterworth Press, and he wrote journal articles for various publications. In addition, he addressed a number of Christian Unions and he was involved in ecumenical dialogue between the Church of Scotland and the Church of England and with the Faith and Order Department of the World Council of Churches.

His time in Beechgrove was busy and took a toll on his health and marriage.

> It was often late in the evening that I used to get home after visiting the housebound, sick and spiritually needy people. It made me realise how guilty I was in leaving Margaret alone in the Manse so long, while I charged about Aberdeen so much each week in my unceasing visitation of parishioners. The strain on her was one of the main factors in my decision to leave Aberdeen when the call came to return to Edinburgh.[40]

During his decade of pastoral ministry in Alyth and Aberdeen Torrance sought to think through the ministry of Word and Sacrament theologically, to preach the Word of God, and to point people to the triune God of grace and the saving power of the gospel of God crucified. He never regretted his time in pastoral ministry but looked on that time with fondness. He often said that in his lectures he would draw upon his pastoral experience and that students found that very helpful. Theology (*theologia*) was for Torrance worship (*eusebia*) and vice versa. Thus, Torrance's sermons from this decade of his life form something of a "Church Homiletics" which must be consulted along with his mature academic monographs—what I earlier called, with obvious reference to his mentor Karl Barth, his "Church Dogmatics"—if one is to comprehend the contours of Torrance's Christian dogmatics.

The General Style of the Sermons

In general, the 477 sermons preached between 1940 and 1950 take an expositional mode, develop three clear points, and conclude with a summary application. The introduction to a sermon would typically set the text in its literary context, retell the biblical story of which it was a part, or engage the audience with some link between the text and the current context. Torrance would then state what in the text he would have the congregation focus on or think about, and would follow that up with the basic exposition. In these sermons we see Torrance expound the central themes of the Gospel to his congregations from across the canon of Scripture.

KEY THEMES IN TORRANCE'S SERMONS

The sermons of this period are remarkable in many ways. In what follows I make mention of nine key themes evident throughout the hundreds of sermons from this time of

---

[40]"Aberdeen. 1947–1950," SC, 10:12.

Torrance's ministry. There are other themes, to be sure,[41] but these strike me as the most immediate and pertinent to his preaching over this period.

1. Clarity of Expression

The first point to notice is that the sermons do not include any excessive technical theological vocabulary. Given that Torrance studied classics at Edinburgh and from 1936 at least could read and speak German, it is all the more surprising he did not use more technical language through this decade of his preaching. The language is very simple, basic even, and not liable to ambiguity. Torrance draws on the range of biblical terms and not a few times provides some of the Greek or Hebrew words with their meanings, but it never gets bogged down in etymological or philological detail, nor is the language so technical as to leave the everyday congregant, his "dear friends" as he called them, confused. Early in his career and up until the late 1960s Torrance was something of a champion of much of the biblical theology movement, finding Gerhard Kittel and Gerhard Friedrich's *Theologisches Wörterbuch* ("Theological Dictionary") especially useful.[42] Torrance would be instrumental in the eventual translation of the multivolume work into English. And yet, here, we find no exaggerated exegetical discussions or technical verbosity. I find this remarkable restraint on Torrance's part admirable.

2. Lack of Secondary Sources

Second, Torrance very rarely quoted from secondary sources or made mention of theological figures. Barth and others do appear from time to time, but that is the exception, not the rule. Tempted as he must have been to imitate or replicate pieces from the sermons of John Calvin, Hugh Ross Mackintosh, James S. Stewart, Karl Barth, or Emil Brunner, for instance, those he had either heard preach or had read collections of their sermons, we do not find this to be the case. We do know that Torrance was highly impacted by a number of influential figures. During his BD studies at Edinburgh he notes the influence of James Denney, *Jesus and the Gospel, Christianity Justified in the Mind of Christ, The Christian Doctrine of Reconciliation*, of which the latter work "opened my eyes to the cosmic significance of Redemption."[43] H. A. A. Kennedy, *The Theology of the Epistles*, is also noted, a work "which made an immense impact on my own understanding of the Gospel and greatly deepened my grasp of the doctrine of *grace* as utterly free and unconditional."[44] The hugely popular work of James S. Stewart, *A Man in Christ*, was also significant "in which the central Pauline concept of union with Christ penetrated more deeply than ever into my life and thought."[45] Finally Torrance "made a point of reading all Mackintosh's books and all those of Karl Barth that were then available, and found myself becoming more and more deeply involved in the tide of

---

[41]Eschatology is another feature of the sermons, given the backdrop of the War and Torrance's involvement with the World Council of Churches at the time. This theme has been treated in detail by Stanley S. MacLean, *Resurrection, Apocalypse, and the Kingdom of Christ: The Eschatology of Thomas F. Torrance* (Eugene, OR: Pickwick Publications, 2012), where Torrance's sermons are used as primary resource material.

[42]*Theological Dictionary of the New Testament*, 9 vols., ed. Gerhard Kittel and Gerhard Friedrich, trans. Geoffrey Bromiley (Grand Rapids, MI: Eerdmans, 1974), from the original *Theologisches Wörterbuchzum Neuen Testament*, 9 vols. (Stuttgart: W. Kohlhammer Verlag, 1933–73).

[43]"Itinerarium Mentis in Deum: My Theological Development," SC, 10:12.

[44]Ibid.

[45]Ibid.

theological renewal."⁴⁶ The influence of such figures is obvious in Torrance's sermons, but indirectly, discreetly, and behind the scenes as it were. Instead of citing secondary sources at length, Torrance chose to let the biblical texts speak for themselves. When he does cite an "authority" it is brief and serves the point of the message.

What Torrance does reference throughout his sermons is the Canon itself. In terms of how he reads Scripture Torrance says he was influenced by one his early teachers Norman Porteous, who was one of Barth's first PhD students. Torrance thus reads the New Testament through Old Testament eyes, reinforced by William Manson's handling of the New Testament in the light of the Old Testament, and Edwin Hoskyn's commentary on John, *The Fourth Gospel*.⁴⁷ He then reads the Old Testament in light of the New Testament and has no qualms about finding Christ in the Old Testament. Christology was, after all, the key to the meaning of Holy Scripture.

A good example of this is seen in his understanding of The Lord's Day. The Lord's Day is the distinctively Christian name for the day of rest and worship. It is founded on the Old Testament concept of the Sabbath but reinterpreted in the light of Christ's resurrection. "The Early Church regarded the Sabbath as a festival of creation, but the Lord's Day as the festival of re-creation."⁴⁸ And further, "The Sabbath means that all creation is summoned to offer praise and worship to God, and man above all offers that praise, as the priest of creation, as it were."⁴⁹ This canonical approach was tied to a certain form of hermeneutic Torrance championed called "depth-exegesis." From Manson's second-year lectures he learned the practice of "depth-exegesis" which "served to open up new dimensions in our understanding of the Gospels and of the liturgical and eschatological teaching in the New Testament."⁵⁰ This is made explicit in Torrance's 1967 editorial to Manson's collected works, *Jesus and the Christian Life*. Depth-exegesis is the ability to see through the text of Scripture to the reality to which it points—Christ himself. This is perhaps one of the most significant aspects of Torrance's preaching.

3. *Use of Illustrations*

The third remarkable feature of the sermons is that, unlike much contemporary Presbyterian preaching, or at least preaching which is Presbyterian and Reformed, Torrance is not disinclined to use illustrations to serve the point of the message, even illustrations from his own experience. Once again, there is no sense of self-indulgence from the pulpit, no hint of any self-aggrandizement. Yet Torrance does provide a good supply of illustrations which no doubt kept the congregation focused on the point of the text being preached, encouraged the congregant to participate in the message, and at times revealed to the congregation the personal character of their minister, often in vulnerable ways. This no doubt accounts in part for the intimate friendships which were made between Margaret and Thomas Torrance and the "dear friends" of Alyth and Aberdeen. Torrance also made mention of current events in his illustrations, not least of which was the War and its aftermath. At times his sermons were politically charged, but in ways which sought to be on the side of the Kingdom of God and not the city of man. He had no qualms about naming Adolf Hitler—both in the sense that here was a "man of evil," and in the sense

---

⁴⁶Ibid., 20.
⁴⁷Ibid., 11.
⁴⁸"The Lord's Day," SC, 38:1.
⁴⁹Ibid., 2.
⁵⁰"Itinerarium Mentis in Deum: My Theological Development," SC, 10:12.

that here even this man was not far from the Kingdom if his "enemies"—the Church—would but love him and his kind as Christ commanded us to.

4. Preaching for a Decision

A fourth feature of Torrance's sermons was an occasion to apply the text and not merely examine it. Torrance's sermons were expositional not exegetical, he was preaching for a decision not for mere mental assent. In a draft of a lecture Torrance asserted:

> Surely the uniqueness of the preaching of Jesus demands a correspondingly special form of transmission and surely that is what we do have. That preaching cannot be handed on by mere reporters of history, for the latter cannot see the decisive factor that this Jesus discloses and authenticates Himself as the Christ—and what they can see—the Rabbi and exorcist who failed—they will hardly consider worth reporting. But in actual fact the oldest strata of the synoptic Gospels contain no mere historical reports, but reproduce the message and proclamation of Jesus Himself in the form of new preaching. The whole history of the Gospel transmission is to be understood as an evangelistic transmission of the preaching and self-disclosure of Jesus, that others may believe.[51]

When dealing with prophecy, which he did regularly in his sermons through Isaiah and Revelation for example, he has that rare talent of making the prophecies real-worldly and related to today. He did this in ways which did not betray a facile application of some biblical timeline to the headlines of the day, but more in the way that Barth once suggested we preach—with the Bible in one hand and a newspaper in the other. He was able to apply to his congregation the truths of Scripture in practical ways that did not shy away from the force of the texts.

The applicatory nature of the sermons is a striking feature: Torrance's directness in appealing to his congregants to repent, to believe, to offer worship, to give, to love, to enjoy God's creation, to act rightly, and all manner of other godly activities, but most of all, the invitation for every man, woman, and child to participate in the life of God in Jesus Christ by means of the Holy Spirit. He would write a book published in 1980 entitled *The Ground and Grammar of Theology*, in which he would argue that the Trinity is the foundation and language of all our thoughts and relations with God Almighty.[52] Throughout his sermons of this period we hear Torrance appealing to the triune God in just this way and providing his congregants with a number of ways to understand that truth and to make it their own.

5. Theological Interpretation of Scripture

A fifth and not very surprising feature of these sermons is that they are theological.[53] Torrance often provided alternate interpretations of a given text before saying that no matter what interpretation one takes, it may be applied in this way or that, given

---

[51] "The Historical and the Theological Approach to Jesus Christ Who Is Self-Disclosed in His Preaching," SC, 16.

[52] Thomas F. Torrance, *The Ground and Grammar of Theology* (Charlottesville: The University of Virginia Press/Belfast: Christian Journals, 1980).

[53] I have written about this aspect of Torrance's sermons in detail in Myk Habets, "Theological Interpretation of Scripture in Sermonic Mode: The Case of T. F. Torrance," in *Ears That Hear: Explorations in Theological Interpretation of the Bible*, ed. Joel Green and Tim Meadowcroft (Sheffield: Sheffield Phoenix Press, 2013), 44–71.

that underneath the various interpretations lies a deeper theological truth. In his major monograph of 1996, *The Christian Doctrine of God*, he makes this point clear:

> Any faithful interpretation of the Scriptures operates on different levels, the linguistic and the conceptual level, but unless the interpreter participates in the movement of God's unique self-revelation through Christ and in the Spirit which gave rise to the Scriptures and has left its imprint upon them, he or she will fail to understand them in their deep spiritual dimension and will be blind to their essential truth content.[54]

Often the sermons are expositions of the intent of a text, a line of a text, and sometimes of an entire passage (with Old Testament narratives for example).

Torrance was committed to a high view of Holy Scripture, but he eschewed any form of strict foundationalism and even at this early stage of his career he was a long way from the fundamentalism that was so common across Britain and America. In his memoirs we read:

> So far as my view of Holy Scripture was concerned, I had been brought up to believe in its verbal inspiration, but my mother had taught me to have an objective and not a subjective understanding of the Word of God. This did not lesson but rather deepened my sense of the divine authority and verbal inspiration of the Bible which mediated to us the Gospel of salvation. She taught us to adopt a Christ-centred approach to the Holy Scriptures, for Christ was the Word of God made flesh—in him Word and Person are one, and it is therefore in terms of the living personal Word of God incarnate in Christ that we are to hear God addressing us in the Bible. My epistemological realism did not detract from that fact, but it did lead me to object to a crudely fundamentalist and objectivist understanding of the Scriptures and to mechanistic and rationalistic concepts and propositions in theology.[55]

Torrance thus preached theologically, from a center in God and not in ourselves, and sought to expound the great truths of the Bible in contemporary terms for his congregants.

6. Christ Focused

A sixth feature of Torrance's sermons is the radical Christocentrism they exhibit. This, again, is not surprising given his later theology in which he is clear that knowledge of God comes by Jesus Christ so that Jesus Christ alone is the place whereby God and humanity meet. In seeking to define theology Torrance wrote:

> Its object is the man Jesus Christ present here today as He was yesterday through the Holy Spirit in the witness of the Old and New Testaments and therefore God Himself in His truth, that is in His revelation—the God who reveals and judges man's sin, takes it upon Himself and forgives it, the God who gives man the hope of eternal life and in doing so takes man into His service.[56]

Preaching Christ crucified and risen again was the keynote of Torrance's sermons.

> Jesus Christ the object of theological thought is an historical reality—indeed a historical reality witnessed to in definite documents, those of the Bible. In the same gospel in which it is written that the Word became flesh Jesus has called Himself the

---

[54] Torrance, *The Christian Doctrine of God*, 38.
[55] "Itinerarium Mentis in Deum: My Theological Development," SC, 10:8–9.
[56] "The Basic Forms of Theological Thought," SC, 56:4.

> *Way*. Therefore theological thought must not stray across country but keep to the way. It must assume the form of Biblical exposition. Where the church whose thinking it is, lives by the Bible. Theological thought has no choice in the matter because it is determined and limited by its historical and historically attested object. It cannot free itself from history and construct itself from its own resources ... As theological thought it can only be exposition of the Bible.[57]

And further:

> Jesus Christ as the object of theological thought is however finally the life, that is to say the actual salvation of the man who believes in Him. Therefore He forces theology which is determined and limited by Him, inevitably to go beyond exposition and criticism and become proclamation. For this reason the ancients named the whole of theology *doctrina*, teaching. By that they meant (in contrast to a later corrupt use of the word) precisely this, that theological thinking is a practical type of thinking a type of thinking which applies to man and his real life and may be therefore no merely contemplative abstract form of mediation.[58]

7. *The Inseparability of Incarnation and Atonement*

As an extension of the last point, that Torrance's sermons are theologically rich and Christ-centered, I want to note two specific aspects of that theological robustness, the first of which is the inseparability of Incarnation and Atonement in his sermons. Reflecting on his preaching, Torrance stated in 1994, "This is the most astonishing part of the Christian message, 'God crucified,' as Gregory Nazianzen expressed it."[59] Elaborating on that comment he states: "It is the preaching of Christ crucified that lies at the very centre of the Christian Gospel—if only because the Cross, as H.R. Mackintosh once wrote in a Gospel tract, is 'a window into the heart of God.'"[60] Critiques of Torrance's academic works have often entertained the suspicion that he was more concerned with Incarnation than Atonement, or even that the Atonement played no real part in his theology. While that is patently untrue, even of the academic works, his sermons bear this out all the more. Alluding to the language of John Calvin he stated, "I believe that if the church is to be faithful to its calling it must concentrate, as I have said, on the uniqueness of Christ, but Christ clothed with his Gospel as the crucified and risen Lord."[61]

One of the principal ways in which Torrance draws out the connection between the person and work of Christ is in his emphasis upon the vicarious humanity of Christ and the great exchange wrought by God in Christ for us and our salvation. In clarifying the centrality of Christ for evangelical preaching we read: "That is the way in which the *katallage*, the wondrous exchange of the atoning and reconciling cross of Christ, operates, by making the shameful things that divide us from him into the very things that bind us to him in life and death forever. Such is the unlimited power of the Cross of Christ."[62]

---

[57] Ibid., 5–6.

[58] Ibid., 8.

[59] Thomas F. Torrance, *Preaching Christ Today: The Gospel and Scientific Thinking* (Grand Rapids, MI: Eerdmans, 1994), 27. This is an edited version of "Preaching Christ Today": An address to the Scottish Church Theology Society (January 21, 1993).

[60] Ibid., 27.

[61] Ibid., 30.

[62] Ibid., 34.

Torrance goes on to say that it is at the Eucharist that this truth can most powerfully be displayed.

In 1994 Torrance was asked to give advice to those starting out in ministry. In terms of preaching he suggested:

> If I were starting again as a young minister entering his first charge, I would do my best to engage in a Christ-centred ministry, i.e., one in which Christ has supreme place over all institutions, I would preach the gospel of unconditional grace, of reconciliation through the incarnation, passion and resurrection of Christ, and seek to find ways of working that out in the life of the church and the community. Evangelism and ecumenism go together.

In addition he wrote:

> I would give a great deal of my time to teaching my people the great Christian truths and the meaning of prayer and worship through, with and in Jesus Christ. I would try to develop in the congregation crystal clear and certain convictions and to translate into their own prayer and daily life their participation in the vicarious activity of the Holy Spirit as mediated through Jesus Christ and as he who mediates Jesus Christ to us.[63]

In the sermons of the 1940s we see in Torrance's actual practice an application of his own advice, where these themes become central to his preaching.

8. *The Inseparability of Jesus Christ and God the Father*

A second major theological theme evident in Torrance's sermons is the inseparability of the being and act of Jesus Christ with God the Father. In a work reflecting on the place of Christ in preaching we read:

> If you really believe that Jesus is God become incarnate you will have no trouble with the miracles. No! What overwhelms me is the sheer humanness of Jesus, Jesus as the baby at Bethlehem, Jesus sitting tired and weary at the well outside Samaria, Jesus exhausted by the crowds, Jesus recuperating his strength through sleep at the back of a ship on the sea of Galilee, Jesus hungry for figs on the way up to Jerusalem, Jesus weeping at the grave of Lazarus, Jesus thirsting for water on the Cross—for that precisely is *God* with us and one of us, *God* as "the wailing infant" in Bethlehem, as Hilary wrote, *God* sharing our weakness and exhaustion, *God* sharing our hunger, thirst, our tears, pain and death. Far from overwhelming us, God with us and one of us does the very opposite, for in sharing with us all that we are in our littleness and weakness he does not override our humanity but completes, perfects and establishes it.[64]

Furthermore:

> Now let me turn back to *the unbroken relation in being and act between Jesus Christ and God the Father* upon which the very substance of the Gospel rests. Cut the bond of being and act between Jesus Christ and God and the bottom falls out of the Gospel, for

---

[63]"If I Were to Start Again," in *A Newsletter for Presbyterians* (May/June 1994), np. Originally a piece in *The Presbyterian Outlook*, SC, 75.
[64]Torrance, *Preaching Christ Today*, 13.

then all that Jesus was, said and did is only of transient moral significance. But if Jesus Christ really is God incarnate, and divine and human nature are inseparably united in his one Person in an utterly unique way, then Jesus Christ himself in the undiminished fullness of his humanity and deity becomes the very center of the Church's mission. To preach Christ to men, women and children today we must proclaim him in his uncompromising singularity and transcendence as the one Lord and Saviour of the world.[65]

And preach Christ in this way he did.

9. The Sacraments

A final feature of Torrance's sermons from this time is the emphasis he gives to the sacraments of Baptism and the Eucharist. We have already seen how important seasons of Holy Communion were to Torrance. In a short article written in 1976 Torrance laid out twelve theses on the Pascal Mystery of Christ and the Eucharist. Included in the theses is a familiar theme in Torrance's work, that fact that "the immediate key to the understanding of the Eucharist is to be sought in *the vicarious humanity of Jesus Christ, the priesthood of the Incarnate Son.*"[66] Explaining this point further he writes, "From our side, it is union with Christ in his vicarious humanity and participation in his vicarious self-offering, both through the Spirit, that are the determinants in our interpretation of the real presence and the eucharistic sacrifice."[67]

Reflecting on the eschatological dimensions of the Eucharist we read:

> We do not offer Him. He offers Himself anew for us at each Eucharist; and we, His Body, the Church, offer ourselves to Him as we spiritually feed upon His sacrifice, receiving His Body and Blood. Eschatologically this is better described in terms of "Real Action", rather than in terms of "Real Presence", the former referring to the category of *time* and the latter to that of *space*, and rather suggesting theosophical atmosphere over against moral. What happens is something *personal* and *ethical* rather than purely *metaphysical*.[68]

Continuing to explicate this sense of the Eucharist Torrance looks to unpack the sense of *anamnesis* as follows:

> Following Dom. Gregory Dix, I would suggest that this all appears in the word *anamnesis,* which unfortunately has become translated in our English Bible as "in memory of", as if the Lord's Supper were merely a convenient symbol and nothing more—a kind of memory-quickener. The sentence *touto poiete eis tēn emēn anamnesis* is capable of another translation than that of "this do in memory of me": "Do this for my re-calling", where "re-calling" has the sense of actually bringing back. As in the time Process Jesus could actually give His Body and Blood to the Disciples *before* they had been offered on Calvary, so in the same process He can actually give the same Body and Blood *after* they have been offered.[69]

---

[65]Ibid., 27.
[66]Thomas F. Torrance, "The Pascal Mystery of Christ and the Eucharist," *Liturgical Review* 6 (May 1976): 6.
[67]Ibid.
[68]"The Sacraments and Eschatology," SC, 16:8.
[69]Ibid., 8–9 (slightly altered).

In the communion sermons of the 1940s this aspect of the Eucharist is brought out time and time again. It was supremely at the celebration of Holy Communion that all the theological and homiletical themes treated already come together in supreme fashion and thus form one of the central windows into Torrance's thought. He writes:

> It is supremely at Holy Communion that Christ comes into the midst like that, for there the Gospel is communicated to us not in word only but in action, and in the real presence of the Redeemer: *Christ for us,* as we break bread, and drink wine, the body and blood of the Saviour who died on our behalf; *Christ in us,* as we feed upon the Bread of Life and become incorporated into the Body of Christ; *Christ with us,* as we rise from the table and go to our homes knowing that we carry from that blessed communion the power of the Resurrection and the peace of the Lord Jesus in our hearts.[70]

Conclusion

To know the triune God of grace is to worship him. This is the heartbeat of Torrance's homiletics. As these sermons from the 1940s testify to, worshipful response to the knowledge of God in Jesus Christ by the communion of the Holy Spirit is the goal of good preaching and Torrance set himself to that goal as a faithful minister of the Kirk of Scotland and as a professor of Dogmatics.

ANALYSIS OF ARCHIVAL SERMONS OF THOMAS FORSYTH TORRANCE

The sermons of this period are held in the Thomas F. Torrance Manuscript Collection, housed at Princeton Theological Seminary. In the collection are 477 sermons preached by Torrance between the years 1940 and 1950. Most of these are typed 5 inch x 8 inch original manila paper copies contained in small manila envelopes with the text, title (if any given), and places preached recorded on them. There are a number of handwritten sermons as well, and some in German. There are other sermons included in the Archive, from his term as Moderator of the General Assembly of the Church of Scotland (1976–77), and sermons from various chapel services, society meetings, and special occasions.[71]

It was only due to Torrance's son, Iain Torrance, that these sermons remain, as we are told in a letter from Torrance to Alister McGrath in 1997, "Iain in Aberdeen has a large suitcase of my old sermons and documents which I was going to destroy but he rescued them!"[72]

---

[70]"Beechgrove Church Publications" (April 1949), SC, 20:4, col. 1.

[71]In addition to archival sermons there are several published collections, notably Thomas F. Torrance, "A Sermon on the Trinity," *Biblical Theology* 6 (1956): 40–4; *When Christ Comes and Comes Again* (London: Hodder and Stoughton, 1957, reprint, Eugene, OR: Wipf & Stock, 1996); *The Apocalypse Today* (London: James Clarke, 1959); "Trinity Sunday Sermon," *Ekklesiastikos Pharos* 52 (1970): 191-9; *Preaching Christ Today* (Grand Rapids, MI: Eerdmans, 1994); "The Evangelical Significance of the Homoousion. Sermon on John 5:17," *Abba Salama* 5 (1974): 165–8; "Sermon on St John 17:17-19," preached at the Consecration of Dr. Alastair Haggart as Bishop of Edinburgh, December 5, 1975, *Ekklesiastikos Pharos* 8 (1976): 226–31; "The Pre-Eminence of Christ," Sermon to the General Assembly of the Church of Scotland before H.M. the Queen, *Expository Times* 89 (1977): 54–5; and "The Light of the World." A Sermon. *The Reformed Journal* 38 (December 1988), np.

[72]"Letter to Alister E. McGrath" (December 8, 1997), SC, 108:1.

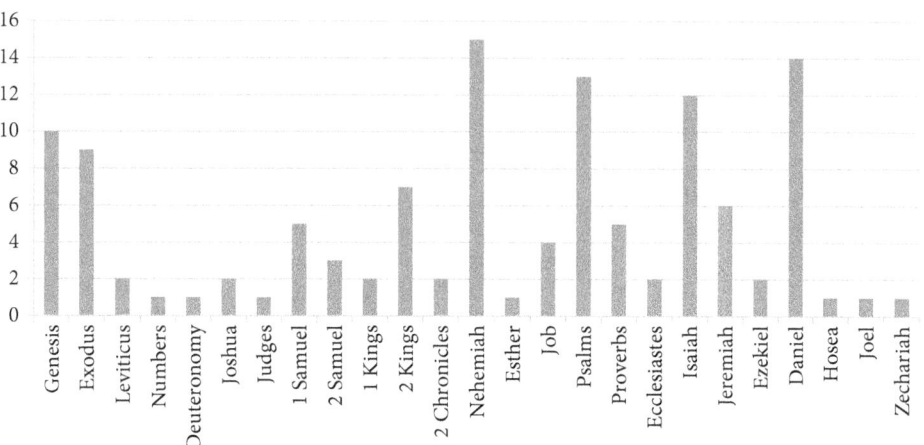

Figure 1 Primary text Old Testament frequency.

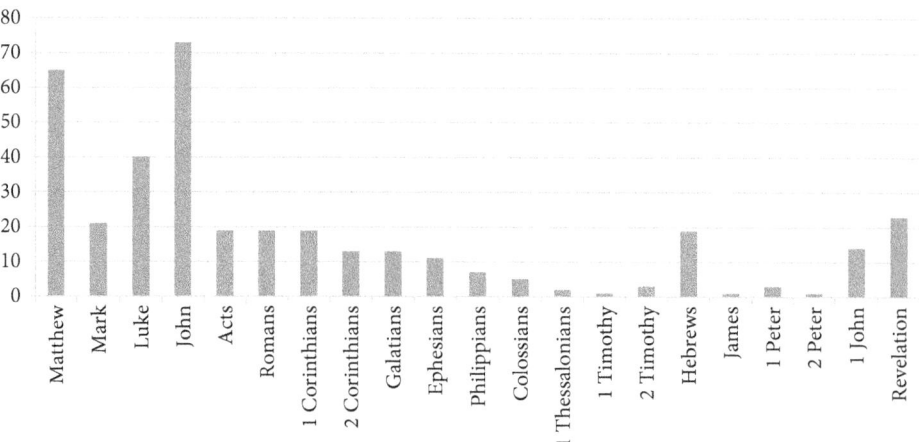

Figure 2 Primary text New Testament frequency.

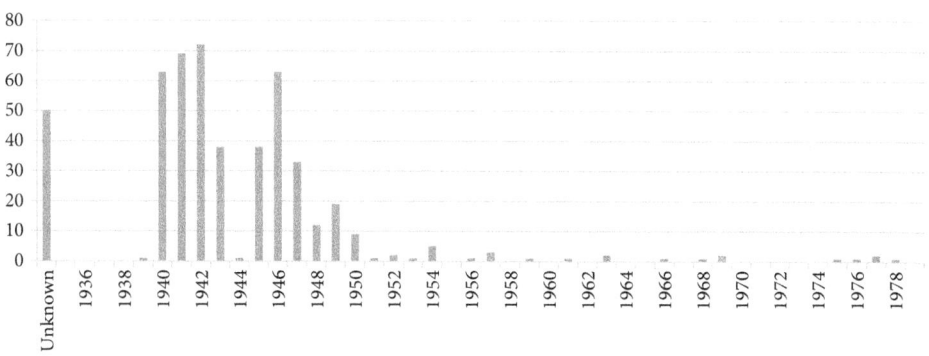

Figure 3 Number of sermons by date first preached.

CHAPTER EIGHTEEN

The End of Ministry

Thomas F. Torrance and Eschatology

ANDREW PURVES

Eschatology is directed toward the end or the consummation in the final *parousia*; it is directly related to the *eschaton*, the last Word and act of God in Christ, the *Eschatos*. Eschatology is the teaching of the church that the acts of God run throughout time to their end; they are teleological as well as eschatological, for time and space are themselves gathered up in the fulfilling of God's purpose for his creation.[1] The whole created universe (or universes) of things visible and invisible is brought within the range of this consummation, leading to a new heaven and a new earth.

The theological themes of eschatology and ministry run consistently together throughout much of the writing of Thomas F. Torrance. The reason is that the primary, and only saving ministry, is that of Jesus Christ, who is the Lord who comes and comes again. There is an eschatological cast in all of Torrance's writing, for he took his theological direction from the eschatological emphasis characteristic of Scripture. Central to his understanding was the inevitable tension for faith between the witness to Christ in history, especially in his cross and resurrection, the awareness of the presence of the ascended Christ now, through the living Spirit, and the anticipation that he must yet come again to fulfil his ministry, all within the one *parousia* or advent of his saving mission. Thus faith, living between the first and second advents, is cast in an inner eschatological framework tied unbreakably to the past, present, and future ministry of Christ.

The explication of this fundamental aspect of Torrance's theology is necessarily selective within this brief discussion. Nevertheless, a number of themes stand out for presentation. We begin with a general discussion of Torrance on eschatology. What is the relation between eschatology and teleology that takes redemption and creation seriously? Specific expression of this relation is given in his work on the ascension and *parousia* of Christ, which introduces us to the notion of an eschatological pause within the tension of presence and coming. An example of this "pause" is found in Torrance's notion of eschatological reserve, which is the time of the evangelical mission of the church. At this point we will look at Torrance's study of the eschatology of the Reformation, with reference to Luther, Butzer, and Calvin. Torrance also gave important commentary on the relation between eschatology and Eucharist, centered in our participation in the vicarious humanity of Jesus. The interlocking of Christ's ministry for us, in its past,

---

[1] Thomas F. Torrance, *Space, Time and Resurrection* (Edinburgh: Handsel Press/Grand Rapids, MI: Eerdmans, 1976), 150–1.

present, and future aspects, the church's ministry and Christian hope all fall within the scope of Torrance on eschatology.

GENERAL REMARKS

Torrance developed a realist, historical perspective on eschatology. The primary issue is whether God really acts or not with what God has created, creating a primary reciprocity between God and us, and, indeed, with all creation. Given the first advent, the incarnation of Jesus Christ, and anticipating the second when he comes again, understood as the one *parousia* of Christ, Torrance expounds his doctrine of the church and its ministry. That is to say, Torrance argues for an eschatological pause at the heart of the *parousia* within which it is understood that the reign of Christ is already established with his resurrection and ascension yet still anticipated as we look for his final revelation and manifestation in glory, for the new heaven and the new earth. Torrance insists that in the New Testament *parousia* is singular, comprising Christ's birth, life, death, resurrection, ascension, and coming again as an extended event. It is at once the Kingdom of God in history, and the final coming of Christ in glory. The church lives within the "space" between having and hoping.

For Torrance the core issue is who came and will come again. The focus is on *Eschatos* (last one) rather than on *eschaton* (last event). The church awaits the apocalypse, the revelation or unveiling of history already invaded and conquered by Jesus Christ when the new creation, as yet hidden, will appear as the new heaven and earth. The glory of Christ's full majesty, for now hidden within the humanity of Jesus, and especially in his cross, will be revealed for who he was, is and will be. The Kingdom of God has entered the world in the life and death of Jesus, though for now veiled in history, must yet be unveiled as Christ will stand transfigured for all to see.

This argument is given in a series of sermons on the Revelation of St. John that Torrance published in 1959 under the title *The Apocalypse Today*,[2] giving the character of his early thinking. (These sermons were preached during his ministry at the Barony Church, Alyth, and Beechgrove Church, Aberdeen, before his appointment to the faculty of the University of Edinburgh.) The theme of these sermons is the church in tribulation, yet it is the place where the Lord reigns, for now under humiliation through his cross. Amid the chaos of history—these sermons were preached during the Second World War—there is a hidden history already written about the destiny of the world. Torrance creatively calls it "a heavenquake," amid the chaotic earthquakes of history, whereby God has acted decisively in Jesus Christ against all evil, even though for now that remains hidden for most people, and opaque and veiled even for the saints.

Torrance is consistently adamant, across all his writing, that eschatology must not be cut adrift from history, both past and future. The emphasis must be placed on an historical rather than a purely spiritual future when Christ will come again. This is developed, somewhat sketchily, and again in an early missive, previously unpublished, as an addendum to the posthumously published New College lecture notes given in Edinburgh throughout his professorship.[3]

---

[2]Thomas F. Torrance, *The Apocalypse Today* (London: James Clarke/Grand Rapids, MI: Eerdmans, 1959).
[3]*Thomas F. Torrance, Incarnation: The Person and Life of Christ*, ed. Robert T. Walker (Downers Grove, IL: IVP Academic/Milton Keynes: Paternoster, 2008), 298–9.

Torrance wonders why it is that the church failed so soon after the beginning, formative years, to take into its whole life and thought the eschatological thinking of the early church. Even after the Reformation the churches soon lost the eschatological note that was characteristic of its teaching during that period. This is in spite of the fact that the eschatological cast is characteristic of all Scripture. Eschatology is forced upon the mind of the church by its confession of Jesus Christ, who fills the whole vista of faith as the reality of the Kingdom of God here and now, yet who will come again. Faith looks for the time when the hidden presence of Christ and his reign will be unveiled, and he will be seen in glory. Torrance insists, then, on the essential relation between Christology and eschatology. Faith rests upon this dual ground: knowledge of the ascended Christ in his Word, through the Spirit, and keeps the eschatological relation at the very center of what is believed. As noted, faith exists within the tension of having and not having, a tension secure, however, in God. Torrance writes, "The more seriously the person of this Jesus is taken, and the more the emphasis upon the word throws faith back upon the historical events of Jesus Christ, the more faith is poised upon historical fulfilment, that is upon the expectation that this same Jesus will reveal himself personally in the actuality of history."[4] Faith rests upon both a past and a future event, and as such is rightly expressed as hope. Torrance, then, stands opposed to a docetic eschatology, with his insistence on a future not just for humankind, but for all creation. That is, he stands opposed to eschatology as mystically conceived as a static and timeless reality in which nature is transposed into supernature, and that which is recognizable here becomes unrecognizable there.[5] In sum, to weaken the relation between eschatology and history means that faith, as through and through eschatological, becomes lost. And history without eschatology finally means the end of history and meaninglessness for the creation.

Torrance turns to a discussion of the nature of New Testament eschatology in order to ground his view of an imminent advent of the Kingdom of God in time as belonging to the core of faith. It is in this way that he did not fall into the trap of a time–eternity dialectic, in which time finally is not taken seriously insofar as it has no future. He sought, rather, to establish a doctrine of new time in reconciliation with God, time enfolded within the grace of God in history.

What is the biblical view of time, and of the relation between the Kingdom of God and history? Torrance locates the clue in a twofold aspect of Old Testament eschatology: the Kingdom is bound up with creation and is a pure act of God.[6] That is to say, the Kingdom of God is not the product of the stream of history, as a causal process immanent within history, but is a free act of God in history. In the New Testament, however, that which hitherto was future oriented is understood to have broken into the present in Jesus Christ, albeit in a hidden way, although it will be revealed in fullness in the future intensively in temporal and historical encounter with Christ in a new heaven and a new earth. Once again there is the note of tension, between having and hoping, between a future advent and a realized presence.[7] But above all, the emphasis rests upon the person of Jesus, reflecting both his past life and ministry and, after his ascension, on his real presence

---

[4] Ibid., 300.

[5] Thomas F. Torrance, *Kingdom and Church: A Study in the Theology of the Reformation* (Edinburgh: Oliver and Boyd, 1956, reprint: Eugene, OR: Wipf & Stock, 1996), 3.

[6] Torrance, *Incarnation*, 314.

[7] Ibid., 315.

through the Spirit, and in expectation of his coming once again. What will be unveiled in the future is a reality, hidden for now, but fully present.

This perspective on Jesus and the Kingdom of God is the embedded basis for the ministry of the church in which the prophetic and apocalyptic dimensions of the gospel are held together as *telos* (end or goal) and *eschaton* (final consummation).[8] That is to say, the New Testament teaches that the final judgment of God at the end of time will involve creation and history. History and creation have a future in God's final redemption. Creation and redemption are here taken with utmost seriousness. Thus, Torrance writes not of the future of the reality of the Kingdom of God as such, but of its full manifestation so that the essential tension between the time of the present but hidden reality and the time of the same reality manifest in the future is maintained.[9] In this way we have to do here, with Jesus Christ, with new time in the midst of old time. The new time is as yet concealed under the form of old time. Remarkably, Torrance refers to a sort of hypostatic union having taken place in the person of Jesus Christ between the eternal and the temporal, the holy and the sinful, in the form of new time even amid the world's estrangement from God.[10]

The end, *telos*, then, must be thought of eschatologically, and the eschatological, teleologically, for the end is the unveiling of the reality hidden in Christ within history as the new creation promised in the resurrection of Christ. God's purposes are eternally bound up with creation, time and space. The incarnation means in part that while God is not limited by space and time, it affirms the reality of space and time for God in the actuality of God's relations with us and of our relations with God. Because Jesus is the incarnate Lord of space and time, Torrance on occasion stressed the relation between eschatology and teleology, as noted above. This relation inevitably raises the relation, then, between eschatology and the future of the physical universe(s); or, put differently, the relation between eschatology and science must come into view. "It will not do," he writes, "to hold our theological conceptions and our natural scientific conceptions apart in entirely disparate realms."[11] How do we speak of continuity and discontinuity in our expression of the future of the physical universe(s) from an eschatological perspective?

SPACE, TIME, AND THE ASCENSION OF JESUS

The commentary on a general introduction to Torrance on eschatology was taken mostly from the Appendix to *Incarnation: The Person and Life of Christ*. It is reckoned this was written in the early 1950s, though revised for publication posthumously in 2008. We turn now to his mid-career writing where the material is covered in depth in *Space, Time and Resurrection* (1976), to look at Torrance's teaching on the resurrection, and especially on the ascension of Jesus, where he reflects on the *parousia* of Christ and Christ as Lord of space and time. Again, we will see that eschatology and the person and ministry of Christ are profoundly intertwined.

Torrance insists that the resurrection of Jesus Christ was an event in history as the resurrection of the body, and that all docetic conceptions mean in the end that we have a

---

[8] Ibid., 317.
[9] Ibid., 334.
[10] Ibid., 335.
[11] Torrance, *Space, Time and Resurrection*, 179.

ghost for a savior.¹² How is it an event in history when it bursts through the limitations of space and time? What does it mean to say the resurrection happens within history when it cannot be captured within the closed continuum of cause and effect? For Torrance, the resurrection of Jesus is a new kind of historical happening.¹³ It has the same kind of continuity and discontinuity as the virgin birth of Jesus. It involves space and time in terms of new creation yet within the frame of the old creation. That is to say, it involves the redemption of space and time that breaks free from what he calls logico-causal necessity.¹⁴ While an event within history, we must interpret the resurrection theologically if we would understand it on its own terms. Thus, in the resurrection time is not annihilated but recreated.¹⁵ Eschatology and teleology combine in Christ, though as yet still in a hidden way. But as the new in the midst of the old it brings with it the capacity to create for us new and appropriate categories of thought with which to apprehend and speak of it appropriately and objectively.¹⁶ That is, the resurrection as an historical event is to be interpreted in accordance with its nature as that is disclosed to us—a familiar theme in Torrance's epistemology. More specifically, because of Pentecost and our union with Christ through the Holy Spirit, we have access to the essential mystery that confronts us in the resurrection of Jesus.

The church lives in two times. It lives in the time of this passing world, amidst decay unto death. The church also lives in the time of the new creation, the time of the risen and ascended Lord, in a world already made perfect in him. As the church in the old time, the church is crucified with Christ; it lives under the cross. As the church of the new time, the church lives in hope.

Torrance notes how difficult it is to think these two "times" together, especially with regard to individual persons.¹⁷ When the believer dies, he contends, he or she goes to be with Christ and is in his immediate presence. In the light of old time, however, the believer is dead, waiting for the final *parousia* of Christ. This differential view of time is only possibly thought through in Christ, as believers and the church live between the times of the resurrection and Pentecost and the time of the final advent.

Torrance, of course, wrote extensively on the relation between theology and natural science, where he made very important contributions. But his treatment of the relation between theology as eschatology and the future of the physical universe(s), or of the believer's future physical existence, is lacking much contribution beyond formal statements. What does it mean to say, for example, that the resurrection of Jesus is a new kind of historical happening? What sense is there in insisting that in the new creation there will be a real experience of time without decay? David Wilkerson, writing as both an astro-physicist and theologian, makes the important point that given his interest in the relation between theology and science Torrance is disappointing in actually describing what it means for space–time to be healed and restored.¹⁸ Of course Torrance's comments

---

¹²Ibid., 87.

¹³Ibid., 88.

¹⁴Ibid., 93.

¹⁵Thomas F. Torrance, *Theology in Reconciliation: Essays towards Evangelical and Catholic Unity in East and West* (London: Geoffrey Chapman, 1975), 98.

¹⁶Torrance, *Space, Time and Resurrection*, 177.

¹⁷Ibid., 102.

¹⁸David Wilkerson, *Christian Eschatology and the Physical Universe* (London: T&T Clark, 2010), 131.

in that regard were measured just because of his emphasis on the need for eschatological reserve when discussing these matters.

Now let us turn to Torrance's teaching on the ascension of Christ, to that event in which he was fully installed in his kingly ministry which stretches from his ascension to the final advent, which is the end of ministry. Torrance notes, however, that while Christ's ascension is his exaltation to power and glory, it is nevertheless through the cross, crucifixion, and sacrifice.[19] Thus the ascension involves the veiling of his majesty, and a holding back of his power. Further, in the humanity of the ascended Jesus he ever lives to present humankind before the Father as our continuing High Priest, offering himself in his endless self-oblation, while always praying for us as our advocate and intercessor. Again, this familiar Athanasian theme in Torrance's theology is to be noted: Christ brings God to us, and us to God, in the unity of hypostatic ministry to us and for us. And in so doing, he sends us the Holy Spirit, making of the church a royal priesthood participating in the one priesthood of Christ, and validating and empowering the proclamation of his Word on earth.

The ascension is to be understood as the corollary to the incarnation. How then is it to be understood in terms of space and time? Once again Torrance invites differential thinking. As Christ became human without ceasing to be God, and so lived in space and time without leaving the throne of God; he ascended to the Father in the fullness of his human being.[20] With the ascension of Christ, created space and time, far from being dissolved, are confirmed in their reality before God, though the expression of this defies our categories shaped by earthly space and time, which now must nevertheless be allowed ineffably to point beyond what they designate here and now to what is transcendent. Statements about the ascension, then, are closed at our human end, as it were, but infinitely open at God's end. Only Jesus Christ can hold this tension in place, for he alone is the place where God and humankind meet. Torrance must now speak for himself:

> As in the incarnation we have to think of God the Son becoming man without ceasing to be transcendent God, so in his ascension we have to think of Christ as ascending above all space and time without ceasing to be man or without any diminishment of his physical, historical existence … In the incarnation we have the meeting of man and God in man's place, but in the ascension we have the meeting of man and God in God's place, but through the Spirit these are not separated from one another.[21]

Torrance often used the illustration of the Byzantine icon to make his point. With an icon there is a deliberate reversal of perspective. Instead of the coherence of the picture maintained by converging lines into the back of the picture at a finite point, so to speak, Byzantine art made the lines of perspective diverge so that they never meet but reach out into infinity. At one end, the icon stands in bounded space and time; at the other end, it transcends all limitations, becoming a window into heaven. In like manner, statements about Christ's ascension cannot be enclosed within the finite limits of creaturely determinations but open out beyond themselves to bear witness to the infinite mystery of divine transcendence.

---

[19] Torrance, *Space, Time and Resurrection*, 111.
[20] Ibid., 126–7.
[21] Ibid., 129.

Torrance makes an important corresponding point: in his ascended withdrawal from space and time as we experience it, Christ sends us back to the historical Jesus as the covenanted place in space and time which God has appointed for the meeting between God and human beings. Our relation with Christ is through the historical Jesus.[22] This is a thoroughly anti-docetic move. We know God in Christ within the frame of earthly existence. The ascension, in effect, sends us back to the incarnation and to the historical Jesus. In a familiar image from Torrance, we must not go behind the back of Jesus Christ, to some kind of *theologia gloriae,* but must seek God where God has given himself to be sought, in the man Jesus of Nazareth. There is a limit placed on our knowledge corresponding to a proper eschatological reserve.

As noted, Torrance teaches that believers live within the eschatological tension formed by Christ's presence through the Spirit and yet awaiting his final advent when he comes again. There is only one *parousia* of the one Jesus Christ, however, and it is understood in such a way that there is no separation between incarnation, ascension, and final coming. But the effect of the ascension, in one regard at least, is a kind of interval within the midst of the one *parousia*. Here Torrance introduces an important image: there is, he says, an eschatological pause which makes it possible for us to speak of a first advent and a second or final advent of Christ.[23] Christ delays his coming in glory to the time when the eschatological pause will end and we shall see him face to face. The period of the eschatological pause is the time of the church, a time also of deep teleological ambiguity, yet given by God for the proclamation of the Gospel to all peoples that they may repent and believe. And the church is sustained in mission and waiting during this pause by eating and drinking sacramentally the body and blood of Christ, until he comes again. (We will return to the relation between eschatology and Eucharist in due course.)

Torrance always remained the evangelical preacher. He understood that in Christ the *eschaton* had broken into history. However, were people confronted openly with the *eschaton* in the Word and presence of Jesus they would be faced with the final judgment. So the breaking in of the Gospel is veiled in the form of parable and is presented in such a way as to bring people face to face with last things and yet leaves them time for decision which could not happen were the *eschaton* fully realized. The interval of time between incarnation and final advent is the time for the Word of forgiveness and the act of healing; it is the time of *kerygma* and grace; it is the time of the necessary eschatological reserve between the Word of the Kingdom and its coming in glory, as time for freedom and decision. Even for the individual believer this eschatological pause is a time of ambiguity amid this-worldly anxieties, and in which we are a mixture of good and evil, trusting alone in the mercy of God, and summoned to look away from ourselves to Christ. For true life is hidden with God in Christ. Yet the day awaits when this gracious withdrawal will end and the new creation will be revealed. It will be a day of judgment by God. Those whose judgment upon sin by God has long been suspended in order to leave room for salvation will be condemned as those who have chosen evilly to defy the love of God. It is this interval, pause, and reserve that creates the urgency for the time of the church, the time between cross and *parousia*.[24]

---

[22]Ibid., 133.

[23]Ibid., 145.

[24]Torrance, *The Apocalypse Today,* 97; Torrance *Conflict and Agreement in the Church.* II: *The Ministry and the Sacraments of the Gospel* (London: Lutterworth Press, 1960), 159; Torrance, *Space, Time and Resurrection,* 146; and Torrance *Atonement: The Person and Work of Christ,* ed. Robert T. Walker (Downers Grove, IL: IVP Academic/Milton Keynes: Paternoster, 2009), 406.

TORRANCE ON THE ESCHATOLOGY OF THE REFORMATION

Torrance wrote extensively on the history of theology, covering an enormous range of material. Thus, his work on the eschatology of the Reformation, of Luther, Butzer, and Calvin, takes its place in this account, published as *Kingdom and Church: A Study in the Theology of the Reformation*.[25] It is mostly an expository account. Picking up on themes already noted, he describes the eschatology of the Reformation as an eschatology concerned with movement and history.[26] The Reformation thought of the end of the world as having already occurred, as last things are being wrought out in history. He characterized it as a return to the realist, historical perspective of biblical eschatology. The new age inaugurated by Jesus Christ was linked with the mission of the church as all history was now moving under the impact of God's Word toward its goal in Jesus Christ.

Torrance's exposition falls under three heads: the eschatology of faith—Martin Luther; the eschatology of love—Martin Butzer; and the eschatology of hope—John Calvin. As should be expected, Torrance found Calvin's eschatology of hope to be the most helpful, and undoubtedly it profoundly shaped his own thinking.

For Luther, according to Torrance, the whole of history, life, and theology is interpreted in the light of ultimate judgment, making Luther's thought thoroughly eschatological.[27] Thus justification was the ultimate act of God's eschatological grace anticipating God's final vindication of the sinner. The believer possesses a righteousness which is real, though not yet fully realized. Righteousness lies under hope, meaning for Luther that the believer lives between having and not having. It is the eschatological dialectic of the *justus et peccator*.[28] Thus the believer lives in two kingdoms, of the world and of the Spirit, and the church lives in the overlap of these two ages. The Kingdom of God, for Luther, is an invisible Kingdom, a hearing but not a seeing Kingdom. It is the Kingdom of Christ who rules through his Word. Christ has his Kingdom from his eternity with the Father, and it is also the Kingdom in which he remits sins and governs his church. But for now, that Kingdom is veiled, though it may be grasped in faith.[29] According to Torrance, this means for Luther that we exercise faith within the framework of divine reserve. The church in faith waits for God's final action and does not attempt to force God's hand. Neither church nor state can assume absolute or ultimate power. But the church as an eschatological community can look forward to a life above and beyond.[30] While eschatology carries with it a joyful ethic even within the broken structures of this world, it remains for now the church under the cross. Again, we see the having and not having, in which the person of faith reaches out in longing for an ever-deeper assurance of forgiveness amid *Anfechtung*—however translated as trial, temptation, affliction, tribulation—a real suffering over anxiety about personal salvation.

Torrance's brief critique consists in noting Luther's weak stress on the renewal of the whole creation. More pointedly, the believer, he suggests, does not live on the resurrection side of the cross. Luther, according to Torrance, puts forth a doctrine of consolation in

---

[25]Torrance, *Kingdom and Church*, 6.
[26]Ibid., 2.
[27]Ibid., 10.
[28]Ibid., 15.
[29]Ibid., 27.
[30]Ibid., 56.

Anfechtung rather than an actual anticipation of the final victory of Jesus Christ. "*Ein feste Burg* will ever remain one of the great hymns of the Church, but it expresses only one side of the eschatology of the Reformation."[31]

Torrance's remarks on Martin Butzer are considerably briefer than the treatment given to Luther and Calvin. (Yet in highlighting *Von der waren Seelsorge* as "the all-important little work," Torrance points to what is perhaps the most important text of pastoral theology from the Reformation period).[32] Torrance see Butzer as making a great effort to get behind medievalism to restore the teaching of the ancient Catholic Church. While Luther stressed the Word of God, Butzer, and Calvin, stressed Word and Spirit in inseparable conjunction. This charismatic element allows Torrance to write of Butzer's eschatology of love, emphasizing the love of God that is shed into our hearts by the Holy Spirit.[33]

Butzer's major work was *De Regno Christi,* published in England in 1557. Butzer was concerned to establish the Kingdom of God in England (where he lived in exile from Strasburg). He sought to reorganize life in conformity to the Gospel of Christ. Butzer believed, according to Torrance's exposition, that the Kingdom of Christ stretches over both believer and unbeliever, compacted into a communion of love by the Word and Spirit. He taught that Christians must live their faith in true and active love for all people.[34] In this way the future life is lived, which already began in us through faith and which will be perfected by Christ at his coming again. Through faith and works of love we taste here and now something of the future life.

Thus Butzer laid great stress on the eschatological relation between the future life and life today. He was convinced that the whole creation belonged to the Kingdom of God. His doctrine of the church as a *Communio renatorum*, a born-again or revived community, and his notion of the *Regnum Christi* as including an external reign in the state, combined to give his eschatology of love present force. Torrance was clearly attracted to Butzer's eschatology of love, with its practical anticipation in present life of the values of the Kingdom of God.

Torrance's treatment of Calvin's eschatology of hope is the lengthiest of the three, and seeks to show how eschatology penetrated into the heart of his faith. He begins with a discussion of an early work by Calvin, *Psychopannychia*, 1534, 1536, and 1542. It was Calvin's attempt to expound the biblical teaching that the souls of believers after death are alert, not asleep, in and with Christ, praising him, and awaiting the resurrection of the body.[35] In contrast to Luther, Calvin's eschatology was activist. He stressed the mighty acts of God and the work of the church, waiting for final redemption. The church lives on both sides of the resurrection, in the heaven lies with Christ, and engaged still with the sufferings of the cross. Thus Calvin, according to Torrance, could hold in tension reflection on the future life and the unceasing ministry of the church.

Torrance argues that the clue to Calvin's eschatology is found in the expression "Christ in our clothing."[36] That is, everything he has to say is in terms of Christology. His focus is on the new humanity in Jesus Christ in which believers share through union with Christ.

---

[31] Ibid., 72.
[32] Ibid., 73.
[33] Ibid., 73–4.
[34] Ibid., 81.
[35] Ibid., 90.
[36] Ibid., 93.

Union with Christ means increase and growth, eschatological growth in Christ. Torrance notes that Calvin thinks primarily in terms of the church rather than individuals, and thus of the Kingdom of God manifest in the growth and extension of the church.[37] In this way, the church and the Kingdom of God are held closely together in dynamic interface.

Torrance is surely correct to emphasize Calvin's central doctrine of union with Christ. Through union with Christ believers are ever nourished by Word and Spirit, partaking of his new humanity. "Eschatology," writes Torrance, "is the analogical transposition of Christology to the whole understanding of the Church ... (E)schatology is the doctrine of the Spirit and all that *union with Christ through the Spirit* involves."[38] That is, faith is eschatological because it is Christologically determined, that Christ may become ours, and we his. Christ's resurrection is the subject and pledge of our resurrection. Through union with Christ we are sharers in Christ's ascension. In this way, faith merges into hope in an essential relation.[39] Salvation is complete, but enjoyment of it is delayed.

According to Torrance, election and eschatology are twin doctrines which must not be separated. Calvin took his cue from Butzer in this regard, speaking of the Kingdom in terms of eternal election and the coming of the will of God on earth. Thus, there is the conjoint notion of the Kingdom prepared for the elect from the beginning yet growing and advancing to the end of the age.[40] Now Calvin believed that all people are willed by God to be saved and that divine judgment is an accidental characteristic. He has no notion of a double decree. Throughout God has the one will of grace, which is to save all humankind. According to Torrance, it is only when election is separated from eschatology that a remorseless logic demands a double decree.[41] Torrance cites Calvin: "When the Word of God blinds or hardens the reprobate, it belongs truly and naturally to themselves, but it is accidental as respects the Word."[42] The gospel is preached for salvation, and that alone is proper to it. We make our own choice turning from life to death, condemned out of our own mouths and acts. Thus for Calvin, election is the *prius*, and eschatology the *posterius*, with the Christian life understood to be lived between the two.

Torrance notes that Calvin writes of the reign of Christ leading up to the reign of God, of which it is the anticipation.[43] Thinking in terms of Christ and his Gospel, his Kingdom is already complete. But insofar as we think of the Kingdom of Christ as the church, we must think in historical terms of growth and increase, as the reign of Christ between his two advents, distinct yet overlapping. And for now, the Kingdom of Christ is hidden under the cross; we live in the time between, the time for patience and mission, yet looking for the age to come. It is within the interlude, as it were, the time of the church, that the church has the ministry of the Word and sacraments. Torrance notes in particular Calvin's notion of the interlude as eschatological reserve.[44] And all orders of the church are held in eschatological suspension, to be regarded as the scaffolding of the church by means of which the church is built up as the Body of Christ, so that his face is in some measure reflected in the church.

---

[37] Ibid., 95.

[38] Ibid., 101.

[39] Ibid., 103.

[40] Ibid., 105.

[41] Ibid., 107.

[42] Ibid., 106, cited from the Comm. on Mark 4:12.

[43] Ibid., 114.

[44] Ibid., 137.

Clearly Torrance found in Calvin eschatological themes that rise to the surface in his own work. In his closing comments contrasting Luther and Calvin he makes that plain. Calvin, for Torrance, has the more robust Christology. In particular, Calvin placed great emphasis on union with Christ and the resurrection, for partaking of Christ's new humanity is the substance of the believer's faith and hope.[45] The believer lives on the side of the resurrection, although the final glory is suspended until Christ comes again. Further, Torrance judges Luther's understanding of the relation between time and eternity to be a point in time, while Calvin taught that God used the whole course of time within which the church has its life. Thus the emphasis is placed on the relation between Christ's ascended Lordship and the church's pilgrimage and mission on earth. The church experiences the real presence of Christ, though that is to be distinguished from the real presence at the *parousia* as eschatological glory. The church, then, for Calvin, according to Torrance, really participates in the vivifying flesh of Christ, in his new humanity. It is where the Kingdom and priesthood of Christ are found that a true church is to be found, although the church will only share in Christ full revealed glory after the present period of tribulation and humiliation for the sake of the Gospel.

ESCHATOLOGY AND THE EUCHARIST

Torrance wrote two long discussions on the relationship of the Lord's Supper to eschatology.[46] He also included a brief discussion of Calvin's teaching of that relationship from the material referenced above.

Torrance's early work on the Lord's Supper was in preparation for intercommunion among the churches, seeing in the Eucharist the divinely given sacrament of unity. For Torrance, in the presence of the eschatological Christ in the Eucharist all barriers to intercommunion are broken down.[47] In fact, the New Testament regards baptism and Eucharist as the same event, both having to do with incorporation into Christ, baptism being all-inclusive and final, while the Eucharist is the continual renewal of that incorporation in time.

Baptism and Eucharist are signs belonging to the fullness of time, charged with the power of the resurrection of Christ and enshrining in time the great mystery concerning Christ and his church. The whole significance of these signs is bound up with the ascension, and through the Spirit, with the real presence of Christ.[48] Torrance emphasized that the crucial point for Calvin is the ascension and what it implies. Calvin speaks at once of union with Christ in the eating and drinking of the Supper, but also of the eschatological distance that must be observed. While Christ is indeed poured into us at the Supper, he remains at a great eschatological distance from us and is not mixed with us.[49] For Calvin, as for Torrance, the *sursum corda* is important, for believers must rise heavenward. But they do so insofar as in the Eucharist there is both the *katabasis* of the living Lord, whereby in the Spirit he comes down among us, and an *anabasis*, in which by the Spirit he bears the church up with him to the throne of God.[50] It is only by the Spirit that

---

[45]Ibid., 140.

[46]Torrance, *Conflict and Agreement in the Church*; and *Theology in Reconciliation*.

[47]Torrance *Conflict and Agreement in the Church*, 192.

[48]Ibid., 161.

[49]Torrance, *Kingdom and Church*, 130.

[50]Torrance, *Conflict and Agreement in the Church*, 189.

believers are united with Christ while remaining separated by space. For the Reformers in general, the Supper is the taste and experience already of the age to come. According to Torrance, the Sacrament of the Lord's Supper takes place therefore in "two times," in the overlap of the present age and the new age that has overtaken us in Jesus Christ and is already actual in our midst through His Spirit. The new age is sacramentally unveiled in anticipation of the great unveiling of the Kingdom of Christ at the final *parousia*.[51] But "when Christ comes again and the Marriage Supper of the lamb is consummated, the sacraments will give way to literal reality."[52]

For Torrance the sacraments do not have to do simply with the relation between the present and the future. They are concerned with a union between the church in history and the new creation. They are characterized as having the nature of essential mystery. Because that union will be fully revealed in the future we must speak about them in terms of eschatology. The eschatological tension here implied is the tension between a present but hidden reality and the time of that same reality revealed in the *parousia*.[53]

In Torrance's view, in the Lord's Supper the church is given to taste and experience, although veiled, the powers of the age to come. As such, the church and its ministry fall within the eschatological pause between the first and second advents when Christ, as it were, holds back the full power and majesty of his presence. There is both a sacramental fulfilment and an eschatological suspension. Yet it is through the Lord's Supper that the church is renewed in its being during that time, this age of grace, "taking shelter under Christ's advocacy and in thankful pleading of His passion in the knowledge that once and for all we have been reconciled to God in Christ and now for ever have a place in Christ's Self-consecration on our behalf and Self-presentation before the Face of the Father in Heaven."[54] While for Torrance "the key to the understanding of the Eucharist is to be sought in the *vicarious humanity of Jesus, the priesthood of the incarnate Son*,"[55] its celebration takes place within the time of the eschatological pause, looking backward with thanksgiving to the historical ministry of Christ and anticipating with hope redemption with his coming again in glory. It is for all who believe in Jesus Christ, that each may taste the powers of the new age through sacramental incorporation.[56]

The Lord's Supper is the eschatological meal of the Kingdom of God. By way of that meal the Kingdom is realized here and now, but within the conditions of this passing world.[57] Torrance, in line with Calvin, directs attention to the objectivity of Christ as the central issue rather than to the rite itself or to the experience of the believer. Central is union with Christ in his life, death, resurrection, ascension, and coming again. Christ is the content of the Supper, with two essential moments: "the night on which he was betrayed," and "until he comes again." Torrance cites Calvin with approval in reference to the words regarding the body and blood, that the whole energy of the sacrament consists in these words.[58] The church in its celebration is both bound to Christ's specific history and related to the advent of Christ at the end of history. "Through the Eucharist

---

[51] Ibid., 139.
[52] Ibid., 162.
[53] Ibid., 164.
[54] Ibid., 151.
[55] Torrance, *Theology in Reconciliation*, 110.
[56] Torrance, *Conflict and Agreement in the Church*, 160.
[57] Ibid., 169.
[58] Ibid., 185.

the Church becomes, so to speak, the great arch that spans history, supported by only two pillars, the Cross which stands on this side of time, and the coming of Christ in power which stands at the end of history."[59] For the church there is an inevitable tension between this fallen world and the new creation, for in the Supper the wholeness of union with Christ is received only sacramentally in the brokenness of time, and the more that wholeness presses for complete unveiling at the *parousia,* the more evident it becomes that the church's existence is broken up.[60] Nevertheless, living in the power of the resurrection, the church must refuse to be imprisoned within history.

The church lives under the veil of the *eschaton*: "until he comes again." For Torrance, the Eucharist displaces the action of the church by the action of Christ. The risen and ascended Christ is the true celebrant at the Table, "and unless that eschatological substitution, the *mirifica commutatio*, as Calvin called it, is recognized, the Eucharistic sacrifice becomes but a pagan ceremony."[61] Thus the liturgical action of the church is displaced suspends the liturgical action, and makes it point away from and beyond itself. The *Maranatha* is an essential element of the Eucharistic action. Thus the Lord's Supper celebrated by the church after the resurrection takes on the sacramental character of the presence of Christ until he comes again, remembering the past history of Jesus both before and after his resurrection, as also anticipating his return. For Torrance, as for Calvin, the Lord's Supper is a meal of sustenance until that future fulfilment, filled with the presence of the incarnate Christ.[62] In the Lord's Supper there is both a sacramental fulfilment and an eschatological suspension, held in dynamic tension.

Torrance advanced the doctrine of the real presence of Christ, what he called the eucharistic *parousia*.[63] This is the actual presence of Jesus Christ. How he is present is inexplicable, for he is present through the Spirit, and that presence remains a mystery. But until he comes, the form instituted by Christ in the Eucharist is the form of humiliation, the breaking of body and the shedding of blood figured and represented in the fracture of the bread and the pouring out of the wine. The Eucharist is the God-given place appointed within our time and space where heaven and earth, eternity and time, fully meet and are united, and where God and humankind are reconciled.[64] The real presence which Christ gives the church in the Eucharist is objectively grounded in the presence of God to himself. Thus attention is not directed at the Eucharist, but rather through the Eucharist to its real ground in the paschal mystery of Christ.

Torrance's powerfully Christologically controlled teaching on the eschatological perspective on the Lord's Supper is a robust part of his legacy. The continuing theme of the eschatological pause is especially highlighted, for it runs through all of his writing on church and ministry. Jesus Christ as a present, experienced reality, although veiled for now, is the anticipation of the future coming with power and majesty at his final unveiling as Lord of all. As Lord of all, Christ will be revealed as Lord over the whole creation, of the universe(s). The Lord's Supper is the sacrament for humankind, given to the church, to strengthen and sustain its mission to bear the Gospel to all things in life and ministry. Torrance cites Calvin to the effect that under the class of sacrifice which we call Eucharist

---

[59] Ibid., 171.
[60] Ibid., 173.
[61] Ibid., 178.
[62] Ibid., 129.
[63] Torrance, *Theology in Reconciliation*, 119.
[64] Ibid., 121.

or thanksgiving are included all the duties of love. When we embrace our brethren with these, we honor the Lord himself in his members. Also, included are all our prayers, praises, thanksgivings, and whatever we do in the service of the worship of God. All these things finally depend upon the greater sacrifice, by which we are consecrated in soul and body to be a holy temple to the Lord.[65]

Taking shelter under Christ's intercession to the Father and his advocacy on our behalf, and in thanksgiving, we share in Christ's self-consecration, and are called thereby into a royal priesthood. Centered in the Supper, entirely in a spirit of thanksgiving, we offer our lives and ministries to the Father "by the right hand of Christ," citing the Edinburgh Reformer, John Knox.[66] Everything here in union with Christ, and thereby in communion with the Father, all of which is the gift of the Spirit. The Church that partakes the Supper is committed to engage in Christ's mission of reconciliation, to proclaim the Gospel to all nations and to live it out as a fellowship of reconciliation bringing healing to a divided world.

---

[65]See Torrance, *Conflict and Agreement in the Church*, 149.
[66]Ibid.

NAME INDEX

Anatolios, Khaled 103
Anderson, Ray vii, x–xi, 8, 85–100, 214, 216, 251–3, 255–6
Anselm 45, 108–9, 119–20, 184, 254
Apollinaris 185
Aquinas 1, 109, 120, 162, 170
Aristotle 118, 146
Athanasius 1, 3–4, 7, 13, 16–17, 49, 70, 102–3, 107–10, 133, 135, 164–70, 172–3, 180, 184–5, 209, 212, 219, 240, 251, 260
Augustine 16, 31, 56, 107, 165, 170, 186

Baillie, John 16, 38, 43, 173
Baker, Matthew 3, 34, 53, 64, 220
Balic, P. Carolo 119
Balthasar, Hans Urs von 72–3
Barth, Karl vii, ix–x, 1–3, 5–8, 11, 13–18, 20, 22, 25, 28–32, 34, 37, 39–41, 43, 45, 48–9, 52, 56, 67–85, 88–90, 95–6, 99, 101–2, 105, 107–10, 127, 129–30, 132, 134–5, 137, 139, 155, 159, 166, 169–72, 180–2, 189, 193, 208, 210, 212, 216, 220, 223–4, 226, 245, 256, 260, 264, 267–70
Barth, Markus 78
Barr, James 37, 43, 177
Basil the Great of Caesarea 22, 30
Bauman, Michael 192
Bebbington, David W. 175
Behr, John 103
Bhaskar, Roy 120
Binning, Hugh 180
Bonhoeffer, Dietrich 88, 90, 95, 97, 174
Brahe, Tycho 121
Brent, Charles H. 51
Browning, Don 98
Bruce, Robert 41–2, 44, 106, 180
Brunner, Emil 16, 39, 264, 268
Buber, Martin 159
Bultmann, Rudolf 19, 71, 80
Butzer, Martin 277, 284–6

Calvin, John 1–2, 13–17, 31, 42, 44–9, 82, 100–2, 105–8, 135, 155, 170, 178, 180, 183, 216–17, 229, 235, 237, 261, 267–8, 272, 277, 284–9
Campbell, John McLeod 38, 44–6, 179–80
Carnell, Edward John 87
Cass, Peter 180, 185, 188, 246
Cheyne, A. C. 47
Clark, Thomas 39
Colyer, Elmer 11, 52, 107, 112, 181, 183, 187, 208, 216, 225, 259
Constantinides, Chrysostom 53
Congar, Yves 3, 34, 52
Costello, John 49
Craig, Archie 43
Craig, John 42, 46, 213
Cullmann, Oscar 37
Cyril of Alexandria 16, 165, 180–1, 187, 210, 221

Deddo, Gary W. 155, 159, 209
Denney, James 45, 175–8, 268
Dickson, David 45
Dragas, George Dion 53, 106, 241, 256

Einstein, Albert 28, 49, 80, 112–14, 118, 137, 181, 189
Epiphanius 167–8, 170, 172
Ernest, James 103
Eugenio, Dick O. 174, 244, 248, 251, 254

Fergusson, David 49, 85–6, 90, 253, 256
Feyerabend, Paul 123
Feynman, Richard 118
Flett, Eric G. 230, 257
Florovsky, Georges 34, 52–3, 60, 63–5, 108, 251
Forbes, John (of Corse) 45, 106
Forsyth, P. T. 175, 178
Fouyas, Methodios 53
Fraassen, Bas C. Van 120–1
Fry, Christopher 87

NAME INDEX

Galilei, Galileo 123
Gödel, Kurt 124
Gordon, James 45
Gregory of Nazianzus (Nazianzen) 22, 30, 105, 108, 164–6, 168, 171–2, 177, 180, 185, 245, 251, 272
Gregory of Nyssa 30, 177
Grotius 45
Gunton, Colin 34, 103, 127–9, 177, 248

Habets, Myk 1, 48, 53, 64, 70, 82, 136, 219, 241, 248, 251, 270
Heidegger, Martin 71
Herrmann, Wilhelm 38
Hesselink, John I. 51–2
Hieb, Nathan 90
Hilary 165, 170, 185, 273
Holmes, Christopher R. J. 161, 247, 257
Hubbard, David Allan 87
Hunsinger, George 1–2, 7, 65, 70, 79, 217, 219–20, 233, 235
Hunsinger, Deborah van Deusen 92

Infeld, Leopold 118
Ip, Pui Him 103–4
Irenaeus 109, 180, 185, 226
Irving, Edward 186

Jenson, Robert 34
Jewett, Paul King 87
Jüngel, Eberhard 34, 85

Kennedy, H. A. A. A. 268
Kierkegaard, Søren 87, 108, 247
Kernohan, R. D. 211
Kettler, Christian 86–7, 187, 207, 209, 216, 257
Kirkpatrick, J. M. 44
Knox, John 42, 44–6, 180, 290
Kuhn, Thomas S. 115, 119
Küng, Hans 34

Lakatos, Imre 118–19
Lamont, Daniel 16, 37, 48
La Montagne, Paul 72–5, 82
Leighton Robert 45
Leitch, James W. 39
Lewis, Alan E. 166
Lindbeck, George 65
Luther, Martin 206, 277, 284–5, 287

Macaulay, A. B. 38
Mackintosh, Hugh Ross 13, 16, 23, 37–41, 176, 178, 186, 224, 248, 263, 265, 268, 272

MacLaren, Alexander 261
MacLean, Stanley S. 224, 229, 239–40, 268
Macleod, Donald 46–7, 186, 246
Macmurray, John 28, 48–9, 88–9
Manson, William 266, 269
March, Robert H. 118
Maréchal, Joseph 24
Maxwell, James Clerk 28, 49, 181
McCall, Thomas 118
McDowell, John C. 136
McFague, Sallie 177
McGrath, Alister 1–3, 5, 48, 52–3, 224–5, 241, 248, 254–5, 257, 260–1, 275
McIntyre, John 173–4, 256, 260
McKinnon, Donald 264
McLelland, Joseph 105
McPake, John 40
Melanchthon, Philip 181
Milligan, William 41
Miskotte, Kornelis 88
Moltmann, Jürgen 166–7, 170–2
Molnar, Paul D. 2, 4, 11, 57, 65, 70–1, 79, 82, 186, 237–8, 256
Morrison, Ruth Helen Bell 43
Musgrave, Alan 118–19

Neidhardt, W. Jim 226
Nestorius 187
Nigh, Adam 15, 210
Noble, Thomas 105, 256–7

Origen 7, 177

Pannenberg, Wolfhart 34, 181
Parker, Joseph 261
Philippou, Angelos J. 53
Phillips, Gerard 52
Philoponos, John 28, 111
Plantinga, Alvin 114
Polanyi, Michael 28, 49, 87, 115, 136–7, 208, 233
Pope Paul VI 1
Porteous, Norman 39–40, 269
Purves, Andrew 92, 176, 183, 220, 243, 253, 256–7, 277

Radcliff, Alexandra 209, 247, 253–4, 257
Radcliff, Jason 3, 23–4, 52, 56, 64, 103–4, 180
Rahner, Karl 3, 24, 34, 52, 107
Ramsey, Ian T. 177
Redman Jr., Robert R. 40
Reid, J. K. S. 267
Riddell, J. G. 48

NAME INDEX

Ritschl, Albrecht 16, 39, 175
Rutherford, Samuel 45, 180

Schillebeeckx, Edward 24, 34
Schleiermacher, F. D. E. 3, 16, 31, 39, 71, 80, 98
Schultz, Walter 83
Scott, John 43–4
Shepherd, Albert L. 240
Smail, Thomas 215–16
Small, Joseph D. 241
Smith, William Robertson 175
Smith, George Adam 175
Smith, Ronald Gregor 88
Sobrino, Jon 90
Sonderegger, Katherine 171
Soskice, Janet 177
Spear, Margaret Edith 7, 51
Speidell, Todd 3, 15, 34, 53, 86–7, 97, 209–10, 216, 247, 253–5, 257
Stamps, Robert 219
Stevick, Travis 112, 115, 117, 119–20, 123–4
Stewart, J. S. 265, 268

Thiemann, Ronald F. 138
Thurneysen, Eduard 98

Torrance, Andrew B. 118
Torrance, Annie Elizabeth (Sharpe) 51
Torrance, Iain R. 7, 275
Torrance, James B. 88, 174, 211–12

Van Kuiken, E. Jerome 185–6, 245–6
Vischer, Lukas 105

Walker, Robert 105–6, 175
Walls, Roland 88
Webster, John 34, 85–6, 90, 127–9, 210, 212, 220, 234, 253
Wilkerson, David 281
Williams, A. N. 171
Williams, Rowan 137
Winslow, Lisanne-D'Andrea 83
Wotherspoon, H. J. 44
Wright, David 43
Wright, Ronald Selby 44

Ziegler, Geordie 238, 244, 248, 250–1, 253, 256–7
Zizioulas, John 34, 53, 88, 91, 107, 146

SUBJECT INDEX

advent Lord (*see parousia*, second coming) 2, 22, 179, 191, 228–30, 235, 238, 241, 277–81, 283, 286–9
analogy 48, 72, 74, 76, 80–1, 193, 195, 198, 202, 226, 235, 240, 250
   analogy of being 226
   Christological 193, 198
anthropology 4, 16, 49
   Calvin's 16
   philosophical 20, 87, 124, 127, 146, 173
   transcendental 24
   theological 15, 23, 87, 92, 96
Apollinarianism (Apollinarians) 218
apologetic 28, 39, 48, 127–8
a posteriori thought 113, 133
a priori thought 132, 145
Arianism (Arian) 57, 108–9, 132, 245, 251
ascension 8, 16, 22, 41, 45, 79–80, 85, 152, 179, 185, 190, 215, 219–20, 228–30, 241, 247, 253, 266, 277–80, 282–3, 286–8
atonement 8, 14, 16, 20, 22, 25, 30, 38–9, 41–2, 44–7, 57, 71, 75, 85–6, 94, 148
   cross 5, 7, 61, 78, 82, 86, 90, 100, 151, 166–7, 169, 175–6, 178–9, 182–5, 187, 191, 198, 214–15, 217, 219, 235, 240, 272–3, 277–8, 281–6, 289
   forgiveness 25, 40, 91, 94, 96–7, 99, 160, 176, 262, 283–4
   hell 178–9, 215, 220
   limited 47–8, 107, 158, 160, 173–88, 191, 197–9, 207, 209, 212, 215, 217–18, 220–21, 243–4, 247, 249–50, 272
   parousia (*see* advent Lord, second coming) 2, 22, 179, 191, 228, 230, 235, 238, 241, 277–8, 280–1, 283, 287–9
   punishment 252
   reconciliation 21, 26, 32, 55, 59–60, 62, 69–70, 77, 79, 81–2, 89, 92–3, 95–6, 99, 109, 116, 136, 140, 148–50, 156, 160, 165, 178, 182–3, 190, 197, 228, 230, 236, 238–9, 241, 249, 253, 255, 273, 279, 290

salvation 2, 26, 44, 47–8, 58, 91, 109, 122, 148–9, 158, 160, 164–6, 169, 171–2, 174, 183, 187, 193–4, 196–8, 200–1, 209–10, 212–16, 220, 228–9, 235, 245–7, 249–51, 254, 262, 271–2, 283–4, 286
   second coming (*see* advent Lord, *parousia*) 236, 241
   soteriology 15, 23, 29, 31, 110, 173–5, 180, 190, 193, 208, 221, 224, 244
   soteriology (Pelagian/semi-Pelagian) 31, 42, 247, 251
Augustinianism (Augustinian) 25, 30–1, 48, 89, 105, 109, 235
authority 14, 19, 21, 25, 27, 33, 56–7, 71, 75–6, 98–9, 137, 269, 271

baptism (*see* sacraments) 3, 23, 31, 42–4, 48, 58–9, 78–9, 97, 154, 198–9, 219, 233, 235–6, 248, 250, 252, 254, 274, 287
Biblical Interpretation (biblical theology/ biblical scholarship) 12–13, 15–20, 25, 29–30, 38, 43, 47, 67–8, 73, 99, 101, 107–8, 120–1, 134, 137–8, 143–6, 154–5, 159, 170, 172, 175–7, 179, 181–2, 190, 192, 202, 218, 233–4, 237, 239, 245, 248, 254–5, 260, 267–8, 272, 279, 284–5

Chalcedon 152–4, 184, 214, 245, 249
   Chalcedonian 40, 135, 181–2, 194–5, 207, 210
Christ (*see* ascension, Atonement, Christology, incarnation: *homoousion*, resurrection)
   High Priestly Mediation 23, 79, 84, 177, 207, 214–16, 218, 252, 266, 282
   homoousial 135, 163, 165, 169–70, 172
   homoousion as the ontological and epistemological linchpin of theology 4, 22, 54, 133
   reconciler 68, 99
   revealer 6, 69, 133, 135

SUBJECT INDEX

Christology 3, 5–6, 15, 23, 26, 40, 45, 54, 66, 68, 73, 75, 77–8, 90, 93, 109, 129, 131, 136, 161, 169, 171, 173–5, 181–3, 189–90, 193–4, 198, 200, 202–3, 207, 223–5, 229, 248, 269, 279, 285–7
- ascension (*see* ascension)
- adoptionist 3, 6, 67–8
- Ebionite (adoptionist) 3, 67, 251
- from below 181
- Chalcedonian (*see* Chalcedon)
- centrality of Christ and incarnation 30, 38, 44, 117, 131, 190, 207, 213, 262, 264, 266, 272
- Christ's active and passive obedience 213
- Christ's suffering 166–7, 285
- docetic 67–8, 79, 250, 280, 283
- Eutychian (Eutychianism) 245, 251
- God-man 183, 190, 199, 204
- hypostatic union 40, 68, 78, 81, 132, 135, 178–84, 188, 190, 192–6, 200–3, 207, 213–14, 221, 225, 230, 243–5, 250, 280
- incarnation (*see* incarnation)
- monophysitism 6
- Nestorian 6, 107–8, 245, 251
- passibility/impassibility 166–7, 170
- realist 66
- resurrection (*see* resurrection)
- Vicarious humanity of Jesus (*see* death, faith of Jesus) 8, 23, 26, 29–30, 32, 58, 78–9, 85–6, 88, 91, 93–7, 136, 174, 180, 184–7, 207, 210–21, 228, 244, 247, 249, 257, 263, 266, 272, 274, 277, 288

communion with God 135, 179, 191, 239, 250

covenant (covenantal logic) 31–2, 55, 69, 77, 89, 147, 149, 157, 159–60, 163, 177, 181–2, 218, 227–8, 232, 237, 239, 283

creation 5, 15–16, 22, 28, 30, 55, 61–2, 70–1, 83, 93, 99, 116, 118, 130–1, 134, 140, 145, 147, 151–2, 154–8, 169, 182, 187, 201, 204–8, 218–19, 226–31, 233, 236–7, 240, 244, 250, 254, 269–70, 277–81, 283–5, 288–9
- contingence (contingent) 4, 7, 22, 111, 120–2, 124, 130–1, 139, 183, 208, 226
- new creation 22, 55, 182, 187, 228, 230, 236, 240, 278, 280–1, 283, 288–9

creator (creator/creature relation) 22, 32–3, 78, 134, 151–2, 169, 178–9, 183, 196, 204, 210, 216, 221, 226, 251, 253

critical realism (*see* realism) 72

death 38, 42, 45–7, 49, 58, 61, 78, 80–1, 86, 91–2, 96, 151, 163, 174–9, 182–3, 185–7, 190, 212, 217, 228, 246, 272–3, 278, 281, 285–6, 288
- death of God theologies 19
- vicarious 210, 228

deistic thinking 4, 28, 63, 134, 156–7, 160, 208

demythologizing 19

determinism 156, 158, 208–9, 219, 250

dialectic (dialectical theology) 38, 40, 72–4, 83, 95, 130, 279, 284

dogmatic theology 8, 12, 21, 23, 80, 109, 129, 131, 140, 223

dualism 4, 29, 31, 34, 62–3, 80–1, 89, 93–4, 107–9, 132–33, 146, 236

ecclesiology 8, 16, 23, 25, 32, 41, 52, 54, 56–7, 63–4, 66, 84, 146, 223–41

ecumenism (*see* intercommunion) 8, 11, 15–16, 20, 25, 34, 51–66, 172, 225, 273

election (*see* predestination) 2, 25, 32, 45–6, 156, 160, 179, 182, 195, 211, 247, 249–50, 252, 286

eschatology 2, 8, 15–16, 41, 214, 220, 224, 229, 239, 268, 277–81, 283–8
- apocalyptic 29, 262, 280
- eschatological 2, 22, 55, 57, 60–2, 133, 179, 215, 229–31, 233, 235, 240–1, 269, 274, 277, 279–80, 282, 284–8
- eschatological dialectic 284
- eschatological pause 277–8, 283, 288–9
- eschatological reserve 92, 96, 283, 286
- eschatological suspension 286, 288–9

eternity 2, 83, 153, 209, 279, 284, 287, 289

ethics 7, 15, 20, 32, 85, 90, 97, 120, 144, 244, 247, 249, 252–5, 257
- forensic view of justification 30, 45, 177–9, 185, 187, 212, 217
- justification by faith (grace) 3, 29, 70, 135, 207, 216
- legalism 14, 31, 221, 247
- license 221
- sanctification 27, 148, 160, 179, 186–7, 216, 220, 230, 232, 236, 243, 245–9, 252–3, 257
- self-justification 217, 249

faith 3, 5–8, 13–14, 18–19, 21–3, 25–6, 28–9, 32–3, 39–40, 42, 44, 46–8, 51–2, 54, 58, 61, 68–71, 76, 79–83, 92, 96–7, 99, 106–7, 129, 134–5, 153–5, 157, 160, 162, 173, 181–4, 187–93, 195, 198–9, 201–2, 204–7, 211–13, 215–17, 219, 221, 224–5, 228, 236, 240, 243, 247, 249–50, 252–3, 257, 259–60, 262–3, 267, 277, 279, 284–7
  deposit 25, 54, 132
  vicarious faith of Christ 26, 78, 187, 191–2, 199, 205, 212–13, 216
faith of Jesus 207, 211
fideism 115
freedom (divine and human) 78, 100, 128, 134, 140, 158–9, 165, 167, 171, 204, 206, 213, 216, 218–21, 226–7, 232, 244, 283

gnostic 109, 152
god-consciousness 4, 80
Gospel 1, 3, 7–8, 15, 19, 21, 23, 25, 31, 35, 39, 43–44, 46–8, 54–6, 58–9, 61–2, 67, 71, 79, 91, 94–5, 98, 100, 106–7, 109, 122, 156, 158, 162–4, 168, 171–2, 174, 179, 181, 184, 187–9, 206, 211, 220–1, 224, 228, 231, 235–9, 248–9, 252–3, 259–61, 263–4, 266–73, 275, 280, 283, 285–7, 289–90
grace 3, 5, 7, 16, 18, 22, 29, 31–2, 34, 41, 43–44, 64, 71–2, 74–7, 80–4, 90–2, 96, 98–9, 105–7, 109, 116, 122, 128–9, 132, 134, 139–40, 157–60, 172, 182, 187, 191–2, 194–6, 199, 201, 203–4, 206–8, 210–11, 216–17, 220–1, 226, 232, 235, 247, 249–51, 253, 262–3, 267–8, 273, 275, 279, 283–4, 286, 288
  unconditional 220, 247, 253, 263, 273

hellenistic 132, 146, 152, 251
hermeneutics 8, 11, 16, 52, 139, 170
historical Jesus 5, 196, 201, 214, 283
Holy Spirit 4–7, 22, 26, 39, 41, 45, 54–9, 62, 67–70, 74–9, 81–4, 93, 98–9, 101, 105, 109–10, 122, 141, 145, 148, 150, 151, 157, 160, 162, 164–6, 169, 173, 179, 184, 186, 199, 209, 213–14, 217–19, 225, 227, 231, 236, 238, 241, 244, 246, 249–52, 259, 270–1, 273, 275, 281, 285
  Filioque 2, 23, 70, 136, 168
  Pentecost 6, 65, 81, 204–5, 214, 227, 249, 252, 257, 281
  pneumatology 15–16, 20, 26, 136, 174
  theosis 23, 64, 161, 207, 219–21, 248–9, 251
hope 79, 91, 97, 100, 159–60, 184, 215, 228, 239, 271, 278–9, 281, 284–8
hypostatic union (*see* Christology)

incarnation 4–5, 8, 14, 16, 20, 22–3, 30, 32, 38–9, 42–7, 55–7, 61, 67, 69–71, 80, 82–3, 85–92, 94, 96, 98, 106, 131, 145, 148–9, 152–3, 156–7, 171, 173–90, 192–204, 207, 209–17, 223, 225–8, 231, 243–5, 249, 251, 272–3, 278, 280, 282–3
  anhypostasis 8, 31, 187, 192, 194–8, 200, 206, 245, 250
  enhypostasis 8, 31, 154, 187, 192–8, 200, 204, 206, 245, 250
  homoousion (*homoousios*) 4, 22, 30, 34, 54, 104, 106–10, 124, 133, 138, 152–3, 158, 162–6, 173, 180, 183–4, 275
  logos 74, 107, 117, 130, 139, 146, 149
intercommunion 60, 63, 65, 224, 287

Jesus
  Christ (*see* Christology)
  mediator 22, 26, 29–30, 34, 46, 57, 68, 79, 93, 133, 140, 148, 164, 177, 179, 190, 212, 237, 239
  obedience (*see* obedience)
  person 6, 38, 122, 181, 193–4, 197, 204, 206, 214, 225, 245–6, 252
  truth 6–7, 12, 18, 25, 27, 29–30, 33, 35, 40, 54, 61–2, 68, 70–82, 89–90, 92, 94, 96–8, 100, 105–6, 113–14, 116, 118–21, 124, 132, 135, 137–8, 141, 146–7, 149, 151, 158–63, 168, 172, 187, 190, 197–8, 200–2, 205, 209, 211, 214, 221, 230, 232–4, 243, 254, 263, 270–1, 273

kerygma (kerygmatic) 27, 54, 89, 100, 181, 233–4, 236, 283
Kingdom of God (Christ) 2, 59, 96, 157, 160, 177, 207, 229, 269–70, 278–80, 283–8
Knowledge of God 14, 22–3, 26, 33, 49, 54, 67–73, 75–8, 80–3, 89, 93, 111, 113, 116, 122–3, 130–1, 133–7, 139, 141, 192–4, 201, 207–8, 233, 260, 271, 275
  from a center in God 21, 27, 71, 75, 83, 271
  kataphysic 112, 123

non-conceptual 71
stratification 123

legalism 14, 31, 221, 247
Latin Heresy 31, 107–9, 210

ministry 8, 14–16, 21–3, 32, 37, 41, 43, 46, 55, 57, 80, 85–9, 92–9, 143, 145, 148, 150, 182, 187, 189, 198–200, 207, 215, 219, 224, 229, 233, 236–8, 248, 252, 254–6, 260–1, 264–5, 267–8, 273, 277–89
ministry of women 99
miracle 5–6, 18, 78, 83, 204, 206, 252, 263, 273

natural theology 2, 14, 16, 28, 32–3, 38–40, 70, 72–3, 79–84
"new" (reconstructed) natural theology 2, 14, 28, 30, 70, 72–3, 79, 81–2
Nicaea 54, 56, 107–8, 167, 184

obedience 23, 26, 49, 61, 70–1, 78–9, 82, 135, 140, 160, 171, 181–2, 184, 187, 198, 212–13, 216, 218–19, 221, 235, 239, 246–7, 252, 260
onto-relational understanding of Persons 22, 143–60, 221
ousia 147, 152–3, 155, 164, 167, 171, 184

pantheism (Panentheism) 4, 156–7
parousia 2, 22, 179, 191, 228, 230, 235, 238, 241, 277–8, 280–1, 283, 287, 288–9
pelagian 31, 42, 247, 251
pneumatology (*see* Holy Spirit)
prayer 23, 27, 32, 43, 78–9, 90, 94, 163, 191, 199, 211–12, 214–15, 252, 255–6, 261, 265, 273, 290
predestination (*see* election) 2, 44, 46–8, 158, 178, 194, 210

realism (realist) (scientific objectivity) (epistemology) (Christocentric ecclesiology) 3, 14, 21, 28, 37–8, 46, 49, 54, 58, 63–4, 66, 72–3, 75, 117, 120–1, 128, 155, 226, 254, 271, 278, 284
resurrection 16, 22, 38, 42, 45, 58, 61, 67, 71, 78–82, 99, 151–2, 159, 163, 176, 178–9, 182–3, 185, 187, 190, 196, 198, 212–13, 215–17, 219, 228, 246–7, 249, 269, 273, 275, 277–8, 284–9

revelation (self-communication) (self-revelation) 4–6, 8, 15–16, 18–19, 21, 23–4, 26–9, 31, 33, 39, 40, 44, 48, 54, 67–70, 72–5, 77, 80–3, 86, 89, 92–6, 98–9, 108–9, 116, 121, 127–41, 143–52, 154–5, 158, 161–2, 164–5, 179–84, 190–1, 202, 204, 209, 211, 223, 228, 232–5, 254, 262–3, 270–1, 278

sacraments 1, 15–16, 32, 34, 42–4, 58, 78–9, 82, 84, 192, 199, 213, 223, 231, 233–6, 250, 274, 286, 288
baptism 3, 23, 31, 42–4, 48, 58–9, 78–9, 97, 154, 198–9, 219, 233, 235–6, 248, 250, 252, 254, 274, 287
Lord's Supper (Eucharist) 3, 23, 40–2, 44–5, 52, 58–9, 62, 65, 78–9, 97, 106, 199, 217, 219, 224, 233, 235–6, 250, 263, 266, 273–5, 277, 283, 287–9
real presence 41, 45, 58, 274–5, 279, 287, 289
scientific theology 4, 6, 13, 27, 88, 93, 111, 123
Scots Confession 45
second coming (*see* advent Lord, *Parousia*) 236, 241
self-communication (*see* revelation)
soteriology 15, 23, 29, 110, 173–5, 193, 208, 221, 224, 244, 251
soteriological suspension of ethics 247, 253–4
subjectivism 18, 73, 80
symbolic (mythological) thinking 4, 19, 22, 24, 26, 33, 75, 80–1, 117, 139, 209, 235, 254

Trinity (trinitarian theology) 3–4, 6–8, 11, 17, 22, 28, 31, 33–4, 52–4, 63, 67–71, 75, 83, 98, 103–5, 107, 110, 123, 145, 151–2, 154–5, 160–74, 184, 190–1, 208, 220, 223–7, 229–30, 232, 240–1, 243–4, 249–51, 260, 270
derived deity 168
modalism 30, 164
monarchy (*Monarchia*) (*arché*) 30, 107, 168
perichoresis (perichoretic) (coinherence/coinherent) 23, 30, 133, 135, 138,

154–5, 163–5, 168–70, 209, 218, 244
Socinianism (Unitarianism) 176
subordinationism (subordination) 2, 22, 30, 70, 168
tritheism (tritheist) 164, 166, 172
triunity 131, 153

universalism 156, 158, 220

Westminster Confession 38, 40, 45, 47–8, 180
worship 20–1, 23, 26–7, 32, 35, 41, 79, 94, 122, 146, 154–5, 157, 160, 164, 166, 177, 192, 199, 211–13, 215, 218–9, 229, 233, 237, 244, 249, 252, 255, 260–1, 264–7, 269–70, 273, 275, 290

www.ingramcontent.com/pod-product-compliance
Lightning Source LLC
Chambersburg PA
CBHW080535300426
44111CB00017B/2734